HOLLAND

FODOR'S TRAVEL PUBLICATIONS

are compiled, researched, and edited by an international team of travel writers, field correspondents, and editors. The series, which now almost covers the globe, was founded by Eugene Fodor in 1936.

OFFICES

New York & London

Fodor's Holland:

Editor: Richard Moore
Associate Editor: Thomas Cussans
Area Editors: Maren and Robin Dannhorn
Editoral Contributors: Robert Brown, Frances Howell, Ira Mayer, John Mayer
Maps: Jeremy Ford, Bryan Woodfield
Drawings: Elizabeth Haines

FODOR'S

HOLLAND

1988

Fodor's Travel Publications, Inc.
New York & London

ISBN 0-679-01522-1
ISBN 0-340-41794-3 (Hodder & Stoughton)

CONTENTS

CONTENTS

SUPPLEMENTS

SECURITY NOTE

As in most other western industrialized countries, standards of personal safety and security have declined in Holland over recent years, but there is no reason why this should interfere with the enjoyment of visits by foreign travelers, provided that basic and common-sense precautions are observed.

In Holland the areas where greater care should be taken are all in major cities, where drug-related problems are worst. In Amsterdam and Rotterdam, particularly, do be cautious about entering "red light" areas at night. The district around both Amsterdam's and Rotterdam's Central Station should be avoided. Bag-snatching and pickpocketing occurs mostly in rail stations and in street markets, so keep a close watch on baggage at all times. Women should use a shoulderbag and keep it tucked under the arm, or worn with the strap across bandolier fashion. Use hotel safes for valuables, rather than taking them around while sightseeing (in cities only is this necessary), and keep a note of travelers' check numbers, separate from the checks themselves, in case they are lost or stolen. If possible do not leave luggage in a self-drive car while touring.

FOREWORD

The Netherlands is one of the smallest countries in Europe, yet it offers an immense diversity of worthwhile experiences to the traveler. Its varied and eventful history and the great cultural energy of its people have created a veritable treasure house of ancient and picturesque towns and buildings, filling its many museums with countless beautiful works. Even the lush green landscape has been created by the tireless determination of its people in the fight against the encroaching sea.

The Dutch love and respect their past and have done more than most nations to preserve their historic heritage, but they also have a progressive approach towards the creation of new and efficient facilities—railways, roads, hotels and other amenities for the traveler.

The visitor will be enchanted by the many old towns, the beautifully-tended small villages and landscapes so unlike any other place in the world. Every Dutch person seems to love growing things. One can see this not only from the carefully maintained farms and tiny house gardens, but also from the indoor plants, seen in such abundance in almost every home. In short, the Dutch truly care about their environment, and the traveler can enjoy the results of their efforts on even the shortest visit.

Some visitors stay only briefly in Holland, concentrating on such major tourist centers as Amsterdam, Den Haag, Delft and Rotterdam. This is a pity, as there are so many charming and unusual smaller towns and villages to see, each with its own special attractions and individual appeal. The country is small, roads, rail and bus systems are extremely good and whether one is seeking culture and sightseeing, or natural and scenic beauty, or sport and recreation, Holland has so very much to offer.

The Dutch themselves love traveling and there are many inexpensive sightseeing tour programmes with special low price fare arrangements to help them, and the foreigner, to enjoy the country to the full.

Perhaps the best way to see the Netherlands is by self-drive car, or, for those on a tighter budget, by the rail and bus fare concessions available. Caravanning is extremely popular with the Dutch and there are excellent campsites with all the latest facilities. An even closer way to discover the country is by bike, which can be hired locally, and for which there are even specially arranged tours.

Particularly deserving of attention are Holland's unrivaled water sports facilities. Around the IJsselmeer (the old Zuyder Zee) are a number of well-equipped yachting harbors which make boating of all kinds a delight, with the additional bonus of being able to go eel-fishing with local boatmen. The many huge inland lakes and the vast network of waterways turn much of Holland into Western Europe's aquatic paradise for all who love boats, fishing and water sports in general. You can hire a boat of your own, or join an organized cruise, lasting from a few hours to several days.

Apart from its proverbial attractions, Holland has some rather unusual ones as well: in Oudewater you can go through the ordeal of finding out whether you're a witch; in Drenthe Province there are stone graves of prehistoric giants; Limburg has the world's largest autograph book (and what's more, made of stone); Friesland in the north has mummies as well as lakes, and still farther north is the fringe of islands which millions of birds have made a paradise of their own.

In fact, there are so many things to see and do in Holland that it has been impossible to cover them all in this book. But the well-organized Netherlands Board of Tourism (NBT), which has several overseas branches, has prepared a splendid range of specialized brochures giving full information about the many ways to make the most out of a holiday in Holland. These booklets, most of which are free, are admirably supplemented by others issued by the various provincial tourist offices (VVV) each of which concentrates on its own area.

* * *

You can be as extravagant as you wish, but there is really no need to limit yourself to the best hotels and restaurants. All over Holland there is plenty of excellent accommodation available at reasonable prices, with the certainty of everything being spotlessly clean and with cheerful service, while the restaurants offer a wide variety of food to suit all budgets. Not only is the choice that is available ample, but so are the helpings. Frequently Dutch restaurants will load their tables with delicious dishes, which only the most ravenous eater could hope to empty. The dishes often contain exotic food, derived from the days when Holland had colonies in faraway places.

All in all, therefore, Holland offers much. Short distances and superb transportation, lovely scenery, art, history, and of course, the people. The old saw about the people being the main attraction in the country holds particularly true for Holland. Crowded into their flat plains and polders with an astronomical population density, they have evolved a dignified way of life in which friendship and hospitality play a major part. They are also accomplished linguists: the number of English-speaking Dutch is so high that you are never at a loss for words in Holland. In that respect, this foreign country is not very foreign. World travelers themselves, the Dutch know how to make a visitor feel at home.

*

Our editorial burdens have been greatly lightened by the kind support of the Netherlands Board of Tourism offices, both in Holland and London, as well as by the various provincial VVVs throughout the country. We would also like to thank Maren and Robin Dannhorn for their efforts on our behalf.

*   *   *

While every care has been taken to ensure the accuracy of the information contained in this guide, the publishers cannot accept responsibility for any errors which may appear.

All prices quoted in this guide are based on those available to us at the time of writing. In a world of rapid change, however, the possibility of inaccurate or out-of-date information can never be totally eliminated. We trust, therefore, that you will take prices quoted as indicators only, and will double-check to be sure of the latest figures.

Similarly, be sure to check all opening times of museums and galleries. We have found that such times are liable to change without notice, and you could easily make a trip only to find a locked door.

When a hotel closes or a restaurant produces a disappointing meal, let us know, and we will investigate the complaint. We are always ready to revise our entries for the following year's edition should the facts warrant it.

Send your letters to the editors of Fodor's Travel Publications, 201 E 50th Street, New York, N.Y. 10022. European readers may prefer to write to Fodor's Travel Guides, 9–10 Market Place, London W1N 7AG, England.

FACTS AT YOUR FINGERTIPS

 SOURCES OF INFORMATION. In this book you will find most of the information needed to plan and organize a trip to and through Holland. However, if you do require further or more specialized information, contact the Netherlands Board of Tourism (NBT). They can supply information on all aspects of travel to and around the country, from which type of vacation is best suited to your needs and purse, to special interest and recreational travel facilities. They produce copious amounts of information, much of it free and all of it useful.

Their addresses are:

In the U.S.: 355 Lexington Ave., 21st Floor, New York, N.Y. 10017 (tel. 212–370–7367); 225 N. Michigan Ave., Suite 326, Chicago, Ill. 60601 (tel. 312–819–0300); 605 Market St., Suite 401, San Francisco, Ca. 94105 (tel. 415–543–6772).

In Canada: 25 Adelaide St. East, Suite 710, Toronto, Ont. M5C 1Y2 (tel. 416–363–1577).

In the U.K.: 25–28 Buckingham Gate, London SW1E 6LD (tel. 01–630 0451).

Once in Holland there are over 400 local tourist offices, known as VVV. They are usually located near railway stations or market squares, at major border crossings and key tourist places of interest, and are extremely helpful and efficient. They too can supply large amounts of information on their locality (excursions, reduced-rate travel cards, entertainment, restaurants etc.). Most can help you to obtain accommodations, for a small fee.

We give addresses of the local VVV offices in each Practical Information section.

 HOW TO GO. The best and most economical way to visit the Netherlands, especially from North America, is on a package tour. The number and variety of these increase yearly, and most offer excellent value for money. Their principal advantages are that the two single most expensive components of a vacation—getting there and accommodations—are generally very competitively-priced, and are arranged for you. At the same time, most packages offer considerable flexibility. You can, for example, buy an all-inclusive, pre-paid package, which gives you flight, accommodations, meals and excursions—all at a fixed price—leaving only incidental expenditure (drinks, shopping, laundry etc.) for you to pay for during your trip. For those making a first visit and unsure of where to visit or how to get around, this is frequently an excellent introduction to a country. Many, however, might find this type of trip too stifling or regimented. There is also the drawback that you might find your fellow packagees—from whom there is no escape—dull, though of course at the same time you might well get on fine.

Alternatively, therefore, there are packages which give you flight and accommodations only, with optional pre-paid meals and excursions. To a large extent, this sort of semi-independent package gives you the best of both worlds.

Other options available include fly-drive, to include the airfare and self-drive car hire, and which is particularly appropriate for a small country like Holland and suitable for those who want the maximum independence, though here costs tend to be steeper. Similarly, special interest packages, again offering varying degrees of flexibility and independence, are also available. Popular themes include sailing, bird-watching, castle touring, painting, photography, art and culture tours, gourmet tours and much else besides.

TRAVEL AGENTS. Regardless of whether you plan to visit Holland independently or take a package, it is advisable to consult a reputable travel agent. If you are only after an inexpensive flight, at the very least he will be able to guide you through the impenetrable maze of trans-Atlantic air fares. But if you want to buy a complete package, or even have an entire itinerary devised (which will prove expensive) he will be able to recommend the most appropriate for your particular needs. He will also be able to arrange insurance and other paperwork. A good travel agent can save you time, money and a good deal of inconvenience, and is an invaluable extra source of information.

If you are in any doubt which agent to contact, consult the American Society of Travel Agents, 4400 MacArthur Blvd., N.W. Washington, D.C. 20007, or the British Association of Travel Agents, 53 Newman St., London W.1.

TOUR OPERATORS. Full details of the many operators offering trips to Holland are available from the NBT overseas offices. But such is the range of tours available from both North America and the U.K. (in some cases taking in the neighboring countries of Belgium and Luxembourg as well) that a summary of some of the more typical is of interest. (All details are for 1987 only—check for latest information).

Tours from the U.S. If you just want to glance around, Holland is a popular stop on numerous 2- and 3-week tours of the continent. Maupintour's "Grand Europe," for example, trots through 11 countries in 32 days, allotting 2 for Holland. If, however, you'd like to take a slightly less hurried look, there are still a number of possibilities.

One of the more interesting, luxurious, and expensive ways to see the country is by barge. *Floating Through Europe* (271 Madison Ave., New York, N.Y. 10016) offers several trips through the country's canals. Each is organized around a theme—"Tale of Two Countries" (Holland and Belgium) or "Tulips and Spring Flowers"—which decides the choice of sights and activities during the trip. Trips are 6 days and 6 nights, or 4 days and 3 nights; accommodations and most meals are on board; and there are daily stops for exploration on shore. 6-day trips cost approximately $1,600 per person (double occupancy) from May to October. 4-day trips are about $700 under the same conditions.

For those who prefer to keep their feet on solid ground, *Maupintour* (1515 St. Andrew's Dr., Lawrence, KS 66044) offers (in addition to the tour mentioned above) "Holland Holiday," an eight-day trip that includes stops in Den Haag, Rotterdam, Amsterdam and Delft. Sights seen include the Keukenhof Gardens, the Royal Delft Blue Pottery Works, and the Alkmaar Cheese Market. Cost is $1,498 plus airfare.

Extra-Value Travel (437 Madison Ave., New York, N.Y. 10022) offers several standard package tours through Holland, such as "The Best of Holland" (6 days, $374 per person, double occupancy), "The Best of Holland and Belgium" (6 days, $336 per person, double occupancy) and "Grand Tour of Holland and Belgium" (7 days, $688 per person). All leave from New York.

U.S.-based tour operators offering travel to Holland also include:
American Express, 822 Lexington Ave., New York, N.Y. 10021.
Caravan Tours, 401 N. Michigan Ave., Chicago, IL 60611.

The Cortell Group, 770 Lexington Ave., New York, N.Y. 10022.
Cosmos Globus-Gateway, 95–25 Queens Blvd., Rego Park, N.Y. 11374.
Travcoa, 4000 MacArthur Blvd., Ste. 650E, Newport Beach, CA 93660.
U.K.-based tour operators offering holidays in the Netherlands are numerous and include the following:
Anglia Holidays, Norwich Airport, Norwich NR6 6ER (tel. 0603–43764).
Chequers Travel, Maybrook House, Queen's Gardens, Dover, Kent CT17 9AH (tel. 0304–204515). Trips to Dutch Grand Prix (cars) and other motor sporting events.
Global, Glen House, 200 Tottenham Court Rd., London W1P OJP (tel. 01–637–3333).
Page and Moy, 136 London Rd., Leicester LE2 1EN (tel. 0533–552996). Grand Prix tours.
Prospect Art Tours Ltd., 10 Barley Mow Passage, Chiswick, London W4 4PH (tel. 01–995–2163). Art tours.
Thomson Holidays, Greater London House, Hampstead Rd., London NW1 7SD (tel. 01–387–9321). Weekends and short breaks by air, rail and coach. Amsterdam and the Bulbfields, Honeymoons and Special Occasions.
Time Off Ltd., 2a Chester Close, Chester St., London SW1X 7BQ (tel. 01–235–8070). Amsterdam packages, air or sea transportation.
Townsend Thoresen Holidays, Enterprise House, Avebury Ave., Tonbridge, Kent TN1 1TH (tel. 0732–365437).
Travelscene, 94 Baker St., London W1M 2HD (tel. 01–486–6411). Trips to the Bulbfields, and Amsterdam.

 YOUTH TRAVEL. The following organizations are the major sources of information for all aspects of youth travel in both Holland and Europe in general. They also have (or can get) information about student jobs, all-inclusive tours, language courses, study programs and other student and young persons' travel. A useful source of information, particularly for youth traveling in Holland, is the Stichting Bureau Internationale Jongeren Kontakten, 2 Prof Tulpstraat, Amsterdam 1018 HA (tel. 020–250821).

One major student exchange organization is the A.F.S. International Program, 313 East 43rd St., New York, N.Y. 10017. Their head office, in Holland, is at Keizergracht 722, 1017 EW, Amsterdam (tel. 020–269481).

The Council on International Educational Exchange *(CIEE),* 205 East 42 St., New York City, N.Y. 10017, for summer study, travel and work programs and travel services for college and high school students, and a free Charter Flights Guide booklet. Their *Whole World Handbook* ($7.95 plus $1.00 postage) is the best listing of both work and study possibilities abroad.

The Institute of International Education, 809 United Nations Plaza, New York, N.Y. 10017, provides information on study opportunities abroad and administers scholarships and fellowships for international study and training. Their New York office has a visitors' information center; and there are smaller offices in Chicago, Denver, Houston, San Francisco, and Washington.

Volunteers for Peace, Tiffany Road, Belmont, VT 05730, recruit foreign volunteers for U.S. organizations hosting work camps, and they refer American volunteers to work camps in over 30 countries. Generally the volunteer arranges and pays for his or her own transportation but receives room and board in exchange for labor. The $10 annual contribution ($6 for low income individuals and students) includes their booklet *International Work Camps* and a subscription to their newsletter.

Student/Youth Travel Agencies. Among the leading specialists in the field of youth travel are the following:

Arista Student Travel Assoc., Inc., 11 E. 44th St., New York, N.Y. 10017. Student and young adult tours.

Bailey Travel Service, Inc., 123 E. Market St., York, PA 17401. School group escorted and independent tours.

Campus Holidays, 242 Bellevue Ave., Upper Montclair, NJ 07043.

Harwood Tours & Travel, Inc., 2428 Guadalupe, Austin, TX 78705. Specializes in quality escorted, co-educational motorcoach tours to Europe for students of high school and college age. Equipment used for tours is private motorcoaches seating 30–40 students.

Osborne Travel Service, Inc., 3379 Peachtree Rd., N.E., Atlanta, GA 30326. American Teens Abroad Program is designed for high-school teenagers. The College Tour Program is for ages 18–26. College students apply for the latter program on a wait list basis. Both budget and quality trips available.

Travel Plans International, Inc., P.O. Box 3875, Oak Brook, IL 60521. Quality high school and college student tours planned according to specifications.

Perhaps the single most important aid to youth travel throughout Europe is the International Student Identity Card. It will help young people to get special youth or student discounts in many useful ways—travel, theater, museum passes, etc. The card is also essential if you plan to take any Intra-European Student Charter flights, an inexpensive and fast way to get around once you arrive, and to get into student lodgings and restaurants. Similarly, you must have a card to get the excellent Eurail Youth Pass. Within Holland the most important address for contact and information is the Netherlands Youth Hostel Center, Prof. Tulpplein 4, 1018 GX Amsterdam (tel. 020–264433).

The ISI Card can be obtained at all of the General Student Travel Service Organizations. You can also get it from the Council on International Educational Exchange, 205 East 42 St., New York, N.Y. 10017; and 312 Sutter St., San Francisco, CA 94108. Canadian students should apply to the Association of Student Councils, 187 College St., Toronto, Ontario M5T 1P7. It is generally easier and cheaper to get all special membership cards and passes *before* you leave home, for example, membership in your national youth hostel association, international student card, student rail pass, International Driving Permit, etc.

 HANDICAPPED TRAVEL. Facilities in Holland for handicapped visitors are generally good. The Netherlands Board of Tourism produces an informative free brochure, *The Handicapped,* which lists many hotels, restaurants, museums, places of interest, etc., with facilities for handicapped visitors.

Otherwise, the major sources of information are: *Access to the World: A Travel Guide for the Handicapped,* by Louise Weiss, available from Facts on File, 460 Park Ave. South, New York, N.Y. 10016; the *International Air Transport Association,* 2000 Peel St., Montreal, Quebec H3A 2R4, for their pamphlet *Incapacitated Passenger's Air Travel Guide;* the lists of commercial tour operators who arrange travel for the disabled published by the Society for the Advancement of Travel for the Handicapped, 26 Court St., Brooklyn, New York 11242; and the Travel Information Center, Moss Rehabilitation Hospital, 12th St. and Tabor Rd., Philadelphia, Penn. 19141.

The main source for information in Britain for all advice on handicapped travel is The Royal Association for Disability and Rehabilitation (Radar), 25

Mortimer St., London W1N 8AB (tel: 01–637–5400). Another possibility is Mobility International, 52 Union Street, London SE1 1TD (tel. 01–403 5688). Mobility International Holland's contact address in Holland is Postbus 165, 6560 AD Groesbeek (tel. 08891–1744).

 WHEN TO GO. The main tourist season in Holland runs from about mid-April to mid-October, the peaks coming at Easter and in June to August. The weather will be at its best during this period and the country's many beaches at their most inviting during the long summer days. The Dutch, themselves, take their holidays in July and August.

However, perhaps the ideal time to visit Holland is during April and May, the height of the bulb season. Short of an unusually early spring, the bulb fields will still be colorful and some even in their prime until the end of May. Be warned, however, that at Easter hotels and other amenities are full to bursting.

Climate. Summers can be excellent, but beware sudden rains and cold winds, particularly by the sea. Winters on the other hand tend to be dull and wet, though there are a fair number of clear bright days.

Average afternoon temperatures in Amsterdam are:

	Jan.	Feb.	Mar.	Apr.	May	June	July	Aug.	Sept.	Oct.	Nov.	Dec.
Fahrenheit	41	41	46	52	60	65	69	68	64	56	47	41
Centigrade	5	5	8	11	16	18	21	20	18	13	8	5

Seasonal Events that might influence your visit to the Netherlands:

January sees the height of the concert and theater season in Amsterdam, Den Haag, and Rotterdam. Not only can you enjoy performances by Amsterdam's renowned Concertgebouw Orchestra and the Residency Orchestra at Den Haag, but there are any number of more intimate performances of chamber music, piano, violin, voice recitals, and touring companies. There is also an annual film festival in Rotterdam.

February This is carnival time, especially in the south. Major carnivals are held 7 weeks before Easter. Towards the middle of the month, the RAI automobile show attracts car fanciers to Amsterdam for 10 days of ogling the new models. In the second half of the month, the West Frisian Flora is held in Bovenkarspel, North Holland; this is a bulb show.

March sees the traditional International Spring Fair at Utrecht, an 8-day event. Towards the end of the month the famous Keukenhof flower gardens open at Lisse in the heart of the bulbfields between Haarlem and Leiden. In mammoth hothouses and outdoors you can enjoy the best in hyacinths, narcissi and tulips until end May. The miniature city of Madurodam in Den Haag opens at end March (until the third Sunday in October). In Maastricht the annual Antique Dealers' Fair is held.

April starts off with the costume re-enactment in Den Briel/Brielle south of Rotterdam, of the capture of the town from the Spaniards in 1572 by the Dutch Sea-beggars. Then come the openings of the Biblical Open-Air Museum at Groesbeek, near Nijmegen, and of the Efteling fairyland park and recreation center at Kaatsheuvel, near Tilburg, both of which continue into October. The last Friday of the month marks the start of the lively Friday-morning cheese market at Alkmaar (until mid-September), so popular that it eclipses the Thursday-morning cheese market at Gouda, which deserves to be better known. And on the 30th of the month, all Holland celebrates "Queen's Day" with parades, funfairs, and pretty decorations honoring the House of Orange.

Meanwhile the bulbfields have been bursting into great expanses of blooms that are unique in the world. The climax, of course, is the brilliant flower parade usually held on the last Saturday of April, starting from the medieval market square of Haarlem by the historic Town Hall and Great Church and then winding its way slowly through Bennebroek, Hillegom and Lisse to Noordwijk. Each year a different theme is selected for this event, and prizes are awarded to the sponsors of the most original and artistic floats. The other major bulb fields are between Haarlem and Leiden at: Hillegom, Katwijk, Lisse, Noordwijk, Rijnsburg, Voorhout, Warmond, Sassenheim, Vogelenzang and De Zilk. Between Haarlem and Den Helder, the major places to see the bulb fields are: Castricum, Limmen, Heiloo, Egmond, Heermskerk, Bergen, Schoorl, Langedijk, Julianadorp and De Zijpe. Throughout the bulb season, outdoor shows are held at the Keukenhof at Lisse. Regular, weekly antique fairs start in Breda, Den Haag and Amsterdam.

May commences with World War II Memorial Day when a two-minutes' silence is held at 8 P.M. on the 4th. The following day, May 5th, is Liberation Day, celebrating the end of World War II and German occupation. The 2nd Saturday in May is both National Cycling and Windmill Day. On this day every mill all over the country will be working and many open for visits. In the middle of the month Flag Day is celebrated at the three big herring ports of Scheveningen, IJmuiden and Vlaardingen, with the exciting race back to port with the first new salted herring for Queen Beatrix and other Dutch personalities. There will also be trips to the Betuwe where the apple and pear trees are in blossom. Centered in Leeuwarden, the Friesian Eleven Towns Walk attracts large crowds.

June launches the three weeks' Holland Festival of music, ballet, and drama. Held mainly in Amsterdam, a different foreign country is selected annually as a theme and participants are invited from abroad. The "Old Music Festival" is held in Utrecht, while other cultural festivals are presented in smaller centers. The more experimental, modern theater has its own festival in Amsterdam, the Festival of Fools; well worth visiting but crowded. The permanent International Rose-growing Competition is in Westbroek Park, Den Haag and it opens alternatively in Den Haag, Amsterdam and Rotterdam and Delft. It lasts about three weeks, but do check dates in advance. The Harlingen-Terschelling international yachting race is held. From mid-June until the end of August, every Thursday morning, West Friesian folklore market in Schagen. In Hoorn another traditional market, every Wed. 9–5 P.M., features folk dancing and craft demonstrations— open till end of August. International Motor Grand Prix, Assen. The Thursday cheese market in Gouda opens mid-June until mid-August.

July is highlighted by the international organists' competition at Haarlem, making use of the magnificent instrument in the St. Bavo Church. Sports come into their own, with the first of several regattas at Oude-wetering, and the Kaag Week regatta at Warmond. On one of the last Thursdays of the month at Middelburg you can watch Zeeland farmers and their wives in traditional garb as they try to run a lance through a suspended ring while riding in a decorated gig. Second week, in Meijel, Limburg, Festival of over 70 old crafts. Mid-July, North Sea Jazz Festival, Den Haag. End July, traditional Horse Fair, Voorschoten, South Holland. The International Rose Exhibition, in Den Haag, presents over 20,000 species of 350 varieties. The Schnitger Recitals, concerts by internationally known organists, are held in Zwolle. The Purmerend cheese market operates every Thursday morning. In Medemblik's Romantic Market, traditional products are brought in by barge and there are demonstrations of old crafts. A summer festival is held in Nijmegen as part of its International Four-Day Walk.

August has many sporting events. Sailing enthusiasts participate in regattas at Loosdrecht and Muiden before entering the all-important Sneek Week, in Friesland, all at the start of the month at delightful Sneek, near Leeuwarden. The very popular Military Tattoo, which used to be held in Delft, now takes place in Den Haag in late August. The Zaansche Schans Annual Festival, a traditional market with craft displays and so on, is held in Zaandam. First Saturday in August, Flower Parade, Rijnsburg-Leiden-Noordwijk. Third Saturday, Flower Parade at Leersum (Utrecht).

September is the traditional time of flower processions at Aalsmeer, and at Zundert, near Breda, usually during the first two weeks. Tiel in Gelderland stages a fascinating fruit harvest procession. Rotterdam enters the picture with its International Horse Jumping Show which attracts the world's best professionals and amateurs, including Olympic champions. September also sees the International Trotting Grand Prix of the Netherlands at Groningen. On Prinsjesdag, on the traditional third Tuesday in September Queen Beatrix rides in her golden coach drawn by eight horses to the opening of parliament at the 13th-century Knights' Hall, Den Haag, a splendid pageant. 's-Hertogenbosch holds an international song competition.

October is an important time in the university city of Leiden because it marks the anniversary of the lifting of its historic siege in 1574. Delft's Prinsenhof Museum hosts the Classical Art and Antique Fair, which lasts about three weeks; but dates vary, so check in advance. Mid-month, "Herfstflora," autumn flower show, Laren, North Holland.

November sees the shop windows begin to fill with gifts and traditional edibles for Sinte Klaus Day and his arrival on the 3rd or 4th Saturday in Amsterdam, where he is welcomed by the Lord Mayor. Downtown Amsterdam and Den Haag are festooned with colored lights strung over the streets. International Flower Show in Aalsmeer. For children, the highlight of **December** is the 5th (Saint Nicholas's Eve), the traditional Dutch occasion for exchanging gifts. Christmas, once a purely religious festival in this country, has now turned into a real holiday season.

 PASSPORTS. Americans. Major post offices throughout the country are now authorized to process passport applications; check with your local post office for the nearest one. You may also apply in person at U.S. Passport Agency offices in various cities; addresses and phone numbers are available under governmental listings in the white or blue pages of local telephone directories. Applications are also accepted at most County Courthouses. Renewals can be handled by mail (form DSP-82) provided that your previous passport is not more than eight years old. New applicants will need:

1. A birth certificate or certified copy thereof or other proof of citizenship;
2. Two identical photographs 2 inches square, full face, black and white or color, on nonglossy paper, and taken within the past six months;
3. $35 for the passport itself, plus a $7 processing fee if you are applying in person (no processing fee when applying by mail). For those under 18 the cost is $20 for the passport, plus a $7 processing fee—again, with no extra fee when applying by mail;
4. Proof of identity that includes a photo and signature, such as a driver's license, employment ID card, previous passport, governmental ID card. Social Security and credit cards are *not* acceptable.

Adult passports are valid for ten years, others only for five (and are not renewable). You should allow a month to six weeks for your application to be processed, but in an emergency, Passport Agency offices can have a passport readied within 24–48 hours, and even the postal authorities can indicate "Rush" when necessary.

If you expect to travel extensively, request a 48- or 96-page passport rather than the usual 24-page one. There is no extra charge. Record your passport's number and date and place of issue in a separate, secure place. When you have pictures taken for passports, have extra copies made, especially if you plan to travel extensively. You'll need photos for your International Driver's License. The loss of a valid passport should be reported immediately to the local police and to the Passport Office, Dept. of State, Washington, D.C. 20524 or to the nearest U.S. consular office when abroad.

Britons. Apply for passports on special forms obtainable from your travel agency or from the main post office in your town. The application should be sent to the Passport Office in your area (as indicated on the guidance form) or taken personally to your nearest main post office. It is advisable to apply for your passport 4–5 weeks before it is required, although in some cases it will be issued sooner. The regional Passport Offices are located in London, Liverpool, Peterborough, Glasgow and Newport. The application must be countersigned by your bank manager, or by a solicitor, barrister, doctor, clergyman or Justice of the Peace who knows you personally. You will need two photos. The fee is £15. A larger, 94-page passport can be obtained for an extra charge.

British Visitor's Passport. This simplified form of passport has advantages for the once-in-a-while tourist. Valid for one year and not renewable, it costs £7.50. Application may be made at a local post office (in Northern Ireland at the Passport Office in Belfast); you will need identification plus two passport photographs—no other formalities.

Canadians. Canadian citizens may obtain application forms for passports at any post office; these are to be sent to the Bureau of Passports, Complexe Guy Favreau, 200 Dorchester West, Montreal, P.Q. H2Z 1X4, with a remittance of $21, two photographs, and evidence of Canadian citizenship. You may apply in person to the regional passport offices in Edmonton, Halifax, Montreal, Toronto, Fredericton, Hamilton, London, Ottawa, Hull, Quebec, St. John's, Saskatoon, North York, Victoria, Windsor, Vancouver or Winnipeg. Canadian passports are valid for five years and are non-renewable.

Visas. Visitors to Holland from the U.S., Canada, the U.K., Australia and New Zealand, plus most European and Commonwealth countries do not require visas to enter Holland for stays of up to three months. South African visitors will need a visa.

Health Certificates. These are not required from any country.

TAKING MONEY ABROAD. Traveler's checks are still the standard and best way to safeguard your travel funds; and you will usually get a better exchange rate in Europe for traveler's checks than for cash. Your choice of branch will depend on several factors. American Express checks are widely known, Bank of America has some 28,000 correspondents throughout the world, Thomas Cook about 20,000. The best-known British checks are Cook's and those of Barclays, Lloyds, Midland and National Westminster banks.

Major credit cards are accepted in most large hotels, restaurants and shops but most do not accept all cards, so check at each place in advance. Out of major cities, credit cards are not so widely accepted.

Britons holding a Uniform Eurocheque card and cheque book—apply for them at your bank—can cash cheques for up to £100 a day at banks participating in the scheme, and can also write cheques for goods and services—hotels, restaurants, shops—again up to £100.

We give details of Dutch currency and exchange rates on page 16.

 HEALTH AND INSURANCE. Travel insurance can cover everything from health and accident costs, to lost baggage and trip cancellation. Sometimes they can all be obtained with one blanket policy; other times they overlap with existing coverage you might have for health and/or home; still other times it is best to buy policies that are tailored to specific needs. But, insurance is available from many sources and many travelers unwittingly end up with redundant coverage. Before purchasing separate travel insurance of any kind, be sure to check your regular policies carefully.

Generally, it is best to take care of your insurance needs *before* embarking on your trip. You'll pay more for less coverage—and have less chance to read the fine print—if you wait until the last minute. Best of all, if you have a regular insurance agent, he is the person to consult first. Flight insurance, often included in the price of the ticket when the fare is paid via American Express, Visa or certain other major credit cards, is also often included in package policies providing accident coverage as well. These policies are available from most tour operators and insurance companies. While it is a good idea to have health and accident insurance, be careful not to spend money to duplicate coverage you may already have . . . or to neglect some eventuality which could end up costing a small fortune. For example, Blue Cross Blue Shield policies cover health costs incurred while traveling. They will not, however, cover the cost of emergency transportation, which can often add up to several thousand dollars. Emergency transportation *is* covered, in part at least, by many major medical policies such as those underwritten by Prudential, Metropolitan and New York Life. Again, check any policy carefully before buying. Note that most insurance issued specifically for travel does not cover pre-existing medical conditions.

Several organizations offer coverage designed to supplement existing health insurance and to help defray costs not covered by many standard policies, such as emergency transportation. Some of the more prominent are:

Carefree Travel Insurance, c/o ARM Coverage Inc., 120 Mineola Blvd., Box 310, Mineola, N.Y. 11510 (tel. 516–283–0220), offers insurance, legal and financial assistance, as well as medical evacuation arranged through InterClaim. *Carefree* coverage is available from many travel agents.

International SOS Assistance Inc., P.O. Box 11568, Philadelphia, PA, 19116, has fees from $15 a person for seven days, to $195 for a year (tel. 800–523–8930).

IAMAT (International Association for Medical Assistance to Travelers), 417 Center St., Lewiston, N.Y. 14092 in the U.S. (tel. 716–754–4883); or 188 Nicklin Road, Guelph, Ontario N1H 7L5 (tel. 519–836–0102).

Travel Assistance International, the American arm of *Europ Assistance,* offers a comprehensive program providing medical and personal emergency services and offering immediate, on-the-spot medical, personal and financial help. Trip protection ranges from $35 for an individual for up to eight days to $220 for an entire family for a year. Full details from travel agents or insurance brokers, or from Europ Assistance Worldwide Services, Inc., 1333 F St., N.W., Washington, D.C. 20004 (800–821–2828). In the U.K., contact Europ Assistance Ltd., 252 High St., Croydon, Surrey (01–680 1234).

The British Insurance Association, Aldermary House, Queen St., London E.C.4 (tel. 01–248 4477), will give comprehensive advice on all aspects of vacation travel insurance from the U.K.

Loss of baggage is another frequent inconvenience to travelers. It is possible, though complicated, to insure your luggage against loss through theft or negligence. Insurance companies are reluctant to sell such coverage alone, however, since it is often a losing proposition for them. Instead, this type of coverage is usually included as part of a package that also covers accidents or health. Should you lose your luggage or some other personal possession, it is essential to report it to the local police immediately. Without documentation of such a report, your insurance company might be very stingy. Also, before buying baggage insurance, check your homeowner's policy. Some such policies offer "off-premises theft" coverage, including the loss of luggage while traveling.

Trip cancellation coverage is especially important to travelers on APEX or charter flights. Should you be unable to continue your trip during your vacation, you may be stuck having to buy a new one-way fare home, plus paying for the charter you're not using. You can guard against this with "trip cancellation insurance." Most of these policies will also cover last minute cancellations.

 LANGUAGE. Dutch is a relatively impenetrable language to most English speakers, but except in the most out of the way places (and sometimes not even then) you are unlikely to have any difficulties. English is widely spoken in all major tourist centers—hotels, restaurants, rail stations etc.—while at all tourist offices there will always be at least one fluent English speaker, though the odds are there will be more. Indeed, you are liable to find that even bus conductors and street cleaners speak pretty good English. But nonetheless, if you can manage a few words or phrases in Dutch, it will be appreciated. See our *English-Dutch Vocabulary* for useful words and phrases.

 DUTCH TIME. Holland is on Central European Time, six hours ahead of the East Coast of the States, nine hours ahead of the West Coast. It is one hour ahead of the U.K.

 GETTING TO HOLLAND FROM NORTH AMERICA. By Air. Amsterdam's Schiphol Airport is a major gateway to Europe, with direct flights from many cities in the U.S. and Canada and through flights from most other cities. Flying to Holland is both easy to arrange and, given the perpetual battle for customers among the major airlines, relatively inexpensive. We give details below.

However, be warned that though fares may be low and flights numerous, long-distance flying today is no bed of roses. Lines and delays at ever-more-crowded airports, perfunctory in-flight service and shrinking leg-room on board a giant jet with some 400 other people, followed by interminable waits for your luggage when you arrive, are the clearest possible signals that the glamor of air travel—if it ever existed—is very much a thing of the past.

Unfortunately, these problems are compounded when flying to Europe by the fact that many flights from the States are scheduled to arrive first thing in the morning. Not only are you in for a night's discomfort on the plane, but you arrive at the start of a new day to be greeted by the confusion (some would say chaos) of a modern airport. To make life even more difficult for the weary traveler, many hotels will not allow you to check in before noon or even 1 P.M. giving you as much as six hours with nothing to do and nowhere to go.

There are a number of steps you can take, however, in order to lessen the traumas of long-distance flying. The first and possibly most important of all is to harbor no illusions about the supposed luxury. If you approach your flight knowing that you are going to be cooped up for a long time and will have to face delays and discomforts of all kinds, the odds are that you will get through it without doing terrible things to your blood pressure or being disillusioned—but there's no point expecting comfort, good service and efficiency because you won't get them.

The right attitude is half the battle, but there are a number of other practical points to follow. Wear comfortable, loose-fitting clothes and take off your shoes. Try to sleep as much as possible, especially on night flights; this can very often mean not watching the movie as it will probably be shown during the only period when meals are not being served and you can sleep. If you have difficulty sleeping, or think you might, take along a light sedative and try to get a window seat in order to avoid being woken up to let the person next to you get to the toilet or being bashed by people walking down the aisle. Above all, avoid alcohol, or at least drink only a little. The dry air of a pressurized airplane causes rapid dehydration, exaggerating the effects of drink and jet lag. Similarly, drink as much water as possible. Finally, once you arrive, try to take things easily for a day or so. In the excitement of being in a new place, especially for the first time, you can very often not realize how tired you are and optimistically set out sightseeing, only to come down to earth with a bump. Whatever you do, don't have any business meetings for at least 24 hours after arriving.

Fares. With air fares in a constant state of flux, the best advice for anyone planning to fly to Holland independently (rather than as a part of a package tour) is first to shop around for all possible information, check with a travel agent and let him make your reservations for you. Nonetheless, there are a number of points to bear in mind.

The best buy is an Apex (advance purchase excursion) ticket. First class, Business and even the misleadingly named Economy, though they give maximum flexibility on flying dates and cancellations as well as permitting stop overs, are extremely expensive. Apex, by contrast, is reasonably priced and offers the all important security of fixed return dates (all Apex tickets are round trip). In addition, you get exactly the same service as flying Economy. However, there are a number of restrictions: you must book, and pay for, your ticket 21 days or more in advance; you can stay in Holland no less than and no more than a stated period (usually six days and six months); if you miss your flight, you forfeit the fare. But from the point of view of price and convenience, these tickets, plus special charter flights, certainly represent the best value for money.

If you have the flexibility, you can sometimes benefit from last-minute sales tour operators have in order to fill a plane. A number of brokers specializing in such discount sales have also sprung up. All charge an annual membership fee, usually about $35–45. Among these: *Stand-Buys* Ltd., 311 W. Superior, Suite 414, Chicago, IL 60610, (312–943–5737); *Moments Notice,* 40 E. 49th St., New York, N.Y. 10017, (212–486–0503); *Discount Travel Intl.,* 114 Forrest Ave., Narbeth, PA 19072, (215–668–2182); and *Worldwide Discount Travel Club,* 1674 Meridian Ave., Miami Beach, FL 33139, (305–534–2082).

Charter flights are also available to Holland, though the number has decreased in recent years. Again, a travel agent will be able to recommend the most reliable. Many professional, trade, sporting and student associations also have access to reduced group fare arrangements. If you belong to any such bodies, do check with them, as savings can be substantial.

GETTING TO HOLLAND FROM THE U.K. By Air.

Flying to Holland from the U.K. is simple and relatively inexpensive. There are some 12 flights daily from London (Heathrow) to Amsterdam by British Airways and KLM (Royal Dutch Airlines). Flying time is approximately one hour. The long-awaited direct rail link to the center of Amsterdam is now open and this makes access much easier. To Rotterdam, Eindhoven and Maastricht, NLM, an off-shoot of KLM, have daily direct flights; also from Heathrow; Rotterdam Airlines, with five flights daily, has the best service from Gatwick. British Caledonian also have four flights daily to Amsterdam and three on weekdays to Rotterdam from Gatwick. Or the maverick Virgin flies to Maastricht daily from Gatwick. Their flights connect with their services from the States. London's new City Airport is open, just a few minute's away from the City and in the old dockland area. Brymon fly four times a day to Amsterdam, while Eurocity Express serve both Amsterdam and Rotterdam.

Holland is also well served by flights from provincial U.K. airports. Air UK operate direct services to Amsterdam from Aberdeen, Edinburgh, Humberside, Leeds/Bradford, Norwich, Southampton and Stansted. From Birmingham and Manchester British Airways and NLM serve Amsterdam, while British Midland fly from the East Midlands. On both of these last two routes there are two flights daily on weekdays. British Midland operates from several midlands points, and Dan Air from Cardiff and Bristol.

Fares. Fares from London to Amsterdam have been turned topsy-turvy by the £55 return by KLM/British Airways from London to Amsterdam. This fare is only available on certain flights, and can only be booked two days in advance, so check carefully with your travel agent before booking. Standard fares remain the same, from around £73 return, providing that you pay for your ticket at the time of booking and your stay in Holland includes at least one Saturday night, to around £170 return in Club Class. The Virgin fare to Maastricht is very attractive at around £35 single. It is likely that fares will remain static in 1988; the promises of an open market for fares between London and Amsterdam have yet to lead to super-low offers.

GETTING TO HOLLAND FROM THE U.K. By Train.

The simplest route from London to Rotterdam, Den Haag and Amsterdam is from London (Liverpool Street Station) to Harwich (Parkeston Quay) then by Sealink ferry to the Hook of Holland and by train to Amsterdam. This is the classic route, with first and second class accommodations on both train and ship. Additionally, the terminals are designed for ease of interchange between ferries and trains. The daytime services from Harwich are usually made by the new

British Ferries flagship—a veritable floating hotel! The overnight crossing is made by the new Dutch vessel Queen Beatrix which is of similar standard.

The daytime journey sets out from London at 9.40 in the morning and arrives in Amsterdam around 9.30 P.M. If time is tight the overnight service is excellent —but note that during the high, summer, season it is essential to reserve both train seats and sleeping accommodations well in advance. For this overnight service you travel by the conveniently timed 7.40 P.M. EuroCity "Benjamin Britten" from London (Liverpool Street) which connects with the night Harwich ferry, reaching Holland at 6.30 the following morning. Sea crossing time is from 7 to 9 hours, depending on day or night sailing.

From the Hook of Holland there are frequent train services. It is possible to be in Rotterdam for example just before 7.30—if you are in a hurry—and, by EuroCity express in Amsterdam just after 9. From Rotterdam Central Station (C.S.) the Dutch Inter-City network fans out to serve most parts of the country.

An alternative route to Holland from London is via Dover and Ostend. This route is slightly quicker than that via the Hook of Holland due to the shorter sea crossing but is only suitable for travelers with light luggage due to the large number of changes involved. The service leaves London (Victoria Station) at 8.15 for Dover to connect with the mid-morning Jetfoil to Ostend. Fare is £ 88.30 return plus £6 for Jetfoil, each way. The Jetfoil has slashed the crossing time from around 3½ hours by ferry to a mere 75 minutes! From Ostend to Amsterdam the quickest way is to travel to Antwerp in Belgium and then change to one of the expresses from Paris bound for Rotterdam and Amsterdam. Rotterdam is reached just after 4.30 in the afternoon and Amsterdam just after 5.30. The channel crossing on this route can also be made by conventional car ferry instead of Jetfoil, but being slow this rather defeats the object! This Dover– Ostend route is not recommended for overnight travel—go via the Hook of Holland.

A third possible route from London is via Sheerness on the Isle of Sheppey (on the North Kent coast) to Vlissingen in the southwest of Holland. This route is not recommended for travelers with heavy luggage due to the number of transfers which have to be made; but it is still a useful alternative. First travel from London (Victoria) to Sittingbourne where you change to the local train to Sheerness, from where there is a bus connection to the Olau Line ferry terminal. There is only one day time and one overnight sailing, the latter berthing at Vlissingen at 7 the following morning. There is a bus service to the railway station from which there is a good service of Inter City trains direct to Rotterdam, Den Haag and Amsterdam.

Fares. British Rail in conjunction with Netherlands railways have introduced very attractive fares to Holland (when traveling via Harwich/Hook) the second class return fare from London to *any* station in Holland is £48 or £62 using the Standard Return on the day or night service (sleeping accommodations are extra). These tickets are valid for two months, and they allow you to break your journey en route. For shorter visits the five-day excursion returns are ideal—the return fare is around £36 using day sailings and £47 by night. There are special offers for children.

For those under 26, Transalpino Travel offers fares which are even cheaper than British Rail, though not by much. A return to Amsterdam works out at around £35. Transalpino's head office is at 71–75 Buckingham Palace Rd., London S.W.1 (tel. 01–834 9656). You must take your passport along when buying a ticket.

Note: These fare details were compiled after the railways had reacted to the new cheap fares to the Netherlands from the UK. But rail/ship fares may well

TO	HOLLAND			BELGIUM	
From:	Rotterdam	Hook of Holland	Vlissingen (Flushing)	Zeebrugge	Ostend
Hull	N			N	
Felixstowe				T	
Harwich		S			
Sheerness			O		
Dover				T	TR

Operators: N = North Sea Ferries; O = Olau line; S = Sealink; T = Townsend Thoresen; TR = Thoresen/RTM

FERRY SERVICES FROM THE U.K. FOR TRAVEL TO HOLLAND

change due to currency fluctuations. Check before traveling. For information
telephone British Ferries 01–387–1234; North Sea Ferries 0482–796145; Olau
Line 0795–666666; Townsend Thoresen Ferries 01–734 4431; Sealink 01–834
8122.

GETTING TO HOLLAND FROM THE U.K. By Bus.

The best and most economical way for budget travelers.
Hoverspeed, as part of the International Express network, run an express coach service from London, Victoria Coach Station to Amsterdam, Den Haag and Rotterdam. From April
through September there are two departures daily. Passengers cross the channel
on the hovercraft and the complete journey is very quick, taking just under 10½
hours. This service is difficult to beat either on speed or price, the single fare
to Amsterdam is only around £23. Students under 26 travel even more cheaply.
Details from Hoverspeed Ltd., Freepost, Maybrook House, Queens Gardens,
Dover CT17 9BR (tel. 0304 216205) or your travel agent.

Several overnight International Express services run to Breda, Rotterdam,
Amsterdam, The Hague, Utrecht and Gronigen. Expect to pay about £20.
Details from International Express, the Coach Travel Center, 13 Regent St.,
London SE1Y 4RL (tel. 01–439 9368).

GETTING TO HOLLAND FROM THE U.K. By Car.

There is a wide choice of routings for motorists going to
Holland. There are two main direct routes from London. First, there is the Sealink ferry service from Harwich (Parkeston Quay) to the Hook of Holland. The day-time crossing takes
around 6¾ hours and the night sailing around 8. Road connections on the
English side of the North Sea are now greatly improved with the opening of the
Chelmsford bypass.

Secondly, there is the Olau Line service from Sheerness to Vlissingen. This
is especially attractive due to the ease of access along the A2/M2 from London.
The service of one day-time and one night-time sailing is operated by two large
modern and very comfortable ships. The sea crossing takes between 7–8½
hours. From Vlissingen there are excellent motorways to all parts of Holland.

You might also want to use the services from Dover to Belgium, generally
quite useful for getting to Holland. However, the number of sailings has declined
markedly—ruling out the main attraction of this route! Things will not improve
again until British Ferries can regain access to a Belgian port—having been
forced out by a new agreement between Townsend Thoresen and RTM. In
mid-1987 an unseemly squabble was still going on! So it's anyone's guess what
the situation will be in 1988. The crossing time on these routes varies around
3½ hours depending on the route. However, the ships are generally older, less
comfortable and smaller than those used on the main crossings. Motorway links
between Belgium and Holland are excellent. The full choice of routes and
operators is listed in our table.

For the direct sailings from Harwich and Sheerness it is essential to book well
in advance, especially if cabin accommodations are required. Late bookers stand
a much better chance on the shorter route from Dover where services are more
frequent.

Fares. As one would expect, fares are highest on the longer crossings. For
example, £310 for two adults and a car under 4.5 meters. The fare includes berth
and meals on the night crossing Hull to Rotterdam or Zeebrugge, while the
Hook of Holland route works out at around £210 overnight, plus cabin. Com-
pare this with around £165 for a daytime crossing from Dover to Zeebrugge.

During the winter months all the ferry companies offer special deals, mostly just for the ferry crossing but some with hotel or self-catering accommodations in Holland.

CUSTOMS. There are three levels of duty-free allowance for visitors to Holland. For travelers arriving from outside Europe the allowances are:

400 cigarettes or 100 cigars or 500 grams of tobacco; plus one liter of spirits more than 22% proof or two liters of spirits less than 22% proof or two liters of liqueur wine, plus two liters of wine; plus 50 grams of perfume; plus other goods to the value of Fl. 500.

For travelers arriving from a non-EEC country *or* from an EEC country but who have bought goods in a duty-free shop, the allowances are: 200 cigarettes or 50 cigars or 100 cigarillos or 250 grams of tobacco; plus one liter of spirits more than 22% proof or two liters of spirits less than 22% proof or two liters of liqueur wine, plus two liters of wine; plus 50 grams of perfume; plus other goods to the value of Fl. 125.

For travelers arriving from an EEC country, the allowances for goods, provided they were *not* bought in a duty-free shop, are: 300 cigarettes or 75 cigars or 400 grams of tobacco; plus one and a half liters of spirits more than 22% proof or three liters of spirits less than 22% proof or three liters of sparkling wine or three liters of liqueur wine, plus five liters of non sparkling wine; plus 75 grams of perfume and 37.5 centiliters of toilet water; plus other goods to the value of Fl. 890.

All personal items may be imported duty free, provided you take them out with you when you leave. Tobacco and alcohol allowances are for those 17 and over. There are no restrictions on the import and export of Dutch currency.

DUTCH CURRENCY. The monetary unit in Holland is the *gulden* (guilder or florin), written as Fl. Notes are in denominations of 1,000, 250, 100, 50, 25, 10 and 5 guilders. Coins are 2.5 guilders, 1 guilder, 25, 10, and 5 cents. Be careful not to mix up the 2.5 guilder and the 1 guilder coins as there is not much difference in size. Bank notes have a code of dots that can be identified; this is for the blind.

At the time of writing (mid-1987), the exchange rate for the guilder was Fl. 2.03 to the U.S. dollar and Fl. 3.35 to the pound sterling. However, these rates change constantly, so check them carefully while planning your trip and during it.

Changing Money. Changing money is easy in Holland. You can do so either at banks (open 9–4, Mon.–Fri.) or through the many GWK bureaux de change offices. These are located in main stations, airports, key border crossings and in a number of major tourist centers. They offer good rates, and some stay open late during the summer. Hotels and some shops will also change major foreign currencies, but usually at less than favorable rates. GWK will also accept major credit cards to obtain cash.

HOTELS. Dutch hotels are generally excellently-run, spotlessly clean and extremely comfortable. The larger cities are well-equipped with hotels in all price categories —indeed some of the very top hotels are as good as any in the world—while more moderate and inexpensive hotels nearly always provide good basic levels of comfort and service. In rural areas, standards are more modest, but you can still be sure of a warm welcome and normally not inconsiderable comfort and service. English is spoken by desk clerks and waiters in all, including the smallest, hotels.

Don't be surprised if your waiter hands you your room bill after you finish breakfast and are preparing to leave. This is typical of smaller establishments and is in fact really quite convenient as it eliminates further delay at the time of your actual departure.

It is usually possible to make reservations either by writing or calling hotels, but there is an excellent reservations system operated by the Netherlands Reservations Center. They are able to make reservations for up to 1,600 hotels throughout the country; this service is free. Write Netherlands Reservations Center, P.O. Box 404, 2260 AK Leidschendam. Alternatively, most VVV offices operate accommodations services for a small fee. We give addresses for VVV offices in the *Practical Information* sections at the end of each regional chapter.

Prices. We have divided all hotels that we list into four categories—*Deluxe* (L), *Expensive* (E), *Moderate* (M) and *Inexpensive* (I). These grades largely correspond with the official NNTO system of hotel grading which is based on the international star system. Thus, 5-stars is the equivalent of our Deluxe, 4-stars the equivalent of Expensive, 3- *and* 2-stars the equivalent of Moderate and 1-star the equivalent of Inexpensive.

Two people in a double room can expect to pay (prices in guilders, including service charge and VAT):

	Amsterdam	Large Town	Rural Area
Deluxe	300—600	220—350	—
Expensive	200—300	140—230	130—250
Moderate	100—200	90—150	70—140
Inexpensive	75—100	60—90	40—80

Hotels frequently have rooms in more than one price category. It's very important to check what price your room is before taking it. Such factors as size of room, whether it has private bathroom or shower, view, etc., all affect the price. Some hotels charge more during the top demand periods like Easter, and many charge less during their off-seasons, when worthwhile savings can often be made. Many smaller and cheaper hotels do not have attached bathrooms, so check when booking. Also note that many older city hotels do not have elevators (lifts), their steep narrow stairs being difficult for older travelers.

 YOUTH HOSTELS. Holland has over 50 youth hostels, mostly providing very clean dormitory style accommodations but very few other facilities. In order to use them, you must be a member of the International Youth Hostels Federation. Bed and breakfast costs around Fl. 17 a night, including breakfast. Hostels in cities tend to get very full in the summer. Full lists of all youth hostels may be had from the Netherlands Youth Hostel Center, NJHC 4 Prof. Tulpplein 1018 GX, Amsterdam (tel. 020–264433) or from any branch of the NBT or VVV.

 CAMPING. There are some 2,000 camp sites in Holland, 450 of which are listed in the NBT's *Camping* brochure. Prices vary according to site and facilities, from FL. 20 to Fl. 30 per night for a family of four people in a tent or caravan. Specialized information is available from the Nederlandsche Toeristen Kampeer Club (NTKC), 11 Daendelstraat, Den Haag, and from the NBT and VVV offices. Note that camping outside these official sites is generally forbidden in Holland. Camping huts are also available along some hiking and cycling routes. Cost for a hut, sleeping 4, is approx. Fl. 40. Details and reservations through NRC, P.O. Box 404, 2260 AK Leidschendam.

 BED AND BREAKFAST. These are found all over Holland and are very popular. Most are family-run and very inexpensive. There is no overall national listing of bed and breakfast places, but many VVV offices have local lists. However, they can get very full in high summer. Prices for a double room range from Fl. 18 to Fl. 35 per person, including breakfast.

 STAYING WITH A FAMILY. The Amsterdam VVV office runs a "Get in Touch with the Dutch" scheme whereby visitors can meet local people. This can range from a coffee or perhaps a meal with a local family through to staying with a family for your whole vacation. A number of tour operators also arrange such vacations.

 RESTAURANTS. The complex and rewarding subject of eating in Holland is covered in our Dutch Food and Drink chapter (see page 69). However, a number of general points should nonetheless be noted.

First remember that the Dutch like to eat early—normally around six or seven in the evening. Even the most expensive restaurants tend therefore to be closed by 10. Most, however, only accept last orders earlier than this. Most can also, especially the better ones, get very full, so it is nearly always advisable to book ahead. Credit cards are generally, but not universally, accepted—always check if yours will be or you could find yourself in a very embarrassing situation. Note also that more expensive restaurants usually have dishes in more than one price category, so that what appears an expensive restaurant can sometimes prove quite reasonable if you choose carefully. All Dutch restaurants are legally obliged to display their menus in the window; study them carefully and you could find yourself a bargain. Keep your eyes open, too, for the excellent-value Tourist Menu. This always costs Fl. 18.75 (by law) and must have three courses. All restaurants serving them have a sign in the window.

Prices. We have divided the restaurants in our listings into three categories— *Expensive* (E), *Moderate* (M) and *Inexpensive* (I). These grades largely correspond with the official Dutch grading of restaurants which is based on a star system. Thus 4-stars, the top category, is the equivalent of our Expensive, 2- *and* 3-stars the equivalent of Moderate and 1-star the equivalent of Inexpensive.

Price guide, per person (in guilders), excluding drinks but including service and VAT:

	Amsterdam		Rural Area	
	Lunch	Dinner	Lunch	Dinner
Expensive	70 up	90 up	40—60	70—100
Moderate	40—60	50—90	20—35	30—50
Inexpensive	15—25	20—40	10—20	15—30

TIPPING. All hotels and restaurants in Holland include 15% service and value added tax. Small extra gratuities can be added for special help or service, but are not expected. Give the doorman, for example, 50 cents for calling a cab, and it is customary to leave any odd small change when paying a bill.

Hairdressers and barbers have inclusive service prices, but they do expect a tip. Taxis in almost every town have a tip included in the meter charge, but here again the fare is usually made up to the nearest guilder by the user. Where the tip is not included, add the odd 50 cents.

The official minimum for railway porters is Fl. 2.50 a bag. Ushers at cinemas, theaters and concerts are usually given 25 cents for showing you to your seat although this is not necessary. Hat-check attendants expect at least 25 cents, but more according to the type of place. Washroom attendants get 50 cents as a general rule.

CASINOS. Holland is not really a gambling country, but there are nonetheless a number of casinos, the main ones being at Amsterdam, Rotterdam, Scheveningen, Valkenburg and Zandvoort. All are open daily, all year round. They offer roulette or black jack and of course have bars and restaurants. Admission for a day (for those over 18 only) costs from Fl. 7.50 or Fl. 25 for a week. Minimum stakes are small, from around Fl. 2 to Fl. 10. Dress need not be terribly formal, but a reasonable degree of smartness is expected. Opening hours are usually 12 noon to 2 A.M.

NIGHTLIFE. There is considerable contrast within Holland between the out and out raunchiness of Amsterdam and Rotterdam and the rather subdued nightlife everywhere else. Nightlife prospects are given in the relevant regional and city chapters.

CINEMA, THEATER AND MUSIC. Cinemas throughout the country have American and English movies, mostly with Dutch subtitles though occasionally dubbed into Dutch. Check whether the movie you want to see is dubbed or not.

The theater scene in Holland is very active, with both Dutch and touring companies at large. There is a good chance therefore that you will be able to catch an English production in one or more of the larger cities. VVV offices have details of all current and forthcoming productions and can also usually provide tickets. Similarly, concerts, opera and ballet thrive in Holland, and you should normally be able to get into a performance or two. Again, check with the VVV office in the town where you're staying.

WATER SPORTS. Facilities for all kinds of water sports exist in abundance throughout Holland. Yachting, wind surfing, water skiing, diving, dinghy sailing etc. can be enjoyed more or less anywhere along the country's winding coastline. VVV offices have details on where to hire equipment and other facilities in their area while the NBT can supply details of vacations centered around water sports. Of special note are the many traditional Dutch sailing boats which can be hired. The NBT has a brochure on this, *Traditional Sailing;* as well as others on *Boat Hire* and *Sailing Schools.*

SWIMMING. Apart from the indoor pools in most towns, Holland offers plenty of opportunity for swimming in the open air. There are numbers of attractively landscaped pools and lidos, while the beaches along the 150 miles of the North Coast and the shores of many of the lakes provide wonderful swimming. But you should be careful to observe the warnings of both police and lifesavers as much of the coastline has uncertain currents, in some places quite treacherous. Open air pools are usually available from about May to mid-September. Some hotels have swimming pools of their own. For information apply to local VVV offices.

FISHING. Angling in Holland is excellent, and there are almost as many opportunities as for sailing. The inland waters offer simple fishing, while the more adventurous angler can do as much deep-sea fishing as he wishes from beaches or ports along the coast. There are even opportunities for fresh-water salmon and trout fishing in the conserved Zeeland waters. Fishing is very well organized, and the waterways are kept amply provided with new stocks every year. Angling is, along with cycling, the most popular Dutch outdoor recreation nowadays.

Sea fishing is not subject to any restrictions and there are no close seasons. In some coastal towns special fishing trips for anglers are organized. Fishing in coastal waters (Waddenzee and the inlets in Southwest Holland) is also without restrictions as long as the fishing is done with no more than two regular rods, one special rod, a bob or smelt fishing gear.

For inland fishing there are restrictions and a close season, the restrictions covering the types of fish that can be caught as well as the times that you can fish. Among other restrictions, fishing in inland waters with certain types of rod and bait is prohibited from 16 March (in rivers from 1 April) through 31 May, and also between one hour after sunset and one hour before sunrise. A license is needed for inland fishing; these can be obtained at any post office. A local permit is also usually required, obtainable from fishing clubs and associations. The NBT produces a detailed leaflet, *Fishing,* for anglers, covering all types and locations.

GOLF. There are public 9-hole or 18-hole courses at Brielle, Rhoon and Rotterdam in Zuid-Holland province, Velsen/IJmuiden and Alkmaar in Noord-Holland, Wuwse Plantage in Noord Brabant and Alphan a.d. Rijn. All are open to anyone, with green fees from Fl. 12 to Fl. 35. Throughout the country there are also 26 club courses, some of which offer visiting memberships. Overseas offices of the NBT or local VVV offices will advise. For details of inclusive golf arrangements call Golf-Line 020–645453.

TENNIS. Tennis is reasonably popular in Holland and there is an abundance of good courts, often in the larger hotels. Visitors can always arrange to play in local clubs, although it is advisable to take one's own equipment.

Holiday resorts very often have their own tennis courts and the hire of a court varies in price from Fl. 20 to Fl. 40 per hour. During the winter months there are facilities for indoor tennis in several cities. Advance bookings are usually necessary.

In the second half of July the Dutch Open Championships are always held at the "Melkhuisje", at Hilversum; an indoor world tennis tournament is held in Rotterdam in the first week in April and in mid-August the Dutch National Championships take place at Scheveningen.

WALKING. There are many opportunities for exploring the country on foot. Practically all the year round walking associations organize tours over various distances.

Well-known are the four-day walking events in Apeldoorn and Nijmegen in July, the flower bulb tours ("Jan Pastoors") in Haarlem in early May, the South Limburg round trip for three days in May/June, the Zeeland Three-day Tour in mid-May and the Amersfoort Two-day Tour at the end of June. For information contact NWB, Rubenslaan 123, Utrecht (tel. 030–517389) and the KNBLO, Valkenbosplein 18, Den Haag (tel: 070–394846).

All VVV offices will provide information about walking events in their area. VVVs issue walking routes and publications such as *De Voetsporen* of the Staatsbosbeheer organization (Forest Commission) and *Wandelingen in Boswachterijen* (Forestry Walks). Dutch Railways organize walking tours through woodland and heather areas, orchards, beaches and tours for dune wanderers.

RIDING. For those who prefer four feet to their own two there are many opportunities to hire horses. Rates are usually between Fl. 15 and Fl. 25 per hour. A small number of hotels operate riding schools of their own.

There are also horsemen's and pony camps for children which can cope with all comers from the novice to the most experienced. Show jumping is popular in Holland with several international events taking place annually in Amsterdam, Breda, Den Haag, 's-Hertogenbosch, Rotterdam and Zuidlaren. In addition there is an international military show jumping event in Boekelo.

The NBT produce a detailed brochure *Horseriding*. Or contact the NHS, Postbus 456, 3740 Al Baarn (tel. 02154–21841).

TELEPHONES. The telephone system in Holland is excellent and thoroughly reliable. All towns and cities have area codes which you must use if you are calling from outside that area. (We give area codes for all towns, cities and villages in the hotel and restaurant listings in the Practical Information sections that follow each regional chapter). Long distance and international calls are easily made; country codes are given in telephone directories. If you wish to make a call via the international operator, all of whom speak English, dial 0010, but this service is not available through coin-operated booths.

Be sure to read the instructions if you are calling from a public phone booth as there are a number of different types. Low rates are charged between 6 P.M. and 8 A.M. and from 6 P.M. on Fridays to 8 A.M. Mondays. Always have plenty of coins available for long distance calls. Local calls cost 25 cents.

However, whatever you do, avoid making calls, especially long distance calls, from your hotel room. Hotels regard telephone calls as a secret source of revenue and sometimes charge as much as double the actual cost.

MAIL. The Dutch post office is as efficient as the telephone service, thanks in part to the modest size of the country and the concentration of population.

Airmail letter rates, to Europe up to 20 gr., 75 cents, to U.S.A. and Canada up to 10 gr., Fl. 1.30. Postcards, to Europe 55 cents, to U.S.A. and Canada 75 cents. Aerogrammes, 60 cents to Europe, Fl. 1 to U.S.A. and Canada.

READING MATTER. Most major English-language newspapers and periodicals are sold in Holland, though only in larger cities. In addition, many bookshops sell a wide range of English-language books.

CLOSING TIMES AND PUBLIC HOLIDAYS. National holidays in Holland are: New Year's Day, Good Friday, Easter Monday, Queen's Day (April 30), Liberation Day (May 5), Ascension Day, Whit Monday, Christmas (December 25–26). Shops are open weekdays from 8.30 or 9 till 5.30 or 6. Some are also open from 7–9 P.M. on Thursdays or Fridays. Many of the smaller neighborhood shops close during the lunch hour from 1–2. All shops are compelled by law to close one half-day each week; this may be during the morning or afternoon, and varies from shop to shop. Most of the department stores are closed Monday mornings, while some restaurants close one evening a week, usually Mondays. Banks are open from 9 to 4 Monday through Friday, closed Saturdays.

Be sure to double check all opening times of museums and galleries on the spot. Hours and closing days are not standardized and we have found that such times are liable to be changed with no notice at all, due to staff shortages, strikes, fire and Acts of God, and you could make a trip only to find a locked door.

ELECTRICITY. The standard in Holland is 220-volt, 50-cycle alternating current. So most American appliances will need transformers to convert them to 220-volt operation. Some hotels have only 120V, while others have wall-plugs allowing for either 220 or 120V. Dutch wall outlets (mains) require a larger plug than the kind used in the United States.

BABY-SITTERS. These can be obtained in many Dutch towns through students' organizations, especially for the evenings. Rates are from Fl. 5 to Fl. 8 an hour until midnight and up to Fl. 12 afterwards. Check with your hotel, or the local VVV office for details.

GUIDES. There is an official organization for guides in the Netherlands: GUIDOR, P.O. Box 404, AK Leidschendam (tel. 070–202500). Guides can be hired, by the hour. They are qualified and multi-lingual. Alternatively, many VVV offices can advise on knowledgeable people to show you around.

GETTING AROUND HOLLAND. By Air. Royal Dutch Airlines under the banner of NLM City Hopper operate several domestic services connecting the major cities. There are several flights each way on weekdays between Amsterdam and Eindhoven, Amsterdam and Maastricht; Amsterdam and Groningen, Amsterdam and Enschede. There are also flights from Rotterdam to Maastricht and Eindhoven, and Groningen to Enschede and NLM can arrange special charter flights for groups. However, distances between major cities are not great and the possible time saving over train or car is usually not worth while, especially when transfer times city center–airport are taken into account.

GETTING AROUND HOLLAND. By Train. Rail services in Holland are very good—in fact trains in the
central areas of the country are so frequent that it is not
really necessary to consult a timetable! Nearly all the
lines are electrified and the trains literally sprint the short distances between
stations, while the main cities are linked by a frequent service of modern,
comfortable Inter-City trains. If you intend traveling much by train buy a copy
of the Netherlands Railways domestic timetable (*Spoorboekje,* price Fl. 6.50).
This can be purchased in advance from any NBT office, or from Netherlands
Railways (NS), 25–28 Buckingham Gate, London SW1E 6LD (tel. 01–630
1735), or in New York at 355 Lexington Ave., New York, N.Y. 10017 (tel.
212–370–7367), or from any railway station in Holland. If you are arriving by
air at Schiphol, there is now a direct rail service to Amsterdam, Utrecht and
Rotterdam. This new service operates hourly throughout the night—ideal for
awkwardly timed flights.

Fares. Rail fares in Holland are very inexpensive, but there are several special
tickets which reduce the cost even further! If you intend to travel only within
the Netherlands the best buy is one of the all-line Rail Rover cards. They are
available for one, three and seven days, for both first and second class travel.
The one-day Rover costs Fl. 52 second class, Fl. 78 first. The three-day Rover
costs Fl. 79.50 second class, Fl. 118.50 first. The seven day Rover costs
Fl. 109.50 in second class and Fl. 161.50 in first. For some of the Rover tickets
it is necessary to show your passport. Travelers holding railcards can also buy
a special "add on" Public Transport link Rover ticket which gives unlimited
travel on all public transport—buses, trams, metro—both in towns and countryside. For a weekly Rover this add-on costs only Fl. 19.75. The link cards and
the Rail Rover tickets can be bought in advance in the U.S. and the U.K. or
after arrival, at all main stations. A passport plus photo is required.

If you wish to travel within Belgium and Luxembourg as well as Holland,
then the Benelux Tour Rail ticket, valid for all three countries, is the best buy.
The ticket gives unlimited travel on 5 days out of a total period of 17 days. When
you buy the ticket, state on which date the 17 days begin and then as you go
along, validate the ticket for the days on which you wish to travel; they don't
have to be consecutive. The tickets can be bought for Easter, the Summer
(beginning of June to end of August) and Christmas. The price is Fl. 199 in
second class if you are over 26, Fl. 140 for those 12 to 26. The Benelux Tour
Rail card can be obtained in advance. Check with Netherlands Railways offices
or your travel agent.

Other good-value rail tickets include weekend returns, available for the cost
of a day return plus Fl. 3, and evening returns for travel after 6 P.M.; these cost
the single fare plus Fl. 4.50. Ideal for families is the Gezinstoerkaart (Family
Rover) which gives an entire family unlimited travel for any four days out of
ten, at a bargain price of Fl. 200 in first and Fl. 140 in second. Available in June,
July and August only. If there's a small group of you (unrelated) then consider
the Multi Rovers which give unlimited day travel for small groups of two to six
people. Netherlands Railways run many special inclusive day tours from the
main stations to places of interest ranging from the picturesque villages border-
ing the old Zuiderzee to a trip up the Euromast in Rotterdam. These are called
"Dagtochten"—day trips; there are also half-day tours. Only brief details are
available in the U.S. or U.K.—ask for the full list of over 150 excursions when
you arrive in Holland. If you have bought a Rail Rover/Tour Rail card you can
still go on the NS day-out programs. They simply charge you for the admission
to the places of interest before you set off but still at a bargain all inclusive price,
so you don't lose out.

Finally a quick word about train services. Because local and inter-city trains are so frequent, travelers are actively discouraged from making short journeys on international trains by charging supplements for travel on them. Note that many of the local electric trains often consist of two portions going to different destinations—the train divides en route—so check the platform indicator to make sure you're in the right section.

GETTING AROUND HOLLAND. By Bus. Holland has an excellent bus network between and within towns. The areas served by the various bus companies are shown in the NS railway timetable. For full details write to Streekvervoer ESO, Postbus 19222, 3501 Utrecht, Holland. In addition to the domestic bus network many companies operate tours to, and excursions around, Holland, plus offer a wide range of sightseeing trips to the principal cities and places of interest. These can be booked easily on the spot and at local VVV offices. For transportation in major cities the best buy is *strippenkaart* tickets which can be used on all bus, tram and underground services. These are purchased from post offices, or at railway stations and some VVV offices. Each card has 15 strips, which are canceled by the driver as you enter the bus. Price Fl. 8.45.

GETTING AROUND HOLLAND. By Car. Holland has one of the best road systems in Europe, which, together with the small size of the country, make it possible to visit the most distant regions in a few hours. Four and six-lane divided highways join Amsterdam with Leiden, Den Haag, Rotterdam, and points south to the Belgian border. Even better are the east–west expressways that connect Amsterdam, Den Haag, and Rotterdam with Utrecht, Arnhem, and the German border. Tempting as these multi-lane expressways may be, we recommend that drivers choose the smaller local roads, which are usually well signposted, are not congested, and are much more interesting, with views of farms, houses and gardens, instead of just open countryside.

Throughout the country, six-sided route signs placed by the Royal Dutch Touring Club (ANWB) indicate particularly picturesque routes for sightseeing. There are 41 of these routes in all. The Netherlands Board of Tourism also issues a road map with marked and numbered touring routes of special interest with, on the reverse side, descriptions of the places en route.

On the open highway, the maximum speed limit is 80 km.p.h. (50 m.p.h.). In cities and other built-up areas the maximum speed is 50 km.p.h. (31 m.p.h.) unless you see a blue sign with white lettering that reads "70 kilometer toegestaan," which authorizes a maximum of 43 m.p.h. The speed on motorways is 100 km.p.h. (62 m.p.h.). Driving is on the right.

Streetcars (trams) have priority over all other traffic (except police, ambulances, the fire department, and the like), whether they come from the left or right and whether or not they cross a priority road. If there is no island for passengers getting off a streetcar, it may not be passed when stopped.

In general, traffic from your right has priority over you even if it is emerging from a narrow side street and you are proceeding along a broad boulevard. Many Dutch drivers will insist on this right of way, as will cyclists, even if you have to stop suddenly. Certain major city streets are considered priority roads, in which case you'll see an orange-colored diamond-shaped sign with a white border posted every hundred yards. Traffic on streets that enter such a priority road is warned by a white triangular-shaped sign with a red border that it must yield the right of way.

One slightly confusing traffic regulation is: when approaching a crossing in the middle of which is a traffic pylon or policeman, you pass *in front* and not round the back, if wishing to take the left-hand turn.

Main highways are patrolled from about 7 A.M. to midnight by members of Wegenwacht, who are expert mechanics. They will help foreign drivers although they make a charge to non-members of their organization.

Parking in the larger towns is difficult, and expensive so drivers should consider parking on the outskirts and using public transport.

A valid driving license is required. Proof of third-party insurance (green card) is no longer obligatory within the Common Market countries (which includes Holland), but until this becomes general practice, it is better to carry it with you, especially if you might be motoring through other lands in Europe. Every car must carry a first aid kit and a standard luminous red triangle for use during a breakdown.

Note. Legislation in Holland aimed at reducing road accidents is very tough on drinking. Highway patrols are empowered to stop any driver and give him a breathalyzer test on the spot and if results show an alcohol content higher than the prescribed level, the driver is not allowed to continue the journey by car and must accept a roadside summons. If desired, a blood test will also be made at the nearest police station. Fines for excess alcohol are heavy, and serious cases result in a jail sentence. The permitted level is very low: more than two glasses of sherry, two beers or even a double Scotch can get you in trouble.

A word of advice: ignorance of the law is not an acceptable excuse. The traffic problem being what it is, driving and parking offenses are dealt with severely, although foreigners are usually treated courteously. Zebra crossings now offer the pedestrian right of way, but be very careful before stepping on to one.

Fuel. Gasoline (petrol), or in Dutch *benzine,* is available everywhere in Holland, and all motorways and highways are well supplied with service stations, although these are gradually becoming of the self-service type. A liter of super-benzine costs Fl. 1.50 and normal grade Fl. 1.45, but these prices are constantly liable to change. Note that, for security reasons, it is very unwise to leave any baggage in a parked car.

For those unused to the metric system:

Liters	Imp. Gallons	U.S. Gallons
1	0.22	0.26
5	1.10	1.32
10	2.20	2.64
25	5.50	6.60
40	8.80	10.56

Car Hire. For self-drive or chauffeur driven cars, *Avis* has offices at the airport. Keizersgracht 485 (tel. 020–262201) and at Nassaukade 380 (tel. 020–836061); *Hertz* at the airport and Overtoom 333 (tel. 020–122441), and *DIKS* at Gen. Vetterstraat 55 (tel. 020–178505), all in Amsterdam.

Car hire rates vary considerably, so it pays to shop around if you have time. Among the lower cost hiring companies are *Budget,* in Amsterdam at Overtoom 121 (tel. 020–126060), *InterRent,* at Amstelveenseweg 294 (tel. 020–730477), and *Europa Car,* Overtoom 51–53 (tel. 020–184595). Daily rates start at around Fl. 49, to include, usually, the first 100 km, with extra mileage at 49 cents, with the driver paying for gasoline. There are also special rates for longer hiring periods. In addition to cars, it is possible to hire camper vans, sleeping two to six people, which saves hotel costs. Leading operators include *Achilles Princes,* s'Marijkestr. Den Haag (tel. 070–477474), and *Mecodam Motorhomes,* Argonautenstraat 98 (tel. 020–792491), in Amsterdam.

Roadmaps. If you plan to tour Holland intensively, you may wish to buy the excellent maps published by either of the two Dutch motoring organizations, the KNAC or the ANWB. The local VVV and NNTO also have road maps.

Kilometers into Miles. This simple chart will help you to convert to both miles and kilometers. If you want to convert from miles to kilometers read from the center column to the right, if from kilometers into miles, from the center column to the left. Example: 5 miles—8 kilometers, 5 kilometers—3.1 miles.

m		*km*	*m*		*km*
0.6	1	1.6	37.2	60	96.5
1.2	2	3.2	43.4	70	112.2
1.8	3	4.8	49.7	80	128.7
2.4	4	6.3	55.9	90	144.8
3.1	5	8.0	62.1	100	160.9
3.7	6	9.6	124.2	200	321.8
4.3	7	11.2	186.4	300	482.8
4.9	8	12.8	248.5	400	643.7
5.5	9	14.4	310.6	500	804.6
6.2	10	16.0	372.8	600	965.6
12.4	20	32.1	434.9	700	1,126.5
18.6	30	48.2	497.1	800	1,287.4
24.8	40	64.3	559.2	900	1,448.4
31.0	50	80.4	621.3	1,000	1,609.3

GETTING AROUND HOLLAND. By Bike. No description of getting around Holland would be complete without a section on cycling, certainly the best way to explore the larger cities and also a delightful method of getting around the countryside, given reasonable weather!

There are 11 million bikes in Holland and there are over 6,200 miles of special lanes and tracks for them. The NBT produces an excellent brochure giving full details, and each local VVV office can provide details on hiring, plus special tours and itineraries in their area. Hiring usually costs around Fl. 6 a day or FL. 22 upwards per week. Most firms require a deposit of between Fl. 100 and Fl. 200. For a brochure detailing over 60 special cycling routes, contact NRTU, Postbus 326, 3900 AH Veenendaal (tel. 08385–21421).

Don't forget that bicycles can be hired at many railway stations—rail travelers get a discount rate. In high summer it is well worth reserving your bicycle a day in advance. Full information is given in the leaflet *Fiets en Spoor* which is available from Netherlands Railways. If you are taking your own bicycles please note that the carriage of bicycles on trains is severely restricted and that they have to be paid for! Netherlands Railways will give full details on request. For organized inclusive tour plans, contact *Ena's Bike Tours,* P.O. Box 2807, 2601 CV Delft.

CUSTOMS ON RETURNING HOME. If you propose to take on your holiday any *foreign-made* articles, such as cameras, binoculars, expensive timepieces and the like, it is wise to put with your travel documents the receipt from the retailer or some other evidence that the item was bought in your home country. If you bought the article on a previous holiday abroad and have already paid duty on it, carry with you the receipt for this. Otherwise, on returning home, you may be charged duty (for British residents, Value Added Tax as well). In other words, unless you can prove prior possession, foreign-made articles are dutiable *each time* they enter the U.S. The details below are correct as we go to press. It would be wise to check in case of change.

U.S. Residents may bring in $400 worth of foreign merchandise as gifts or for personal use without having to pay duty, provided they have been out of the country more than 48 hours and provided they have not claimed a similar exemption within the previous 30 days. Every member of a family is entitled to the same exemption, regardless of age, and the exemptions can be pooled.

The $400 figure is based on the fair retail value of the goods in the country where acquired. Included for travelers over the age of 21 are one liter of alcohol, 100 cigars (non-Cuban) and 200 cigarettes. Any amount in excess of those limits will be taxed at the port of entry, and may additionally be taxed in the traveler's home state. Only one bottle of perfume trademarked in the U.S. may be brought in. Unlimited amounts of goods from certain specially designated "developing" countries may also be brought in duty-free; check with U.S. Customs Service, Washington D.C. 20229. Write to the same address for information regarding importation of automobiles and/or motorcycles. You may not bring home meats, fruits, plants, soil or other agricultural items.

Gifts valued at under $50 may be mailed to friends or relatives at home, but not more than one per day (of receipt) to any one addressee. These gifts must not include perfumes costing more than $5, tobacco or liquor.

Military personnel returning from abroad should check with the nearest American Embassy for special regulations pertaining to them.

Canadian Residents. In addition to personal effects, the following articles may be brought in duty free: a maximum of 50 cigars, 200 cigarettes, 2 pounds of tobacco and 40 ounces of liquor, provided these are declared in writing to customs on arrival and accompany the traveler in hand or checked-through baggage. These are included in the basic exemption of $300 a year. Personal gifts should be mailed as "Unsolicited Gift—Value Under $40." Canadian customs regulations are strictly enforced; you are recommended to check what your allowances are and to make sure you have kept receipts for whatever you have bought abroad. For details ask for the Canada Customs brochure, "I Declare."

British Residents. There are two levels of duty free allowance for people entering the U.K.; one, for goods bought outside the EEC or for goods bought in a duty free shop within the EEC; two, for goods bought in an EEC country but not in a duty free shop.

In the first category you may import duty free: 200 cigarettes or 100 cigarillos or 50 cigars or 250 grammes of tobacco (*Note* if you live outside Europe, these allowances are doubled); plus one liter of alcoholic drinks over 22% vol. (38.8% proof) or two liters of alcoholic drinks not over 22% vol. or fortified or sparkling wine; plus two liters of still table wine; plus 50 grammes of perfume; plus nine fluid ounces of toilet water; plus other goods to the value of £28.

In the second category you may import duty free: 300 cigarettes or 150 cigarillos or 75 cigars or 400 grammes of tobacco; plus 1½ liters of alcoholic drinks over 22% vol. (38.8% proof) or three liters of alcoholic drinks not over 22% vol. or fortified or sparkling wine; plus five liters of still table wine; plus 75 grammes of perfume; plus 13 fluid ounces of toilet water; plus other goods to the value of £163 (*Note* though it is not classified as an alcoholic drink by EEC countries for Customs' purposes and is thus considered part of the "other goods" allowance, you may not import more than 50 liters of beer).

In addition, no animals or pets of any kind may be brought into the U.K. The penalties for doing so are severe and are strictly enforced; there are *no* exceptions. Similarly, fresh meats, plants and vegetables, controlled drugs and firearms and ammunition may not be brought into the U.K. There are no restrictions on the import or export of British and foreign currencies.

THE DUTCH SCENE

THE DUTCH WAY OF LIFE

Dignity and Comfort

What the Dutch are today results mainly from two influences—water and religion. Both have stamped themselves on the Netherlands landscape, where they stare you in the face in the form of dikes and churches, and on the personality of the Netherlanders, though here these two influences may not always be so apparent.

To understand the Netherlander you have to know that about half of his compact little country has been wrested from the sea and that he stands over it in ceaseless vigil to prevent its reconquest, maintaining dams against the flood and running pumps to empty out the water infiltrating from below. That is the meaning of the sturdy dikes and quaint windmills of the Dutch countryside. He is holding his country aloft to keep it from slipping back into the sea. No one has given the Dutchman anything; he has worked hard for what he has and must go on working to keep it.

The sense that life is no frolic is reinforced by their Calvinist beliefs; or perhaps Calvinism was attractive to such a people. After the Reformation, Holland was a great Protestant fortress in Europe. Today the Roman Catholics, who a century ago were a small minority in the south, number about 40 percent of the population and, owing to a higher birth-rate, are increasing their numerical ratio. But it was a leading Catholic who said, "In Holland, the Catholics are Calvinistic,

31

too!" Until recent years, Holland was a country of Sunday blue laws, although the Dutch are now operating more in harmony with modern liberality in these matters. Indeed in some cities, notably Amsterdam, any notion of censorship or puritanism has long since been abandoned with an unusual vigor. But there are still two or three rural villages where you are in danger of assault if you try to take photos on the Sabbath.

A grim fight for economic survival and a grim religion have made the Dutch basically serious, determined, fiercely independent, hard-working, law-abiding, helpful, and hospitable. They have a sense of order, an inclination towards communal organization, a devotion to tradition and written precedents, and a passion for cleanliness and neatness, although in the late '60s and early '70s, the "absolute freedom" idea tended to turn Holland into a mecca for drop-outs creating a situation which the generally tolerant Dutch found hard to control effectively.

The water both unites and divides the land. The latticework of rivers and canals make every part of the Netherlands easily accessible; commerce and culture flowed freely through the country long before it was knitted together by railways and highways. Yet, paradoxically, the same water has created isolation, separating the north from the south, the islands from the mainland, one village from another. Because of this a day's drive will take you through many different collections of dialects and accents, customs and costumes. The dark, hard-bitten Protestant farmers of the island of Walcheren have little in common with the more jovial, Catholic farmers of Brabant just over the causeway. The people of Amsterdam have a different accent from those of Haarlem, a quarter-hour away by train.

The water has had other effects. The North Sea, gateway to the great currents of international trade, has brought to the west wealth, urbanity, denser population. The south and east are more agricultural, more insular, more tradition-bound. The Netherlands is many regions; the sea, the rivers, and the canals help to account for the differences.

It seems no mere coincidence that religious lines roughly follow water lines. One speaks of "above" or "below" the Moerdijk to denote the regions north and south of the great estuary, but also to signify the Protestant and Catholic parts of the country, though the religious line has been growing more fuzzy in recent years.

Perhaps even more than the water, religion both unites and divides the Dutch. Nowhere else in Europe is there such a compartmentalization of society into denominational groups. Schools, hospitals, and similar benevolent organizations are administered by Roman Catholic or various Protestant confessions with state subsidies. A bare handful of newspapers are independent, the rest identifying themselves with Catholic, Protestant, or Socialist ideologies, as do radio and television organizations.

This factionalization penetrates every aspect of life. A Catholic house painter, for example, might typically be educated at a parochial school, join a Catholic sports club, meet a Catholic spouse at a denominational young people's dance, read a Catholic newspaper, subscribe to a Catholic weekly magazine, listen to the Catholic radio station, vote for the Catholic party candidates, trade at Catholic stores, spend his holidays on Catholic-sponsored excursions, have his appendix removed in a Catholic hospital, and end his days in a Catholic old peoples' home on a Catholic-managed old-age pension, all without ever knowing his Protestant neighbor, whose life might follow a similarly limited pattern. Indeed, Catholics distinguish themselves from Protestants by wearing their wedding ring on the third finger of their left instead of on the right. The distinction can be misleading, however, because a gold band often doubles as an engagement ring, in which case Protestants wear it on their *left* hands and Catholics on the *right.* Fortunately for the future of Holland, this pattern is beginning to change, especially in the larger urban centers to which the more ambitious and liberal youth of the countryside escape.

A Profile of the Dutch

In talking of the Dutch way of life, the aspects that the visitor does not immediately see have been purposely stressed. This background may help in an understanding of the Dutch personality, customs, and manners that will be discussed later.

With the big reservation that there is much diversity even in this little country, this is what the Dutch are like:

They are first and foremost home-loving people. The French and the Italians may make the café or bistro the center of their social life, but not the Dutch. They stay at home, in the bosom of the family—and an ample bosom it is, because the Dutch are still inclined to take literally the Biblical admonition to be fruitful and multiply. It is no wonder that the jam-packed people must plow the bottom of the sea in their frantic effort to avoid bursting out of their country.

The Dutch rise early and go to work by car, by bicycle, or by public transport. The end of the day is marked by an early dinner (6 P.M. is not considered too early). Then the evening is spent comfortably at home. They pore over the evening newspapers, which have been delivered. (Evening papers are more popular than morning editions because the Dutch do not believe in skimming through the headlines.) They may look at television, listen to the radio, play chess, practice a musical instrument, or they may just sit. This lifestyle, however, is changing with the under-35s, who prefer livelier diversions and know how to provide them.

Because home provides the center of life, a great deal of time and expense go into it, especially those parts that are open to public view. The living room must be ample and comfortable. More often than not it is over-furnished and over-endowed with knick-knacks and potted plants. Particularly in cities, it will likely be the front room of a private house, its broad windows offering the nocturnal passerby an unobstructed view of family and guests, the most notable exception to the Dutch insistence on privacy. To draw the curtains would suggest that something illicit was intended . . . and would deprive the neighbors of the opportunity to admire and envy the new television set, the oil painting on the wall, the tableau of tourist gewgaws from holidays in Italy and Spain.

Competing with the home as a source of material satisfaction the automobile parked in front of the house now broadens the average Dutch family's leisure horizons. Although parking is difficult and distances are short enough to warrant greater use of public transport (especially in such a densely-populated country), the Dutchman makes greater use of the car than any other European. With one car to every four inhabitants—not counting at least half as many mopeds and bicycles as there are people—even the excellent network of motor highways, seen in 32.5 kilometers (20 miles) of roads per square kilometer compared with 17.8 in West Germany and 15.8 in Belgium, cannot carry peak time and holiday traffic without creating long queues. At busy weekends even the six-lane motorways often have three-mile files of waiting cars.

Almost every house has flowers—a cheerful garden, be it only a two-by-four plot, or pots and vases full of tastefully arranged blossoms. For here is where the Dutch may fool you. They may seem formidably stiff and unromantic, but the love of flowers is a national characteristic. Their love of tidiness, too, is obvious from the meticulous care they take of their farms, public parks and even the open countryside—which always seem so clean and free from rubbish.

They will perplex you in other ways too. Without being very articulate about it, they are likely to enjoy music and to adore painting. It isn't for nothing that many provincial towns have their own symphony orchestra and almost every village at least one brass band and a choral society; it is no accident that museums are crowded, even in winter when the tourists are gone. This is, of course, a land of museums; with over 500, they have more, relative to the size of population, than any other country.

They are also a nation of sun-worshippers, which can easily be understood in a country where there is precious little sun to worship. They build big windows to let in whatever sunlight there is and, if Sunday happens to be bright, the whole family rush off to the beach or to the field to thrust their faces to the sun. Almost every Dutch person seems to be able to go to Italy, Spain or France for a holiday in the ceaseless quest for sunlight. A decade ago, the Dutch talked of sun with a kind of starved ardor. But today, they revel in being able to follow the sun on a grand scale.

Orderliness of Manners

If you visit Holland, you are likely, of course, to meet Dutchmen and women (though some resourceful British and American travelers have managed to avoid this, to a great extent, by staying at tourist hotels and then speeding through the countryside). They have their own manners and values, and it might be helpful to know something about them to avoid misunderstandings. It should be added, however, that you need not be too nervous about mistakes because the average Netherlander is supremely tolerant, not given to touchiness and has had sufficient contact with foreigners to make allowances for whatever mannerisms may not be understood. Hospitality towards foreigners and a willingness to make allowance for their transgressions are so great, particularly in western Holland, that some resident foreigners who have learned to speak Dutch make a practice of sticking to English to get the benefit of the preferential treatment reserved for strangers.

Social intercourse in the Netherlands is marked by fixed forms, literalness, and time-saving efficiency, and rests on the principle that everyone is a member of the same community. When a Dutch person walks into a train compartment, barbershop, or even washroom, they say "Good morning" or "Good afternoon" to all present and the rest are expected to reply. In a business or social gathering, he will introduce himself individually to everyone else, which is accomplished by a lightning handshake while barking out his surname. Unless the individual is accustomed to foreigners, he or she will be surprised by your greeting of "Hello!" or "How do you do?" Indeed, the latter form of greeting may bewilder her, and you might be stared at rather blankly, or treated to a description of how she *does* feel. The Dutch form of self-introduction is actually remarkably efficient and a boon to the harried hostess who does not remember the names of all her guests. If you, in the Anglo-American manner, enter a social gathering without introducing yourself personally to all the people who are present, they may be upset by your apparent casualness.

The Dutch are punctual in their appointments and expect you to be the same. If you are tardy, remember to make profuse apologies or they may feel slighted. Promptness in Holland is not a superficial thing; it springs from a sense of orderliness and from a feeling that it is an impermissible imposition to waste the time of others. There is a growing tendency to more casualness and less strict punctuality, but the Dutch are still more than likely to bring a bouquet of flowers, especially if it is the first visit to your home.

Because the Dutch tend to be literal, you must avoid saying any casual things that you do not exactly mean. If you say, "Drop in some time when you are in the neighborhood" as a rhetorical remark, they may, to your surprise, visit you. If you say, "I'll get in touch with you in a few weeks," they fully expect you to do it. They, on the other hand, mean precisely what they say and you can usually depend on it.

At first meetings, the Dutch are reserved to the point of seeming brusque. This is not because they are cold or hostile, but because they regard over-friendliness as an imposition on you. They have a strong sense of privacy, which is maintained in spite of the constant elbow-rubbing in this crowded country, and they will also respect your privacy. They will warm up considerably after subsequent meetings, if you encourage them to do so. However, do not expect vivacity. The flowery word with the light touch is not a Dutch characteristic. In sum, the Dutch, in their everyday contacts, are stiff, but dependable; reserved, but friendly; unimaginative, but intelligent and intellectually curious.

The Dutch way of life is ruled by rigid laws of etiquette, which you should try to understand, even if you do not observe them. A shop attendant will concentrate on one customer until she is ready to leave the shop, and will then see her to the door. This is vexing if you happen to be in a hurry, but it's no use trying to rush things. The other customer will look at you indignantly, and the attendant will get nervous.

Decorum and Coziness

Set forms of politeness run through every activity in which persons come in contact and, more than in most countries, formality is an accepted standard of all classes and groups. This is the country where breakfast will be served by a waiter in white tie and tails in a restaurant that you would consider second-class at home. *Dank u wel* (thank you) and *Als 't U blieft* (If you please) constantly interlard conversation. "Yes" and "no" are rarely spoken without being followed by "sir" or "madam." In Holland, these are not empty forms, but living courtesies among a people with tremendous respect for other human beings. There are set stereotypes for addressing letters. For example, a letter to you would probably be addressed *"Weledelgeboren Heer Smith"* (the "very nobly born Mr Smith"). Don't let it go to your head! If you were, say, a member of a baron's family, you would be addressed as "The highly well born . . ." Every rank in society has its form of address, though, increasingly, the more egalitarian forms *dhr* (Mr) and *mevrouw* (Ms or Mrs) are used.

The "Dutch treat" really exists. If you eat or drink with them, you are fully expected to pay your share—calculated down to the last cent—unless it has been decided in advance that you are a guest. You will be left in no doubt about the situation. If you are asked, "May I invite you?" or "Will you be my guest?" you know where you stand. A suggestion to "Join me for lunch" or "Let's have dinner together!" usually means Dutch treat. If a Dutchman does pay for you, normally you are expected to reciprocate at the first convenient opportunity. All of this does not apply if you, as a foreigner, are a guest in a Dutch home. Home hospitality to a visitor can have no counterpart, and none is expected. But you will cause delight if you take along a plant or bouquet, or send one the next day.

You can learn a great deal about a nation from its language. There are two commonly-used words in Dutch with so many connotations that they cannot be accurately translated. One is *deftig,* a concept that includes the qualities of dignity, respectability, decorum, and propriety. The other is *gezellig,* which embodies the ideas of coziness, comfort, and pleasure. Both are values highly cherished by the Dutch. You must see a septuagenarian granddame, managing to remain stately while astride a bicycle, to realize the *deftigheid* that is Holland. The word has, unfortunately, fallen into disrepute among the young and has taken on the connotation of stuffiness and sham. But the yearning for respectability is dying hard.

For all their Calvinism, the Dutch love earthly pleasures, and the gold seal of approval for a comfortable living room, an animated party, a pleasant chat over beer or a *borrel* (a nip of Dutch gin) at a sidewalkk café is the word *gezellig.* The Dutchman has fulfilled a primary aim in life if he or she manages to exude *deftigheid* while reveling in a *gezellig* evening. If these sound like bourgeois values, it is no wonder, The Dutch are essentially a bourgeois nation.

But the Dutch language also betrays the sentimentality beneath the *deftig* exterior in the profuse use of diminutives. In his doll's house of a country, it is not surprising that to make something small is also to invest it with affection. The Hollander's darling son Piet is called *Pietje*. And the beloved five o'clock nip of gin is a *borreltje*.

Another thing that betrays the sentimentality concealed behind a stolid exterior is the calendar of birthdays and other anniversaries, which often hangs in the bathroom. This may seem to you an odd place to hide such a calendar, but you must remember that the Dutchman does not wear his heart on his sleeve. Birthdays are really celebrated—usually by keeping open house for the entire day. And woe betide the relative or friend who fails to put in an appearance bearing a bunch of flowers or a small present. Even small occasions, such as the anniversary of the office-boy or a secretary joining the office, have to be celebrated with cream cakes all round.

A Feeling for Organization

Dutch society is characterized by a high degree of organization. The density of the population makes this both necessary and possible. Almost everything the housewife needs is delivered to her door—not just milk and newspapers, but soap, meat, groceries, vegetables, fruit, bread. If she lives above the ground floor, she may have a pulley-operated basket with which she sends down her order and pulls up the supplies. This system of home delivery is possible because almost all Netherlanders live in closely settled areas. However, high wages, shortage of labor, and tall apartment buildings have combined to limit severely this personal service, a trend probably assisted by the competitive supermarkets and shopping centers springing up in residential areas.

The Dutch love to organize themselves, and they form societies for almost every conceivable purpose. On Sundays you will see hiking societies marching out, in serried ranks, for their self-regimented weekend pastime. There are religious, political, philanthropic, and social associations of every sort. Trade groups, chambers of commerce and research bodies multiply. Along with the associations go "plans." There are plans to drain what is left of the Zuider Zee, to industrialize marginal farm areas, to improve towns, and to raise the mortgage on the local tennis club.

The system of government is a constitutional monarchy, at whose pinnacle stands the throne, now occupied by Queen Beatrix, a modern, well-educated, and democratic woman who treats her function as a vocation rather than a divine right. She lives with her husband, Prince Claus, and her three sons in a palace situated in a wood on the outskirts of Den Haag (The Hague), called Huis ten Bosch. There is very little protocol. The children attend a progressive school and are shown no special favors. Queen Beatrix spent four years as an ordinary student at Leiden University. Of her sisters, Irene, has two sons and two daughters; Margriet, who also studied at Leiden University, married a commoner, Pieter van Vollenhoven, and has four sons; Christina, the youngest, married a Cuban exile working as a teacher in the States in 1975. Although they are royal, this family epitomizes the middle-class virtues which have made the Dutch respected throughout the world, while at home, they have the sincere support of most of the Dutch people.

Dutch politics are ordinarily as placid as the people themselves and are seldom discussed, except in dramatic situations, such as occurred with the Lockheed scandal, in which Prince Bernhard, husband of the then Queen, Juliana, was involved, and the South Moluccan kidnappings, and hijackings of 1975 and 1977. In these situations, every Dutchman had an involved and morally thoughtout, if individual, opinion. This does not mean that the average citizen has no interest in the government. At the same time that he deplores bureaucratic waste and inefficiency, he may secretly envy his neighbor who has a safe job as a governmental civil servant or in the highly organized municipal administration that keeps track of his every change of address and every family detail. At the same time that he complains about endless red tape and stifling regulations, he may be urging a local ordinance to prevent unfair competition in his particular business by prohibiting competitors from keeping open after 6 P.M.

Domestic politics are dominated by problems typical of the '80s such as unemployment and the health of the economy. Increasingly, there also appears to be a tendency towards separating economic from religious issues. So intertwined are church and state, however, and so strong is the conviction that the moral approach to problems is the only correct one that this movement continues to be slow.

Nevertheless, in spite of the basically provincial attitudes of the Dutch, who apparently still prefer to concentrate on national, or even local, issues, a growing internationalism is forced upon them. Membership of the European Economic Community (EEC) and NATO have opened up their horizons and is gradually encouraging them to view themselves, however reluctantly, as part of a larger European whole. Support for membership of such multinational organizations, with the resultant responsibilities for more than the immediate community group, is not universal among the Dutch, and the same independent attitudes that characterized their long and fierce struggles for independence during the Middle Ages now makes them apprehensive about the possible loss of national identity.

But the Dutch today are essentially what they have always been—conservative, respectful of authority and orderliness in their society, while at the same time very ready to fight to preserve their independence and traditional values should it, once again, prove necessary.

HOLLAND, PAST AND PRESENT

The Netherlands' Distinctive History

There has been something special about the Dutch since the dawn of history. There has had to be. Who else would have chosen to live in a vast swamp by the edge of a steadily encroaching sea? Who else would have had the courage and the hardihood to eke out a precarious existence on the fringe of Europe where land merged into water and fog crept in with the tide?

A kind of glacial afterthought, much of Holland is uninhabitable, or ought to be. For more than 2,000 years the Dutch have refused to admit this fact, however, and their stubborn perseverance has made farmland out of lake bottoms, forests out of bogs, and a marvelously green and fertile nation where once there was little more than a tidal marsh. Yet in addition to conquering this inhospitable land, they learned enough about geography, art, finance, and self-government to inspire the rest of the world in almost every department of knowledge.

Little is known about the origins of the earliest tribes that settled in this unpromising region. They are assumed to have been Germanic, though of different stocks and customs. The inhospitable nature of the country and the incredible hardships imposed by wind and water caused them to be regarded with superstitious awe by their more fortunate kinsmen to the east.

Especially in the northwestern province of Friesland, the tribes constructed great mounds or *terpen* of earth as a protection against the periodic inundations. They built their homes and farmhouses on top of these artificial hills, which are still characteristic sights in the Frisian landscape, especially in the region between Harlingen and Leeuwarden. Many of the mounds have been excavated and have yielded such a profusion of Roman pottery as to indicate a thriving trade with the south.

The Romans were relative latecomers, however, first invading the northern lowlands in 12 B.C. Even earlier settlers left behind huge graves constructed of ponderous stones brought down from Norway by the glaciers of the Ice Age. These megalithic *hunebedden* are scattered throughout eastern Holland along the present border with Germany. The greatest concentrations are in the province of Drenthe (or Drente) especially around Emmen and Borger.

Trade rather than conquest seems to have been the primary motive of the Roman penetration. They levied a tax on cowhides, which the Frisians exchanged for bowls and implements manufactured in workshops in Italy and France. Despite more than three centuries of occupation, the Romans left behind few traces other than a number of Latin words that were so thoroughly assimilated into the language that modern Dutchmen are scarcely aware of their origin.

After A.D. 300 the Roman power began to crumble along the northern edges of their Empire in the face of Germanic migrations from the east. The Franks were chief among those who invaded Holland, but they never succeeded in conquering the hardy Frisians. King Chlodowech (Clovis) of the Franks was converted to Christianity in 496, but the Frisians continued pagan for another two centuries, partly because they identified the new religion with the hostile Frankish tribes.

Willibrord, a missionary from Northumbria in England, who better understood the Frisian temperament, succeeded where others had failed, although King Radbod of the Frisians restored the pagan gods briefly in 714. With one foot in the baptismal font, so the legend runs, he asked a number of awkward questions about the state of grace of his ancestors. When informed by Willibrord that they would spend eternity in hell, Radbod withdrew his foot and vowed that he would, too. Once the obstreperous king was laid to rest, however, Willibrord continued his efforts, and the Frisians have been Christian ever since.

The Saxons, who had settled east of the IJssel River, were even harder to convince. Ultimately Charlemagne, Emperor of the Franks, imposed virtue upon them at sword's point. Scarcely was this nominal unity established than Charlemagne died, and some 30 years later his grandsons divided their heritage. Charles ruled in the west—the France of today—while Louis fell heir to the east—roughly Germany. Lothair was to have the rest—Italy and a long, narrow middle kingdom stretching across Europe to the North Sea. Before long this synthetic northern limb had been amputated from the Italian body with the result that most of present-day Holland passed into German hands, whereas much of what is now Belgium fell under the control of the western or French kingdom.

Life in the Middle Ages

The complex dynastic conflicts of the early Middle Ages in Holland were of little concern to the half-civilized peoples who struggled to wrestle a living from the land while holding off the sea. Assuming they didn't starve or drown, these early Dutch peoples had permanently to guard against the prospect of being robbed, enslaved, or murdered during Viking raids that would materialize out of the morning mist, lay waste a village, and as suddenly disappear. Because of the abundant tidal estuaries and inland waterways, hardly any community was safe from these fierce Norwegians and Danes who later had the audacity to besiege Paris itself.

Defense of the most vulnerable areas was entrusted to counts who built castles near the most important river mouths. (The one at Muiden, about seven miles east of Amsterdam on the IJsselmeer, dates from the 13th century and has been made into a delightful museum). Other strongholds were erected inland at critical points. Seeking the security of a well-garrisoned fortress, traders and craftsmen would settle nearby. Gradually towns grew up with a merchant core whose wealth created a new, dominant class that looked to the counts for protection against the petty quarrels of the lower feudal orders. By the 14th century the military function of the towns was overshadowed by the manufacturing and trading that were soon to make the Low Countries the most prosperous corner of Europe.

Apart from the Frisians, who never acknowledged a hereditary ruler, the Netherlands during the late Middle Ages was a composite of regions owing allegiance to the Duke of Brabant, the Bishop of Utrecht, the Count of Holland (a province whose capital was at Den Haag), and similar rulers. Except for the Count of Flanders (present-day Bruges, Ghent, and Ypres in Belgium) who owed allegiance to the king of France, these lords were vassals of the German emperor. Although these ties were more personal than political, they had much to do with the later involvements of the nation-to-be in the wars and dynastic struggles of France, Germany, and England.

The Burgundian Ascendancy

The first phase of this contest for control of the mouths of the Rhine, Maas (or Meuse), and Scheldt was the northern advance of Burgundian power, beginning in 1384 when Philip the Bold, Duke of Burgundy, succeeded his father-in-law as Count of Flanders. His grandson, Philip the Good, acquired Brabant and Limburg by bequest, and in 1433 added Holland, Hainault and Zeeland by cession.

When Philip the Good called together delegates from all the low countries in 1465, he startled them by introducing a tax measure. Previously, taxes had been requested from the various states individually, which he now proposed to regard as a collective entity. His son, Duke Charles, acquired Gelderland and Zutphen by bequest, and continued this centralizing tendency by establishing a mercenary standing army in place of local militia. He also set up a court that began reviewing and revising decisions of the provincial tribunes. Within the provinces, the duke was represented by *stadtholders* whose councils were dominated by learned jurists, many of whom were burghers rather than aristocrats.

When Charles fell at Nancy (1477) while fighting the Swiss, the States-General was quick to reassert its independence by forcing his daughter, Duchess Mary, to sign what was termed the Great Privilege, a document that abolished the army and the central court and modified the provincial councils. Her son, Philip the Fair (1478-1506), disregarded these concessions obtained under duress. Nevertheless, they formed the nucleus of democratic protest against arbitrary rule, a thorn in the side of absolutism that festered into open rebellion before the end of the 16th century.

Spain and the Protestant Revolt

Shortly after Columbus returned from his first voyage to America, Philip married Joanna, daughter of Ferdinand of Aragon and Isabella of Castile. In 1500 at Ghent in present-day Belgium, Joanna presented Philip with a son, Charles, who became King of Spain through his mother, Duke of Burgundy (and the Low Countries) through his father, and Charles V, Emperor of the Holy Roman Empire upon the death of his paternal grandfather, Maximilian. To these vast holdings, Charles added Friesland, thus bringing together under one sovereign what later became the Republic of the Seven United Provinces.

Charles, a sensible and enlightened ruler, continued the centralizing policies of his Burgundian predecessors. Seeking to integrate all the Low Countries under a single allegiance, he forced Francis I of France to relinquish his fiefs of Flanders and Artois. Although the Low Countries were technically a part of the empire, in 1548 he induced the Diet of Augsburg to free them from direct imperial jurisdiction. From this moment on, the region that today comprises Belgium, Luxembourg, and the Netherlands was potentially a single state.

However, there were also many significant factors working against unity. First was the question of language. Charles maintained his court at Ghent, Brussels, or Mechelen in the south, never at Den Haag, Amsterdam, or Utrecht. French speech and manners prevailed over Dutch, and the *stadtholders* whom Charles sent north had little in common with the blunt and often outspoken burghers they were supposed to rule. The French tongue became so identified with foreign rule that only the genius of Voltaire and Rousseau could restore its respectability 200 years later.

Religious controversy was even more divisive. The Holy Roman Empire, closely allied to Rome both politically and spiritually, had played a leading role in maintaining the status quo of the Church during the Reformation, the great schism that rent the Church during the early 16th century. The Low Countries on the other hand, in common with much of the rest of northern Europe, had for the most part sympathized with the great reformers of the Church and had embraced the new Protestant faith. But despite the lasting polarization caused by the Reformation in the Low Countries, the moderation and wisdom of Charles V prevented the outbreak of religious war. (This moderation, however, was only relative and did not prevent the burning of books by Martin Luther in 1522, prime mover of the Reformation, or the appointment of an Inquisitor in the same year). Nonetheless, the seeds of much greater religious conflict had already been sown.

William the Silent, Father of the Netherlands

Towards the end of 1556, a moving event took place at Brussels that culminated in the emergence of the Netherlands as an independent state. Charles V, leaning on the shoulders of German-born William, Prince of Orange, addressed the assembled delegates from all the Low Countries with an eloquence that left much of his audience in tears. The time had come, he told them, to relinquish the burdens of empire in favor of his son, Philip II, whom he recommended to their loyalty and devotion. Tears ceased to flow, however, when Philip began to speak. Not only did he use Spanish, being unable to converse in Dutch or French, but there was a certain rigidity about his outlook that suggested an ever greater void between his subjects and their new ruler. Four years later, in fact, Philip left the Low Countries, never to return.

His nemesis was the same William whose sturdy shoulder had supported the aging Charles at Brussels. One of five sons of the Count of Nassau-Dillenburg, William inherited extensive estates in the Netherlands as well as the principality of Orange in southern France at the age of 11. Raised a Lutheran by his mother, William was allowed to take possession of his estates only on condition that he become a Roman Catholic, live in the Netherlands, and take part in the Burgundian court at Brussels. This was done, and the young prince soon became a favorite of the emperor. He also kept his ears open and his mouth discreetly shut, a characteristic that earned him the Dutch sobriquet of Willem de Zwijger, more aptly translated as William the Taciturn than the usual William the Silent.

During William's youth, Calvinistic teachings had taken firm root among those whose fathers and grandfathers were inspired by the Reformation. So extensive had this heresy become that one of Philip's parting instructions to William was to arrest a number of prominent citizens in the provinces of Holland and Zeeland and bring them before the inquisition. William attempted to do so, but only after secretly warning the victims in advance. Thousands more followed their example and fled the country. Then, in 1566, exasperated mobs pillaged churches and monasteries. Philip responded by sending the Duke of Alva to restore order and William, having professed Protestantism, departed for Germany to raise an army in defense of his adopted country.

At first the Spanish duke prevailed, beating down all resistance and defeating two of William's attempts to invade from Germany. Soon his brutal methods united the Low Countries in despair, however, and city after city renounced its allegiance to Spain during 1572 and 1573.

Haarlem, Naarden, and Zutphen were among the many towns that were crushed and sacked. Alkmaar and Leiden withstood prolonged sieges, Catholics and Protestants joining hands to resist the hated Alva, who was presently recalled.

The struggle continued, however, and gradually became anti-Catholic as well as anti-Spanish, especially after the massacre of the Protestant Huguenots in France. Struck down by an assassin at Delft in 1584, William was succeeded by his son Maurice, only five years after the Union of Utrecht had established a nation of seven provinces. First Henry III of France was offered the crown, then Queen Elizabeth of England, but both refused. In 1585 Robert Dudley, Earl of Leicester, arrived at the head of an English force to assist the Dutch and was appointed a quasi-regent. His mission was a military and political failure, and when he returned to England in disgrace in 1587, the States-General emerged as the governing body of the reluctant republic. A revitalized army under Prince Maurice cleared the infant nation of Spanish troops before the end of the century.

When Philip II closed Portuguese ports to Netherlands ships, the Dutch sailed to Java to obtain directly the spices that formerly had come via Lisbon. A few years later in 1602, the East India Company was chartered. In due course it was followed by the West India Company, which took a leading part in settling Nieuw Amsterdam, later New York City.

In 1609 a 12-year truce was signed with Spain. Taking advantage of the toleration granted Protestant refugees, various groups of English separatists settled in Holland. A congregation at Leiden, fearing that the end of the truce in 1621 would result in new conflicts with Spain, sailed from Delfshaven in what is today Rotterdam aboard the *Speedwell.* Transferring to the *Mayflower* when their own ship proved unseaworthy, they reached the coast of New England late in 1620 and founded a colony at Plymouth.

Holland's Golden Age

Holland's independence was not fully recognized until the Treaty of Westphalia in 1648, at which time the vigorous young republic found itself embroiled with England over commercial rivalry at sea and with France over the southern provinces (today Belgium) that were still a part of Spain. There were domestic troubles as well, dominated by a painful struggle to build a unified nation out of seven jealously independent provinces. England was brought to her knees in 1667 when a Dutch fleet under De Ruyter blockaded the Thames with 80 ships and caused a panic in London. A year later, Britain, Holland, and Sweden were allies in an attempt to forestall Louis XIV of France from occupying all of the Spanish Netherlands. Hardly was the ink dry on this Triple Alliance than England under Charles II was again conspiring with the French against the Dutch.

Imperiled from every side, the States-General rejected the policies of Cornelis and Johann de Witt, allowed them to be slaughtered by a mob at Den Haag, and appointed 21-year-old William III commander in chief of the army and navy. Miraculously, he succeeded in beating down these threats, assisted by the former arch-enemy, Spain, and by Protestant sentiment in England that forced Charles II to conclude peace long enough to marry Mary, daughter of the Duke of York, to the redoubtable William. In 1689, James II having been chased into French exile, William was crowned king of England, which he ruled in conjunction with Mary until his death in 1702.

These confused events, culminating in the Treaty of Utrecht in 1713, tend to obscure the golden age that flowered magnificently in the 17th century, only to fade gracefully during the 18th. Despite a population of only a million in 1600, the Dutch were the most prosperous and solvent people of Europe. Herring fishing, the East and West India companies, whaling, and a vast fleet of merchant ships brought abundant profits from abroad. The hard work of skilled craftsmen, many of them religious refugees from other countries, made Holland foremost in every branch of industry: weaving, pottery, rope-making, sugar-refining, diamond-cutting, paper manufacturing, and printing—not a hand was idle.

Nor did learning lag far behind. Each province was proud of its university, that of Leiden setting the standard for the rest. Latin was still the language of scholarship; thus students of every nationality were able to take part in the revival of learning that produced such men as Hugo Grotius, the founder of the study of international law; Christiaan Huygens, the physicist; Anton van Leeuwenhoek, the first to study microscopic organisms; Spinoza, the philosopher; and many others. Dutch explorers gave their names to corners of the earth as remote as Spitsbergen and Staten Island, Tasmania and Cape Horn. Among painters of the period were such giants as Rembrandt, Vermeer, Carel Fabritius, Frans Hals, Jan Steen, and Hobbema.

Decay and Revolution

This great burst of creative activity exhausted itself by the end of the century, which saw the beginning of an era of decadence. Though France was a constant danger to the state politically, the speaking of French, the aping of French manners, the imitation of French fashions replaced the boundless energy and vitality of the 17th century. Continued frictions with England led to wars that left Holland substantially stripped of her colonies, a state of affairs that inspired early recognition of the United States of America, the lionization of John Paul Jones, and three substantial loans to the struggling young republic. When the States-General voted to accept John Adams as the new nation's envoy, he wrote home that "the American cause has gained a signal triumph in this country."

In Holland there was a popular reaction against the House of Orange, inspired by the Declaration of Independence and the revolutionary writings of Montesquieu and Rousseau. Prussian intervention was necessary to bolster the vacillating policies of William V, who fled to England in 1795 when Dutch patriots swept into Amsterdam with the backing of revolutionary France. The new Batavian Republic was short-lived, however. In 1806 it was forced to accept Louis Bonaparte as king, whom Napoleon removed four years later after a British force had landed in Zeeland.

When the House of Orange was restored in 1815, the son of William V stepped ashore at Scheveningen as William I, who styled himself as 'sovereign prince' not only of the seven provinces but of the southern Low Countries that had passed from Spain to Austria. His autocratic if well-intentioned policies soon antagonized the more populous, predominantly Catholic south. An appeal to the Great Powers to intervene in the ensuing revolt had the unexpected result of British support for a separate Belgium kingdom under Prince Leopold, son-in-law of King George IV. A Dutch army under William's son, the Prince of Orange, invaded Belgium and defeated Leopold in a lightning, 10-day campaign, but in vain. The new kingdom was restored and guaranteed by the Great Powers in a settlement that William I refused to recognize until 1839. A year later he abdicated.

William II (1840-49) and William III (1849-90) saw the personal rule of the monarch further abbreviated by the growing tide of liberal sentiment. Parliamentary government gradually took form as political parties came to the fore. Queen Wilhelmina was only 10 when William III died, so her mother, Queen Emma, served as regent until her 18th birthday in 1898.

Holland succeeded in remaining neutral during World War I, but despite vigorous attempts to do the same in 1940, the country was invaded by the Nazis in May that year and rapidly overrun. Within four days the great port of Rotterdam had been severely bombed and reduced almost entirely to rubble. Despite occupation by the Nazis during the war, the Dutch managed to contribute significantly to the Allied cause and through the efforts of an effective resistance to create endless and often serious difficulties for the occupying forces. The liberation of Holland in 1945, in which the resistance played a leading part, was a vital step in the subsequent defeat of the Nazis.

Similar reverses were encountered in the Dutch colonies in the East, all of which were conquered by the Japanese, whose cruelty toward their newly-subjugated peoples if anything exceeded that of the Nazis. These years of suffering were also ended in 1945, but were almost immediately followed by a long-drawn out fight for independence, most notably, and violently, in Indonesia. The Dutch bowed to the inevitable and in 1949 granted full independence to their colonies, adding the usual proviso that all their former colonials could if they so choose settle in Holland itself, an offer eagerly accepted by many.

Another momentous event had also occurred a year earlier in 1948 when, after 50 years of rule, Queen Wilhelmina abdicated in favor of her daughter, Juliana, who was herself to abdicate in 1980, stepping down for her daughter, the present Queen Beatrix.

Modern Holland: Progressive and Prosperous

Holland's development in the post-war years has largely followed that of the rest of the West; spectacular progress and affluence throughout the '50s and '60s followed by economic stagnation and recession in the latter part of the '70s and into the '80s. Nonetheless, the country has remained predominantly prosperous and successful.

It has had some unusual problems to tackle, but has at the same time retained, and in many respects extended, its reputation for civilized and tolerant behavior. Perhaps Holland's greatest difficulty has been in providing for a rapidly expanding population—now some 14 million, a three-fold increase since the beginning of the century. Despite having expanded her total area dramatically through massive land reclamation schemes, Holland remains one of the most densely populated countries in the world with, at 413 people per square kilometer, almost twice the population density of Japan. Though there has been a significant degree of emigration—principally to the U.S., Canada, Australia and New Zealand—this has been more than compensated for by large scale immigration from her former colonies in Asia and South America. The integration of these immigrants has been achieved with the minimum of social disruption. Nonetheless in recent years a number of programs have been introduced to aid former immigrants wishing to return to their original countries. With the advent of large-scale unemployment in the '80s, which has had the unfortunate but inevitable effect of making ex-colonials less welcome, these programs have been substantially stepped up. Despite these efforts, it is still projected that by the year 2000 the Dutch population will have reached 15 million.

Economically, Holland is today coping with a difficult trading climate and world recession more successfully than many industrialized countries. Having benefitted immensely from the creation of the EEC, which takes over 70 percent of their total exports, Holland, poor in raw materials and natural assets other than gas, is now concentrating on the development of high technology industries. She has also been successful in attracting a large number of multi-national corporations, many of whom have large plants here. As a consequence, unemployment has been held at relatively lower levels than in many other EEC countries.

Politically, Holland has remained one of the most stable and enlightened of the Western democracies. Indeed some might argue that the country has taken its traditional tolerance and liberality too far, as reflected in the large number of active political parties and the consequent steady stream of coalition Governments they have produced. But though consensus may at times have been difficult to achieve, the country has broadly continued on a moderate, reforming path since the war, while at the same time consistently referring major issues to the electorate. Today such questions as the stationing of American nuclear missiles on Dutch soil, Holland's continuing and vital role in NATO, and environmental conservation are in the forefront of popular debate. In common with a number of European countries, a discernible swing to the Right has occurred since 1982 on the more important topical issues.

The changes in Dutch social life over the last 20 years have been every bit as great as the country's economic progress. Though more rural areas may have retained their basic conservatism and bourgeois attitudes, Holland has otherwise become a byword for permissiveness and official tolerance. The results of this open mindedness have not all been desirable—witness the endless sex shops and strip joints, many truly Fellini-esque in their excesses, in Amsterdam's red light district, or the unfortunates who congregate around Amsterdam's central station at night attracted by the city's easy drug laws. At other times, only an earnest banality has arisen, nowhere better illustrated than by the famous all-nude productions of the once-conservative Netherlands' Ballet Company, with performers dancing naked among the audience.

But for the most part, this toleration and readiness to listen to the other man's point of view have produced a caring, progressive, and genuinely enlightened and intelligent society, placing a high priority on education, social spending and on maintaining an admirable standard of living for its people, but at the same time understanding full well that the quality of life cannot be measured by economic prosperity alone.

DUTCH ARTS, CRAFTS AND LETTERS

Merchants and Old Masters

Dutch art speaks with many voices, and is sometimes blithely silent —as though smugly aware that tradition, in the long haul, will overtake the periods that turn out daubs and make do. To find a beginning to the tradition (traditions would hit it off just as well), one could go back just as far as one felt like and begin to make out one's plausible case. One could begin with the Romans' brief hegemony over the land that was to become the Netherlands. Next might come the relics, in the southeast of this territory, of Byzantine influence, when the Middle Ages were young and unlabelled. One could do worse than say that before the 14th century there was no Dutch art. Instead, there were a number of foreign influences working away at the fashioning of a native art. There were Germanic elements, and, in the 14th century, came French elements.

Claus Sluter, who was born in Haarlem about the middle of the 14th century, was the most important sculptor of his time. But at an early age he moved to Dijon, in France, to work for the dukes of Burgundy, so when his Dutch talent developed, it was outside Holland. At Dijon he fashioned great tombs testifying to the grandeur of the dead nobility.

He has been called the first of the modern sculptors, and his realism, his plastic expressionism, and his individual treatment of figures influenced the art of sculpture in Europe until the end of the 15th century.

The greatest painters at this time, when the dukes of Burgundy ruled the lands that were one day to become known as Holland and Belgium, were undoubtedly Hubert and Jan van Eyck. Born at Maaseik, near Maastricht, in the second half of the 14th century, the two brothers did not represent a sudden and unexpected upsurge of painting. Although they are regarded as the founders of the Flemish School, their work, heralding the beginning of the Renaissance in the north, was the result of a long and integrated line of capable artists, but their genius eclipsed their precursors. Hubert's life is an almost complete mystery. Jan, his junior by 19 years, was first employed by John of Bavaria, and was then engaged by Burgundy's Duke Philip the Good. He worked in Bruges, mightily developing the art of portraiture. As a favorite of the Duke he also went on a pilgrimage and several secret missions. In 1428 he accompanied an Embassy to Portugal where he painted two portraits of the Infanta Isabella as well as taking part in negotiations on behalf of Philip, who was suing for her hand.

The style developed by his Flemish School, so finely represented in its early stages by Albert van Ouwater (1400-80) and his pupil Geertgen tot Sint Jans (1465-93), has become known as "primitive." As in Italy, the northern quattrocento looked back into its own past, and used what it found there to produce new ideals. In Italy the model was antiquity. In the Netherlands, where an energetic bourgeoisie looked out toward a wider world, the Gothic style lent its ancient idiom to the new art. This is why northern Gothic seems to have lasted for so long. But the outer shell was animated by a new and vigorous force.

But there was another fundamental difference between the development of the Italian and Northern Renaissances, a difference that was particularly pronounced in the Low Countries and that was to exert an enormous influence on Dutch arts. In Italy, and to some extent France as well, patronage of the arts was the almost exclusive preserve of the Church and the ruling families. Painting, sculpture and architecture were accordingly either courtly and aristocratic in character or religious. In the Low Countries on the other hand, especially after the Reformation and into the 17th century, patronage was principally in the hands of a powerful and influential merchant class. The necessary consequence of this was that the arts were predominantly bourgeois in character; that is, portraiture, especially group portraits, landscapes and views, and flower painting—all basically forms concerned with the real world as opposed to the largely idealized world of Italian paintings —were most common. And of course the existence of this wealthy merchant class, able and willing to patronize the arts, was, in addition to shaping the character of Dutch arts, crucially important to its continued existence and development, the primary precondition of all sustained artistic endeavour being the means to practise it.

From Bosch to Hals

However, at the end of the 15th-century, Dutch art was still funda-
mentally medieval in character, as the nightmare visions of Hieronymus Bosch (c. 1450–1516) make very clear—the rational and lucid
paintings of the 16th century were still very much a development for
the future. Bosch is a compelling painter, strangely in tune with modern tastes. His complex religious allegories, which have provoked com-
parisons with Surrealism—a notion that the painter himself would be
at a complete loss to understand—present an endlessly fascinating and
detailed vision of late medieval concerns. Unfortunately the exact
meaning of much of his haunted world is not known, but his success
may be judged from the fact that many of his best pictures belonged
to Philip II (and are accordingly now housed in the Prado in Madrid).

Among other leading figures of this period was Cornelis Engelbrechtsz (1468–1533), founder of the Leiden School of painting. One
of his most important pupils was Lucas van Leyden, the leading figure
of the artistic transition from the Gothic to the Renaissance during the
early years of the 16th century. Where Engelbrechtsz seemed limited
by formal conceptions, Lucas van Leyden inclined towards the freer
Italian style. His great portraits did much to forward the trend towards
secularizing art. When he died in 1533, aged 37, he was ranked with
Dürer and Marc Antonio Raimondo as one of the greatest etchers of
his time.

Half a century after Bosch, Pieter Brueghel the Elder (1529-69), who
lived during the tumultuous times of the Spanish wars, brought a deep
understanding of the tragedy of destruction, poverty, and illness to his
robust and realistic canvases. And it was in the latter part of the 16th
century that the most characteristic forms of Dutch painting developed. The period as a whole witnessed the development of Holland's
great portraiture; at the same time came a wholesale, religious-inspired
destruction of much of the great Catholic art which had been building
up through the generations. Into the 17th century, the peculiarly Dutch
tradition of group portraiture gradually evolved. Civil groups and
professional societies were soon having large group portraits of themselves painted. The century also saw the quick growth of a number of
tendencies: there were artists who grew great at the art of suggesting
rather than laying bare on canvas. The Dutch were witnessing the full
bloom of the work which earned their artists the title of "painters of
the bourgeoisie". Comparatively little of Dutch art before the 17th
century—except portraits—has survived. The inspiration of Calvin had
led to the destruction of stained-glass windows, church statues, and
canvases.

Frans Hals (1580-1666) has been called the first modern painter. He
succeeded in transfixing on canvas the outward appearance of the
bourgeoisie. A fantastically adept and naturally gifted man, he could
turn out a portrait in an hour. He delighted in capturing the emotions
of a moment—a smile or a grimace—in an early manifestation of the
same impressionist preferences that were to capture art in the 19th
century. He spent most of his life in Haarlem (where much of his work

can be seen in the authentic 17th-century building of the Frans Hals Museum), and he has perhaps justly been called the founder of the Dutch School—a term encompassing the supreme art that flourished for a century.

Rembrandt and the Stirring 17th Century

Rembrandt van Rijn (1606–69), born a quarter-century after Hals, was the greatest of the Dutch School—therefore, perhaps, the greatest Dutch artist of all time. Born in Leiden, the fifth child of a miller, he grew rich from painting and tuition paid by his pupils; for a while his wealth was such that he became a noted collector of art. Into his first works he painted a heap of over-ornamentation, but then, as the years went by, he dug deeper and deeper into the essence of his subjects and portrayed the incessant metaphysical struggle for inner beauty and reason. When his whole material world crashed about him, though he was blackmailed and ruined, he unaccountably continued to turn out art that grew greater and greater. His marvelously skilled use of light and shadow is a text and source of wonder for living artists. A master of landscapes, still-lifes, and Biblical scenes as well as portraiture, his greatness as a painter has tended to eclipse his glory as an etcher and draftsman. In the graphic arts he was the last of the universal men of the Renaissance. His most imposing work, *The Night Watch,* can be seen at Amsterdam's Rijksmuseum. Some of his finest self-portraits hang in the Mauritshuis at Den Haag.

Holland's political golden era came during the second half of the 17th century, and though the art of the day was pale compared to Rembrandt's, it is nonetheless great. With only one million people in the Netherlands, there was nevertheless a superabundance of great masters. Jan van Goyen began fashioning the neglected art of landscape painting (which previous artists had usually been interested in merely as background). So, then, did Albert Cuyp and Jacob van Ruysdael. Jan Vermeer (1632–75) was born in Delft and died in Delft, and for all any historian knows never left the town. There are about 40 paintings ascribed to him. Vermeer brought genre art to its peak; in small canvases of a sometimes overwhelming realism, he painted the soft calm and everyday sameness of scenes from middle-class life, with the subjects caught and held fast in the net of their normal surroundings. His *View of Delft* is considered the greatest of all Dutch town portraits.

Pieter de Hoogh (1629–85) painted pictures that have been called architectural; i.e., the people seem to have been introduced to heighten interest in the buildings and only after the buildings have been painted in. Jan Steen, who was born in Leiden in 1626, painted occasionally great, sometimes biting or humorously satiric, canvases, full of human bustle and animation. He was the painter *par excellence* of the Dutch shopkeeper and his family—the lower middle class. He had trouble finding a market for his art; when he died he is supposed to have had on hand 500 unsold canvases. Gerard Terborch (1617–81) developed a mastery at painting textile texture, and served up a series of thoughtful conversation pieces, posing his subjects talking. He also developed tremendous skill at miniature-scale, full-length portraits. The son of a tax collector, he appears to have done a good deal of traveling and to have painted only in his spare time.

With their strong maritime interests it is not surprising that Dutch marine painters were among the most important painters of their time. The first notable artist in the field was Hendrik Vroom (1566–1640) who worked mainly in his native Haarlem. Simon de Vlieger (1600–53) is known for his peaceful sea themes and as the teacher of two other respected marine artists of the period, Jan van de Capelle (1624–79) and Ludolf Bakhuizen (1631–1708).

Perhaps the best known and admired of all were the van de Veldes, Elder and Younger. Willem van de Velde the Elder (1611–93) was present in a semi-official capacity at a number of the sea battles between the Dutch and British and recorded what he saw with superb depth and craftsmanship. His son, also Willem, (1633–1707) also painted sea battles and, like his father, spent his later years in England, under the patronage of Charles II.

Dutch marine artists, like their colleagues on land, were interested in recording the reality of their subjects and they did so with consumate skill and style. They developed this particular school of painting to a level of mastery seldom challenged elsewhere and their works are prominantly hung in a number of leading galleries.

At the end of the 17th century a decline set in that was characterized mainly by a lack of vigor and individuality and a preoccupation with color and gaudy ornamentation. In the 18th century interest was directed more towards the decorative arts, such as painted panels, ceilings and wallpaper, and the exterior ornamentation of the home.

The 19th and 20th Centuries

Around the middle of the 19th century a new trend became noticeable, the best-known interpreter thereof being J. B. Jongkind. This rebirth of Dutch art, the Den Haag School, as it became known, with painters like Joseph Israels and Jacob Maris, coincided with the French Impressionists. A representative collection of its work (as well as of the Barbizon School) can be seen in Den Haag at the Rijksmuseum H. W. Mesdag, housed in the former home of H. W. Mesdag (1831–1915), who also painted the interesting Mesdag Panorama.

Vincent van Gogh (1853–90), an individualist, the servant of no school, but the unwitting master of many a painter, left Holland to bring his private revolution in art to southern France. But Holland now honors him with a wide-ranging selection of his works in many museums, notably Amsterdam's Rijksmuseum Vincent Van Gogh and the Rijksmuseum Kröller-Müller near Otterlo.

Towards the end of the 19th century Breitner and Isaac Israels founded the Amsterdam Impressionists, followed during the early years of the present century by Jan Toorop and Johan Thorn Prikker, representing the Art Nouveau movement. The Bergen School (called after the resort town of Bergen near Alkmaar), led for a time by the Frenchman Le-Fauconnier, who lived in Holland during World War I, carried on the renewed tradition of vigor and individuality. Hendrik Chabot painted rough-looking peasant figures which closely resemble the work of today's Flemish master, Constant Permeke. Other painters belonging to this school are Kees van Dongen, Jan Sluyters, Leo Gestel, and Piet Mondriaan, whose work during this early period clearly indicates the beginning of Dutch Fauvism. *De Stijl* (Style), a movement that took its name from the magazine published by an *avant garde* post-World War I group, blew simplicity into the cluttered structure of art (and architecture), notably with the work of Piet Mondriaan, Theo van Doesburg, and Bart van der Leck. Van Doesburg and Mondriaan drew canvases made up of rectangles of white and primary colors separated by thick or thin black lines. The period between the two world wars was dominated by two trends, the expressionism of painters like Charley Toorop, Hendrik Chabot, and Charles Eyck, and a form of neo-realism represented by Raoul Hynckes and A. C. Willink.

After World War II the New European School was represented in Holland by the Informal Group. Amongst the best-known modern Dutch painters are Kees van Dongen, Jaap Wagemaker, Willem de Kooning, Sierk Schröder, Karel Appel, Carel Willink, Gerrit Benner, Co Westerik, Bram van der Velde, Corneille, G. Veenhuizen, and Jan van Heel. In more recent years, a small group of painters and sculptors established *Fugare* in Den Haag, a movement whose main purpose is to counterbalance the lack of aim or form they feel is apparent in too much of the work of the younger generation of artists.

In the field of graphic art Holland has a long and rich tradition. The most strikingly original among recent graphic artists was Maurits Escher who died in the early 1970s.

Stained Glass and Sculpture

During the 16th century Holland produced some outstandingly fine stained glass, of which only a small amount survived the Reformation. The best examples, made by the brothers Dirck and Wouter Crabeth, can be seen in the St. Janskerk in Gouda. Although the following centuries saw a large production of attractive work, and the art is still practiced fairly extensively today, it never again achieved the same standard of greatness.

Except for Rombout Verhulst (1624–98), the Dutch have had no sculptor since Claus Sluter they could call of a truly great international character. During the 20th century, however, there has been a tentative resurgence of attempts at creative sculpture, but the current work is hardly inspired. Henry Moore, Zadkine, Arp and Marini have exerted a profound influence. Among the most successful contemporary sculptors are Professor V. P. S. Esser, Wessel Couzijn, Hildo Krop, Mari Andriessen, Lottie van der Gaag, and the Japanese-born Tajiri.

Great Galleries

Among the abundance of public and private art collections in the Netherlands, the two greatest are Amsterdam's Rijksmuseum and Den Haag's Mauritshuis. The former, if not quite in the same class as the Louvre or the Prado in terms of size, still must be ranked among the top half dozen in Europe for quality. It is strongest in the Dutch masters of the 16th and 17th centuries, of course, but is by no means limited to them or even to painting alone. Its collection of prints and etchings is possibly the finest in the world.

The small and intimate Mauritshuis in Den Haag fills the visitor with unabashed delight. This gracious 17th-century former palace houses a collection that boasts only first-class work. Housed in magnificently restored surroundings, its quality is great enough to warrant a lifetime of study.

After these two rank the Stedelijk Museum at Amsterdam and the Gemeentemuseum (Municipal Museum) at Den Haag, both emphasizing 19th and 20th-century Dutch Art. The former is especially noteworthy for its extensive modern collection, the latter for Dutch painting since the 17th century. Rotterdam's museum Boymans-van Beuningen is housed in a delightful modern building, and its collection of paintings is well worth a visit.

A very valuable addition in 1973 was the opening of the Vincent van Gogh Museum near the Stedelijk Museum in Amsterdam. This contains one of the world's richest collections of works of art of one period, in the form of paintings, drawings and letters by Vincent van Gogh placed on permanent loan to the Netherlands State. The artist's full collection of prints and many sketches form part of the treasure, which comprises altogether about 200 paintings and 400 drawings by van Gogh as well as works by his contemporaries like Gauguin, Bernard and Monticelli. In addition to being a unique exhibition, it also serves as a research center, with a library, extensive archives and a studio/ workshop, available to specialists, students and painters.

Among other specialized museums are Haarlem's Frans Hals-museum, the previously mentioned Rijksmuseum H. W. Mesdag at Den Haag (late 19th-century works), and the Rijksmuseum Kröller-Müller near Otterlo (north of Arnhem in central Holland), which has a fine collection of van Goghs.

Collections, or part-collections, are sometimes loaned to other museums at home or abroad, so if there are certain exhibits you particularly want to see remember to check beforehand or you may be disappointed.

Progressive Architecture

Romanesque influences can be detected in the architecture of some of the older towns, especially in the southern provinces. The Pieterskerk in Utrecht is the best example of the Romanesque in the Netherlands. During the Gothic period, when other nations were building gigantic cathedrals, Holland built smaller ones. The marshy ground makes great and heavy building impractical, which accounts for the fact that most of the churches have wooden, instead of stone, vaults.

The Renaissance, when it came to Dutch architecture, was fairly conservative, but only by comparison with the effects it brought in other countries. The baroque, in Dutch architecture, was never to be given free rein. Instead there was developed a form of restrained classicism, the best examples of which are the Mauritshuis and the façade of the Houses of Parliament facing the Vijverberg in Den Haag, and the Royal Palace in Amsterdam.

For a long time, Dutch architects were content to imitate foreign styles, re-creating them in "neo" forms. But there was always that prime necessity to think in terms of the given elements: the marshy ground, the available building materials. Whole towns were built on piles sunk into the swampland. The Royal Palace in Amsterdam, for example, built during the first half of the 17th century, is supported by some 13,600 piles.

It is, perhaps, in the field of domestic architecture that the Dutch have made their most important contribution to the face of Europe. The town houses lining the canals of cities like Amsterdam have much individuality in design and character yet, over all, create an outstanding sense of aesthetic cohesion. In England, much of the riches created by imperial and commercial expansion were poured into great country houses, but in Holland, particularly during the 17th century, wealthy merchants in spices and other trade from the Indies, built on a much smaller scale. Their homes were compact, outwardly relatively re-strained and often served as offices and even warehouses for their owners, as well as homes. But there is no denying their taste, nor the obvious wealth they represented. Old Dutch houses, as in so many manefestations of the Dutch character, reflect the nature of the people: conservative, cautious about wasting space or money, but not above wanting to demonstrate to outsiders how successful they were!

The visitor to any of the older Dutch cities should look carefully at these ordinary houses, they are one of the most delightful and enjoyable aspects of sightseeing.

Another of the most delightful sights on Holland's architectural scene are the *hofjes,* or almshouses. These miniature residences are usually grouped around a central courtyard, and many of them can be visited.

The great Dutch architect, Hendrik Petrus Berlage (1856–1934), had by the late-19th century broken with current styles, substituting for them a rationalist style. Gradually the functionalists supplanted the traditionalists. The Amsterdam School brought the expressionist influ-ence. *Stijl* had a profound influence on architecture, advocating as it did a simplicity and economy of structure, and the doing away with excessive ornamentation. Thousands of buildings (and especially schools) bear the earmarks of the functionalists' concepts. Although in the past building had been based on brick construction, during this century more and more concrete faced with granite, marble, sandstone and so forth is used. The Dutch were the first ever to use glass bricks as structural elements. In buildings everywhere, more and more thought was given to bringing sunlight into the home. Windows grew broader and broader, and now the great expanse of glass in homes and offices is one of the most superficially striking features of the cityscape. World War II, sadly enough, proved a tremendous stimulant to that same architecture, for with wide destruction came the need for exten-sive rebuilding: in the Netherlands, urban planning is a major profes-sion. Today's Dutch architecture is characterized by a sense of order and conciseness. Color is another striking feature—everywhere patently visible, if not always underdone. In the large towns and cities there are few tall buildings, and in the Dutch context a 10-story building may be counted a skyscraper, although blocks of flats with 20 or more floors are now being erected. Modern Dutch architecture is succeeding in achieving considerable variety and attractiveness of design for both industrial buildings and new housing, with Rotterdam in the lead. Urban sprawl has eaten into the landscape—Amsterdam, Den Haag, Rotterdam and Dordrecht are separated only by short stretches of open fields. Within a decade they are expected to have been merged, absorbing the little towns and villages in between, to form one long city along the coast which is known as *Randstad Holland.*

Arts and Crafts

In the decorative arts, as in the fine arts, Holland's artisans and craftsmen first borrowed and copied heavily from foreign teachers. Dutch pottery, for example, was strongly influenced by Spanish and Italian decoration and form. In the beginning of the 17th century Holland evolved a national pottery of its own—the famed blue and white Delftware—though this was, indeed, inspired by Chinese porcelain. The greatest potters were soon centered in Delft, which now produces the well-known Delft blue.

However, a new generation of artist-potters has appeared, started by Christiaan J. Lanooy, continued by Lambertus Nienhuis, and greatly fostered by the well-known Delftware makers De Porceleyne Fles. A great deal of talent emerged from that firm's experimental studio and some lovely ceramics are now being made by artists who have abandoned both tradition and ostentation.

In the manufacture of glassware, foreign sources again provided initial impetus, followed once more by a gradual shift to greater austerity, which finally fashioned itself into a Dutch style. Dutch domestic glass—decanters, wineglasses etc.—reached a high order of design and execution from the 16th century onwards. Basic shapes tended to be simple and solid, but the superb etching and engraving skills of Dutch craftsmen turned them into works of art, which can still be seen and enjoyed in various museum collections of domestic glass throughout Holland. The best modern Dutch crystal comes from Leerdam, and the finest of the Leerdam products are usually the simplest, the most regular, the most blankly austere in design.

Tiles—a third, well-known product of Dutch artisanry—were best made in and about Rotterdam. At first the tiles were used in Dutch floors only, but their popularity and practicality were such that it soon became common practice for whole walls to be covered with tiles, in the Arabic manner.

The Dutch have always loved silver. It represented a solid and portable form of wealth which could demonstrate not only the affluence, but the taste of the owner. As early as the mid-16th century Dutch silversmiths, influenced by designs from Germany (especially Nuremberg and Augsburg), France and Spain, began to produce fine work for the guilds, churches and domestic patrons. Influenced by Gothic forms, but tending towards much heavier pieces than seen in, say, France, Dutch craftsmen evolved their own distinct character and techniques. Utrecht became a major center for silversmiths after the Seven Provinces united in 1579 and, during the 17th century, the craft flourished in other cities, particularly Amsterdam, Haarlem, Leiden and Dordrecht.

The elaborate Dutch version of Baroque style in the mid-17th century dominated European taste, and Dutch craftsmen perfected techniques for engraving on silver never surpassed elsewhere. Dutch silversmiths also favored the use of heavy embossing and high relief, particularly in dishes and plaques. The rich guilds commissioned massive commemorative works and private families often recorded births and marriages with specially engraved pieces. In church plate the influence of the Reformation produced more restrained designs than was generally seen in domestic silver, but overall the quality of Dutch craftmanship was outstanding. It is a tragedy that the constant international and civil wars which racked the country caused much of this magnificent work to be lost, melted down to pay for various military needs, but enough remains in museums in Holland to show how superb was the Dutch control over this rich medium.

Dutch Literature

Dutch literature is one of the anomalies of the country's culture. Since authors, as a rule, write in their native language, Dutch authors are doomed to a limited readership that can be expanded only through translation. There has always been a shortage of skilled translators for Dutch literature. But the Dutch themselves, subjected to a schooltime regime that includes heavy, compulsory doses of French, English, and German, take pride in reading foreign literature in the original language. Perhaps the greatest influences on Dutch literature have come from outside Holland's borders—from the foreign authors whose works Dutch authors came to know so well.

Thomas à Kempis (1380–1471), the German author of the *Imitatio Christi,* made Holland his home and died in a monastery near Zwolle. Desiderius Erasmus (1467–1536), sometimes called the Dutch Voltaire, sometimes The Prince of the Humanists, was born in Rotterdam. Grotius, who lived in the 16th and 17th centuries, wrote the first great texts on international law, especially those concerning the conduct of war. The philosopher Descartes, though a Frenchman, lived in Holland for 20 years, extolling the cool climate, claiming it helped him think more clearly.

Baruch Spinoza (1632–77), one of the philosophy greats of all time, was born in Holland of Portuguese parents who had fled the Inquisition in their home country. He was educated in Holland, lived by working as a grinder of lenses, and developed a pantheistic philosophy that scandalized the Jewish community's theological leaders. Spinoza's first great work—*Tractatus Theologico-Politicus*—published anonymously, pleaded for religious freedom and higher (i.e. scientific) criticism of the Bible.

Perhaps as a reaction to strait-laced morality and narrow-mindedness, Dutch literature is at its greatest in the lyric form. The very strictness of moral injunction has been cast in a soaring form of lyric expression. The greatest Dutch poet was Joost van den Vondel (1587–1679). Vondel wrote classic, often baroque, Alexandrine verse tragedies in five acts, treating subjects of occasional great remoteness and loftiness. Thirteen of his tragedies had Biblical subjects. He was the son of a couple from Antwerp who took refuge from the Inquisition in Cologne, then moved to Amsterdam. From the age of ten, Vondel lived there; for a time he was accountant at the municipal pawn shop. Partly because of poetry's translation difficulties, Vondel is hardly known outside Holland.

The Dutch statesman and poet Jacob Cats (1577–1660), known affectionately as 'Father Cats', wrote poetry about ordinary, devout people in a form easily remembered and quoted. P. C. Hooft was one of the most urbane of poets, who gathered about him, in his castle at Muiden, a group of artists, musicians, and authors. Constantijn Huygens, father of the physicist Christiaan, was yet another of the gifted Dutch versifiers, the fashioner of a spare style which nevertheless managed to bulge with pithiness. Gerbrand Adriaanszoon Bredero was that strangest of all classic Dutch literateurs: a thorough Bohemian.

As in painting, Holland's native literature suffered a long period of something less than greatness during the 20th century. During World War II some great poetry was written by an occasional resistance worker, and in the 1960's and 1970's a young generation of Dutch poets sprang up which attracted attention mainly because they broke all the normal rules of poetry and produced extraordinary works which means something only if you're in the same stream of consciousness.

Though Dutch literature is seldom translated, and its market rarely goes farther than Dutch-speaking Flanders, in Belgium, Dutch authors produce a startling number of works. Three-fourths of Dutch books are first editions. Some of Holland's youngest authors have taken the bull by the horns and now write in English in order to reach a wider public. Among the better-known Dutch authors abroad are Jan de Hartog, Johan Fabricius, Simon Carmiggelt, Hans Martin, Willy van Hemert, Willem Frederick Hermans, Pieter de Vries, Gerard Reve, van Eysselstein and the late Godfried Bomans.

Music and the Theater

Although such composers as Jacob Obrecht (1455–1505), Jan Sweelinck (1562–1621), Alphonse Diepenbrock (1862–1921), and Willem Pijper (1894–1947) had considerable influence upon their contemporaries, rare is the Dutchman who will do much bragging about his country's record in composing music. This attitude is not wholly justified. Research in recent years has led to the rediscovery of a host of minor composers whose work had been relegated to oblivion.

In performing music, however, the Dutch do not bow their heads to anyone. The Amsterdam Concertgebouw Orchestra, which celebrates its centenary in 1988, was led towards European supremacy by Willem Kees, and under the late Willem Mengelberg was believed to have reached the pinnacle of its fame. However, it is continuing to improve its deserved reputation under their conductor Riccardo Chailly. The

Den Haag Philharmonic (Residency) Orchestra is Holland's second-best, and there are a number of cities and towns, such as Rotterdam and Utrecht, boasting orchestras of their own. The Dutch also have their own National Opera Company which gets a great reception all over Europe for the standard of its performances and the imagination behind its productions. Stolid though the Dutch may seem to be, they love music. There are choral societies, chamber music groups, and village bands and fanfares beyond number. In the smaller towns as well as in the larger cities recitals on ancient church organs and famous carillons can be heard regularly.

Nor do the Dutch limit their musical tastes. Every Dutchman will tell you that to hear Bach's St. Matthew Passion performed in the 15th-century church at Naarden at Easter is a unique experience no music-lover should miss, but he will also extol the rollicking tunes churned out by one of the many gaily baroque barrel organs that roam the streets in fair weather. And contrary to what one might have expected, the Dutch are the best exponents of jazz and swing in Europe. To name but a very few of the best performers: the beautiful and sophisticated pianist and singer Pia Beck, Pim Jacobs' Jazz Trio with the brilliant vocalist Rita Reys, the Dutch Swing College Band, the Dixieland Pipers, and a number of pop groups which have won European renown.

There are also many music contests and festivals held all over Holland. At Kerkrade, in the southeast of Holland on the German border, a World Music Festival is held every four years, the next in the summer of 1990. Den Haag is the home of the annual North Sea Jazz Festival, an international event that regularly attracts major stars from abroad.

Perhaps the biggest event is the Holland Festival, which takes place annually during June. Although some programs are presented throughout the country, and a few specialized features take place only in one or other of the smaller towns, the majority of performances are held in and around Amsterdam. Performances of Dutch music, drama and dance are alternated with the best other countries can offer in the field of new theatrical productions, contemporary music and choreography. Although most of the guest programs are provided by neighboring countries, some come from as far afield as Peru or India. The Holland Festival has won generous acclaim from the international press and is now ranked with the renowned Salzburg and Edinburgh festivals.

Faced with the difficulties of a severely limited audience at home and little chance of touring abroad because of the language barrier, the Dutch theater has no chance of counting on a large and profitable run of a single play. Its survival, therefore, depends largely on government subsidies. There is a good deal of traveling by theater companies within Holland and the repertoires are usually large. There is a growing coterie of Dutch playwrights, although there is still a tendency to produce translated performances of foreign plays and musicals. The Dutch do, however, excel in revues, cabaret or *kleinkunst* ("small art" forms). A special mention should be made of the Nederland Dance Theater ballet company which many consider to be among the most important of modern contemporary groups in Europe.

The Dutch are not particularly renowned for their contribution to the cinema. Most of the films that are shown are imported and screened in their original language, with Dutch subtitles.

FOLKLORE AND TRADITIONAL EVENTS

Rich Panorama of Customs and Costumes

As could be expected of a nation with so rich a past and with such veneration of tradition, the Dutch are steeped in their special folklore and folkways. Their tradition, bearing the marks of their history and of their religion, displays itself in their work and in their play, in their dress and in their habits.

We will not subject you here to any deep study of ethnology. But we will try to cover, discursively and impressionistically, enough of the Dutch folklore so that you may understand a little better the strange things you see as you travel through the country. For those more interested in the national ways and habits, we would suggest a visit to the Het Nederlands Openluchtmuseum (Netherlands National Open-Air Museum) at Arnhem, where you can see, spread over acre after acre, samples of Dutch houses, costumes, and rural life, exhibited in a manner that will help you to understand the differences between one region and another.

It is neither true—as you may have gathered from movies and musical comedies—that all Dutch people disport themselves in quaint costumes and wooden shoes, nor—as you may suspect after visiting some of the places where costumes are worn—that they are a sham, invented and perpetuated to gull the guileless tourist. What is true is that at one time regional costumes were prevalent in many parts of the country, that they are dying out under the impact of modern influences, and that they are still holding on in those relatively isolated areas where there is resistance to the machine age.

You will not see traditional lace caps, golden earrings, and billowing skirts in big towns. But there are areas where costumes—mainly worn by women, but also by men in some cases—are the daily dress, the living representation of an ancient heritage. For those interested in costume-hunting, the best grounds are the shores of the IJsselmeer (the former Zuiderzee), the fishing harbor at Den Haag's seaside resort of Scheveningen, the islands of Zeeland, and, to a certain extent, the rural areas of eastern and southern Holland.

If costumes are of more than passing interest to you, then you must not miss the Zuiderzee Museum at Enkhuizen, 33 miles northwest of Amsterdam. An entire floor of this fascinating museum, housed in a building that once belonged to the East India Company, has been given over to sample interiors of homes that are typical of the Zuiderzee region. Each of the authentically furnished rooms is livened by the presence of dummy figures dressed in the local garb. Although the collection is not complete—it does not include areas beyond the Zuiderzee—it is nonetheless fascinating and worthwhile.

Where Regional Costumes Are Still Worn

Best publicized, of course, are the twin towns of Volendam and Marken, a scant dozen miles north of Amsterdam, where costume-wearing and the selling of souvenirs to tourists have become the main sources of livelihood. You can even dress up yourself and have your picture taken, provided you can fight your way through the bus loads of other tourists. Go if you must, but remember that the clothes are the only authentic feature of this commercially orientated parade.

In Volendam, the women wear a blue-striped or black-pleated skirt and a jacket. Young girls wear a bonnet with a high point. The costume is completed by a colorful apron, patent slippers, and a red-coral necklace. The men sport exaggeratedly baggy trousers and, on Sundays, a fascinating jacket, closely fitted at the waist and decorated with a massive silver button and chain.

Over at Marken, a former fishing village sitting high and dry following the completion of yet another Zuider Zee polder, the women wear a long-sleeved shirt under a sort of cotton vest (waistcoat) with red-and-white striped sleeves. On top of this rather masculine get-up they femininely wear an embroidered bodice, a woollen yoke, a sleeveless jacket, and finally another square yoke of flowered cotton. Their headgear is a bonnet with a cardboard form to keep it in shape. The men wear baggy black (or sometimes, in summer, white) trousers, a bright red sash, a blue smock with white collar, a neckerchief, and gold throat buttons. Girls and young boys are dressed alike in checked bibs, bonnets, and aprons. (But white bibs and blue skirts for the boys.)

When you visit Den Haag, you may notice portly ladies doing their shopping in severe black dresses whose hems practically touch the ground. They are wives of the fishermen at nearby Scheveningen, where you will see even more of these dignified matrons going about their business without the slightest trace of selfconsciousness, although the younger generation now usually prefer modern dress. Although the sea-colored shawls, in shades of blue, green, and grey (red-lined black capes in winter) enliven the somber skirts, your eye will most likely be attracted to a pair of gold, horn-like ornaments that protrude from the spotless white cambric bonnets (lace on Sundays) that invariably cover their heads. These oval filigree decorations are part of a gold hair band that is concealed by the bonnet.

Something rather similar is characteristic of the islands of Zeeland in the southwestern corner of Holland, which are less frequented by visitors because of their remote location. The town of Goes is the best center, especially on Tuesday market days. There are marked differences between the dress of Protestants and Roman Catholics. Protestant women wear a bonnet shaped somewhat like a conch shell, and Catholic women a bonnet shaped like a trapezium with a light-blue under bonnet beneath. Catholic women usually wear brighter colors than the Protestants. With the bonnet go the burnished gold "ear irons". The most important element of the South Beveland costume is a yoke combined with a *beuk,* a garment covering bosom and back, often made of flowered silk. Men wear black kneebreeches and silver belt buttons. There are local variations in costume from one part of Zeeland to another.

Less far afield are the twin towns of Spakenburg and Bunschoten on the southern shore of the IJsselmeer, roughly 30 miles east of Amsterdam and near the garden-like cities of Hilversum and Amersfoort. Of the two, Spakenburg is perhaps more interesting, although the costume worn there is more unusual than beautiful. Its chief features are what appear to be shoulder boards, a yoke of brightly-flowered cotton that stands out so stiffly from the neck that a slim girl looks something like a knight in armor and a husky young lady suggests a tackle on an all-star football team. A tight-fitting cap tends to make the head look shrunken above this massive shoulder line, perhaps explaining why the husbands are fishermen and stay away for days on end.

The most charming, most genuine, and most colorful costumes are worn by the farming families that live along the road joining Rouveen and Staphorst, a few miles north of Zwolle, which lies between the IJsselmeer and the German border. Should you detour to include these delightful villages on your itinerary, remember that picture-taking is deeply resented. In the past, if you were to attempt a photo on a Sunday when the pious farmers walk to church in silent files, you would risk physical assault for invading the privacy of these otherwise cheerful villagers; so be sure to ask first.

As for the Staphorst costumes, the women wear bolero-like bodices with black-and-blue striped skirts whose hips have been strangely padded. A wide, deep collar with painted flower motifs is worn except when a woman is in mourning. A red checked cotton neckerchief and large silver show buckles are added on Sundays. Beneath a white lace cap lurk silver "ear irons" with golden curls. The men boast watch chains, gold buttons on a white collar, and a double row of silver buttons on the shirt. Boys and girls dress alike up to the age of three or four.

At Urk, a one-time island that now forms the southwest tip of the Noordoostpolder, about 25 miles northwest of Zwolle, women wear a partly visible corset of light blue on which chamois leather is sewn to prevent wear. The costume itself is stiffened with whalebone. The Urk men wear baggy black trousers held together with silver belt buttons, plus black shirts, shoes, and caps. But remember that even today no cars or even bicycles are allowed within the Urk village center on Sundays. And don't start up your radio either within church earshot.

There is a colorful folklore procession, and traditional Dutch and West Frisian dances are performed each Thursday during July and August in Schagen, North Holland.

Distinctive costumes are worn in other districts and villages of Holland, and if you are interested in knowing about more of them, detailed studies with extensive illustrations may be bought in English editions at larger bookstores in Amsterdam and Den Haag.

Traditional Holidays

The Dutch love food—especially sweets, pastries, and whipped cream—so it is no wonder that many of their holidays are associated with particular delicacies. Most festivals, of course, are religious in origin, still retaining a devotional atmosphere. Here are the significant ones.

December 5th—and not Christmas, as in Great Britain and the United States—is the occasion for exchanging gifts. It is presided over by St. Nicholas, or Sinte Klaus, as the Dutch call him. This is in fact the origin of the name Santa Claus, but unlike the polar Santa Claus, this one makes his entry from Spain. He has the same white beard as Santa Claus, but he is dressed in a sweeping red robe, a red and gold miter, and carries a bishop's golden crook. He is attended by his Moorish servant, Zwarte Piet, or Black Peter. Most Dutch families celebrate the day by meeting in the evening to place shoes by the fireplace which during the night are filled with presents. St. Nicholas himself, however, appears on the 3rd or 4th Saturday in November. In Amsterdam the whole city, including the Queen as often as not, turns up to welcome him as he makes his way from the harbor to the center of the city. He is officially welcomed in front of the Stadhuis, the City Hall, by the Lord Mayor. St. Nicholas then makes a speech of his own, praising or reproaching the people as he sees fit. At the same moment, he and his helpers suddenly appear all over the rest of the country. Six weeks before St. Nicholas Day, shops blossom with marzipan in every shape and form, fondant, *speculaas* (spiced ginger cookies), *taai-taai* (spiced cake) in the form of animals and figures, and nine-inch-tall chocolate initials. Equally characteristic is the *banketletter,* a pastry initial filled with almond paste.

Until recently Christmas itself was not a time of festivity. But almost all over the country now it has been influenced by the Anglo-American customs. So, in addition to still being a family affair Christmas is nowadays little else but a prolongation of the St. Nicholas festival earlier in the month, and in many cases, especially in families where the children have grown up, is celebrated with much more jollification than the earlier feast. Almost every Dutch family now has a Christmas tree, and a thriving new industry has sprung up in the designing, producing and selling of Dutch Christmas cards, while all department stores and stationers' shops also sell a wide variety of cards in English. The shops, too, now treat Christmas as a wonderful second St. Nicholas festival, both in decorations and presents.

Winter celebrations and festivities in Holland immediately suggest the fabulous winter scenes of Pieter Bruegel or Jan van Goyen, to name but two of the many Dutch 17th-century painters who have done so much to color the popular image of Christmas the world over. For some reason, winters never seem quite as snowy or picturesque in Holland these days, but the country's lakes and canals still regularly freeze over and then a series of ice-skating races, whose origins stretch back many centuries, take place. Whole towns and villages turn out to watch, with suitable feasting and drinking afterwards. The most famous is held, conditions permitting, in Friesland in February and attracts country-wide excitement (the saying goes that children here are born with skates on their feet). The race goes by or through 11 towns, hence its name: Elf-Steden-Tocht, simply, the Eleven Town Race. It covers a gruelling 200 km. (125 miles) and starts at seven in the morning, when it is still dark and decidedly cold. Many competitors are still battling their weary way around the final stretches of the course at midnight. But with typical Dutch thoroughness, check points and first aid stations line the route to help those who don't make it.

Easter, as might be expected, features the bunny and the egg, with merry hunts for buried eggs and a special Dutch game called *eiertikken* in which children bump their eggs together to see whose will be broken first. But, in addition, there are some unusual regional customs. In some places in the eastern and southern provinces, "Easter bonfires" are lit to celebrate the spring-blazes that are reminiscent of the old fertility fires. In a few rural places girls are still covered with soot—a direct vestige of another ancient fertility rite.

Among other characteristic holiday customs are *dauwtrappen* (treading the dew), the dawn trip to the country on Ascension Day; the St. John's procession during June in the woods near Laren, ending at the "Old Cemetery", the reputed site of one-time heathen sacrifices; and the Whitsun Crowns in the Frisian village of Hindeloopen, consisting of hoops decorated with fir branches, garlands, paper roses, and eggshells.

Among secular holidays, the most important are the Queen's Day on April 30th, a time when the larger cities are festooned with the royal standard and with clusters of orange-colored balls in honor of the House of Orange; the unique flower parade as many thousands of Dutch people from all over the country file past the front steps of the Royal Palace where the whole Royal Family stands to accept the gifts of flowers; and, in Den Haag, on the third Tuesday in September, when

Queen Beatrix opens parliament, arriving in a golden coach amid much cheerful pomp.

Market days can be witnessed in a wide variety, depending on the region and on what is being marketed. One of the most famous is built around the cheese trade in Alkmaar, which started in 1571 as a special privilege granted by the king. The carrying and weighing are part of an ancient ritual, and you need only see the cheese-laden barrows and costumed porters to realize that this is a tradition buried in antiquity. The market runs on Fridays only, mid-April to mid-September, from 10 to midday. Almost as interesting is the Gouda cheese market on Thursday mornings from 9 to 12.30, mid-June to mid-August. You can sample the cheese in the charming old town hall and watch a color film illustrating how Gouda cheeses are made.

A number of "Folk Markets" are held throughout the year, such as that in Hoorn. From July to mid-August, the market is held every Wednesday with handicraft displays, folk dancing and local craft demonstrations. A similar market is that at Westerbroek in Drenthe. This also displays old crafts, but gives you a chance to admire the delightful old costumes of the area. A newer market is the Kaasmarkt, Cheese Market, at Purmerend. Here, porters wearing the historic uniform of the ancient Cheese Guild, solemnly weigh and carry the cheese. It takes place from 10 to 1 every Thursday, mid-June to mid-August.

Carnival in Holland does not reach the heights attained in the Latin countries, but in the more Catholic south and east there are many festive celebrations worth seeing—especially in such towns as Maastricht and 's-Hertogenbosch (Den Bosch). They are riots of costumes and merrymaking, all presided over by "Prince Carnival". The Dutch Carnival is usually held seven weeks before Easter.

In more recent times New Year's Eve has become another very popular Dutch excuse for merrymaking. Although end-of-the-year balls are held only in the large hotels and restaurants, most Dutch wait up enjoying the special TV or radio programs so that they can participate in street fireworks displays. Amsterdam traditionally rings in the New Year with church bells ringing, ships' sirens in the harbor, rattles, saucepan lids, in fact anything that makes a noise. Doughnuts are usually eaten on New Year's Eve and sometimes a coin is hidden in one of them, or in a cake. Finding it is a mixed blessing as the finder has to treat everyone to cakes or other goodies.

Local Customs and Sports

The fishing ports have age-old local customs, of which the most stirring is the spring departure of the luggers and trawlers for the herring grounds. Once the sailings were filled with poignancy because of the long absence and dangers involved, and an aura of the momentous still surrounds this traditional event. For weeks in advance, herring casks are scrubbed, the boats painted and made shipshape. On sailing day the villages are gaily decorated with flags and there is much excited speculation as to who will bring back the first boatload of new herring—the first cask of which is traditionally presented to the Queen.

IJmuiden, Scheveningen and Vlaardingen take turns in putting on an elaborate festive display.

Traditional sports can still be seen in the Netherlands, such as the Frisian ball game of *kaatsen,* the archery clubs, and *vendelzwaaien,* the banner-waving displays in the south. A typical traditional sport is the Walcheren *ringrijderij,* at Middelburg during August, in which men mounted on horses aim their lances at small rings. The winner receives the Queen's beaker.

DUTCH FOOD AND DRINK

Homelike or Exotic—Always Hearty

Her sons and daughters having ranged the four corners of the earth for several centuries, Holland can offer you a large variety of cooking, while the frequent trips which Dutch businessmen make abroad have served to ensure that the foreign cuisine in Holland, when it is good, is very, very good. If your soul yearns for them, and your pocket-book can stand the strain, *Sole Cardinale, Steak Orloff,* and *Canard à l'O-range* are yours for the ordering.

But real Dutch cooking is made of sterner stuff. Simple, solid nourishment, without any fancy trimmings that might hide the basic high quality of the food, is what warms the cockles of the average Dutchman's culinary heart. As a result, Dutch cooking is often called unimaginative. This is only relatively true. An abundant variety of meat, fish and fowl, vegetables and fruit, at reasonable prices, do not oblige the Dutch cook to resort to ingenuity when preparing a meal. The true Dutch cook is inclined to be lavish with butter and the result is often a strain on the digestive systems of those used to lighter fare.

At the other extreme, Indonesian food, with its variety of spices and exotic dishes, provides a dramatic contrast to the blander Dutch fare. But in between nowadays, almost every large town has a wide range of restaurants specializing in their own brands of 'national' dishes, running from Chinese to Italian, French to Yugoslavian, and even

American to English. Your hotel porter will tell you where to go for any particular kind of food, while most of the local tourist offices (VVV) have restaurant lists which will help you to explore the best in each area.

When to Eat

The mealtime pattern is remarkably uniform throughout Holland. Breakfast invariably consists of several varieties of bread and rolls, thin slices of Dutch cheese, prepared meats and sausage, butter and jam or honey, often a boiled egg, and a pot of steaming coffee, tea, or chocolate. Fruit juices are generally available but not cheap.

Don't be astonished if the waiter presents you with your hotel bill when you have finished breakfast (assuming you are preparing to leave). This custom, especially prevalent at provincial hotels, is actually a convenience and saves you the trouble of having to settle up at the last minute.

The typical lunch is *koffietafel*, which consists of more bread, various cold cuts, cheese and conserves. There is usually a side dish—warm (an omelette, a small individual cottage pie, or the like) or cold (a salad, Russian eggs, or something similar)—to go with it. The whole is washed down with tea or coffee.

The evening meal is usually the major repast of the day and is often eaten quite early—6 P.M. to 6.30 P.M.

Coffee at 11 in the morning (or earlier) and tea at 4 in the afternoon are equally sacred rituals.

What to Eat

Tradition has its place in Dutch eating. Although many dishes which were a part of the Dutch way of life before the advent of heated glasshouses, canning, deep-freeze, and modern transport facilities are now no longer a necessity, people still relish them.

To start with soup, there are two which can be called typically Dutch. *Erwtensoep*—a thick pea soup, usually only available October through March. Often served with pieces of smoked sausage, cubes of pork fat, pig's knuckle, and slices of brown or white bread. The other is *Groentensoep*—a clear consommé, loaded with vegetables, vermicelli, and tiny meatballs.

Hutspot—a hotchpotch of potatoes, carrots and onions with a historical background. When the siege of Leiden was raised on October 3rd, 1574, the starving populace was given, first, salted herring and white bread, then *hutspot* with *klapstuk* (stewed lean beef of which a little goes a long way). This has become such a traditional dish that you will find Dutchmen eating it on October 3rd anywhere from the North Pole to the Equator, from New York to Hong Kong.

Herring—eaten all the year round, the Dutch delight in the salted variety, but especially in "green herring" (those caught during the first three weeks of the fishing season which starts in May). You can eat herring neatly filleted and served on toast as an hors d'oeuvre in any restaurant, but half the fun is buying it from a pushcart, holding the herring by the tail, and gobbling it down like a native. The first cask of new herring is traditionally presented to the Queen.

Rolpens met Rodekool—thin slices of spiced and pickled minced beef and tripe, sautéed in butter, topped with a slice of apple, and served with red cabbage.

Boerenkool met Rookworst—a hotchpotch of frost-crisped kale and potatoes, served with smoked sausage.

Zuurkool—Sauerkraut: "garni" means with streaky bacon, gammon, and sausage.

Stokvis—an old-time favorite few restaurants serve nowadays. If you'd like to try something really different this is your dish. The basis is dried whitefish, cooked in milk and drained, served with potatoes and rice, fried onions, sliced raw onions, chopped dill pickles, melted butter and mustard sauce.

Kapucijners—Marrowfat peas, served with boiled potatoes, chunky pieces of stewed beef, fried bacon cubes, french fried onions, slivers of raw onion, dill pickles, mustard pickles, melted butter, molasses, and a green salad. Believe it or not the result is delicious.

Remember that nearly all the above dishes, like so many traditional dishes in Europe, are winter fare.

Seafood—fish of all kinds is usually well prepared in Holland. Try, for example, *gebakken zeetong* (fried sole) or *lekkerbekjes*—specially prepared fried whiting. Royal imperial oysters, mainly from Zeeland, are still an epicurean dish, while the smaller equally tasty "petites" are also good. Both types, however, are expensive. Dutch shrimps are delicious, but often small. If your purse is well filled, try lobster (but ask the price first), as this is a real luxury. Crab is rarely available. Mussels, on the other hand, are cheap and if you love them there's always a fish restaurant somewhere around, or buy them, fried in batter or pickled, from a fishmonger. Eel is another specialty. It is served either fresh or smoked and filleted, on buttered toast. It has a bouquet and flavor that is more easily praised than described; the smaller-sized eels taste better than the large ones. In this form it normally serves as an hors d'oeuvre. It is also eaten stewed or fried (but again, ask the price first).

Dessert—Here the Dutch, on the whole, do not shine and generally rely on ice-cream or fruit with lashings of whipped cream to carry the day. Dutch pancakes *(flensjes* or *pannekoeken)* in all their dozens of varieties are good. To mention but one, which is a meal in itself, *spekpannekoek* is a pancake measuring about a foot across, and about half an inch thick. It should be loaded with bits of crisp, streaky bacon and be full of air pockets. It is served with apple syrup or molasses. Three other favorites are *wafels met slagroom* (waffles with whipped cream), *poffertjes,* which can only be described as small lumps of dough, fried in butter and dusted with powdered sugar, but which the Dutch insist taste "as if an angel had caressed your tongue", and *spekkoek*—which literally means "bacon cake", probably because it looks like best-quality streaky bacon. The recipe comes from Indonesia and it consists of alternate layers of heavy butter sponge and spices. It tastes delicious and, besides fruit, is the only congruous dessert to a *rijsttafel*

Snacks—Nearly every town in Holland has many snack bars. Here you can get a *broodje* (roll) or sandwich in a hurry. These come in an infinite variety ranging from plain cheese to what amounts to a modest *hors d'oeuvre*. One of Holland's favorites is the *uitsmijter*. This is an open-face sandwich consisting of two fried eggs, laid on a foundation of ham, roast beef or cheese, on slices of buttered bread; potato and meat croquettes have recently become great favorites. The snack bars also offer several kinds of soup, cake, pastry, and ice-cream and some have a menu with two or three *plats du jour,* and to drink, tea, coffee, soft drinks, beer, and maybe wine. The service is usually fast and the cost modest.

What to Drink

Like the kitchen, Dutch bars are for the most part internationally-minded. First-class hotels and top restaurants in major cities have learned to make good martinis and similar cocktails. The indigenous drink, of course, is gin or *jenever,* a colorless, potent beverage that is served chilled, or at room temperature, in shot glasses and should be drunk neat as it does not mix well with any other liquid. Some Dutchmen drink it with cola or vermouth—but unless you have a very strong head avoid deviations. It comes in many varieties depending on the spices used, if any. *Jonge,* or young jenever, contains less sugar, is less creamy, but no less intoxicating than *oude,* or old, jenever. The *Bols* brand, still available in the famous stone crock which, when emptied of its original contents, was often used as a hot water bottle in wintertime, is best-known to most tourists, whereas the Dutch often prefer *Bokma,* although *De Kuyper* and *Claeryn* are also favored brands. If you don't like your gin straight try a *kleine angst* (literally little terror), which is a shot of young jenever with a liberal dash of angostura bitters. Don't gulp your jenever as the Dutch do—remember they're used to it! This innocuous, mild-tasting liquid has a delayed action which might have unfortunate results.

If you don't feel up to the challenge of tasting the Dutch water of life, they have an infinite choice. Besides the many kinds of sherry, vermouth, port and various beverages available in other countries, Holland offers a long list of gins—*bessen-jenever* (red-current gin), *citroen-jenever* (lemon gin), and so forth, as well as *advocaat* (a heavier and creamier variety of egg-nog).

Many Dutchmen drink beer with their meals. You'll make no mistake if you follow their example, because Dutch beer is good, always properly cooled and inexpensive. Imported Danish, English, Belgian and German beer is usually available, at about twice the price. Unless you want one of the heavier varieties just ask for a *pils.*

Better restaurants and hotel dining rooms will nearly always offer you a wine list. If you find the vintage you particularly fancy and don't mind the cost, order away. But unless you have a particular interest in wine, stick to beer or water (which may have to be asked for).

Many restaurants nowadays serve a carafe or individual glasses of *vins du table* which is both palatable and reasonable. But where the wine lists are concerned the wines are generally good and with a wide range, and in comparison with other countries cannot be called expensive, except at the luxury hotels and restaurants.

Dutch liquers, on the other hand, are excellent and reasonable. *Curaçao* takes its name from the island of the same name in the Dutch West Indies. It receives its flavor from the peel of a special variety of orange grown there and is delicious. *Triple Sec* is almost the same thing as Cointreau, though a shade less subtle. *Parfait d'Amour* is a highly perfumed, amethyst-colored liqueur. Dutch-made versions of crème de menthe, apricot brandy, anisette, and similar liqueurs are also very good.

Brand name whiskies from Scotland, Canada and the United States are on sale at prices below those charged at home. But the Dutch produce several quite potable bottled whiskies, as well as several varieties of passable dry gin suitable for nearly all mixed drinks.

Indonesian Cooking

Although Indonesian food tastes good at any time of the day, your digestion will probably appreciate it if you stick to lunch. The best restaurants are in Den Haag, Amsterdam and Rotterdam, although nearly all towns now have good ones. Generally, however, they are nowadays announced as Indonesian-Chinese places, and both types of food are always available. But it is always a good idea to have a chat with the manager, or the waiter, to get an explanation of what the dishes are composed of. This is particularly the case with the Chinese food, although most menu cards have English translations.

The most elaborate Indonesian meal is called a *rijsttafel.* This starts off prosaically enough with soup plates and a dish of plain, steamed rice. The rice serves as a foundation for the contents of anywhere from 15 to 50 dishes, each more delectable than the one before. Some of these are described below. Sit down to this in the mood to stuff yourself, be prepared to feel as if you want to go to bed and sleep it off afterwards (which is what most Dutchmen do) and don't be surprised if you feel hungry again a few hours later. If moderation is your virtue, try the less ambitious *nasi goreng* or *bami goreng* (fried rice or noodles—with choice bits of meat, shrimp, chicken and the like). These are equally delicious and make fewer demands on your palate.

An average *rijsttafel* is usually enough for two people, although you would do well to add one or two extra dishes from among these: *Saté babi,* bite-sized morsels of pork skewered on a wooden spit and cooked in a mouth-watering *pinda* (peanut) sauce, is delicious. *Loempia* is a mixture of bean sprouts and vegetables wrapped in wafer-like pastry and fried in deep oil. *Kroepoek* is a large, crunchy prawn cracker. Fried prawns are a welcome addition. *Daging* is the general name for stewed meat. *Daging smoor* identifies the kind prepared in a black sauce and is particularly delectable. *Daging roedjak, daging besengek,* and *daging oppor* identify variations prepared in red, green and white sauces, respectively. *Bebottok* is meat steamed in coconut milk. *Fricadel* is a forced meat ball, relatively bland and somewhat mushy. *Sambal ati* is liver stewed in a red sauce. *Sambal telor* is an egg in red sauce. *Sambal oedang* are shrimps in a red sauce. *Babi pangang* is pieces of delicious roast suckling pig in a mild spicy sauce.

Ajam (chicken) is served in as many ways as meat. *Sambalans* is a collective term for several varieties of stewed vegetables, some of which you have probably never seen before.

Seroendeng, fried coconut and peanuts, is also called *apenhaar* (monkey hair). *Gado gado* are cold vegetables in peanut sauce. *Atjar ketimoen* are cucumber sticks in vinegar. *Pisang goreng* are fried bananas. *Roedjak* is a compote of fresh fruit in a sweet sauce. *Sajor* means soup, and comes in a variety of guises, but is not a separate course as in most other countries.

To eat your *rijsttafel* you start off with a modest layer of rice on the bottom of your plate, adding a spoonful of each dish, arranging these neatly around the edge, finally filling in the center. It should be eaten with a spoon and fork. On a small dish you'll discover three or four little blobs of red and black paste—these are *sambals.* They are made of red peppers and spices and are generally red-hot. A little goes a long way. If you inadvertently bite into something that is painfully over-spiced the remedy is a large spoonful of plain rice.

Beer, though not Indonesian, is the perfect beverage to accompany a *rijsttafel.* Iced tea, lemonade or mineral water are also excellent. But never wine or milk.

Final Reminders

In nearly all Dutch restaurants, whether the cuisine be French, Indonesian or Serbo-Croatian, a service charge of 15 percent and a Value Added Tax (VAT) are included in the bill. This also applies to a *borrel* (a shot of Dutch gin) or any other drink in a bar or café. If you have any doubts, ask. Unless the service has been unusually attentive, you're at perfect liberty to pocket all your change, just as the average Dutchman does.

Remember, too, that the better Dutch restaurants are fairly formal. If you prefer casual dress at mealtime, pick a modest type of place or you'll feel awkward matching your sportswear against the headwaiter's white tie and tails. Dutch restaurants hardly ever have high chairs or children's portions, so the youngest members of your party will likely fare better at your hotel.

Because the Dutch follow the continental custom of relaxing at the table, allow at least an hour for a simple meal, two for something more elaborate. When short of time (or money) but brave enough to try a really cheap meal, try your hand at one of the "automatieks". A guilder or two in the slot and you pull out: a *croquetje*—a croquette with either veal or beef; a *loempia*—Chinese/Indonesian pancake roll; a *gehaktbal* —meat ball; a *nasibal*—Indonesian-version meat ball, rather hot, with rice; a *huzarensla*—Russian salad (cold hard-boiled egg with lettuce leaf, slice of tomato, gherkin).

If you intend to eat something at an automatiek, take care to have some guilders, as only some have change machines and it is not always possible to get your money changed.

All in all, eating is a delight in Holland, especially as nowadays there is no difficulty in finding places to suit every palate or fancy. True, it is expensive in most places, but the personal attention and service are often worth it. Moreover, a growing number of restaurants all over the country now serve the so-called tourist menu, which provides more than enough food for the average visitor (the Dutch themselves have tremendous appetites), and at a price about half the normal menu rates. So if you are traveling on a budget, look out for the notices which announce "Tourist Menu," which is priced, by law, at Fl. 18.75 for three courses.

A feature in many towns is the street carts and stalls which serve a variety of food. Herrings, to be eaten with the fingers, sandwiches, *brodjes*—rolls containing cheese, meat, or fish, often with salad—are the most common. Another speciality is *bollen,* deep fried balls of crispy batter, usually formed around fruit centres.

The visitor is unlikely to leave Holland hungry or slimmer. It can, in fact, be a real problem for anyone on a strict diet!

SHOPPING

From Diamonds and Delft to Cheese and Cigars

The question of what to take home as a souvenir of the Netherlands has as many facets as one of the glittering Amsterdam diamonds. If your purse and luggage are limited, you can always tuck a piece of pewter into your suitcase, or an antique *koekeplank* (cookie mould) carved with amusing designs. Other possibilities in the same category include pretty enamel ashtrays, blue-and-white Delftware, crystal from Leerdam or Maastricht, a Gouda cheese, or a box of those delicious hard candies called *Haagse Hopjes*.

Amsterdam is the logical place to start for most tourists, although Den Haag, thanks to the presence of the diplomatic colony as well as the European headquarters of many international companies, can offer almost as wide and varied a selection. Venturing farther afield, Haarlem, Delft, Leiden, and in fact, almost every town can also be interesting, as they frequently have more "local" antiques at prices lower than in the large cities. It is astonishing to see the wealth of antique treasures still in Holland, and although many of these come from other countries, some of them are genuinely Dutch, while the remainder can almost always be relied on to be authentic articles from elsewhere. The shops tend to be localized in particular streets or districts, making it easy to shop-hop.

Further, many places like Den Haag or Breda, for example, have antique markets in the town center during summer. These are generally supervised by the local authorities, although of course, no guarantee is given about authenticity. Still, many a good bargain, Dutch and foreign, can be picked up in these marketplaces. Prices are usually reasonable and a little bargaining occasionally makes them more so. Details of the locations of these markets will be found under the Practical Information sections at the end of each regional chapter.

Amsterdam, Home of the Diamond Cutters

During the Middle Ages, Antwerp was Europe's great diamond center. After the Spanish conquest of 1576, many diamond experts fled north to Amsterdam. During the latter part of the 17th century, master gem-cutters from persecuted religious groups all over the Continent found refuge in Amsterdam. This, timed with the discovery of Brazilian diamond fields, gave the industry a tremendous boost. At the French court of Louis XV, brilliants were in high demand to set off powdered wigs. In those days, facets were made by rubbing two diamonds together on a wheel turned by women. Violent protest was voiced by the fairer sex in 1822 when horse-power began replacing feminine hands. At that time, when a shipload of raw diamonds arrived from India or Brazil, there was feverish activity for several months until the cargo was cut and the finished stones sent, with Paris the principal destination, to be sold. Then factories stood idle until a new shipment landed.

Political upheavals throughout Europe during the latter part of the 19th century caused a serious crisis in the diamond industry. Unexpectedly, it was saved by children of a Dutch farmer living near Hopetown, South Africa, who discovered that the pebbles in a nearby stream made marvelous toys. For 500 sheep, 10 oxen, and one horse, one of these twinkling marbles representing 21 carats, found its way to Europe. The diamond rush was on and Kimberley, South Africa, became the big center. In 1870, the first shipment of South African diamonds reached Europe, commencing a trade that today supplies 90 per cent of the world's diamonds.

A visit to one of the modern diamond centers in Amsterdam offers the visitor a brief education in this fascinating business. You will see a demonstration with glass dummies which shows how the diamond is mined, cut, and polished. It is a process which fascinatingly combines modern techniques with the kind of skill only learned through many generations of craftsmen. First, each diamond is examined by experts to determine its exact color, weight, grain, and possible flaws. Then it is decided how it should be cut. Later, the finished product is scrutinized for quality and price. One of the great triumphs of the diamond cutter's art was the work on the world's largest diamond (the Cullinan), which represented over 3,000 carats when it was discovered in Transvaal in 1905 and presented to King Edward VII of England. After months of study, the fabulous stone was split to make the world's largest polished diamond. It was set in the crown of England. Another massive gem from the same stone was placed in the royal scepter and two more have been mounted in a pin for Queen Elizabeth II. The smallest in the world was also cut here as a demonstration of master technique. It weighed ¼ of a milligram; or 1/2,500,000 of the Cullinan.

We are told that it takes an entire day to saw one carat. Next comes the cleaving or shaping by hand, followed by the important polishing process, which gives the diamond its 58 different facets. You will notice that the size of a gem is usually proportionate to the number of grey hairs on the head of its worker, for it takes 15 years of experience to know how to polish the big stuff. The untrained eye can tell a good diamond at one glance by its blue-white color. You could do worse than to choose a sparkling diamond as a life-long souvenir of your visit to Holland—it will cost considerably less than elsewhere. There is also an excellent diamond store in the duty-free Shopping Center at Schiphol Airport.

Solid Dutch Silver

Silver is considered to be another good buy in Holland. The metallic content of its products is guaranteed by special controlling marks. The marks consist of a lion and number, indicating the purity of the silver, either .925 (sterling quality) or the more usual .833, to which may be added the town and maker's mark. Much antique silver was also stamped with the coat of arms of the city of its origin and sometimes the guild mark of its maker.

For example, three crosses topped by a crown was the mark of old Amsterdam, while a stork was the mark used by silversmiths in Den Haag. Indeed by law all Dutch silver must be hallmarked, which makes buying modern silver much easier, but the knowledge of marks on old pieces is a specialized business and one that should be researched very carefully; otherwise, it's best to buy from a reputable dealer, who will explain, and should guarantee, its origin.

A number of museums, large and small, feature collections of fine old silver. Notable are the display in Amsterdam's Rijksmuseum and in the Fries Museum in Leeuwarden or in the Nederlands Goud, Zilver en Klokkenmuseum in Schoonhoven.

The Dutch silver industry in Voorschoten started about 100 years ago in a small shed. It is now known as Van Kempen & Begeer and an enlarged factory stands there on this firm's private property. For silver filigree work and embossed plaques, the Dutch government has set up a school for the cultivation of fine silversmiths and goldsmiths in Schoonhoven.

In recent years a large trade has been built up in Holland in English and Continental silver, especially tea and coffee services, candelabra, and Victorian and Georgian tableware. Prices are admittedly high, but for visitors to Europe who cannot include a trip to England in their itinerary, this sort of souvenir can often be a good buy. All the large Dutch jewellers' shops carry extensive stocks of this old silver.

When looking for not too expensive jewellery as souvenirs, ask to be shown rings, bracelets or brooches and tie-pins with the traditional *Zeeuwse knop* or Zeeland knob pattern: a silver filigree rosette. They make an unusual, original, and not too pricey gift.

Delve into Delft

Most gift counters, hotel lobbies, and china shops are littered with so-called Delftware, much of it mass produced by factories in Gouda. The art of making the authentic blue-and-white earthenware, however, is not extinct.

In the 17th century, 30 different potteries produced Delft china. Now there are only two, of which the Royal Factory at Delft is the most famous. Founded in 1653, it bears the worthy name of De Porceleyne Fles. On the bottom of each object that is produced a triple signature appears: a plump vase topped by a straight line, the stylized letter *F* below it, and the word Delft. The only discernible difference between a new piece of hand-painted Delft and an old one is age. Genuine Delft may be recognized by its color, the fine shine of its glaze, the complexity of its design, and the superlative way it is expressed. The varying shades of blue found in Delft depend on the particular artist. Small scattered leaves known as the parsley pattern are characteristic of many of its pieces. The big floral splotches or simple portraits without detail are usually produced by practicing beginners.

The price of a genuine Delft article is never determined by its size but by the quality of its painting. As every object is hand-drawn, unaided by stencils or tracings, the quantity is exceedingly limited. You can understand that an entire Delft dinner service is rare; it becomes too expensive for the buyer as well as an interminable bore for the artist to complete. On weekdays visitors are welcome at De Porceleyne Fles in Delft (Rotterdamseweg 196) to see its showroom of exquisite museum pieces as well as demonstrations with the potters' wheel, the oven, and the brush. Although blue and white Delft sprinkled with floral bouquets is the most popular, other variations of Delftware do exist.

The milk-white ware, without design, was exclusively for kitchen use during the 17th century. However, in 1936 a small white collection of ridged, petal-edged decorative pieces was started, using the old moulds. Recently, a new line of white has been introduced, featuring sleek smooth forms to suit modern interiors. Also keeping step with the present is an entirely original conception of Delft that alternates black with earthy tones of gray and brown in unusual futuristic shapes, decorated by Wynblad-inspired etchings of people scratched into the glaze, rather than painted below it.

In 1948, a rich red cracked glaze was introduced depicting profuse flowers, graceful birds, and leaping gazelles. (The special cracked texture of this pottery is achieved only after six or seven bakings.) A range of green, gold, and black known as New-Delft is exquisitely drawn with minuscule figures to resemble an old Persian tapestry.

The marvelous Pynacker Delft borrowing Japanese motifs dominated by rich orange with gold, deep blue, and touches of green, has existed since the 17th century. The brighter Polychrome Delft carries a bolder picture in sun-flower yellow, vivid orange, and blue with green suggestions.

Magnificent reproductions of canvases made by 17th-century artists are executed on circular dishes in blue or brown sepia. For a goodish price, you can have your portrait drawn on a Delft plate. De Porceleyne Fles even produces a limited number of unpainted, specially glazed tiles for industrial uses in buildings, bathrooms, and swimming pools.

A commemorative tile or wall-plate could well provide that "different" present. Of the many designs for a new baby, there is one with the child's name, place, and date of birth encircling a grandfather clock, denoting the hour and the minute, and a cradle. Dutch *jenever* and liqueurs, too, bottled in blue-and-white Delftware jugs or Gouda china dolls in national costume make attractive gifts. These items, of course, along with many of the so-called Delft tiles, are found everywhere in souvenir shops, and are seldom made in Delft.

There are, indeed, several Dutch makes of pottery which make good souvenirs. Some have much the same design and color as Delft and are usually somewhat cheaper, while others have their own distinctive designs. The name of the maker is always given on the bottom of the piece, so there is no risk of mistaking it for Delft or any make of English or Continental pottery. In addition to the better known Delft wares, attractive traditional and folk designs of pottery are found in some of the smaller towns, such as Makkum and Warkum, in Friesland.

Pewter Pots and Plates, Crystal

During the 17th century, pewter was a necessary complement to Delft blue plates. However, age is no guarantee that the pewter you unearth in an antique shop is fine. 300 years ago, they made bad pewter just as they do today. Cast in old moulds, Meeuws' handwrought pewter tends to retain the original shapes you see pictured in the museums. Pewter is a mixture of tin and lead. The greater lead content a piece contains, the more worthless it becomes . . . bending easily, tarnishing quickly, and denting without apparent cause. Don't be misled by the bright appearance of those long necked jugs you see in the knicknack shops around town. Look for the heavy duty quality, preferably Meeuws' if it is new, with only five percent lead and an eternal shine.

Leerdam crystal has become famous for its fine design and lovely blue-white color. The forms vary from wide-mouthed champagne glasses balanced on cut stems to generous cornucopian vases to elegant glittery candlesticks to chubby beer beakers. Ask any reliable glass shop to let you see a complete catalogue of stocks and styles. Maastricht crystal, though as beautiful as Leerdam, is generally less expensive. Heavier, more cut, and worked, it often resembles the French Baccarat while its competitor to the north can be compared to Swedish Orrefors.

Dutch cigars are always a good buy as gifts, but bear in mind your Customs quota.

If you do not want to carry cheeses home with you, you might find that cheese accessories such as cutting boards with small glass domes, or specially designed knives, make very acceptable souvenirs.

When you want to take home a pair of clogs, do NOT buy them at a souvenir shop but ask for them when in the country, where the farmers buy them. You'll get them for a much lower price and there will be more choice.

Eatables, Drinkables and Plantables

The Dutch love to eat and drink and their favorite foods provide splendid opportunities for souvenir and gift shopping. Dutch cheeses and the potent *jenever* gin are obvious choices, but Holland also produces a wide range of liqueurs such as *Curaçao,* or *Advocaat,* a type of egg nog, and many flavored with fruit or herbs. Dutch chocolate and a variety of specialized candies cater for those with a sweet tooth, while pickled herring, or smoked eel, are delicious savoury souvenirs.

The bulbfields of Holland are among the country's top scenic attractions and their products are ideal as gifts to take home. One word of warning, here, on the regulations applied by some countries to imports of plants, which may limit the type or quantity of such produce that can be taken home, but commercial growers offering plants or bulbs for sale can advise on these regulations for most countries and will supply appropriate purchases.

A Last Word

If you are leaving the Netherlands by air it might be useful to remember that the tax-free shops at both Schiphol (Amsterdam) and Rotterdam Airports, open for long hours, offer a mouth-watering display of cameras, watches, liquors, tobacco, perfume, jewelry, toys, porcelain, and the flower bulbs and seed for which Holland is so justly famous, at prices which are often lower than in the ordinary shops. Since the standard of duty-free shops around the world is so variable, many of them being far more expensive than the stores just around the corner from you at home, it is a pleasure to be able to record that Schiphol at least is full of genuine bargains.

EXPLORING HOLLAND

AMSTERDAM

City of a Thousand and One Bridges

Nearly 1,000 years ago, so the legend goes, two fishermen and their dog beached their boat on a sandbank where the river Amstel flowed into the IJ, the old Dutch word for water. They settled there, prospered and were joined by others.

By the 12th century their settlement was still little more than a small fishing village, and not nearly as important as the surrounding towns—Kampen and Zwolle to the east, Delft, Dordrecht and Leiden to the south. The village was named after the river and the dam that had afterwards been built there: Amstelledamme.

Despite their insignificance, the people of the village were clearly both shrewd and able. For example, it was only in 1275 that Count Floris V, after many unsuccessful attempts, succeeded in annexing the town to his own lands, and then only after having granted unusual tax exemptions and a lucrative beer-producing monopoly. By 1300 Amstelledamme had grown sufficiently to be awarded a city charter.

Its prosperity continued to increase over the next 200 years. But it was the fall of Antwerp, in what is today Belgium, to Spain in 1576 that provided the major spur to the city's growth. Most of Antwerp's merchants moved north to Amsterdam, bringing their wealth and trading connections.

The city embarked on a period of rapid expansion and fast-growing prosperity. Trade was the corner stone of the city's success. Indeed so successful were the city's merchants, that by 1600 their merchant fleet was larger than those of all the rest of the Low Countries combined. Following the establishment of the East India Company in 1602, the city rose to the peak of its influence and its ships were seen in every corner of the globe. The Bank of Amsterdam, one of the oldest in the world, was established in 1609.

The key to this spectacular mercantile success story was water, or, to be more exact, the canal system, which remains one of the city's most prominent features. The first canals had been built essentially as defensive moats, but by 1600 they came to be used for trading purposes. The building in 1610 of the Herengracht, Keizergracht and Prinsengracht canals in the city center was the first step in turning the city into a vast port. More were gradually added throughout the 17th century, until by the latter part of the century it was possible to unload cargoes in the heart of the city direct from the ships that had carried them there.

By now much of the city's center had assumed its present day appearance. Many of the houses whose upper stories were used for storing this flood of tea, spices, silks, furs, and whatnot, can still be seen. The heavy beams that jut out from their topmost gables lack only a rope and the men to pull it; the patrician mansions seem still to echo with the steps of the "burghers" whose portraits were painted by Rembrandt and Frans Hals.

Water was the city's nemesis as well. Twice during the 17th century the locks were opened and the surrounding countryside flooded in defense against the attacks of Prince Willem II and Louis XIV. In January, 1795, however, the stratagem failed when the temperature fell and the waters froze, thus enabling Napoleon's cavalry to ride across the ice and capture the proud city for France. Even before this time, moreover, the Zuiderzee had begun to silt up. Only ships with flat bottoms and relatively shallow draft could clear the mudbanks, and this during an era when the British were learning to construct stout, deep-keeled vessels that could carry twice the cargo of a Dutch boat twice as fast. Commerce stagnated from the late 17th century until the completion of the North Holland Canal in 1825 and the North Sea Canal in 1876, while England supplanted Holland as mistress of the seas.

The Spanish also had a hand in making Amsterdam great. Not only did they suppress rival Antwerp but the dreaded Inquisition drove out liberal Catholics, Protestants, and Jews alike, many of whom settled in Holland's leading city where religious toleration and freedom of conscience also attracted certain Separatists or Pilgrims from England, some of whom in 1620 set sail for the Americas where they founded Plymouth, Massachusetts. After the revocation of the Edict of Nantes, these Flemish, Spanish, Portuguese and English refugees were joined by French Protestants. Most of the families who sought asylum in Amsterdam were hard-working, thrifty and skilled in trade, craft or industry. Their talents, their money, and their gratitude to the city that had made them welcome had a catalytic effect on the Dutch themselves and their surroundings.

Today, Amsterdam is a bustling, vigorous city. It is the capital of the Netherlands and with its new suburban agglomeration, has a population of about 700,000. The fourth greatest European attraction, after Rome, London and Paris, it celebrated its 700th birthday in 1975.

Exploring Amsterdam

By whatever means you arrive in Amsterdam you will necessarily be struck by the symmetrical rings of canals and the 1,200 bridges lacing them together. There are 160 canals lined by some 7,000 buildings, many dating from the 16th to the 18th centuries. They are the most characteristic features of this delightful bourgeois city whose character is indelibly stamped with the taste and philosophy of the early 17th century. Time has vindicated its builders, and if few of the stately patrician houses are still owned by merchant princes, few have been allowed to fall into disrepair.

A glance at the map confirms the relatively ordered layout of Amsterdam's heart. Imagine a horizontal line with a dip in its middle. The left-hand side of the line is the North Sea Canal, an engineering accomplishment of the first magnitude that cuts a 15-mile swath through what was once sand dunes to provide a direct outlet to the ocean. The right-hand side of the line is the IJ River (pronounced "eye"), which once flowed into the brackish Zuiderzee and thence into the North Sea by a round-about route that led north past Hoorn, Enkhuizen, and Den Oever. Today, of course, the Zuiderzee is a fresh-water lake called the IJsselmeer in honor of this selfsame river. Along both sides of this line is a complex of piers, harbors, drydocks, warehouses, cranes, and other maritime facilities that testify to Amsterdam's importance as a center of world trade.

The dip in the middle of our hypothetical line marks the point at which an artificial island was built to receive the Central Station (1889), whose elaborate towers and cluttered façade were designed by Cuypers in a style that is euphemistically called Dutch Renaissance. The medieval core of Amsterdam, marked by a confusion of waterways that have since been partially filled in (Damrak and Rokin were once canals), is directly below this dip and thus within a few minutes' walk of the station itself. Around this core you'll notice four semicircular rings of canals, with two more at a somewhat greater distance. Planted with elms and lined with gabled, red-brick mansions and storehouses, they are best explored on foot. We seriously advise you to do your exploring with map in hand. The concentrically circular nature of the city's layout makes it terribly easy to start walking in exactly the opposite direction from the one you thought you were going.

A favorite itinerary takes about an hour and follows the east or inner side of the Herengracht from the Raadhuisstraat (behind the Dam and the Royal Palace) to the south and then the east as far as Thorbeckeplein and Reguliersgracht. Americans may wish to detour briefly to the building at Singel 460, today used for auctions, where John Adams obtained the first foreign loan ($2 million) of the infant United States from the banking house of Van Staphorst in 1782. Other loans from

AMSTERDAM

1 Central Station
2 St. Nicolaaskerk
3 Oude Kerk (Old Church)
4 Nieuwe Kerk (New Church)
5 Koninklijk Paleis (Royal Palace)
6 Main Post Office
7 Anne Frank Huis
8 Joordan District
9 Amsterdam Historisch Museum
10 Zuiderkerk (South Church)
11 Museum het Rembrandthuis
12 Zoological Gardens
13 Rijksmuseum
14 Rijksmuseum Vincent Van Gogh
15 Stedelijk Museum (Municipal Museum)
16 Stadsschouwburg (Theater)
17 Joods Museum
Ⓒ Canal Trips - starting points
ℹ VVV Tourist Information Offices

SCALE
0 ———————— 440yds
0 ———————— 400m

this and other houses soon followed to a total of $30 million, a generous Dutch gesture of confidence in the future of America.

Everything within the Lijnbaansgracht or outermost canal is called the Centrum. Everything beyond belongs to the modern development of Amsterdam and is subdivided into West, Zuid (south), and Oost (east). Knife-like, the broad Amstel River pushes its way between Zuid and Oost into the Centrum, where its waters are partitioned into three canals, eventually mingling with the IJ. Visitors may also be interested in Amsterdam's two tunnels, one under the IJ and the other leading to the Zaan area. Perhaps the best introduction to Amsterdam is on one of the frequent canal and city tours. We give full details in the Practical Information section at the end of this chapter.

From the Central Station to the Dam

As you emerge from the Central Station, the Haarlemmerstraat lies just to the right. A tablet at No. 75 (now an orphanage) commemorates the occasion in 1623 when the directors of the Dutch West India Company planned the founding of Nieuw Amsterdam on the southernmost tip of the island of "Manhattes." Two years later the first permanent settlement was made, followed in 1626 by the purchase of a good part of the island from the native Indians "for the value of 60 guilders". In 1664, the colony was seized by the English and renamed New York.

The street directly opposite the station is Prins Hendrikkade, where to the left is Oude (Old) St. Nicolaaskerk. This is one of the oldest parts of the city (the church was consecrated in 1306). It is also the heart of the red light district. The church is notable for its organ, made most famous by the late 16th-century composer Jan Sweelinck. He is buried in the church, as is Rembrandt's wife Saskia. Three stained glass windows, dating from 1555 but extensively restored from 1761–63, and a lovely carillon (complex set of bells) are also worth taking in. During the summer organ concerts are held on Tuesday, Wednesday, Friday and Saturday evening. Admission is Fl. 6.

Beside St. Nicolaaskerk is the tower of the Schreierstoren (the Criers' Tower or Weeping Tower), where seafarers used to say goodbye to their women before setting off to faraway places. At the angle of Geldersekade and Oudezijdskolk, it was erected in 1487 and a tablet marks the point from which Henry Hudson set sail in the *Half Moon* on April 4, 1609 on a voyage that took him to what is now New York and the river that bears his name. The "Weeping Tower" is now used as a combined reception and exposition center and old-world tavern. It also houses the world's first diamond museum. Farther left (east) at No. 131 is the house of Admiral De Ruyter, who, among other things, sought to avenge the English capture of Nieuw Amsterdam by sailing up the Thames and creating a panic in London in 1667.

More or less behind the Schreierstoren at Oudezijds Voorburgwal 40 is the Amstelkring Museum whose façade carries the inscription "Ons' Lieve Heer Op Solder" or "Our Dear Lord In The Attic." In 1578 Amsterdam embraced Protestantism and, just as reformist sects had previously been forbidden by Catholicism, forbade the Church of Rome. So great was the tolerance of the municipal authorities, however, that clandestine Catholic chapels were allowed to exist as long as their activities were reasonably discreet. At one time, there were 62 such institutions in Amsterdam alone. One such was installed in 1663 in the attics of three separate houses built around 1661, whose lower floors were ordinary dwellings. It was in use until 1887, the year that the St. Nicolaaskerk opposite the Central Station was consecrated for Catholic worship, since which time it has been preserved by both Protestant and Catholic owners as a monument to toleration in the midst of bigotry. Of interest are the baroque altar with its revolving tabernacle, the swinging pulpit that can be stowed out of sight, the upstairs gallery, and the display cases in some of the rooms. Organ recitals are given here at 4 o'clock on Sunday afternoons.

Returning to the Damrak, the broad thoroughfare that leads towards the Dam from the Central Station, we pass the piers of excursion boats and reach the Beurs or Exchange, designed by Berlage.

If you continue east another three or four blocks, you pass through the red-light district, known as the *walletjes* or *rosse buurt*. Travellers should exercise caution in this area, as bag-snatching is quite common. Do leave your valuables, passports etc. in the hotel safe. Just beyond is the Nieuwmarkt or New Market dominated by the five-towered Waag or Weigh House. Like the Schreierstoren, it was orginally part of the town wall, in this case a gate. In 1617 it was turned into a weigh house and guildhouse.

The Dam and the Koninklijk Paleis

Instead of turning aside, however, let's continue up the Damrak to the Dam, the broadest square in the old section of town. To the left you'll note the simple monument to Dutch victims of World War II. The 12 urns contain soil from the 11 provinces and from the former Dutch East Indies, now Indonesia. The old name for this part of the Square is Vischmarkt (Fishmarket) where the boats of the fishing fleet would come in and sell their catch. To the north of the Dam is the Nieuwe Kerk, New Church. Dating originally from around 1400, it is in the form of a late-Gothic cruciform basilica. It was expanded gradually until approximately 1540 when it reached its present size. Gutted by fire in 1645, it was reconstructed in imposing Renaissance style. The superb oak pulpit, the great organ (1645), the monumental tomb of Admiral de Ruyter, just one of many famous people buried here, and several fine stained glass windows are all worth noting. Today the church is used also for exhibitions and concerts.

The Koninklijk Paleis (Royal Palace) or Dam Palace, a vast, well-proportioned structure completed in 1655, was built originally to replace the city hall that had stood on the same site but had burned down. Remarkably, it is built on 13,659 piles, an excellent illustration of the problems posed by building on the marshy soil of this part of Holland. The great pedimental sculptures are an allegorical representation of Amsterdam surrounded by Neptune and mythological sea-creatures. The seven archways at street level symbolize the then seven provinces of the Netherlands, although the entrance, oddly enough, is on the opposite side of the building. In 1808 it was converted into a palace for

Louis Bonaparte, Napoleon's brother, who abdicated two years later. Theoretically, it is now the official residence of Queen Beatrix, but she seldom uses it, preferring to live at Huis ten Bosch in Den Haag. The Dam Palace now sees only an occasional reception for a visiting Head of State and the Queen's annual New Year reception of the whole diplomatic corps. Parts of the palace are open to the public, with guided tours being operated every Wednesday afternoon at 1.45 P.M. Opening times vary so check with VVV office.

Directly behind the Palace is the main post office. From here the Raadhuisstraat leads west across three canals to the Westermarkt and the Westerkerk, or West Church, built in 1631 by Pieter de Keyser to plans drawn up by his father, Hendrick (who was also responsible for the Zuiderkerk and Noorderkerk). Its 275-ft. tower, the highest in the city, has a large Emperor's crown commemorating Maximilian of Austria at its summit. It also houses an outstanding carillon. Rembrandt and his son Titus are buried here (lying side by side), and Queen Beatrix was married here. During the summer, one can climb the tower for a fine view over the city.

Opposite, at number six Westermarkt, Descartes, the great French 17th-century philosopher *(Cogito, ergo sum)* lived for a brief period in 1634. The house is identified by a commemorative plaque. Another, more famous house, it found further down the same street. This is the Anne Frank Huis, immortalized in the immensely moving diary kept by the young Anne Frank from 1942–44. The Franks, a German-Jewish family, had emigrated to Amsterdam in 1933, following Hitler's rise to power. They managed to evade the Nazis for over two years after the invasion of Holland in May 1940, before moving into the house in July 1942. Here they hid in empty, barren rooms, reached by a small, cleverly-disguised passage leading off the library, and here Anne kept her sad record of two increasingly fraught years before their inevitable capture and deportation to Auschwitz. A small exhibition of the Holocaust can also be found in the house.

Walking north up the Prinsengracht, you reach the Noorderkerk, built in 1623 by de Keyser (see above). In the square in front of the church, the Noorderplein, there is a bird market every Saturday.

From the Dam you can also turn into the Kalverstraat, the single most important shopping street in Amsterdam, which leads south from the left-hand side of the palace. At No. 92 is the beautiful Renaissance (1581) gate of the Burgerweeshuis or City Orphanage, once a monastery, which has an ever older door around the corner to the right in St. Luciensteeg. The inner court dates from about 1670. The black and red coloring in the coat of arms of Amsterdam was reflected in the uniforms of the orphans; they had one red and one black sleeve.

Continuing down Kalverstraat, turn right into Begijnsteeg, which leads to the delightful Begijnhof, a charming almshouse boasting one of the only two remaining authentic Gothic façades in Amsterdam. Founded in 1346, the houses enclosing the original courtyard date from the 14th to the 17th century. It now adjoins the rehoused Historisch Museum, enlarged and enriched for the 700th anniversary celebrations of the city in 1975. Room after room documents the history of the city with old maps, documents, plans and works of art. Opposite the church, which was given to Amsterdam's English Reformed community more than 300 years ago, is a secret Catholic chapel built in 1671.

Muntplein to Rembrandt's House

The next street to cross Kalverstraat is Spui. A right turn here would bring us to Singel and, following the tram tracks, to Leidsestraat, another important shopping street, which terminates in the Leidseplein with its Municipal Theater and other amusements. On the Singel's west bank, just past the lock by the Open Haven, is what is often erroneously called the narrowest house in Amsterdam. In fact it is just a door giving onto a small alley. The real thing is at number 166 Singel; it's called Den Gulden Fonteyn and houses a gallery.

Continuing straight along Kalverstraat instead, you soon reach the Muntplein with its 1620 Munttoren or Mint Tower, a graceful structure whose clock and bells still seem to mirror the Golden Age. West from the Muntplein is the flower market on Singel canal. Reguliersbreestraat leads east from this point to the Rembrandtsplein where you will find De Gouden Hoffd, a newly restored complex of shops, cafés and restaurants. To the right is Thorbeckerplein, with its bandstand offering concerts every Sunday during summer. Here also many cafés and bars are clustered. From the latter square, the Reguliersgracht or canal leads south across the ring canals, crossing them on picturesque bridges.

We turn left (north) out of the Muntplein, however, and cross Rokin, another shopping street, to the bridge that connects with Nieuwe Doelenstraat, which is lined with some of Amsterdam's leading hotels. It in turn merges with Kloveniersburgwal, on whose left-hand side is the University, founded in 1632 and housed in an 18th-century hospital. Today it has over 10,000 students.

We cross the canal ourselves and follow the Raamgracht east to Zwanenburgwal, where the bridge to the left leads across to Jodenbreestraat. At number four is the house where Rembrandt lived from 1639 to 1658, now the Museum Het Rembrandthuis. It was built in 1606, originally with only two storys. The ground floor was used for living quarters, the upper floor was Rembrandt's studio. For some five years, Rembrandt and his wife Saskia lived here in considerable pomp. But following the death of Saskia in 1642, the great man became increasingly introspective and his business gradually declined, though his output remained as prodigious as ever. Finally, in 1658 he was forced to sell the house to meet the demands of a multitude of creditors, and with his mistress Hendrijke Stoffels, who had originally been his housekeeper, and son Titus, moved to the much less prestigious Rozengracht, beyond the Westermarkt. The house was acquired by the city in 1906, and opened as a museum five years later. It is fascinating to visit, both as a record of life in 17th-century Amsterdam and of the life and working methods of one of Holland's presiding geniuses. It contains a superb collection of Rembrandt's etchings.

As the name Jodenbreestraat suggests, Rembrandt's house was located in the midst of Amsterdam's Jewish quarter. Close by, at Waterlooplein 41, the Portuguese Jew and philosopher Baruch Spinoza

was born in 1632. The Dutch Israelite and Portuguese Israelite synagogues were built between 1671 and 1675, a few hundred yards east.
The Waterlooplein is also the site of the new Stopera building. The
unusual name is derived from its role as Town Hall (Stadhuis) and
Muzicktheater. The Waterlooplein flea market occupies the area
around the Muzicktheater.

At the northern end of Jodenbreestraat is the Zuiderkerk, the third
and final city church on this route designed by Hendrik de Keyser.
Built between 1603 and 1611, it was Amsterdam's first post-Reforma-
tion church. At the other end of Jodenbreestraat, on Jonas Daniel
Meijerplein is an important new museum opened in 1987. The Joods
Historisch Museum is a complex of four synagogues, the oldest dating
from 1670, displaying a wide-ranging religious, ceremonial and social
history collection of the Jewish community.

Jodenbreestraat continues east under different names to the botanical
gardens (Hortus Botanicus), the zoo (Natura Artis Magistra), and the
aquarium, which can be reached by following the tramline. Another
half mile in the same easterly direction brings you to the Tropenmuseum or Tropical Museum. Its aim is to present the problems of the
Third World, and there is a theater (the Soeterijn) showing Third
World movies and plays.

Amsterdam's Museum Quarter

On the southernmost edge of the outer Singelgracht canal, a few
minutes' walk from the Leidseplein, you'll find three of the most distin-
guished museums in Holland—the Rijksmuseum, the Stedelijk Museum and the Rijksmuseum Vincent van Gogh. Of the three, the
Rijksmuseum, easily recognized by its cluster of towers, is the most
important, so do be sure to allot a fair amount of time. It was founded
originally by Louis Bonaparte in 1808, but the present rather lavish
building dates from 1885. The museum contains significant collections
of furniture, textiles, ceramics, sculpture and prints, as well as Italian,
Flemish and Spanish paintings, many of the highest quality. But the
great pride of the Rijksmuseum is its collection of 16th- and 17th-
century Dutch paintings, a collection unmatched by any other in the
world.

Perhaps the single most famous painting is Rembrandt's *The Night
Watch,* commissioned by the Company of Captain Cocq and Lieuten-
ant van Ruytenburg and completed in 1642. The picture was originally
even larger than it is today (a spectacular 14 by 12 feet). But in 1711
it was transferred to the War Council in what is today the Royal Palace,
and it was necessary to cut 26 inches from the width and 11 from the
height. The title of the picture is actually rather misleading. It was long
assumed, quite naturally, that Rembrandt's dark and mysterious picture represented a night scene. In fact, it was only when the painting
was cleaned in 1947 that it became clear that it was a daytime picture.
Nonetheless, the original name has continued to be used. The picture
also had to be restored in 1975 after it was slashed by a crazed visitor.

There is much more in the Rijksmuseum: among the superb collection of over 3,000 paintings are jewel-like vignettes by Jan Vermeer,

landscapes by Ruysdael and Hobbema, pastorals by Paulus Potter, boisterous domestic scenes by Jan Steen, vigorous portraits by Frans Hals, cool interiors by Pieter de Hoogh, peasant scenes by Van Ostade. Allow at least two hours just to sample these riches, then relax in the pleasant restaurant for a snack, before going on to see the 50-odd galleries containing the magnificent collection of furniture, glass, porcelain, gold and silver. A new wing adds art and artifacts from prehistory to 1900. There is also an Asiatic department in the basement.

A few blocks down the road is the Rijksmuseum Vincent van Gogh, opened in 1972. The largest collection of works by van Gogh in the world, the museum contains 200 paintings and 500 drawings by the artist, as well as works by some 50 other painters of the period.

A stone's throw away is the Stedelijk (Municipal) Museum, housed in a late 19th-century neo-Classical pile, with a new wing added in the '50s. The museum has a good collection of modern art, with all the major figures represented. It also arranges frequent and usually stimulating temporary exhibitions.

Diagonally opposite the Stedelijk Museum at the end of the broad Museumplein is the Concertgebouw, which presents a full and varied schedule by two major national orchestras, the Amsterdam Philharmonisch and the Concertgebouworkest. There are also many visiting orchestras. The building has two auditoriums, the smaller one being used for chamber music and recitals. A block or two away in the opposite direction is Vondelpark, an elongated rectangle of paths, lakes and pleasant shady trees. A monument honors the 17th-century epic poet Vondel, after whom the park is named. From Wednesday to Sunday in summer free concerts and plays are performed in the park.

While you are exploring Amsterdam, keep one ear cocked for the unmistakable strains of a street organ. These remarkable instruments pour forth a torrent of sound generated by a bizarre mixture of drums, pipes, cymbals, and the like. The virtuosity of selections—jazz, waltzes, round dances, and martial airs—together with the frescoed façade behind whose carved panels the muses labor so mightily, seem somehow symbolic of this proud city.

One old part of Amsterdam that must be mentioned and is certainly worth exploring is the Jordaan, the area between Prinsengracht and Lijnsbaansgracht. The canals and side streets in this part all have the names of flowers and plants. Indeed at one time, when this was the French quarter of the city, the area was known as *le jardin,* a name that over the years has become Jordaan. The best time to explore the old town is on a Sunday morning when there are not too many cars and people about, or for an evening stroll. The area is attracting a lot of artists and is becoming a "Bohemian" quarter, with rundown buildings turning into restaurants, antique shops, boutiques and galleries.

The Outskirts of Amsterdam

About a mile south of the city is the Olympic stadium, completed for the Olympic Games in 1928 and accommodating 80,000 spectators. Close by is the Haarlemmermeer Station, site of the Electrische Museumtramlijn Amsterdam (City Tram Museum). This is one of the very best spots in town for children. Take a ride on one of the old trams (weekends only) to the Amsterdam woods, where, incidentally, a short walk takes you to the delightful old farm house of Meerzicht.

Just beyond the stadium is one of Amsterdam's proudest achievements: the Bosplan or Forest Park, stretching for several miles, almost to Schiphol Airport. As large as Paris' Bois de Boulogne, twice as big as New York's Central Park, it was started in 1934 as a relief project during the depression. Its more than 2,200 acres is about half woodland and includes mile after mile of bicycle paths, bridle paths, footpaths, and roadways plus an open-air theater, a score of soccer fields, a rowing course 733 meters (2,400 yards) long, and many other sports facilities. The land used for this far-reaching development has been reclaimed at the cost of constructing a 322 kilometer (200-mile) network of drainage pipes. In the past four decades the park has been colonized by birds and other wildlife.

Nearer to Schiphol Airport is Europe's largest artificial ski slope. Called the Meerberg, it's near the Golden Tulip Schiphol Hotel, Hoofddorp.

A visit to the new Amstelpark with its modern sculptures, restaurant, sauna and rose exhibition, is a pleasant way to spend an afternoon. The park is close to the RAI fairground.

Despite some complaints that the city is overpriced, overcrowded and over-rated, Amsterdam remains one of Europe's most charming towns. The Dutch take care to preserve their architecture as well as carrying out innovative expansion schemes stretching out into the surrounding countryside. Some fine examples of continental city-planning and urbanization are to be seen, especially towards the Schiphol area, all of them characterized by the Dutch love of greenery, flowers, parks and decorative waters. There is actually an underground metro whose construction was no small job in sandy soil below sea level.

Call in at the VVV in front of Central Station to get particulars of sightseeing excursions in and around Amsterdam and make hotel or theater reservations. If you feel a little adventurous, ask for the holiday-time plan by which you see Amsterdam on bicycles. The excursion starts around 10, and you collect your tour certificate at 3.15 P.M. with a Dutch drink at a local tavern.

PRACTICAL INFORMATION FOR AMSTERDAM

GETTING TO TOWN FROM THE AIRPORT. The best way to reach the center of Amsterdam from Schiphol Airport is by using the new direct rail link, with three stops en route to Central Station. This runs every 10 to 15 minutes throughout the day and takes roughly half an hour to Amsterdam Central Station. Fare, second class, is Fl. 4.40.

Taxis, readily available, are expensive, costing from around Fl. 40. Many first class hotels provide their own transfer bus.

TELEPHONE CODES. The telephone code for Amsterdam is 020. When dialing from within the city, no prefix is required.

HOTELS. Most hotels in Amsterdam are inside the concentric ring of canals that surround the downtown area. At Easter and in the peak summer months (mid-June to September) they fill to bursting and advance reservations are essential. The VVV accommodations office outside the Central Station can usually find a room for you, however, if you arrive without a booking. (Out of season they can usually also recommend hotels offering discounts). Few downtown hotels have parking facilities.

We have divided the hotels in our listings into four categories—Deluxe, Expensive, Moderate and Inexpensive. In *Deluxe* hotels, two people in a double room can expect to pay from Fl. 300 to Fl. 600, in *Expensive* hotels from Fl. 200 to Fl. 300, in *Moderate* hotels from Fl. 100 to Fl. 250 and in *Inexpensive* hotels from Fl. 75 to Fl. 150. These prices include service charge, VAT and, for the cheaper grades, usually breakfast as well. Most hotels, particularly at the upper end of the scale, have rooms in more than one price category. Be very sure to check *before* making your reservations what category of room you are booking. Deluxe and Expensive hotels all have bathrooms in the rooms; in the lower grades bathrooms are usually down the corridor, but they will always be spotlessly clean.

Prices for single rooms are around 80% of double room costs.

Deluxe

Amstel. 1 Prof. Tupplein; 226060. 111 rooms with bath. Situated on the Amstel River, it has a reputation for solid comfort—and for being the most expensive hotel in the city. Room standard varies a bit. The terrace is delightful in summer. *La Rive* restaurant. Intercontinental chain.

Amsterdam Hilton. 138 Apollolaan; 780780. 276 rooms with bath. Glassed-in floral garden, heated in winter. Boasts the *Terrace* restaurant, *Half Moon Bar* and an excellent, if expensive, Japanese restaurant.

Apollo. 2 Apollolaan (main entrance on Stadionweg); 735922. At the junction of five canals, has 225 rooms each with bath. There is a fine restaurant, private landing stage and a large car park. (Do not confuse this with a less pretentious Apollo close by.)

De L'Europe. 2 Nieuwe Doelenstraat; 234836. Opposite the Muntplein with a view of the Amstel. 80 rooms with bath; newly decorated and more comfortable than its Victorian facade suggests. Excellent restaurant for dinner and *Le Relais* for grills.

Marriott. 19–21 Stadhouderskade; 835151. 400 rooms; excellent dining in the popular *Port O'Amsterdam* restaurant. Several deluxe suites. Right in the city center.

Okura Intercontinental. 175 Ferd. Bolstraat; 787111. 402 rooms with bath, 20 suites, studios and Japanese-style rooms. Several restaurants including the fine *Ciel Bleu,* serving the best Japanese food in Holland. Parking.

Schiphol Hilton. At the airport; 020–5115911. 204 rooms, all with bath; 24-hour room service, ideal for inter-flight business meetings. Indoor pool.

Sonesta. 1 Kattengat; 212223. 425 rooms, all with bath. Well-designed modern hotel with every comfort. *Rib Room* restaurant, *de Serre* and *Koepel* cafés give full range of eating possibilities. Attached to the Sonesta complex are several old houses and a restored Lutheran church, a huge rotunda used for conferences and regular concerts.

Expensive

Alexander. 444 Prinsengracht; 267721. 25 rooms with bath. Is located above (and belongs to) the *Dikker en Thijs* restaurant.

American. 97 Leidsekade; 245322. 185 rooms with bath. Next door to the City Theater, a few minutes from the town center.

Arthur Frommer. 46 Noorderstraat; 220328. 90 rooms. Dinner only in restaurant.

Caransa Crest. 19 Rembrandtsplein; 229455. 70 rooms with bath; restaurant.

Crest. 2 de Boelelann; 429855. 263 rooms with bath or shower, penthouse suites. *Bourgogne* restaurant, coffee shop, bar.

Dikker en Thijs Garden. 7 Dijsselhofplantsoen; 642121. 98 rooms. With *de Kersentuin* restaurant.

Doelen Crest. 24 Nieuwe Doelenstraat; 220722. 86 rooms, most with bath. Traditional, old-fashioned comfort. Ask for a room on the quieter canal-side. Excellent restaurant and bar.

Golden Tulip Barbizon. 7 Stadhouderskade; 185765. Near Vondelpark and Leidseplein, ten minutes from downtown. 240 rooms with bath.

Golden Tulip Schiphol. 495 Kruisweg, Hoofddirp; 02503–15851. No charge for children sharing adults' room. Pets welcome.

Ibis. 181 Schipholweg; 02968–1234. 400 rooms. In Badhoevedorp, near the airport (has shuttle service). Restaurants, 24-hour coffee shop, bar.

Krasnapolsky. 9 Dam; 5549111. 325 rooms, most with bath.

Ladbroke Park. 25 Stadhouderskade; 717474. 183 rooms, most with bath. A step away from the Rijksmuseum and next door to the Vondelpark.

Memphis. 87 De Lairessestraat; 733141. 90 rooms with bath or shower, furnished in French style. Good restaurant.

Novotel. 10 Europaboulevard; 5411123. With 600 rooms and several restaurants, this is Holland's largest hotel. Modern and a little anonymous.

Pulitzer. 315–331 Prinsengracht; 228333. In a row of restored 17th-century houses. 194 rooms with bath. Restaurant, bar. A Golden Tulip hotel.

Victoria. 1–6 Damrak, opposite the station; 234255. 150 rooms, all with bath or shower. Very central.

Moderate

Ambassade. 341 Herengracht; 262333. 27 rooms, all with bath. Beautiful canal-side location. Good value.

Asterisk. 14 Den Texstraat; 262396. 35 rooms, some with bath. Very good value. Closed Jan. and Feb.

Atlas. 64 van Eeghenstraat; 766336. Art nouveau; small but pleasant.

Het Canal House. 148 Keizersgracht; 225182. Delightful American-run hotel. 20 rooms all with bath or shower. Charming building partly dating from 1650. Larger rooms are worth extra cost.

Carlton Crest. 18 Vijzelstraat; 222266. Central but noisy. 150 rooms with bath.

Casa 400. 75 James Wattstraat; 651171. 400 rooms with shower. All the amenities—American bar, two restaurants, sun lounges, plus a nursery for the kids. Closed Sept.—June.

Cok Budget. 30 Koninginneweg, with an annex next door at 1 Koningslaan; 64611. Recently restored, comfortable.

De Gouden Kettingh. 268 Keizersgracht; 248287. Central but quiet; only 18 rooms, most with shower. Good value.

Estherea. 305 Singel; 245146. 70 rooms.

Euromotel Utrechtsebrug. 10 J. Muyskenweg; 658181. On the highway to Utrecht. 140 rooms with shower.

Fantasia. 16 Nieuwe Keizersgracht; 248858. 20 rooms, a few with bath. At the lower end of the price scale. Closed Jan. and Feb.

Mikado. 107 Amstel; 237068. 25 rooms, with bath. Reasonable.

Museum. 2–10 P.C. Hoofstraat; 733918. 150 rooms, only a few with bath.

Poort van Cleve. 178 N.Z.-Voorburgwal; 244860. 110 rooms with bath. Though very central, it breathes antiquity and quietness. Top of this price range.

Prinsen. 36 Vondelstraat; 162323. Centrally located in residential area.

Pullman Schiphol. 20 Oude Haagseweg; 179005. On the main road to Den Haag. 158 rooms with shower.

Rembrant Crest. 255 Herengrach; 221727. 110 rooms with bath.

De Roode Leeuw. 93 Damrak; 240396. 80 rooms, over half with bath. Pleasant sidewalk terrace. Central.

Sander. 69 Jac. Obrechtstraat; 722495. Family atmosphere, excellent service.

Schiller Crest. 26 Rembrandtplein; 231660. 86 rooms with bath. Very central. Has popular sidewalk café and restaurant.

Slotania. 133 Slotermeerlaan; 134568. A bit far from the center, but good connections on city transport. Reasonable prices.

Trianon. 3 J.W. Brouwerstraat; 733918. 58 rooms. Located next to the concert hall, the Rijksmuseum and the van Gogh Museum.

Inexpensive

Hans Brinker Hotel. 136 Kerkstraat; 220687. 52 rooms, no facilities, but extremely inexpensive.

Holbein. 5 Holbeinstraat; 628832. 16 rooms, mostly without bath. Good quality for price.

Kap. 56 Den Texstraat; 245908. 32 rooms, pleasant and family-run.

Museumzicht. 22 Jan Luykenstraat; 712954. 27 rooms, few with bath.

Paap. 39 Keizersgracht; 249600. 20 rooms, some with bath. Closed Jan.–mid-Mar.

Sphinx. 82 Weteringschans; 273680. 36 rooms, 10 with bath.

Wiechmann. 328 Prinsengracht; 263321. 35 rooms, some with bath.

Youth Hostels. There are a number of youth hostels in Amsterdam offering accommodations from Fl. 16.75 to Fl. 25 per night, including breakfast. Full details are available from Stichting Nederlandse Jeugdherberg Centrale, 4 Prof. Tulpplein, Amsterdam; or from the VVV at the Central Station. Two of the best are *Stadsdoelen,* 97 Klovennersburgwal; 246832, and *Vondelpark,* 5 Zanpad; 831744.

Camping. There is a large camp site at 45 Ijsbaanpad (tel. 620916). It is open from April to October but can get very full in high season, so book ahead.

GETTING AROUND. By Bus, Tram and Metro. Armed with a route map, available from the VVV, you should have no trouble getting around. A zonal fare system is used, with metro tickets purchased from automatic dispensers, tram and bus tickets from drivers (all of whom speak English!). One of the most useful tickets is the *Strippenkaart* (strip ticket) from which bits are clipped off as they are used up, according to the number of zones crossed. Don't forget that more than one person can travel on a *Strippenkaart,* it just gets used up more quickly! If you are going to travel around a lot in Amsterdam, buy one of the runabout tickets, *Dagkaart.* These are available for 1 day (Fl. 8.65), 2 days (Fl. 11.60), 3 days (Fl. 14.20), 4 days (Fl. 16.90). Buy them from Central Station or at post offices or GVB ticket counters.

If your travels are taking you throughout Holland, don't forget the public transport Link Rovers which can be added onto the NS Rail Rovers—see page 23.

By Taxi. Taxis are expensive. Flag fall varies from Fl. 2 to Fl. 4, and charges thereafter are Fl. 2 to Fl. 4 per kilometer. Taxis are not usually hailed in the street, but taken from ranks, normally near stations, or at key road intersections. To call a taxi, dial 777777.

On Foot/By Bicycle. Amsterdam is a small congested city full of narrow streets—ideal for exploring on foot. But be sure to get a good map, available from the VVV. Bicycles are available for hire for around Fl. 6 per day. They are perhaps the easiest way to get around, but be careful of the traffic. A high deposit is payable, usually Fl. 100. Details, available from the VVV. Ask about Ena's Bike Tour, a 7½ hour escorted trip to the Vinkeveense Lake, costing Fl. 37.50.

Canal and City Tours. Perhaps the best and most enjoyable introduction to Amsterdam is a boat trip along the canals. Several operators run trips, usually in glass-roofed boats. There are frequent departures from starting points opposite the Central Station, by Smits Koffiehuis, beside the Damrack, along the Rokin and Stadhouderskade (near the Rijksmuseum) and from several other spots. Most trips have multilingual guides, and last from 1 to 1½ hours. They cost from Fl. 7.50 to Fl. 12. Most also take in the busy harbor. A few have facilities for wheelchairs.

Even more delightful are the night-time trips that run in the summer. They are more expensive (Fl. 29–35) but wine and cheese are usually included in the price, and in any case the sight of the city's graceful and dignified 17th-century mansions slipping by in the twilight, their lights glistening in the water, should not be missed. You can also now hire pedal-boats to make your own canal tours. Called Canal-Bike, they cost Fl. 17.50 per hour. For details call 265574.

Bus tours around the city are also available and provide a reasonable introduction to Amsterdam. Price is from Fl. 29, duration around 3 hours. Most of these trips include a brief visit to the Rijksmuseum and to a diamond-cutting factory. Tours on Sundays also include a canal trip.

TOURIST INFORMATION. The main tourist information office (VVV) is at the Central Station (tel. 020–266444). It is open every day in summer from 9.00 A.M. to 9 P.M.; in winter for shorter periods. The office has an accommodations service for those who arrive without reservations; a small fee is charged for this. They can also make theater and excursion bookings (including canal trips) as well as supplying maps, restaurant lists, sightseeing checklists etc. There is always at least one person on duty who speaks English. There is another VVV office at 106 Leidsestraat.

USEFUL ADDRESSES. Travel Agents. *American Express,* 66 Damrak (tel. 262042). *Key Tours* (*Wagonlits Cooks*), 19 Dam (tel. 247310), and at Amstel Hotel, 1 Prof. Tulpplein (tel. 226060). *Holland International,* 54 Rokin (tel. 264466). *De Vries & Co.,* 6 Damrak (tel. 248174).

Consulates. *American Consulate,* 19 Museumplein (tel. 790321). *British Consulate,* 44 Koningslaan (tel. 764343).

Car-Hire. *Avis-Rent-a-Car,* 485 Keizersgracht (tel. 262202). *Hertz,* 333 Overtoom (tel. 122441). *Europcar,* 51–53 Overtoom (tel. 184595). *InterRent,* Amstelveenseweg 294 (tel. 730477). *Budget,* 121 Overtoom (tel. 126060).

All the leading car-hire companies have desks at Schiphol Airport.

MUSEUMS. Amsterdam has over 40 museums, ranging from the quaint and local to the internationally renowned. For the really serious museum-buff, the Museum Ticket will get you into 16 museums in Amsterdam (and dozens more around the country). Issued by VVV offices, it costs Fl. 7.50 for those under 25 and Fl. 21 for those 25 and over. Note that most museums close on Mondays. Note that 1988 has been declared "Museum Year" throughout Holland, with special presentations being made in many places.

Allard Pierson Museum. Oude Turfmarkt. Archeological finds from Mesopotamia, Egypt, Greece, Italy. Open 10–5, Tues.–Fri., 1–5 Sat. and Sun. Closed Mon. Adm. Fl. 2.50.

Anne Frank Huis (Anne Frank Museum). 263 Prinsengracht. The house in which the young Jewish girl Anne Frank, author of the famous diary, hid from the Nazis during World War II. The rooms where the family was hidden are open to visitors and there are other moving wartime exhibits. Open 9–5, Mon.–Sat., 10–5 Sun. Adm. Fl. 5.

Amsterdams Historisch Museum (Historical Museum). 92 Kalverstraat. Housed in a renovated orphanage. Good depiction of the city from earliest times. Interesting coffee and diamond trade exhibits; fascinating collection of jewelry. Fairly good restaurant. Open daily 11–5. Adm. Fl. 3.50.

Aviodome National Lucht- en Ruimtevaartmuseum (Aviodome National Aeronautical Museum). Schiphol. Exhibition of aviation and space travel, past and present, with a glimpse into the future. Open 1 Apr.–31 Oct. daily 10–5; Nov.–31 March, Tues.–Sun. 10–5. Adm. Fl. 5.25.

Begijnhof. Entrance on Spui. A kind of openair museum with a church and nuns' living quarters dating back to 1346.

Bijbels Museum. 366 Herengracht. Biblical antiquities from Palestine, Egypt and Mesopotamia, Open 10–5, Tues.–Sat., 1–5 Sun. Closed Mon. Adm. Fl. 3.

Collectie Six. 218 Amstel. Home of the descendants of Jan Six; you can visit it by obtaining an introduction card from the Rijksmuseum. Ten generations ago Jan Six was, among other things, a patron and friend of Rembrandt, who painted his portrait, which still hangs here. For opening times, check when you obtain the card.

Electrische Museumtramlijn Amsterdam (Amsterdam Tram Museum). In the old Haarlemmermeer Station. Includes rides on old city trams. Sat. and Sun. only.

Filmmuseum Nederlands. 3 Vondelpark. Film reviews, photographs, playbills, shows; library; changing exhibitions. Open Mon.–Fri. 10–12.30 and 1.30–5. Closed holidays. Adm. Fl. 1.

Joods Historisch Museum. Jonas Daniel Meijerplein 2–4. Jewish historical museum housed in four former synagogues. Open daily 11–5. Adm. Fl. 5.

Madame Tussaud. Kalverstraat 156. Tells the story of Dutch people and events through the ages in life-size wax models. Open daily from 10–6, in summer 10–8. Adm. Fl. 8.

Museum Amstelkring Ons' Lieve Heer op Solder (Our Lord in the Attic). Oudezijds Voorburgwal 40. From the outside this is a typical 17th-century merchants' home. On the top floor, however, is a remarkable attic Catholic church that dates from the Reformation when non-Protestants were forbidden to worship. Open Mon.–Fri., 10–5, Sun. 1–5. Adm. Fl. 3.

Museum Het Rembranthuis (Rembrandt Museum). Jodenbreestraat 4. Dating from 1606 this fascinating house was the home of the painter from 1639–1658. Open Mon.–Fri. 10–5, Sun. and holidays 1–4. Adm. Fl. 2.50.

Museum Overholland. 4 Museumsplein. Specializing in very modern art (post-1970), it holds several exhibitions a year. Open Tues.–Sat. 11–5, Sun. and hols. 1–5. Closed Mon.

National Spaarpottenmuseum. 20 Raadhuisstraat. Money-box museum, with over 300 piggy banks and other boxes on display. Open Mon.–Fri. 1–4. Adm. Fl. 1.

Nederlands Scheepvaart Museum (Maritime Museum). 1 Kattenburgerplein. Historical ship models, paintings, prints, maps, nautical instruments. Open 10–5, Tues.–Sat., 1–5 Sun. Closed Mon. Adm. Fl. 5.

NINT, Nederlands Instituut voor Nijverheid en Techniek (Dutch Institute for Industry and Technology). 129 Tollstr. Exhibitions relating to natural science and technology. Open Mon.–Fri. 10–4, Sat. and Sun. 1–5. Closed public holidays. Adm. Fl. 5.

Rijksmuseum. 42 Stadhouderskade. A vast Victorian red-brick building facing the outermost of the city's concentric ring of canals and the country's most prestigious and important museum. Superb collection of Dutch 16th- and 17th-century paintings, plus magnificent Flemish, Italian and Spanish works. Other departments include Asiatic and graphic art, a print room with ancient and modern drawings, a library containing 35,000 books on art, and Dutch sculpture and decorative art up to the 19th-century. Well over 30 galleries of 18th-century furniture, glass, porcelain, gold and silver, make it the largest collection of its kind in Europe. Useful cafeteria available. Conducted tours at 11 and 2.30. Open 10–5, Tues.–Sat., 1–5 Sun. Closed Mon. Adm. Fl. 6.50

Rijksmuseum Vincent van Gogh. Next door to the Stedelijk Museum. Unrivaled collection of 200 paintings, 400 drawings and 600 letters by the artist, along with library and many other documents. Attractive cafeteria with terrace in summer. Open 10–5, Tues.–Sat., 1–5 Sun. Closed Mon. Adm. Fl. 6.50.

Stedelijk Museum (Municipal Museum). 13 Paulus Potterstraat. Excellent collections of modern art, plus good late 19th- and early 20th-century works. Open daily 11–5. Adm. Fl. 5.

Theatermuseum. 168 Herengracht. Documents history of the Dutch theater through prints, drawings, costumes, programs etc. Changing exhibitions. Open 11–5, Tues.–Sun. Closed Mon. Adm. Fl. 2.50.

Tropenmuseum (Tropical Museum). 2 Linnaeusstraat. Exhibits on all aspects of the Third World. Open 10–5, Mon.–Fri., 12–5 Sat. and Sun. Adm. Fl. 4.

Willet Holthuysen Museum. 605 Herengracht. Characteristic and delightful 17th-century merchant's mansion. Open daily 11–5. Adm. Fl. 1.75.

 BOTANICAL GARDENS, ZOO, AND AQUARIUM. These three make up a large complex just to the east of the downtown area along the Plantage Kerklaan; it's well worth a visit particularly as a change from serious museum visiting. Coming from the downtown area, you first reach the *Hortus Botanicus* (Botanical Gardens), with hothouses and nurseries and plants galore. A block further along is the *Natura Artis Magistra* (better known as the Zoo), an excellent example of its type with everything from insects to elephants. Finally, there is the Aquarium, a characteristic representative of the species; one of the highlights here is the electric eels who are periodically stimulated into lighting up a row of bulbs.

ENTERTAINMENT. Music and Concerts. In the music department, Amsterdam's famous Concertgebouw Orchestra ranks among the foremost in Europe. It plays in the Concertgebouw, Van Baerlestraat 98. The same building has a smaller auditorium that is used for chamber music, recitals and even jam sessions. For opera and ballet, the national companies are housed in the new Muzicktheater on Waterlooplein. During the Holland Festival foreign companies also perform. For information on the annual Holland Festival contact—Holland Festival, 21 Kleine Gartmanplantsoer, 1017 RP, Amsterdam.

For details of current performances—including rock and jazz—see *Amsterdam This Week,* a weekly listing of events and entertainments available free from the VVV. The VVV can also make bookings for most performances.

Movie theaters are scattered throughout Amsterdam, the biggest concentrations being on Leidseplein and Reguliersbreestraat. Performances begin at fixed hours, often 1.30, 3.45, 6.45 and 9.30 P.M. Smoking is forbidden in all theaters and movie houses. Sound tracks are usually in the original language with Dutch subtitles, but some are dubbed, so check first. To see what's playing when and where, see *Amsterdam This Week.*

ALTERNATIVE AMSTERDAM. Paradiso, still famous from the drug days of the '60s and the provo's (kabouters), is at 6–8 Weteringschans (tel. 264521). Now has pop concerts, classical music, cinema, workshops, jazz, reading table, café, macrobiotic restaurant, etc., as well as being the Punk center of Amsterdam. Open Tues.–Sat., 8–1 A.M., Fri., Sat. 8–2 A.M.

Akhnaton, 25 N.Z., Kolk, a youth center for young working people as well as students, with performances of theater, concerts, films.

Kosmos, 142 Prins Hendrikkade. Meditation center including yoga, zen, astrology, alternative medicine, herbs, food, film, theater, lectures, café, macrobiotic restaurant and even a sauna.

Melkweg (Milky Way), 234a Lijnbaansgracht, behind the main city theater. A multi-media center with film, theater, video, pop, jazz, poetry, mime, jam sessions, tea rooms with a sweet heady scent in the air, art market, etc.

SHOPPING. Amsterdam's chief shopping streets, which have largely been turned into pedestrian-only areas, are the Leidsestraat; the Kalverstraat; de Nieuwendijk, on the other side of the Dam Square; the Rokin, somber and sedate, where the best antique dealers are found; de Reguliersdwarsstraat, starting at the Muntplein; the Nieuwe Spiegelstraat where a series of old curiosity shops cluster together; the P. C. Hooftstraat strewn with small attractive boutiques favored more by the resident than the tourist; and the Beethovenstraat, which converges with the Stadionweg, where the smart residential south lives and buys.

Markets

There's a lively flea market on the Waterlooplein around the Musicktheater (weekdays only, 10–4). The flower market is held on the Singel during weekdays; a colorful and vivid experience. Noisier, is the bird market held every Saturday in the Noordmarkt. The more studious might be interested in the stamp market, Wed. and Sat. afternoon, at Nieuwwezijds Voorburgwal and the book market at Oudemanhuispoort, held most days Mon.–Sat.

Diamonds

Moving upmarket rather sharply, no visit to Amsterdam is complete without a visit to one of the major cutting houses. Apart from the fascination of watching the cutting, there is usually no pressure to buy. A lucky thing, too—diamonds may be forever, but they are also terribly expensive!

Among the leading cutting houses are:

Amsterdam Diamond Center B.V., 1–5 Rokin; *Coster Diamonds,* 2–4 Paulus Potterstraat; *Gassan Diamond House,* 17–23 Nieuwe Achtergracht; *Holshuysen - Stoeltie B.V.,* 13–17 Wagenstraat; *A. Van Moppes & Zoon B.V.,* 2–6 Albert Cuypstraat.

Most are open from 9–5, and all will be glad to show you around.

Antiques

Amsterdam is one of Europe's leading centers for antiques, from every source, of every type, from every age. The area around Nieuwe Spiegelstraat is full of small antique shops, specialized and general. The Joordan district also has many shops. In addition, there are several important antique markets held each week, featuring stalls for everything from the worthless to the, perhaps, priceless. As well as the flea market on Waterlooplein, other antique markets include: Antiekmarkt de Looier, 109 Elandsgracht, open Mon.–Thurs. 11–5, Sat. 9–5; and from May–Sept. the Antique Fair held each Sun. in the Nieuwe Markt.

Porcelain

Fine porcelain, particularly imported Wedgwood, is obtainable at *Van Gelder & Co.,* J. Rebelstraat (closed Saturdays), or in their narrow branch store at Van Baerlestraat 40. A wide range also to be seen at Focke and Melzer, Kalverstraat, 65 P.C. Hoofstraat, or Okura Hotel shopping arcade.

Books

Book shops have a very large selection of new editions, second-hand books and even collectors' items in many languages, and so are often worth browsing in for half an hour or so. Bargains can also often be picked up during a stroll through Oudemanhuispoort, a unique market, between Kloveniersburgwal and Oudezijds Burgwal. Don't be put off by these tongue-twisting names; they're easier to get to than pronounce. The *Atheneum Bookshop,* 14-16 Spui, is one of the most wide-ranging and pleasant to browse around. *Allert de Lange,* 62 Damrak, opposite the Bijenkorf, has a fascinating range of maps and travel guides. *De Sleghte,* Kalverstraat (also Coolsingel, Rotterdam) is a good place to browse. They sell foreign books as well as Dutch ones and on any topic you can think of. They also sell their own reprints of old Dutch maps, engravings and prints at reasonable prices. Also reproductions. *Antiquariaat,* 14–18 Oude Hoogstraat, for old books.

Miscellaneous

Go to *Jacob Hooy* at 12 Kloveniersburgwal, an old-style delicatessen filled with herb pots and drawers of spices in which the firm has been dealing for well over two centuries. For cheese, make for *De Franse Kaasmaker* at 192 Marnix-straat. They sell 65 different varieties of cheese from many lands.

Most shops have a wide range of French and other foreign clothes, while Dutch ready-to-wear fashions are good quality though more expensive than fashions in Britain or the States. For the young there are many small boutiques, including some interesting second-hand clothes-shops in the Joordan area.

Holland is famous for its cigars. One fascinating old shop for these is *Hajenius,* 92 Rokin, while at *Sigarenmakerij Nak,* 27 St. Pieterspoortsteeg you can see demonstrations of making cigars by hand. Another traditional Dutch craft, clog making, can be watched at *De Klompenboer,* 20 Vorburgwal.

Lazy (or tired) shoppers could do worse than call in at one of the big department stores like the *Bijenkorf,* Damrak, corner Dam Square, where almost everything is obtainable under one roof. Although not quite so large as Macy's or Harrods, it's got just about everything, including a restaurant where the pancakes are quite delicious. Also *Vroom & Dreesmann,* Kalverstraat near Munt Square, *Hema,* and *Marks and Spencer,* 11 Museumsplein.

 RESTAURANTS. Amsterdam has an abundance of excellent restaurants in all price categories offering a wide range of international cuisines. Dutch cuisine is naturally the most common (our *Food and Drink* chapter will introduce you to many of the traditional Dutch specialties you can enjoy here—in typical, unhurried Dutch style, of course) but the city is also famed for its Indonesian restaurants, a legacy of the country's colonial past.

Also recommended for a sample of genuine local life and food are the "brown cafes," so called as they are seldom decorated! They are a cross between a British pub and a French cafe and, apart from the normally exuberant atmosphere, serve good inexpensive food. As well as the many Indonesian restaurants, you might also try Chinese food, usually inexpensive and reliable. Amsterdam, in common with the rest of Europe these days, has its fair share of fast-food hamburger joints which, though hardly characteristic, are inexpensive and good value. Much more characteristic are the city's traditional herring carts; these can be found in many locations throughout the city.

Best value of all is the Tourist Menu. Over 600 restaurants in Holland serve it (look for the sign outside) and the price is always Fl. 18.75, fully inclusive, for three courses. For those on a tighter budget it is excellent value.

Our restaurant lists are divided into three categories: Expensive, Moderate and Inexpensive. Per person and excluding drinks, you can expect to pay from Fl. 70 in an *Expensive* restaurant, from Fl. 40 to Fl. 90 in a *Moderate* restaurant and from Fl. 15 in an *Inexpensive* restaurant. However, these prices can be no more than approximations as most restaurants serve dishes in more than one price category. Similarly, what you drink will affect your bill significantly. So be sure to check the menus posted outside (by law) *before* you go in. The daily *table d'hôte* set menus are best value, even in the most expensive places.

Note also that for more expensive restaurants you should book ahead. Similarly, remember that the Dutch eat early and that many restaurants are accordingly closed as early as 10 P.M. with last orders as early as 9 P.M. outside of the bigger cities. Credit cards are not universally accepted, even in Expensive restaurants, so take cash along for emergencies.

Expensive

Bali. 95 Leidsestraat; 227878. Fast for a day before you come here or you won't be able to finish half the delicious Oriental delicacies you'll be served.

Blue Berry Hills. 138 Kerkstraat; 220689. Cosmopolitan atmosphere, international menu.

Dikker en Thijs. 438 Prinsengracht; 267721. Elegant restaurant serving fine French cuisine; certainly one of Amsterdam's best. The **Café de Centre,** ground floor, for inexpensive lunches and self-service dinner.

Edo Japanese Steakhouse. Kransnapolsky Hotel; 554609. Good range of Japanese specialties.

Excelsior. 2 Nieuwe Doelenstraat; 234836. A close rival of Dikker en Thijs for flawless French cooking and elegant atmosphere. Located in the Hotel de l'Europe, sharing its view of the Amstel river.

Ile de France Rôtisserie. 9 Platmanweg, in Amstelveen (a suburb of Amsterdam); 453509. Quality French restaurant with impeccable food and service.

De Kater. 2–4 Gerard Douplein; 722424. The chef discusses the evening's French specialties with each party. Reservation essential.

De Kersentuin. 7 Dijsselhofplantsoen; 642121. Very modern, *nouvelle cuisine.* Highly recommended.

Molen de Dikkert. 104a Amsterdamseweg, Amstelveen; 411378. French cuisine. Recommended.

Prinsenkelder. 438 Prinsengracht; 267721. Rather formal, but excellent food, if a little expensive. Closed Sun.

Les Quatre Canetons. 1111 Prinsengracht; 246307. Nouvelle cuisine, fresh trout from a trout aquarium, excellent wine list. Closed Sun.

La Rive. 1 Prof. Tulpplein; 226060. International specialties. In Amstel Hotel.

De Silveren Speigel. 4 Kattengat; 246589. Excellent food, but a bit pricey.

t' Swarte Schaep (The Black Sheep). 24 Korte Leidsedwarsstraat; 223021. Dates from 1687, and has one of the largest wine cellars in all of Europe. Cooking is reasonably good, but prices are on the high scale.

Tout Court. 17 Runstraat; 258637. Run by a member of the renowned Fagel family, famed for its French culinary feats. Good for after-theater parties. Closed Mon.

Trechter. 63 Hobbemakade; 711263. High quality French food.

d'Vijff Vlieghen (Five Flies). 294 Spuistraat; 248369. Five ancient houses contain a warren of dining rooms, any of which would grace a museum. Menu includes Dutch specialties; game in season.

Yamazato Oriental Restaurant. 175 Ferd. Bolstraat; 787111. Part of Okura Hotel, this is perhaps the best Japanese restaurant in town. Also in the hotel is the popular *Teppan-Yaki.*

Moderate

Adrian. 21 Reguliersdwarsstraat. French cuisine, good wines.

Beit Hamazon. 57 Anjelierstraat. Kosher restaurant, vegetarian dishes. Open Sun.–Thurs. 4–10.

Bodega Keijzer. 96 van Baerlestraat, opposite the Concertgebouw, the City Concert Hall; 711441. Very good food, warm atmosphere.

T'Brueghelhuys. 20 Smaksteeg; 220537. For dining in a medieval atmosphere. Touristy but fun, set out like a street market complete with minstrels.

China Corner. On Dam Square. For "Dim Sum" lunch.

Dorrius. 336 Nieuwe Zijds Voorburgwal; 235245. A popular businessmen's haunt serving Dutch specialties. Closed Sun.

Fong Lie. 80 P.C. Hoofstraat; 716404. Chinese food for the knowledgeable. Booking essential. Closed Mon.

De Groene Lanteerne (The Green Lantern). 43 Haarlemmerstraat; 241952. Three floors high, this is the narrowest restaurant in all Holland. Crowded with bric-a-brac and atmosphere. Closed Tues.

t'Heertje. 16 Herenstraat; 251827. Authentic Dutch dishes and ambiance. Closed Wed.

Heineken's Hoek. 13 Kleine Gartmanplantsoen; 230700. Good for basic, moderately-priced lunches.

Iboya. 29 Korte Leidsedwarsstraat. Offers live entertainment as you dine.

Istanbul. 770 Keizerstraat. Fine introduction to good Turkish cooking.

Kopenhagen. 84 Rokin; 249376. For Danish snacks; fish specialties.

La Marina. 5 Klove Niersburgwal; 222040. Spanish cuisine.

Mirafiori. 2 Hobbemastraat; 723013. Serving simple, but well-prepared Italian pastas and the like.

Mouwes Strictly. 73 Utrechtsestraat; 235053. Excellent for kosher sandwiches and delicatessen foods. Closed Sat.

De Oesterbar. 10 Leidseplein; 263463. A must for fish-fiends. Wide range of seafood as well as prices.

De Orient. 21 van Baerlestraat; 734958. Worth trying for something different Oriental-style.

Die Port van Cleve. 178–180 N.Z. Voorburgwal; 244860. Fine Dutch herring dishes in vaulted beerhall or old Dutch dining salon.

Restaurant Speciaal. 89 Leliestraat; 249706. One of the best for Indonesian food.

Roses Cantina. 38 Reguliersdwarsstraat; 259797. Lively Mexican restaurant.

Sea Palace. Oosterdokskade (beside the Central Station); 264777. Huge, new floating Chinese (mostly Cantonese) restaurant.

Seoul. 106 Prins Hendrikkade; 223267. Good spicy Korean food.

Sluizer. 45 Utrechtsestraat; 263557. Fish specialties. Popular.

Witteveen. 256 Ceintuurbaan; 724368. Good traditional Dutch cuisine.

Yoichi. 128 Weteringschans; 226829. Excellent Japanese *sukiyaki* and *tempura* menus.

Inexpensive

Bredero Pannekoekenhuisje. 244 O.Z. Voorburgwal; 229461. Pancakes of all sorts. Closed Tues.

Café Rokin. 100 Rokin. Reasonable food, delicious apple pie.

Floreat. 502 Overtoom; 189129. Wide variety of attractive vegetarian dishes.

Golden Temple. 126 Utrecherstr; 268560. Macrobiotic food served with honey muffins.

HaringhandelVisser. Muntplein Haringkar. Typical Dutch herring delights served from characteristic herring cart. Closed Sun. and Mon.

t'Haringhuis. 18 Oude Doelenstraat; 221284. Another herring cart. Closed Sun. and Mon.

Bars

Bols Taverne. 106 Rozengracht. For Bols and many other characteristic Dutch drinks; interesting.

Cafe Americain. 97 Leidsekade. Popular meeting place in the Hotel American.

Cafe Gollem. 4 Raamsteeg. The perfect place for beer lovers; has over 100 different beers, and calls itself a *bierakademie!*

De Drie Fleschjes. 18 Gravenstraat. Another tasting house and one of the oldest, having opened in 1650. After a comprehensive tasting the visitor is not, perhaps, too unhappy that it closes at 8.30 P.M.

Wijnand Fockink. 31 Pijlsteeg. A traditional tasting house. Just east of the Dam at right angles to Warmoesstraat, you'll find this narrow alley. Turn in under the doorway with the naked Bacchus and the date 1679 on it, and you'll discover a pint-sized bar with a drinks list that staggers the imagination. Ask for a *half-en-halfje* (don't inquire too closely as to the contents). When it comes in its cone-shaped glass, don't pick it up but bend down and sip it, at least for the first time around—traditionalists are very firm on this point! It closes at 8 P.M.

Brown Cafes

So named after the tobacco-smoke stained ceilings and walls that never seem to be redecorated, these are a must-see-and-sample aspect of Amsterdam. Great charm and character, in the best "pub" tradition. Among the best of these colorful Amsterdam institutions are:

De Bak. 193 Prinsengracht.
Cafe Nol. 109 Westerstraat.
Dokterje. 4 Rozenboomsteeg.
De Egelantier. 72 Egelantiersgracht.
Hoppe. 18–20 Spui.
De Pilsener Club. 4 Begijnensteeg.
Sing–Sing. 101 Singel.
Het Laatste Oordeel. 17 Raadhuisstraat. Serves over 200 different beers!

 NIGHTLIFE. The nightclubs of Amsterdam have now become much more daring than those in Paris and more notorious than those in Hamburg. Some say they are more exciting in every sense of the word than in any other city. To the tourist they present a strange anomaly, because while on the one hand the Dutch have always been noted for a strict morality verging on puritanism, they are also stern upholders of absolute freedom. The wide wave of sex freedom has certainly engulfed Amsterdam, where its effects are seen not only in the most bawdy nightclubs presenting every type of live show, but also in a rash of porno shops.

Amsterdam's red light district remains one of its chief sexy attractions with scantily-clad girls displaying their charms in bright windows by day and night under the unobtrusive eye of the police. This scene attracts the curious onlooker as well as the participant.

Although the police vice squad tries to stop the most daring of the nightlife attractions, they close their eyes to most of them: indeed, the fact that the most bizarre of them change their location every week or so (from bar to bar, or from houseboat to houseboat) makes police vigilance largely impossible.

For obvious reasons, most of the way-out places do not advertise their location, and sources of information are the usual world-wide ones: hotel porter, taxi driver, head barman or waiter, who will certainly require a tip of, say Fl. 5. But beware—you may find yourself in a "live" show that just might shock you beyond your wildest expectations! Amsterdam also has a number of regular gay meeting places, many of them in and near the Kerkstraat, in which the hetero-sexual has been increasingly accepted during recent years. In Holland, homosexuality is anything but frowned on.

Although at night private rooms become public bars and some discos (such as *Juliana's,* 3 Breitnerstraat) offer more than they appear to, Amsterdam's real nightlife is concentrated in two areas: the Leidseplein and Rembrandtsplein which have a chain of dinner-cum-dancing-cum-floorshow joints. Among other discos currently popular are *Mazzo,* 114 Rozengracht, which presents the latest in pop music videos, and *Zorba de Buddha Rajneesh,* at 216 O.Z. Voorburgwal. Most such clubs charge around Fl. 5 entrance.

All the nightclubs and bars within the three areas mentioned above can be regarded as safe for the tourist in a physical sense, though some may make heavy demands on your purse. The same goes for places recommended by your hotel porter. Wandering off on your own down side streets and back alleys is another matter, and one should be wary about touring the more insalubrious areas at night, especially those where the drug scene is active. This applies particularly to the area around the Central Station.

The regular nightclubs listed below are generally acceptable to all but the primmest of maiden aunts (although some go in for fairly spectacular strip-tease), and are as daring as the average person would want. Most are open from about 10 P.M. to 2 A.M. or even 4 A.M. and serve drinks which are not usually excessive in price. However, they might have moved or changed name, so check your choice with your hotel porter or even with the VVV. The alphabetical list below is not necessarily in order of merit or price.

De Amstel Taverne, Halvemaansteeg, close to Rembrandtsplein. A lively, pleasant gay bar with music.

Bamboo Bar, 64 Lange Leidsedwarsstraat. Informal, inexpensive, relaxing and international. Has the longest bar in Amsterdam.

Be-Bop, 24 Amstelstraat. For slightly more than teenage crowd.

De Bios, 12 Leiseplein. Open from 10 P.M. Entrance fee. Very trendy, for teenagers and up (slightly).

Cab Kaye's Jazz Piano Bar, 9 Beulingstraat. Live music and singing.

Carrousel, 20 Thorbeckeplein. Informal, attended by the top people. Floor-show. Topless waitresses. Take your own instrument along if you have it, for you will be welcomed as a player.

Disco Escape, 15 Rembrandtsplein. Lively pop scene; programs are recorded here for satellite T.V.

Joseph Lam Jazzclub, 8 Van Diemenstraat. Good dixieland music. Closed Mon.–Thurs.

STIP, 161 Lijnbaansgracht. Dance and drive disco; live music.

AMSTERDAM AS AN EXCURSION CENTER

Holland in a Nutshell

There are few parts of the Netherlands that offer the variety of landscape and human activity that is characteristic of the region north and south of Amsterdam. Within the span of a single day you can roll the centuries back from Dudok's modern City Hall at Hilversum to a 13th-century castle at Muiden, from the modern North Sea beach resort of Zandvoort to the dreamy lassitude of Hoorn on the IJssel-meer. You can feast the eye with field after field of flowers, soothe the spirit with solitary walks through the west coast dunes, pursue the ghost of Frans Hals through the streets of Haarlem, and marvel at the wonder of a dike that stretches across open water for 32 km. (20 miles).

Though you would miss much of interest if you left Holland after visiting no more than this corner of the country, there is no other region that so well merits four or five days of your time. For this is the Netherlands in a nutshell, the Holland of storybook villages, peaceful fishing ports, green meadows, tiled rooftops. The flat horizon broken by windmills and distant spires, the scudding clouds chasing their reflection along the motionless surface of a canal, the fresh scrubbed farmhouses, all serve as reminders of the eternal struggle between land and sea, between man and nature.

There are so many impressions, in fact, and so much to see that you must beware of rushing. The four excursions described in the chapter are ambitious in terms of places to visit and things to do. However, most hotels and restaurants are invariably cheaper as you radiate out from Amsterdam, which means that your budget will prove more flexible.

In the province of Noord (North) Holland are Amsterdam and the principal places we are about to visit, while the bulbfields lie in the province of Zuid (South) Holland as well. With the latter, described in later chapters, its economic and political influence has been so great through the centuries that its name has become synonymous for the nation as a whole. The country's official name, of course, is *Nederland* or the Netherlands, just as the language spoken by its citizens is officially called Nederlands. However, the name Holland has come to be accepted in general use, even as the word Dutch is accepted much more universally than it was some years ago. Admittedly, however, there is apt to be some confusion because the two Provinces known as North Holland and South Holland are not geographically in the north and south of the country respectively. Yet, somehow or other, it all works itself out once you get into it.

The province of Noord Holland that we plan to explore extends from the vast dike that encloses the IJsselmeer all the way south to a line that runs very roughly from the North Sea resort of Zandvoort east to Hilversum and then back up to the IJsselmeer again, thus encircling Amsterdam, the principal city and the capital of the country. For the sake of convenience, the island of Texel has been added to the northern limit of this territory and so have the bulbfields to the south, in the companion province of Zuid Holland.

Centuries ago there was no break between this peninsula and the mass of Friesland province on the far side of the IJsselmeer, which was then, as now, a lake. The city of Hoorn, for example, was once the capital of West Friesland though only 40 km. (25 miles) separate it from Amsterdam today. Little by little, however, the sea opened larger and larger breaches in the dunes that once continued north as far as the coast of Denmark. Erosion being a progressive process, the destruction of land proceeded at an even faster pace until West Friesland lay separated from the rest of Friesland by a water gap that was 16 km. (10 miles) wide at its narrowest. Had human ingenuity been unable to arrest this trend, the map of Noord Holland would look quite different today.

With modern skills and technology, however, the sea has been driven back. The first step was the completion of an enclosing dike in 1932 that turned the Zuiderzee into a lake, which has been rechristened the IJsselmeer. With the sea held at bay to the northwest, work has progressed on empoldering—diking off and pumping dry—the pear-shaped body of fresh water that was left to the south and east. The Noordoostpolder was completed in 1942. The Oostelijk Flevoland Polder came dry in the spring of 1957 and the Zuidelijk (Southern) Flevoland Polder was pumped dry by 1968. Progress has been made on the Markerwaard Polder which would turn the present harbors of Volendam, Marken, Edam and Hoorn into small lakes and completely change their economy. The fear of this change is so great, however, that there is a strong degree of resistance among local people to the final draining of this polder, so the remaining area may still be left as a lake.

Exploring the Amsterdam Region

As already noted, distances in this part of the Netherlands are relatively so small that the region can be explored almost at will. For the sake of convenience, however, it is useful to divide our sightseeing into four itineraries, each roughly equivalent to what can be seen in a day, departing from and returning to Amsterdam. It might be helpful first to read the earlier section outlining a four-day itinerary around the IJsselmeer.

The first takes us north up the east side of North Holland along the edge of the IJsselmeer to Volendam, Marken, Edam, Hoorn, Enkhuizen, Medemblik, and on as far as the enclosing dike. The second also runs north, but up the west or ocean coast through Zaandam and Alkmaar to Den Helder and the island of Texel. The third changes direction and heads south to Aalsmeer, then west to the bulbfields, and finally back via Haarlem. The fourth turns east towards Muiden, Naarden, Hilversum, Breukelen, and the Loosdrecht Lakes (dipping here briefly into the province of Utrecht). Readers who plan to drive around the IJsselmeer can include the first and fourth itineraries as part of that trip.

1—AMSTERDAM NORTH TO VOLENDAM, HOORN, AND THE ENCLOSING DIKE

Formerly the first stage of our 216-km. (134-mile) trip was by water, taking the ferry from Amsterdam across the IJ River to the road leading north. Today, however, we may drive over the Schellingwoude Bridge that spans the river to the northeast of the city or use the underwater tunnel. It is amazing how suddenly one is out of Amsterdam and into unspoilt country along this road.

Broek in Waterland is a scant 11 km. (7 miles) up the road. It seems more like a child's playground than a serious-minded community, perhaps because everything seems to be on a miniature scale. Still, it's one of the many towns where so-called Edam cheeses are produced, and if you are passing through in the summertime, you can watch them being made in the farmhouse of Jakob Wiedermeier & Son, just opposite the 15th-century church.

Hardly is the salty odor of curing cheeses out of the air than the towers of Monnickendam's Grote Kerk (Great Church) and Speeltoren signal our next stop. If it's a few minutes before the hour, hasten to the latter, which is the tower of the 18th-century town hall. Instead of bells, a carillon chimes while knights perform a solemn march. Unless they're stuck again. Take another moment to stroll down an avenue of dainty gabled houses to the harbor, and then, on your way back, note the finely detailed 17th-century Waag or Weigh House which is now a restaurant, offering smoked eels as a specialty.

Out of Monnickendam to the east is a small road leading to the fishing village of Marken; once an island, it is now connected to the mainland by a 3 km. (2 mile) long causeway. In spite of its obvious dedication to being a tourist attraction, it is a delightful village, its streets small traffic-free paths and a few of its people still in traditional costume. Despite the comment of one so-called expert that "the baggy knee breeches of the Markenaars give them the look of boatmen from Greece," the effect is more Oriental than Mediterranean. The women's flowered chintzes, inspired by the East Indies, are one reason for the impression. The children were traditionally dressed alike in skirts up to the age of six, the boys being identifiable by the color of their skirts—blue.

Besides costumes, one of the chief attractions here are the houses that line Marken's narrow streets. Seafaring traditions have obviously influenced their construction, with the result that the interiors are as compact and tidy as the cabin of a ship. This nautical overtone has been muted, however, by the porcelain, clocks, glassware, hangings, and other furnishings that have been passed down the ages.

Similarly, look inside the church, where model ships in full sail hang from the ceiling. Remember that Marken, a strict Reformed community, observes the Sabbath to the letter.

From Marken, return to Monnickendam by road and continue north 6 km. (3½ miles) to Volendam, the hub of tourism in this much-frequented region. Instead of getting to Marken along the causeway mentioned above, it is possible to leave your car at Volendam and take a motorlaunch. The trip along the waterfront, lined with old Dutch houses and shops, takes about 25 minutes each way.

A Roman Catholic village in contrast to the Protestant fishermen on the island of Marken, Volendam makes a business out of wearing traditional costumes and encouraging tourists to take pictures. The men sport baggy pantaloons that are fastened with silver guilders instead of buttons. Over these are worn red-and-white-striped jackets and a cap. The women, in turn, have the appearance of birds in flight, thanks to the pointed wings on their white lace bonnets. It is rumored that some of these caps are now made of drip-dry, no-iron nylon, but no one will admit such sacrilege, yet. Be on the lookout for the *zevenkleurige rok* or seven-colored skirt, which, however ungentlemanly the advice, is better viewed from behind than in front. On Sundays a different costume is worn that is more elaborate than the workaday variety.

We continue north 5 km. (3 miles) more along the top of the sea dike to Edam, a picturesque and tranquil little town with a population of 22,000. The center is crossed by canals that have drawbridges and are lined with old houses that boast lovely façades. Edam was once an important port, but today it is best known for its cheese, which is famous all over the world for its distinctive ball-like shape and red skin. These are the characteristics of the exported variety; in Holland Edam cheese is sold with a yellow skin. It is, in fact, produced in a number of provinces. First stop, perhaps, in Edam should be the fascinating Captain's House on the Dam just opposite the Town Hall, now the Edam Museum. Paintings that hang on the walls of its front room will introduce you to some of the town's more remarkable citizens. Most imposing is the lifesize, full-length portrait of Trijntje Kester who was nearly 4 meters (13 feet) tall at the age of seventeen. Pieter Dirksz is equally arresting, thanks to a forked red beard so long that he had to fold it over his arm. Although this tonsorial triumph was possibly a handicap under some circumstances, it didn't prevent his election as mayor.

As you clamber up and down the narrow stairs, peer into the bunk-like beds built into the walls, and stand on the "bridge" with its view of the rooms below, you will see many items of daily usage back in the 18th century. During summer, the *Kaaswaag* or Weigh House features a display on the making of local cheeses.

The 18th-century Town Hall that faces this remarkable building has a green and gold council chamber that ranks it among the most beautiful of all Holland's civic rooms.

The original Grote Kerk, or Great Church, dating from the 15th century, was almost completely destroyed by fire and had to be rebuilt in 1602 and again in 1670. It has a stately charm and some unusually fine stained-glass windows, and has now been fully restored and re-opened to the public each afternoon.

Another great attraction is the bell tower that carries a lovely carillon. This tower was once part of a Catholic church that was destroyed. The tower was left standing, but only just, for a few years ago it began to lean dangerously. The area was evacuated and the tower made safe. It still leans a bit, but not so much as its counterpart in Pisa. The carillon was cast in Mechelen in 1561, and is one of the oldest in the country. From Edam boat trips are available to nearby Purmerend, site of the weekly cheese market in summer, and out across the IJsselmeer.

Hoorn, Ancient Shipping Center

Leaving Edam by road, you continue through rural landscapes along the 18 km. (11 miles) that separate it from Hoorn. You can also continue to follow the sea dike from Edam to Hoorn, but its twistings and turnings require three times as long to navigate.

Don't rush through Hoorn, however. It is certainly not a "dead city"—at least there's nothing ghostlike about the 52,000 people who live there today—and who can tell what its future will be if the Markerwaard Polder places it in the midst of rich farm country? Its development was abruptly arrested in the 17th century when England, not limited to flat-bottomed boats that could clear the sandbanks of the IJsselmeer, eclipsed Holland in the shipping trade. Its importance as a port further declined with the completion of the Noordhollandskanaal linking Amsterdam directly to the sea. It became the sleepy place of today, looking back to the time it sent ships around the world.

Willem Cornelis Schouten (1580–1625) was born here. In 1616 he was the first to round the southern tip of South America, which he named Cape Hoorn (later Horn) in honor of his home town. Another native, Jan Pieterszoon Coen (1587–1629) founded Batavia (now Jakarta), in Java, governed the island from 1617 to his death, and did much to establish Holland's empire in the East Indies. Later, Abel Janszoon Tasman (1603–59) circumnavigated Australia, discovered New Zealand, and gave his name to the island of Tasmania. Here, too, on October 11, 1573, the combined fleets of Hoorn, Enkhuizen, Edam, and Monnikendam defeated a Spanish force within sight of the ramparts and brought the Spanish Admiral Bossu back a prisoner.

As you enter the town and drive along the Kleine Noord, the 15th-century Noorderkerk (North Church) St. Mary's is on your left. A carved panel inside dated 1642 has a horn on each side, the one separating the words *wilt* and *'t-woort,* the other *gaat* and *'t-woort.* Since Hoorn is pronounced the same as *horen* (the verb "hear"), the inscription is a pun: "Be willing to hear the Word," and "Go hear the Word."

In a moment you enter the Rode Steen or Kaasmarkt, the chief square, with a statue of the aforementioned Coen in the middle, the 1609 Waag or Weigh House on the left. This is another of Hendrick de Keyser's buildings; today it houses a restaurant. The 1632 Westfries Museum is on the right. Its gable is decorated with the coats-of-arms of the seven cities of West Friesland whose delegates once sat here, while in its basement are Bronze Age artifacts and a collection of contemporary naive paintings by regional artists.

A lovely fireplace is to be found in the Grote Voorzaal, the hall, as well as several fine guild paintings. A collection of antiques and artifacts of great beauty are exhibited on the first floor, brought here during the 17th century by the East India Company, and there is also a portrait of Admiral de Ruyter by Bol (1667). In addition, there are weapons, armor, silver, porcelain, flags, coins, and much else associated with the history of Hoorn and its region. The whole of the second floor is dedicated to the maritime past of the town.

Turn left down the Grote Oost street, lined by houses whose façades incline perilously forward, perhaps to keep the rain off passers-by, perhaps to flatter the vanity of owners who wanted the ornate fronts to be more easily seen. At the end on the right, just before you cross the canal, are three houses with a frieze that re-creates the sea battle in which Bossu was defeated. Continue across the bridge through Kleine Oost to the East Gate, completed in 1578, the house on top dating from 1601. An inscription in Latin reads: "Neither the watchfulness of the guards, nor the arms, nor the threatening walls, nor the thunder of the hoarse cannon will avail anything, if thou, God, wilt not rule and shelter this town."

Retrace your steps down the Kleine Oost, cross the bridge again, and this time turn left along Slapershaven. Directly ahead is another bridge and, beyond, a house with an unusual façade and 1624 over the door. Next door is the meeting place of the West India Company in 1784.

Follow Oude Doelenkade around the curve of the inner harbor, and you'll see the remarkable tower of the Hoofdtoren, part of the harbor defences of the town and dating from 1532. The belfry on top was added 119 years later. During the 17th century it housed the offices of a company that financed whaling expeditions to the Arctic, a theme commemorated in a carved oak chimney-piece that is now in the West-fries Museum. Note here the row of beautifully restored 17th-century houses along the Veermanskade.

Returning to the central square, we head down Nieuwstraat a short block to Kerkplein. On the left at No. 39 is the Sint Jansgasthuis or St. John's Hospital, a beautiful early Renaissance building with the date 1563, which housed the ill and infirm for more than three hundred years. At the next left-hand corner of Nieuwstraat and Nieuwsteeg is the Town Hall with not one but two stepped gables. A Hieronymite convent was established here in 1385, traces of which can be identified in the present 1613 structure. The magnificent Council Room inside is enlivened with a painting representing the naval victory over Bossu.

From here we turn half-left down Gouw, then left again on Ge-dempte Turfhaven (Filled-in Peat-harbor), until we see a block away on the right, the entrance to Sint Pietershof with the date 1691. Go inside for an impression of one of the most charming of Holland's many almshouses or old people's homes. A convent antedating 1461 once stood here, then an old men's home. In 1639 it was united with an old women's home, and is still in use.

A craft market is held in Hoorn every Wednesday from the end of June until August. Stalls are arranged around the market place with a glassblower, glass painter, lacemaker, weaver, brass worker, sculptor and many others demonstrating their traditional skills.

The journey between Hoorn and Medemblik can be made by antique steam train, which operates during the summer. One can also hire "Zuiderseebotter", traditional fishermen's sailing craft, for an outing on the water.

Enkhuizen and the Zuiderzee Museum

Another 19 km. (12 miles) bring us to a second IJsselmeer port that has declined from roughly 50,000 souls in the 17th century to about 16,000 today. Enkhuizen's herring fleet once numbered 400 vessels, setting sail not far from the massive double tower called De Drom-medaris or Dromedar (1540) whose carillon ranks next to that of Edam. Of interest are the 1688 Town Hall, with a museum on the second floor, and the Stedelijk Waagmuseum, built in 1559, situated at the Kaasmarkt (cheese market). It is the old Weigh House in which cheese and butter auctions took place. Today it is a small municipal museum. We then continue to the waterside and the Binnenmuseum Zuiderzeemuseum, appropriately lodged in the Peperhuis, a former warehouse of the East India Company. Here have been gathered together exhibits that explain much about the fishing, furniture, cos-tumes, architecture, and topography of the entire region that today bears the name of the IJsselmeer. When you have admired the heavy timbers and solid workmanship of the three-centuries-old building, when you've studied the sample rooms with their authentically dressed dummies, when you've marveled over the manner of men who used cannon-size shotguns to decimate a flight of geese, step out the back door and examine the boats and yachts of all periods that are tied up at the pier to illustrate the history of shipbuilding. A large covered hall of ships is continuously being added to with new finds, proving that for centuries, even from Roman times, the IJsselmeer has been the graveyard of ships of all sizes and types. Holland's great problem now is to find space in which to display what are undoubtedly remarkable historical and archeological discoveries. The Wapenmuseum, or Museum of Weapons, has been established in the old prison, which has a picturesque façade dating from 1612.

The greatest touristic achievement in Enkhuizen is the open-air Buitenmuseum Zuiderzeemuseum. Some 130 original buildings, farmhouses, shops, public offices and even a church have been collected from villages and towns around the old Zuiderzee and re-erected along the cobbled streets of this museum, which was first opened in 1983 by the Queen. You reach the Buitenmuseum by ferry from the Enkhuizen-Lelystad dike car park.

On the west edge of town the main road leads left. We keep straight ahead, however, following the signs for Bovenkarspel and Grootebroek. At Hoogkarspel we turn right and follow the country roads north for a total of 21 km. (13 miles) to Medemblik, the third and smallest of our dreaming IJsselmeer cities. We now pass the restored Radboud Castle, which was built in the 8th century by the Frisian King Radboud. In 1288 Count Floris V fortified the castle to keep his recently-conquered Frisian subjects from rebelling. The interior of the castle has been restored to its original state and it is open daily from May 15 to September 15 and on Sunday afternoons for the remainder of the year. Opened in 1985 is the Eerste Nederlandse Stoommachinemuseum, devoted to a fine collection of early steam engines and housed, appropriately enough, in a former steam-powered pumping station.

Also of note in Medemblik is the fine Gothic Bonifaciuskerk, with some late-17th-century stained glass windows and an early-Gothic gate.

As you leave town by the Medemblikkerweg leading northwest to the main highway, keep your eye cocked for the Lely pumping station on the right at some distance from the road. We are now entering the Wieringermeer Polder, completed in 1930, and it was one of the two stations used to pump the water out. It has the unbelievable capacity of 1,500,000 litres (330,000 gallons) per *minute,* yet when you consider that much of the 20,235 hectares (50,000 acres) reclaimed here are 6 meters (18 feet) below sea level, the need for such a vast potential becomes evident.

Three towns were built in the midst of this pentagon-shaped polder: Slootdorp, Middenmeer, and Wieringerwerf. The highway leads us past the last of these, about 6 km. (4 miles) west of the point where the Germans breached the dike on April 17, 1945, only 18 days before the Nazi surrender. The land, of course, was completely flooded, but the polder was pumped dry as soon as the dike had been repaired, and crops were growing again in the fields by the following spring.

Twenty-three kilometers (14 miles) after leaving Medemblik we pass a second pumping station at the northern end of Wieringermeer Polder and cross a corner of the former island of Wieringen to the town of Den Oever, the beginning of the Afsluitdijk or enclosing dike.

Although many men dreamed of running a barrier from Noord Holland to Friesland and reclaiming the IJsselmeer, Dr. Lely was the first to conceive a practical plan, back in 1891. Persuading the government to appropriate the funds required an additional 25 years. Actual work commenced in 1923. The dike you see today is 29 km. (18 miles) long, 92 meters (300 feet) wide, and 6 meters (21 feet) above mean water level. Its top carries a surfaced motor road plus a path for bicycles and another for pedestrians.

At a point slightly more than halfway across, a monument raises its tower above the point at which the dike was closed on May 28, 1932. From its top you can survey the entire project from shore to shore on a fine day, and, if the daring of the scheme has caught your imagination, buy an illustrated booklet describing this and a number of other reclamation plans. Then, turning back after a pause at the café in the base of the monument, we start the 89-km. (55-mile) run back to Amsterdam.

But the Dutch have found more than romance and history in their old IJsselmeer. Apart from the large areas of new land being reclaimed from that historic basin of water, they are now using it for hydraulic studies as well. On the eastern side, near Emmen, the Delft Hydraulics Laboratory has established a large open-air and covered experimental station in which extensive model studies are carried out not only for current and planned Dutch projects but also for hydraulic works intended for countries all over the world.

II—AMSTERDAM NORTHWEST TO ZAANDAM, ALKMAAR, AND TEXEL

This excursion is shorter than the first—183 km. (114 miles)—and takes us up the west coast of Noord Holland to Den Helder, terminus for the boats to Texel (which there won't be time to visit in a single day), then back down through the center of the province to Amsterdam. We are completely away from the IJsselmeer with its memories of days of glory.

We leave Amsterdam by the road that leads to Zaanstad, via the Coentunnel underneath the Noordzee Kanaal or North Sea Canal, another of the mighty engineering works of the Dutch. You'll recall that originally Amsterdam's ships reached the open sea by sailing east to the IJsselmeer and then north. The silting of the IJsselmeer during the 18th century, however, threatened Amsterdam (where during the Golden Age more than 3,000 ships could be counted alongside the busy quays) with extinction unless some new outlet were discovered that could accommodate vessels of deep draft. The North Sea Canal was the solution.

Extending for 24 km. (15 miles) through dunes whose average height is 10 meters (33 feet) above sea level, it reaches the ocean at the fishing village of IJmuiden after passing through a set of locks so vast that the *QE 2* could pass through with 45 meters (150 feet) to spare at each end.

The canal itself was opened in 1876 after 11 years of labor; the present system of locks was completed in 1930 and can cope with a difference in water level of 4 meters (13 feet), although the average is normally about half that. So much salt water is admitted every time the locks are used that the entire IJsselmeer could be contaminated if there were not another set of locks at the Amsterdam end to keep the waterway isolated. The entrance was recently enlarged to accommodate tankers.

For many years the canal had the effect of cutting Noord Holland in half and leaving road traffic dependent on ferries. In 1957, however, a vehicular tunnel was completed in Velsen, while more recently the Coentunnel and the IJ tunnel were finished, giving Amsterdam better connections with northern parts.

The Zaan area, which we enter after crossing the canal, was Holland's great windmill area centuries ago, and although hundreds have been torn down, having been replaced by modern pump engines, you will still see a few scattered here and there. Even more important, if you play golf, is the fact that the district gave birth to the game of *kolf,* the lineal ancestor of today's pastime. There is little resemblance to today's game; then only one club was used which looked like a rather unfortunate combination of hockey stick and polo mallet. The ball, a clumsy leather affair, was half again bigger than a cricket ball or soft ball. You can see some of these primitive implements, by the way, at Den Haag Golf and Country Club.

During the 17th century Holland was renowned as the leading ship-building nation of the world, with Zaandam as its center. One of the many people who came here to study Dutch progress in ship-building, mathematics and physics at first hand was Peter the Great, the enlightened young Czar of All the Russias. Arriving "incognito" in Zaandam in 1697, he worked in the shipyards as Peter Michailov, but local curiosity forced him to take refuge in Amsterdam after one week. Czar Nicholas II (1868–1918) arranged to have the small wooden house his ancestor had inhabited during his short stay in Zaandam turned into a museum, now called Het Czaar Peterhuisje, and in 1911 he presented the town with a statue of Czar Peter, which now adorns the market-place.

A few kilometers up the road is Koog aan de Zaan, notable chiefly for the old (1751) Het Pink windmill, an oil mill which is in operation during the summer. At Zaandijk, a village just east of the highway, is an antiquities museum, called Zaanlandse Oudheidkamer, housed in the 18th-century home of a wealthy merchant. Its rooms are furnished in the typical old *Zaanse* style and represent the life, culture and industry of the district in former times. Even more interesting is the Zaanse Schans plan which is an old windmill village. Strolling round the green Zaan houses and the windmills you'll find yourself back in the 17th century. Definitely worth visiting are an historic grocery shop, a museum containing period rooms, a bakery museum, clock museum, and wooden clog workshop.

This Zaan area, however, has not escaped the Dutch industrial revolution. Side by side with the old buildings still redolent of clever crafts-manship there are now busy factories turning out a host of different products. Yet every effort is being made to retain some of the old-time glamor of the area.

We continue along a secondary road (not the expressway) to Krommenie, a hamlet where everything seems to be on a miniature scale. Gables, pilasters, façades, cornucopias, and sculptured panels abound in this arcadia of two-roomed cottages. Particularly interesting are the houses at 74 Noorder Hoofdstraat and at 65 and 115 Zuider Hoofdstraat.

If it's spring, take the Alkmaar highway and stop at Limmen, a center of the tulip, narcissus, and hyacinth industry, where there is a unique outdoor "tulip museum" in which practically all the original varieties of this wonderful flower are still preserved—and grown. If not, turn north at Uitgeest and follow the country road to Akersloot, the oldest village in this part of the Netherlands according to records that date back to 777. Even more impressive, however, is the Alkmaarder Lake on which it lies, a yachting center crowded with graceful craft. Beyond Akersloot the road follows the west side of a canal all the way into Alkmaar.

Alkmaar and Its Cheese Market

Though Alkmaar is famous today for the Friday-morning cheese market (mid-April to mid-September), it is worth visiting in its own right, too. Its origins go back to the 12th century, but its proudest day was in 1573 when Don Frederico of Toledo, son of the dreaded Duke of Alva, was forced to abandon his siege of the town. This was the first important victory over the Spanish, the first indication that the Dutch could hope to succeed in throwing off the foreign yoke.

The late 15th-century St. Laurenskerk (St. Lawrence's Church) has one of the finest antique organs in the Netherlands, not to mention the tomb of Count Floris V, who overcame the fierce Frisians and built the castle we saw yesterday at Medemblik. The Town Hall, a beautiful Gothic building from 1520, contains the meeting room of the mayor and corporation, in Renaissance style. The Stedelijk Museum is in a historic building, Nieuwe Doelen, built in the early 16th century for the National Guard, and housing a collection of old toys, maps and pictures. But the glory of Alkmaar is the Waaggebouw or Weigh House. Originally a chapel, its steep gables draw the eye upward by a labyrinth of receding planes that culminate in the weathervane. On the hour, pause for a moment to enjoy the chimes and watch the moving figures.

If it's a Friday morning, it won't be easy to tear yourself from the spectacle taking place at your feet. The cheeses arrive at the market by truck (the factory may be as little as one kilometer away), and are unloaded by means of a juggling act that would do credit to any circus as the round balls, weighing 2–6.5 kg. (4–14 lb.), are transferred to barrows that look vaguely like stretchers. At this point the porters or carriers take over. Together they form an ancient guild with the exclusive privilege of handling the cheeses. A "father" directs the activities of the 28 porters and various older workers who assist them. The porters, in turn, are divided into four groups or *veems*. Each group consists of three pairs of carriers and a silver-badged headman who is responsible for seeing that his men are spotless, punctual, and well disciplined, and that the group's scales are correct.

The actual selling of the cheeses takes place in a ring and is consummated by a handclasp that is as binding on both parties as a signed contract. The porters wait until a barrow is piled high with cannonball-sized cheeses. They then attach a leather shoulder sling to the barrow's handles and jog off with a distinctive bobbing gait calculated not to spill the load. At the weighroom the barrow is set on the group's own scales. The total is noted on a blackboard, and then the barrow is carried off to the new owner of the cheeses.

All morning long the twelve pairs of porters jog their way through the crowds of tourists to the Waaggebouw, or Weigh House, and back, gradually building up their tally for the day. The color group with the highest total is made chief guild group until the following week. When the market is over, the porters retire to their own quarters to drink beer, using centuries-old pewter mugs that have been handed down from father to son. Over the fireplace hangs a "shame board" with the names of the men who were late reporting to work or who cursed while on duty. The Waaggebouw was once a Chapel of the Holy Ghost, built at the end of the 14th century, which served as a refuge for needy travelers. It was transformed into a Weigh House in 1582 after Alkmaar's weighing rights were restored.

During the Kaasmarkt, between 11 and 12 noon, the 35-bell carillon bursts into life with a medley of tunes that cascade down the belfry in a golden shower. As a finale, the noon hour is announced, and at every stroke of the bell, a trumpeter blows his horn, doors open, and horsemen burst out of the clock tower, lances held high.

For 300 years cheese has been sold in this fashion at Alkmaar. If today the market is perpetuated for the benefit of tourists (more efficient ways of handling cheese have been developed over the centuries), it is done with a zest that betrays the townspeople's own delight in recalling bygone days when there was time for pageantry.

Close to Alkmaar lies the pleasant village of Bergen, on the edge of the sea dunes and beside a forest. For the past century Dutch artists have settled here where life is pleasant and cheap and the surroundings inspiring. On the village square is an artists' center, with exhibition room and work for sale. Roughly 5 km. (3 miles) due west is Bergen-aan-Zee, a simple, family-type seaside resort similar to Egmond-aan-Zee and Castricum-aan-Zee, which lie farther down the coast to the south.

We follow a local road north, however, towards Schoorl, skirting the edge of the widest and most densely wooded dunes in the Netherlands. We pass through sleepy villages—Bregtdorp, Katrijp, Hargen, Camperduin—that curve gently westward until suddenly we are face to face with the North Sea. Ahead of us stretches a 5-km. (3-mile) gap in the dunes that has been heavily reinforced with piles, breakwaters, and dikes with the collective name of Hondsbosse Zeewering. The road runs alongside the fortifications to Petten, which has been twice submerged by the sea.

The coastal road ducks back behind a new range of dunes for another 10 km. (6 miles) to the dreamy seaside resort of Callantsoog. From there it's a straight run into Den Helder at the northernmost tip of Noord Holland between, in season, fields vivid with tulips and the arrow-straight canal.

Den Helder and Texel Island

Bordered by the rolling North Sea on three sides, set among extensive bulb fields that bloom during April and May, and secure behind heavy dikes, Den Helder is full of surprises. At the end of the 18th century it was a forgotten fishing village visited by seagulls. Then, in January 1794, the Dutch fleet got itself frozen into the ice between Den Helder and Texel Island opposite. A detachment of French cavalry took advantage of this predicament by riding out on the ice and capturing the fleet, one of the few instances in naval warfare when horsemen have been decisive. Five years later the Duke of York landed here with a force of 13,000 Russian and 10,000 English troops, who were subsequently defeated near Bergen by French and Dutch forces based on Alkmaar. In 1811, Napoleon ordered the town fortified.

Today Den Helder is the chief Dutch naval base and training center, recruiting many men and women from the sturdy citizens of the city itself. The Royal Naval College, the Admiralty Palace, an interesting Naval and Lifesaving Museum, the state shipyards, and usually a contingent of vessels can be seen. Standing on the quay you can recall that glorious day in 1673 when a Dutch fleet under the command of admirals Tromp and De Ruyter defeated a combined English and French fleet almost within sight of this coast.

Texel, the largest—25 km. (15 miles) long, 10 (6) wide—and most southerly of the five Wadden Islands, is a scant 3 km. (2 miles) from Den Helder. A good ferry service carrying passengers and cars makes the 20-minute run to the port of 't Horntje. You might prefer to leave your car in the free parking area in front of the ferry terminal in Den Helder and take the passenger ferry. On the other side there are frequent buses from the 't Horntje terminal to different parts of the island. This is also a more economical way to see the island. Less than 13,000 people live in the seven villages scattered about its surface, although during the year it has millions and millions of visitors. For Texel is a bird paradise, a breeding ground (May and June) discovered by the birds themselves and now protected by the island authorities. Its wide dunes, extensive moors, shallow lakes, and wooded clumps form ideal seasonal homes for mating, breeding, and training the young as part of that great miracle of nature known as migration. In the spring the visitors arrive by the million. Almost every known variety of duck and geese, belligerent ruffs and peaceful reeves, avocets and plovers, wagtails and warblers, stately spoonbills and dignified herons, kestrels and bitterns, gotwits and martens—these are just a few of the regulars who turn this island into a bird-lover's treasure-house. The guides who conduct the human visitors around these sanctuaries know just how far the different bird colonies will tolerate inquisitiveness. For the special benefit of bird-lovers the Texel VVV has prepared a brochure on the bird life of the island, including a survey of the different reserves and a checklist of those which can be seen. If you decide to stay here for a few days, there are a number of smallish hotels, some of which make special arrangements for bird watchers, including excursions.

But don't expect to rush around Texel. This is an isle of peace, where you are expected to move quietly, to take your time to see the flocks of sheep grazing so placidly on its pasture, or the millions of narcissi blooming in spring, or its fishing fleet, or farmers who make their special green cheese from ewe milk.

On Texel you can ride, cycle, walk, or take a bus. The seven villages are linked by good though narrow roads, and the rolling dunes and golden beaches are unhampered by restrictions on walking or bathing or picnicking, except in those areas left undistrubed for the birds' breeding grounds.

The whole transport system of the island covering the ferry and bus services are owned by Teso which stands for Texel's Eigen Stoomboot Onderneming, meaning Texel's Own Steamship Society. Owned by the local population, it began by opening the steamer service, and the profits from its activities mainly go towards improving the roads, educational facilities and health schemes of the island. Teso runs several large and modern drive-on-drive-off vessels, giving an hourly service: although in busy periods there is a trip every half hour. Reservation of space is neither necessary nor possible. The journey is a pleasant one and makes it possible to get from Amsterdam to Texel in about two hours.

Over recent years there has been a battle between those who would like to drill for oil and natural gas here, and conservationists. The conservationists have largely won, with the water between mainland and islands being declared a protected area. For recreation there is swimming, sailing and angling along the dykes, for which a permit is needed, obtainable from the post office. It is also possible to camp among the dunes, as many do during summer.

The Den Burg VVV office has prepared a *Birdwalk* leaflet describing a 35-mile walk; birdwatching excursions are organized by the State Forest Dept. Bookings can be made through the Nature Recreation Centre, 92 Ruyslaan, De Koog.

South to Broek op Langedijk

The quickest way back to Amsterdam from Den Helder is via the main highway Alkmaar and Zaanstad, which we have been following or skirting all day. Instead, let's take an extra hour or two to explore a series of country roads and the simple farming communities.

Ten kilometers (six miles) south of Den Helder a left-hand fork leads east to Anna Paulowna, a town strung along the waters of a canal that drains a polder of the same name, honoring the Russian Grand Duchess who married Willem, Prince of Orange, later King Willem II, in 1816. A sharp turn takes us south again until we join a better road at Schagen, the scene of a weekly folklore pageant during July and August. Then southeast to Oude Niedorp and to Noordscharwoude, the beginning of a remarkable 5-km. (3-mile) community that changes its name to Zuidscharwoude and then Broek op Langedijk. On the other side of the main highway, between Bergen and Heerhugowaard, you will find one of the biggest artificial ski-slopes in Europe.

This is the country of a thousand islands. A maze of canals tied together by a web of lovely bridges greets the eye, together with Frisian gondolas gliding back and forth carrying farmers and vast loads. Chances are they are all bound in one direction, towards the auction hall that claims to be the world's oldest (1887), largest, and most remarkable vegetable market. This is now a living museum "Broeker Veiling," Broek op Langedijk, where you can buy your fruit, vegetables and flowers at auction.

Below Broek op Langedijk we rejoin a main highway for another 5 km. (3 miles). When it forks right for Alkmaar, we turn left and follow an arrowlike country road east across the middle of the Schermer Polder, whose midpoint is marked by the village of Stompetoren. Just before entering Schermerhorn, we climb out of this polder only to descend, just beyond, into the even older (1612) Beemster Polder, perhaps the most beautiful in all Holland. This is an orchard area whose fruit trees burst into blossom between the end of April and early May. Some of the original farmhouses still stand, bearing such dates as 1682 and 1695, and can be seen on the right-hand side of the road less than two kilometers south of Midden Beemster.

Working our way east around the right-angle corners of this grid-iron-shaped paradise, we soon enter Purmerend, which stands on high ground in the middle of the Beemster, Purmer, and Wormer polders. The church, which dates back to 1358, has been extensively restored and has a fine baroque organ (1742), but the major attractions are the tremendous pig, cattle, and horse market on Tuesday mornings and the historical Kaasmarkt. The cheese market is centuries old and is held at the foot of the Town Hall. Every Thursday morning, 10–1 P.M., from the second in June until the third in August, cheese porters, dressed usually in white with only blue or red ribbon distinguishing their guild, and sporting straw hats, show the public how they taste, weigh and buy the cheese.

From Purmerend a 16-km. (10-mile) stretch of highway leads back to Amsterdam.

III—AMSTERDAM SOUTH TO AALSMEER, THE BULBFIELDS, AND HAARLEM

This is the shortest of our excursions—112 km. (70 miles) if the bulbfields are in bloom, otherwise 77 (48)—and the most beautiful. Hardly are we out of Amsterdam on the main highway leading south to Den Haag and Rotterdam than we drop down into the Haarlemmer-meer Polder, the largest and most important in the Netherlands until the enclosing dike was completed. For centuries this lake—23 km. (14 miles) long—was a constant threat to Haarlem and even Amsterdam as well as to the ships that sailed across or fished in its waters. A gale or even a sudden change of wind was enough to pile its waves against the dikes along its sides.

As early as 1617, one of Holland's most talented engineers and windmill designers, Jan Adriaansz Leeghwater, conceived a plan for diking and draining the Haarlemmer Meer. The book in which he described his scheme for using 160 windmills went through seventeen editions, but the capital investment required was too great for those days and the success of so ambitious an undertaking was too problematic. Not until 1851 with the advent of steam powered pumps did his dream become a reality.

These thoughts fresh in our mind, we turn off the main road and follow the signs pointing to Schiphol Airport, which lies located in the northeast corner of this vast polder, a circumstance that makes it unlike any other airfield in the world. To begin with, the runways are 4 meters (13 feet) below sea level, a statement you can verify as you drive along the top of the dike that keeps the polder dry.

Schiphol is the most important commercial airport in the country and one of the busiest and best-equipped airports in Europe. At Schiphol is the national aviation museum Aviodrome, with its striking aluminum dome. It contains displays depicting man's adventures in the air since the days of the Wright brothers, with many early planes as well as scale models of aircraft and space ships.

Past the entrance to Schiphol, however, we continue along the top of the dike another 5 km. (3 miles) or so to Aalsmeer, and on past it for another mile. Then turn left to 313 Legmeerdijk, where you will see the Centrale Aalsmeerse Bloemenveiling, the world's most important flower auction hall. There are five auction rooms, two for potted plants, two for cut flowers, and one for bulb flowers. Buyers begin bidding as early as 7.30 A.M. and continue until everything has been sold, usually about 11.30, five days a week. In a single year up to three billion flowers and 220 million plants are sold here, coming from over 4,000 nurseries. Annual turnover is around Fl. 1.5 billion. From the visitors' gallery you can watch this fascinating spectacle.

The flowers arrive by truck or barge and are sorted out into lots. A sample is selected from each lot and held up for the assembled buyers to see. The auctioneer then sets in motion what looks like a vast clock with numbers around the rim and in the middle. The numbers in the middle correspond to the seats in which the buyers sit, each of which has an electric button. The numbers around the rim represent prices for ten bunches of flowers or plants similar to the sample being displayed. A pointer, like a huge minute-hand, begins to move, but instead of starting at low prices and working up, it begins at high prices and moves backwards. The instant it reaches a price acceptable to the most eager buyer, he presses his button, the minute-hand stops, and the number of his seat lights up on the clock face. This proceeds at the rate of roughly 600 lots per hour.

Once sold, the flowers are taken to the packing and delivery sheds. Those intended for export are skilfully wrapped in tissue and light-weight cardboard boxes, rushed to nearby Schiphol Airport, and are being admired in Stockholm, Paris, and London flowershop windows before the end of the day, all within 12 hours of the time they were cut.

Those for sale in Holland are loaded in trucks and dispatched to shops all over the country.

Even in the depths of winter when the roads are slick with ice and the canals half frozen, bargefuls of huge cherry chrysanthemums, roses, carnations, and lilies appear in the Aalsmeer auction rooms, together with a wonderful array of cyclamens and miniature azaleas, both popular as Christmas presents.

And in September when the town goes all out for its Bloemencorso or flower festival, something over two million blossoms are used for the huge decorated floats, a sight that attracts thousands of flower fanciers to Amsterdam's Olympic stadium.

Holland's Bulbfields

Still dazzled by the sight of so many flowers in one place, we retrace our route for half a kilometer or so to the edge of the Haarlemmermeer Polder, where we plunge west across its middle on a road so straight that we are through Hoofddorp or "Head Village" before we realize it. On the far side of the polder, just as the road climbs slightly to go over the western dike, a strange building on the right attracts our eye.

This is the Cruquius Pumping Station, one of three steam-powered stations that pumped out the Haarlemmermeer Polder. It was in continuous use until 1933, when it was converted into the Museum de Cruquius that well merits a stop. Besides explaining by means of working models how a polder drainage system works, it contains a relief map of the entire Netherlands which can be flooded at will and then pumped dry in a vivid demonstration of the fate that would overtake the country if all the dikes were to give way (producing a rise in sea level calculated at 49 meters, or 160 feet!). Models of various kinds of windmills can be seen here as well as an explanation of how major dikes are constructed today. Don't overlook the Cruquius pump, an engineering giant with eight beams transmitting power to as many pumps from a single cylinder with 3-meter (10-foot) stroke. The pumps had a capacity of 386,400 liters (85,000 gallons) per minute and operated for 84 years, due to, or possibly despite, the forest of levers, pipes and gauges.

The delightful garden city of Heemstede lies on the higher ground just outside the Haarlemmermeer. If the bulb season is past, we continue west to Zandvoort. Let's assume, however, that it's April or early May and turn south for Bennebroek and the most important bulbfields.

Such great progress has been made in producing new varieties of the main bulb plants that the calendar is no longer quite the tyrant it used to be. Still, there is a general progression in this part of Holland from daffodils and narcissi from the end of March to the middle of April, early tulips and hyacinths from the second week of April to the end of the month, and late tulips immediately afterwards. An early or late spring can move these approximate dates forward or backward by as much as two weeks.

The art of bulb-growing, by the way, has been a Dutch specialty since the first tulip was brought to Holland from Turkey in 1559. In 1625 an offer of 3,000 florins for two bulbs was turned down, but the speculation in bulbs became a mania during the years 1634–1637, as irrational and popular as stock market speculation in the late 1920's, when fortunes were made—and lost—in a single day. Individual bulbs worth thousands of guilders had their pictures painted in tulip books that enjoyed a similar vogue. Only during the last 60 years has the scientific approach prevailed. Today's experts diagnose the rarest tulips illustrated in the books that have survived as suffering from viruses that caused abnormal (and beautiful) coloring or shape.

The bulbfields themselves extend from just north of Leiden to the southern limits of Haarlem, but the greatest concentration is limited to the district that begins at Sassenheim and ends between Hillegom and Bennebroek. In a neat checkerboard pattern of brilliant color the fields stretch out as far as the eye can see.

The apparent artificiality of the sharply defined rectangular fields is not a concession to taste. It is part of the businesslike efficiency of an industry that has made the bulb one of Holland's most important export commodities. It must be remembered that here the bulb, not the flower, is the most important part of the plant. When the flowers bloom, the heads are cut off, leaving only the green stalks. The children play with the discarded blooms, threading them into garlands which they sell to passing motorists or use to make floral mosaics.

Let's follow the main Hillegom-Lisse-Sassenheim road south from Heemstede. This is the core of the bulb-growing district. Along the road you may notice flower mosaics on one side or the other. These are worked out, petal by petal, by the local residents in competition with each other, usually reaching their peak just before the annual Bloemencorso or flower parade. Held, usually, on the second or third Saturday in April, this procession is a highlight of the year in this part of Holland. Dozens of magnificent floats, covered with multicolored blooms, are prepared and put on display, first in Lisse. The main procession, accompanied by marching bands, starts in Haarlem and covers a 10 km. (6 mile) route through Bennebroek, Hillegom, Lisse, Sassenheim and Nordwijkerhout to Noordwijk, by which time it is evening and the floats are illuminated. They remain on show for the rest of the weekend at the Koningin Wilhelmina Boulevard in Noordwijk.

Keukenhof Gardens

Lisse, the middle of the three main bulb towns, is noted for its Keukenhof Gardens, but we keep straight ahead to Sassenheim, turning right (west) into the bulbfields at the north edge of town. At Loosterweg we head north again, following the zigs and zags of this country lane as it passes through the very heart of the fields so overburdened with color. Presently we are back at Lisse again, and follow the signs for Keukenhof. In Lisse, at 219 Heereweg, is a museum devoted to the history and cultivation of bulbs.

From the end of March to the end of May the 28 hectare (70 acre) Keukenhof Gardens, founded by leading bulb-growers, are a living open-air flower exhibition that is unique in the world. As many as 5–6 million bulbs blossom here together, either in the 5000 sq. meters of hothouses or in flowerbeds along the sides of a charming lake. Holland's leading bulb-growers have joined together to make this old estate a permanent treasure house of floral beauty. It is open from late March to late May, daily from 8 A.M. to 7.30 P.M.

Here you can always see the lively "meisjes" (girls) who stroll around as guides and hostesses dressed in costumes dating from the lifetime of Jacoba van Beieren, who had her hunting lodge here in the 15th century, and who was in succession Dauphiness of France, Duchess of Gloucester and Countess of Bavaria.

Spring is not the only time of the year when this man-made tide of color bursts the dikes and floods the fields around Lisse. Just as the many hues of hyacinths and tulips march across the countryside in disciplined ranks during April and May, so in July and August does the stately gladiolus welcome visitors to his domain. Then, in September, the dahlia takes over by way of emphasizing the horticultural preeminence of these sandy fields by the North Sea. A further Lisse attraction is the Huys Dever, a keep dating from 1375 and providing a setting for exhibitions and concerts.

From Keukenhof, Loosterweg III leads to North Holland and to Vogelenzang, whose names means "song of the birds". Birds there are, too, in profusion, for this is the wooded edge of the dunes that next lead us due west to the cosmopolitan seaside resort of Zandvoort. Just north of Vogelenzang you can visit the nursery of a leading bulb grower, Frans Roozen, with exquisite gardens, greenhouses and fields of blooms. Up to 1,000 varieties are grown here. Open daily from 9–5 during April and May for the tulip show, and from July through September for summer flowers. Entrance is free.

At Zandvoort is the 5-km. (3-mile), closed circuit for motorcycles and cars where international races are held during June and July. The coastal road turns abruptly inland a mile or so beyond the entrance to the Zandvoort track, leading us back through dunes to Bloemendaal, or Flowerdale, whose open-air theater is used by visiting companies for Shakespearean programs. In addition, it offers a miniature lake, botanical gardens, and an aviary.

Along the coast, within easy reach of Lisse, are a number of beach resorts, large and small. The best known, in addition to Zandvoort, are Noordwijk and Katwijk.

Haarlem, Home of the Arts

In the heart of Haarlem we find the earliest center of Dutch art. Lying in the shadow of a nest of lovely medieval buildings in this 740-year-old city of 154,000 people is the Frans Halsmuseum housing a fine collection of masterpieces by this famous Dutch painter and other artists who worked here in the 16th and 17th centuries. The building, 62 Groot Heiligland, in which the display is presented, was originally one of 25 picturesque old almshouses dotted around the lovely Grote or St. Bavo Kerk, completed in the 16th century having been under construction for over a hundred years. Known as Oudemannenhuis, it was built largely by the Ghent architect Lieven de Key (1560–1627).

The Grote Kerk is girdled with souvenir shops literally growing out of its walls and buttresses. The interior as well as the outside of this imposing structure reveals to the trained eye the architecture of three centuries. Above all, look at the organ, one of Europe's most famous, with three keyboards, 68 registers, and 5,000 pipes. Built in 1738 by C. Mueller, it has been played on by Mozart and Händel, and many more modern masters of that form of music. Organ recitals are given all through the summer on Tuesdays and Thursdays and there are important international organ music festivals held annually in early July. Over recent years it has been extensively restored and is open to visitors from Mon.–Sat. 10–4.

The genius of Frans Hals (c.1580–1666) has not only established itself in his peerless paintings, but has also influenced such painters as Buytewech, Terborch and Brouwer. Hals is one of the finest portrait painters that Holland has ever produced, and his corporation pieces, paintings of the guilds of Haarlem, are to be admired in the museum. The setting for these arresting paintings, some amazingly virile and some unbelievably peaceful, is in itself a gem of artistry.

In the center of Haarlem, around the great market square, the whole story of Dutch architecture can be traced in a chain of majestic buildings ranging through the 15th, 16th, 17th, 18th, and 19th centuries. With a smile and perhaps a little bravado you can enter most of them, from the Town Hall, originally the 14th-century hunting lodge of the counts of Holland, with its candle-lit and tapestried Council Chamber, to the Meat Market, of all places, one of Holland's greatest Renaissance buildings of the beginning of the 17th century. Externally it is unique, for nowhere in the country is there such a fine sweep of stepped gables that invite you, had you a giant's stride, to clamber up to the pinnacle that almost pierces the scudding clouds. No longer does this fanciful building serve the butcher's needs. Today, it often houses the most adventurous of modern art exhibitions and is part of the Frans Hals Museum, known as *De Hallen.*

Housed in its remarkable collection of architecture, Haarlem offers a variety of museums. In the Teylers Museum, besides a fine collection of the Hague school of painting, you can see an unexpected collection of original sketches and drawings by Michelangelo, Raphael and other non-Dutch masters, against a background of fossils and other petrified remains. Of more recent date is the impressive Sint Bavo Basilica, designed by Cuypers and built between 1895 and 1906, with the towers completed in 1930. The red brick building is a complex of fanciful towers and roofs, on a considerable scale. Over 100 meters long and 60 meters high it has beautiful stained glass windows, sculptures and pictures and is open daily from April to October. Organ concerts are held here each Saturday at 6 P.M.

Each Saturday during the blooming season there is a colorful flower market in Grote Markt, and every year on the last Saturday in April a spectacular flower parade between Haarlem and Noordwijk.

Spaarndam's Statue to a Legend

A couple of kilometers or so northeast of Haarlem is a statue to a legend, a statue that proves once again the power of imaginative fiction. You may recall the young boy Pieter who appears in the pages of an American book called *Hans Brinker or the Silver Skates*. The story goes that he discovered a hole in a dike one afternoon and plugged it with his finger while waiting for help to come. All night long he stood vigil until, when help finally arrived the following morning, he was dead, having heroically saved Haarlem from destruction.

So many people have asked where Pieter lived and where he performed his brave deed that the Dutch finally felt compelled to do something about the legend. In 1950 Princess Irene, accompanied by her mother Queen Juliana, unveiled a memorial, if not to Pieter, then to the courage and devotion of Dutch youth through the centuries. The place selected was Spaarndam, a choice as logical as any and more picturesque than most. Even if no dike could be saved by so puny an instrument as a boy's finger, the memorial has been cunningly placed so that the motorist who stops to admire it can plug the flow of traffic around with 100% effectiveness. Needless to say, most Dutch people, when asked, know nothing whatever about the legend. It is one of those happy fictions that has the ring of truth.

Following the signs for Zwanenburg, we rejoin the main Haarlem-Amsterdam highway, and are back in the city of canals in 30 minutes.

IV—AMSTERDAM SOUTHEAST TO MUIDEN, NAARDEN AND HILVERSUM

The last of our four Amsterdam-based trips takes us along the southern edge of the IJsselmeer to the garden district of Gooiland, a 120-km. (75-mile) excursion that reaches into what is technically Utrecht Province long enough to see the Queen Mother's palace at Soestdijk, Queen Beatrix' palace of Drakenstein at Lage Vuursche where she lived until she moved to Den Haag after her Coronation, and the costume villages of Spakenburg and Bunschoten, and the pleasant woodland town of Baarn.

First stop is Muiden, 18 km. (11 miles) east of Amsterdam, whose castle, Muiderslot, stands on the right (east) bank of the Vecht River at its confluence with the IJsselmeer. As early as the beginning of the 10th century, a wooden tollhouse was erected on this site. Gradually it was rebuilt and enlarged. The castle, a red brick building, became a fortress after 1205 to guard the banks of the Vecht, and was reconstructed by Count Floris V of Holland who was assassinated here by noblemen in 1296. From 1621 the Muiderslot was the meeting place of a circle of poets and intellectuals led by P. C. Hooft (1581–1647), and brought together celebrities like Vondel, Grotius and Maria Tesselschade. This group became known as the Muiderkring. After Hooft's death, the castle was neglected, but in 1948 its interior was restored to the state of Hooft's day. A half hour spent exploring its galleries and enjoying the view of the IJsselmeer is well spent, especially in view of the fact that Holland has relatively few such relics of sterner times.

About 6 km. (4 miles) farther east is Naarden, a fortified town of 19,000 souls whose star-shaped ramparts and moats have been miraculously preserved despite a succession of bloody sieges and massacres. Here the dreaded Spanish Duke of Alva refined the art of torture; and here the French broke through in 1672. In comparison with other European walled cities it seems more like a toy fort, although observed from the air it shows correctness of design and stern obedience to the principles of self-protection. The 17th-century Bohemian pedagogue Comenius lived and died here (a special chapel perpetuates his memory) and the 1601 Dutch Renaissance Town Hall is charming inside. Thanks to outstanding acoustics, the 15th-century church is the locale for an annual performance of Bach's St. Matthew Passion.

Bussum, practically next door, wears a more modern aspect. So much so, in fact, that Holland's first television studios were established here amid the comfortable homes, wide boulevards, and public buildings.

Beyond Bussum we enter Gooiland, a region of lakes and woods whose scenic beauty has attracted the well-to-do from Amsterdam and elsewhere. Just 6 km. (4 miles) farther along is Laren, famous as an artists' colony. About the turn of the century, artists of Den Haag School, attracted by the paintability of the district, congregated here and formed a group known as the luministen. Others joined them until today there are over a hundred modern painters and sculptors living in the neighborhood whose works are displayed from time to time in the Singer Memorial Foundation with its collection of paintings and engravings by the American artist William Singer, Jr.

Baarn (in the province of Utrecht), the other town of the wealthy, lies just south of the road we take to the costume towns of Bunschoten and Spakenburg, the latter with a fine IJsselmeer yachting harbor. The distinctive feature of the women's clothing here is the Kraplap, made of brightly flowered cotton, shaped like a cuirassier's breastplate and starched to about the same rigidity. The men's costumes have died out.

Retracing our tracks to Baarn, we turn south with Soestdijk as our goal. A vaguely semicircular building by the side of the highway is the palace of the Queen Mother and Prince Bernhard, who may emerge with no fanfare in their own car.

Heading back towards Baarn a third time, we swing west along the Hilversum road, which runs past the Hooge Vuursche castle hotel.

Hilversum up the Vecht to Breukelen

Hilversum has two claims to distinction: it is the home of Dutch radio and TV broadcasting, and renowned for the outstanding modern architecture designed by Dudok. Although broadcasting is a state monopoly in the Netherlands with the government imposing a monthly license fee, the six stations are under Catholic, Protestant, Socialist, and independent management. Their studios, the schools, the public baths, and most particularly the angular Town Hall are among the outstanding examples of the architect's art.

Emerging on the west side of Hilversum we follow the road to Loenen, presently crossing the middle of the popular Loosdrecht Lakes, one of the most attractive swimming and yachting centers in the Netherlands. Loenen itself graces the west bank of the Vecht River, whose outlet into the IJsselmeer we saw during our visit to the castle at Muiden. The district from here south along the river to Breukelen and Maarssen enjoyed a great vogue during the second half of the 17th and the first half of the 18th century among prosperous Amsterdam merchants who built country houses beside the water in a style already showing signs of decadence, an abandonment of the austere classical line in favor of French influences. Many of these homes have been restored during recent years by wealth Amsterdamers, and if the result is hardly Dutch, the effect is none the less delightful as the road winds and twists around each bend of the Vecht. These old patrician houses are best seen by taking a boat trip on the river, or by bike or car along the banks.

We continue as far as Breukelen in the province of Utrecht, or possibly half a kilometer beyond to the 13th-century Castle of Nijenrode, on the right-hand side of the road, today a training school for Dutchmen planning to represent their companies abroad. Breukelen itself is just another sleepy town drowsing by the river bank, but Americans may be startled to learn that it gave its name to Brooklyn, which still retains memories of the Dutch who founded it. On the water side of the village is the Breukelen bridge, rather more modest than its famous counterpart, since the river is no more than 6 meters (20 feet) wide at this point.

From Breukelen a 2 km. (1 mile) link to the west brings us to the express highway that runs from Utrecht north to Amsterdam, a distance, from this point, of only 25 km. (16 miles). So enchanting is the Vecht district, however, that you may prefer to follow the river downstream to Loenen once again before turning west for the highway back to our starting point.

This is a delightful region to sample the country hotels, of which there are many—often in old buildings in charming surroundings.

MOTORING AROUND THE IJSSELMEER

In addition, or as an alternative to the tours listed above, a circuit of the IJsselmeer is one of the most interesting trips you can make in Holland. You can start anywhere, of course, though Amsterdam will be a logical choice for many visitors, especially those who wish to rent a car for the purpose. A number of the places included on the itineraries mentioned below are described in this chapter, others in the chapters devoted to their respective regions.

Although it's possible to drive around the IJsselmeer in a single day, you are advised to allow at least two days for the journey. If you can spare three or four days, include one or two other stops en route.

Two-Day Itinerary

Amsterdam north to Volendam (brief pause), Edam (visit Kaaswaag museum), Hoorn (visit De Waag or Weigh House in central square, also harbor), Enkhuizen (visit Zuiderzee museums) for late lunch, then via Hoogkarspel and Wervershoof to Medemblik (brief pause) and Den Oever where the enclosing dike begins. In the middle, at Breezanddijk, is a monument with a tower that affords an outstanding view, where you can stop for tea or coffee. At the north end of the dike, turn south at Bolsward for Workum, Hindeloopen (pause for drive through town on the sea wall), Koudum (by-passing Staveren), Rijs, Sondel, and Lemmer, where a fast road takes you across the Noordoostpolder to Emmeloord. There are few, and mostly small, hotels in these country towns and the best bet for overnight accommodations is Bolsward, Sneek or Emmeloord.

From Emmeloord, take the small road to Urk (best chance for parking is by the harbor) for costumes and a breath of the IJsselmeer, before continuing east to Ens with a brief pause at Schokland to see the island and its minuscule museum. Continue southeast to Kampen, then swing southwest to Elburg (bypassing Zwolle) for an impression of its gridiron layout and almshouses. Nunspeet and Hierden are next along the secondary road, which runs just north of the motorway. Drive slowly for a glimpse of local costumes. At Harderwijk, drive north along the dike as far as the Hardersluis pumping station (visit) for an impression of Holland's newest polder, then back to Harderwijk and on to the costume villages of Bunschoten and Spakenburg via Putten and Nijkerk. After a stop to sample Spakenburg, you return to Amsterdam by the main highway, detouring briefly at Naarden and Muiden. This makes a very full two days and assumes two early starts.

Three-Day Itinerary

The first day is the same as the Two-Day Itinerary above, stopping overnight at Emmeloord, or Sneek.

In the morning you visit Urk and Schokland, as above, but instead of turning south at Ens you continue east to Vollenhove and St. Jans-klooster, where you take the causeway across the delightful Beulaker Wijde to the crossroads De Blauwe Hand, turning left (north) from there for Giethoorn, the village that has canals and footpaths instead of streets. After a half-hour visit here, you continue east to Meppel, then swing south and turn off the main highway to drive through the costume villages of Staphorst (being sure not to take any pictures of the pious people who live there without their express permission) and Rouveen Zwolle is next (brief visit), followed by Elburg (visit as on Two-Day Itinerary) and Harderwijk, via Nunspeet and Hierden.

The trip out to Lelystad and a visit to the Nieuwland Information Center is interesting because of the impression you gain of what is involved in reclaiming land on so vast a scale.

The morning of the third day, cut east and slightly south to the villages of Lage Vuursche and Soestdijk for a glimpse of respectively

Drakestein and Soestdijk palaces. Then swing over to Baarn and north-west through Laren to Naarden. Turn south once more to Hilversum, cut west across the pleasant Loosdrecht Lakes to Loenen, on the banks of the delightful Vecht River, lined with 17th-century country houses built by wealthy Amsterdammers. Turn south to Breukelen, which gave its name to New York City's famous borough.

From Breukelen follow the express highway back to Amsterdam if it's late in the day. If not, follow the Vecht River back to Loenen where, about 2 miles beyond, you can follow the east side of the Amsterdam-Rijn Canal north to Weesp and Muiden for a visit to Muiden Castle before returning to Amsterdam. Since the creation of the Bijlmermeer suburb of Amsterdam and new expressways, the smaller roads have been rerouted, so follow the signposts carefully, but it is worth the effort as the drive is so much more interesting.

Four-Day Itinerary

This is an elaboration of the above. Allow yourself more time to explore Hoorn, Enkhuizen, and Medemblik, then cross the enclosing dike and spend the night in charming Sneek, or in Bolsward.

The next morning, head north for Leeuwarden (visit), west to Fra-neker (visit), then south to Bolsward, where the route into Emmeloord is the same as for the previous two itineraries.

The third and fourth days are the same as the second and third days of the Three-Day Itinerary.

In this tour you would be well advised to plan to spend an hour or so at the Dolphinarium at Harderwijk. This is an enthralling experi-ence, because not only do the dolphins put up a remarkable circus performance but the directors also run a dolphin research station studying the habits and language of these delightful creatures. It is open daily from March to October.

Not very far from Harderwijk is the Flevohof Park, a remarkable composite "working" exhibition of everything agricultural and hor-ticultural in Holland. It gives the visitor a day on a farm, with every form of visual display, and there is a host of fun entertainment for the children, water sports, etc. Open daily from April to October. A side-trip out of Harderwijk, 32 km. to the north, is to Lelystad, where one can visit the Nieuw Land Information Center, with remains of ship wrecks recovered from the reclaimed Zuider Zee.

Instead of returning to Amsterdam at the end of any of these tours, you can easily leave the shores of the IJsselmeer at Hilversum and turn south for Den Haag via either Utrecht, Woerden, Alphen a/d Rijn, and Leiden, or (more direct and much faster) Utrecht and thence by the express highway straight to Den Haag, with a brief stop in Gouda.

PRACTICAL INFORMATION FOR THE
AMSTERDAM REGION

WHEN TO GO. As in the case of Amsterdam itself, the best time to visit its surroundings is from **May** to the end of **September,** with **July** and **August** being the peak months to avoid. Because of the bulbfields, the first week of May is possibly the best moment of all if flowers are high on your list of things to see. If spring comes early, however, the peak of the tulips, hyacinths, and narcissi can be as early as the middle of April, with nothing but heaps of discarded blooms left in the fields a fortnight later. The annual Bloemencorso or Flower Parade through the bulbfields takes place on the last Saturday in April, running from Haarlem to Nordwijk.

Because the bulbfields are such an unpredictable factor, they should not be given too much weight in the scheduling of your trip, especially if it is to be a brief one. There will still be plenty of flowers to see in May no matter what. Here are some of the other attractions:

The Keukenhof Gardens always open in late **March** nowadays and can be visited until the end of May. The last Friday in **April** is the traditional beginning date of the sprightly Alkmaar cheese market, which continues every Friday morning until late **September.** *May 4* is Memorial Day. Haarlem is the site of the International Organ Competitions in early **July.** During the first two weeks in **August** international sailing regattas are staged at Loosdrecht, Muiden and Medemblik. In early **September,** Aalsmeer stages its annual flower parade, to Amsterdam and back.

TELEPHONE CODES. We have given telephone codes for all the towns and villages in this chapter in the hotel and restaurant listings that follow. These codes need only be used when calling from outside the town or village concerned.

HOTELS AND RESTAURANTS. Because few tourists consider staying anywhere else but Amsterdam or Den Haag when they visit this corner of the Netherlands, hotel accommodations are relatively simple (with the notable exception of Hilversum). Moreover, most of the towns are so small that good restaurants are also scarce. If you are a little adventurous, however, and willing to put up with quarters that are spotlessly clean if simple, then there is no reason why you should feel bound to Amsterdam. Your reward will be a more leisurely pace through the countryside, the opportunity to come in closer contact with the Dutch, and noticeably lower hotel costs.

In many instances, the restaurant of the leading hotel may be the best place to stop for a meal. If so, no restaurant recommendations are made in the listing that follows. If you see *paling* (eel) on the menu, remember that it's often a specialty of the house. If you have your doubts, at least try the smoked variety as an appetizer on a piece of toast.

We have divided the hotels and restaurants in our listings into three categories—Expensive (E), Moderate (M) and Inexpensive (I). We give prices for hotels and restaurants in the *Facts at Your Fingertips* (see pages 17–18). Most hotels, particularly at the upper end of the scale, have rooms in more than one category and a consequently wide range of prices. Remember, too, that many restaurants have dishes in more than one category, so be sure to check the menu outside *before* you go in. Look out too for the excellent-value Tourist Menu.

Figures in brackets after place names are mileage from Amsterdam.

ALKMAAR (22 northwest). Site of Holland's most interesting cheese market. *Alkmaar Motel* (M), 2 Arcadialaan; 072–120744. *Marktzicht* (M), 34 Houttil; 072–113283. *De Nachtegaal* (M), 100 Langestraat; 072–112894.

Restaurants. Hotels *Marktzicht* and *De Nachtegaal* both have good restaurants. *Le Bistrot de Paris* (E), 1 Waagplein; 072–120023. French, centrally located near Weigh House. *Rôtisserie rue du Bois* (E), 3e van den Boschstraat; 072–119733. *t' Guiden Vlies* (M), 20 Koorstraat; 072–112451. *Koekenbier* (M), 16 Kennemerstraatweg; 072–114386. Excellent Scandinavian buffet.

BAARN (23 southwest). *De Hooge Vuursche* (E), 14 Hilversumsestraadweg; 02154–12541. 27 rooms with bath. Luxurious castle-hotel on the road to Hilversum; Extensive grounds, terraces, fountains, dancing. *De Prom* (M), 1 Amalialaan; 02154–12913. 40 rooms.

BENNEBROEK (14 southwest). **Restaurant.** *De Oude Geleerde Man* (M), 51 Rijksstraatweg; 02502–6990. Highly recommended.

BERGEN (26 northwest). Once famous for its artists' colony. *Elzenhof* (M), 78 Doorpstraat; 02208–12401. 30 rooms, modest prices for quality. *Marijke* (M), 23 Doorpstraat; 02208–12381. 45 rooms. Inexpensive for quality. *Zee-Bergen* (M), 11 Wilhelminalaan; 02208–97241. One of the best.

BERGEN AAN ZEE (3 west of Bergen). Quiet family seaside resort. *Nassau-Bergen* (E), 4 Van der Wyckplein; 02208–97541. 28 rooms, most with bath; sauna, solarium; near the beach. *Prins Maurits* (M), 7 van Hasselstraat; 02208–12364. 25 rooms mostly with bath. *De Stormvogel* (I), 12 Jac. Kalffweg; 02208–12734. 14 rooms.

BLOEMENDAAL (13 west). A garden suburb of Haarlem, 3 miles from the sea. *Iepenhove* (M), 4 Hartenlustlaan; 023–258301. 40 rooms, some with bath. *Rusthoek* (M), 141 Bloemendaalseweg; 023–257050. 22 rooms, 10 with bath.

Restaurant. *Bokkdoorns* (E), 53 Zeeweg; 023–263600. First class French cuisine. Recommended.

BOVENKARSPEL (67 northeast). *Het Rode Hert* (M), 235 Hoofstraat; 02285–11412. Romantically-housed in a 16th-century inn.

BUSSUM (16 east). On edge of the charming Gooiland district. *Golden Tulip Hotel Jan Tabak* (E), 27 Amersfoortsestraatweg; 02159–59911. 100 good modern rooms. Pool, gardens with tennis. 30 mins. from Schiphol. *Gooiland* (M), 16 Stationsweg; 02159–43724. 24 comfortable rooms. *Hotel Cecil* (M), 25 Brinklaan.

Restaurant. *Auberge Maître Pierre* (E), 16 Stationsweg. On the pricey side, but worth it.

CALLANTSOOG (39 northwest). Small, seaside family resort. *De Wijde Blick* (M), 2 Zeeweg; 02248–1317. Small, with a good restaurant.

CASTRICUM (20 northwest). Quiet town on edge of the dunes, 3 miles from the beach. *Kornman* (I), 1 Mient; 02518–52251. 10 rooms, some with bath. **Restaurant.** *'t Eethuisje* (M), 53 Dorpsstraat; 02518–52043.

DEN HELDER (48 north). Important naval base and ferry terminus for island of Texel. *Beatrix* (E), 2 Badhuisstraat; 02230–14800. 40 rooms, excellent, with pool, sauna, etc. *Forest Hotel* (M), 43 Julianaplein; 02230–18141. 30 rooms. *Motel den Helder* (M), 2 Marsdiepstraat; 02230–22333. 75 rooms. *De Branding* (I), 44 Badhuisstraat; 02230–16057. Small, family-style.

DEN OEVER (45 north). Southern terminus of the enclosing dike that leads to Friesland. *Wiron* (M), 20–24 Voorstraat; 02271–1255. *Zomerdijk* (M), 65 Zwinstraat; 02271–1404. *De Haan* (I), 4 Oeverdijk; 02271–1205. Small with a good restaurant.

EDAM (14 northeast). *Damhotel* (M), 1 Keizersgracht; 02993–71766. *Fortuna* (M), 7 Spuistraat; 02993–71671. Small and cosy.

EGMOND AAN ZEE (25 northwest). Seaside resort. *Bellevue* (E), A-7 Boulevard; 02206–1387. 50 rooms near the beach. *Golfzang* (M), 19–21 Blvd Ir. de Vassy; 02206–1516. 20 rooms. *Sonnevanck* (I), 114–116 Wilhelminastraat; 02206–1589. Small, good quality.

EMMELOORD. *t'Voorhuys* (M), 20 De Deel; 05270–12441. Modern rooms and facilities with reasonable restaurant.

ENKHUIZEN (35 northeast). Attractive old walled city. *Het Wapen van Enkhuizen* (M), 59 Breedstraat; 02280–13434. 15 rooms with bath or shower. *Die Port van Cleve* (M), 74 Dijk; 02280–12510. 20 rooms, near the old harbor. *Du Passage* (M), 8 Paktuinen; 02280–12462. Small with good restaurant.

GIETHOORN. *Jachthaven Giethoorn* (M), 128 Beulakerweg; 05216–1216. Near the charmingly peaceful village.

HAARLEM (12 west). *Carillon* (M), 27 Grote Markt; 023–310591. Central. *Golden Tulip Lion d'Or* (M), 34 Kruisweg; 023–321750. 40 rooms. **Restaurants.** *Le Chat Noir* (E), 1 Bakkumstraat; 023–317387. French and worth the price. *De Coninckshoek* (E), 1–5 Koningstraat; 023–314001. Recommended. *Dreefzicht* (M), in the woods. *Lantaern* (M), with an Old Dutch interior. *Los Gauchos* (M), 9 Kruisstraat; 023–320358. An Argentinian steak house.

HILVERSUM (20 southeast). *Het Hof van Holland* (E), 1 Kerksbrink; 035–46141. 55 rooms with bath. *Hilfertsom* (M), 28 Koninginneweg; 035–232444. 37 rooms, some with bath. **Restaurants.** *Het Zwarte Paard* (M), la Larenseweg. *Me Chow Low* (M), 25 Groest. *Palace Residence* (M), 86 s' Gravelandseweg. *Rôtisserie Napoléon* (M), in the Hotel de Nederlanden at nearby Vreeland. A local favorite.

HOORN (25 north). Historic seaport. *De Keizerskroon* (M), 31 Breed; 02290–12717. The oldest in town. *Petit Noord* (M), 53 Kleine Noord; 02290–12750. 34 rooms, all with bath; pleasant restaurant.

Restaurants. *Oude Rasmolen* (E), 1 Duinsteeg; 02290–14752. French cuisine, superb quality. *De Waag* (M), 8 Roode Steen; 02290–15195. Fish specialties. *'t Wapen van Hoorn* (M), 20 Dubbele Buurt; 02290–19402. French cuisine.

IJMUIDEN (16 northwest). Gateway to the North Sea Canal. *'t Zwaantje* (M), 93 Kennemerlaan; 02550–31008.

KATWOUDE, near Volendam (see below). *Katwoude Motel* (M), 1 Wagenweg; 02993–65656. 30 rooms.

LAREN (18 southeast). Artists' colony just outside Hilversum. *De Witte Bergen* (E); 05783–86754. 50 rooms with shower. *Herberg t'Langenbaergh* (M), 1 Deventerweg; 05783–1209. 10 rooms.

Restaurant. *Auberge La Provence* (E), 2 Westherheide; 035–87974. Excellent French restaurant with superb sea food.

MAARSSEN (10 southeast). *De Nonnerie* (M), 51 Lange Gracht; 03465–62201. 10 rooms.

Restaurant. *Wilgenplas* (M); 03465–61590. Excellent food.

MEDEMBLIK (64 north). *Het Wapen van Medemblik* (M), 1 Oosterhaven; 02274–3844. 28 rooms; good quality for the price.

Restaurant. *Twee Schouwtjes* (M), 27 Oosterhaven; 02274–1956. Good restaurant in 16th-century house. By the harbor.

MONNICKENDAM. *De Posthoorn* (M), 43 Noordeinde; 02995–1471. Also has excellent restaurant. *De Waegh* (M), Haven; 02995–1241. Small and delightful, overlooking a canal near the harbor.

OUDERKERK (4 south). Sleepy village on the Amstel river. *t'Jagerhuis* (M), 4 Amstelzijde; 02963–1432. 25 rooms; closed Dec.

Restaurant. *Klein Paardenburg* (E), 59 Amstelzijde; 02963–1335. One of the region's best.

SASSENHEIM (10 south of Haarlem). *Motel Sassenheim* (M), 8 Warmonderweg; 02522–19019. 30 rooms with bath; recommended.

SCHAGEN (38 northwest). *de Roode Leeuw* (M), 15 Markt; 02240–12537. 24 beds, some with bath.

TEXEL ISLAND (60 north). Reached by ferry from Den Helder; most hotels close during the winter. At **De Koog**, on Texel's west shore: *Het Gouden Boltje* (M), 44 Dorpstraat; 02228-755. 15 rooms, closed Nov.–Dec. *Opduin* (E), 22 Ruyslaan; 02228–445. 42 rooms with bath. Pool, sauna, solarium, etc. *De Pelikaan* (M), 18 Pelikaanweg; 0228–202. 30 rooms.

Restaurants. *Taverne* (M), 296 Dorpstraat; 02220–585. Sole is their specialty. *Tubantia* (M), 133 Pontweg.

At **Den Burg,** the island's capital: *den Burg* (M), 2 Emmalaan; 02220–2106. 18 rooms. *De Lindeboom* (M), 14 Groeneplaats; 02220–2041.

Restaurants. *De Graven Molen* (M), 4 Gravenstraat; 02220–2204. Small with good fish menu. *De Raadskelder* (M), 6 Vismarkt; 02220–2235.

VELSEN (18 northwest). **Restaurant.** *Taveerne Beeckestijn,* 136 Rijksweg; 02550–14469. Located in an annex of Huis Beekestijn, an 18th-century mansion with period rooms.

VOLENDAM (14 northeast). *Spaander* (M), 15 Haven; 02993–63595. 90 rooms. *Van Diepen* (M), 35 Haven; 02993–63705. 18 rooms; good restaurant.

WIJK AAN ZEE (17 northwest). Quiet seaside resort. *De Klughte* (M), 2 Van Ogtropweg; 02517–4304. 20 rooms; breakfast only. *Het Hoge Duin* (M), 50 Rijkert Aertsweg; 02517–5943. 27 rooms, all with shower. Situated on the dunes, 130 feet above sea level; restaurant specializes in sea food; good value. *Welgelegen* (I), 2 De Zwaanstraat; 02517–4323. No bathrooms attached. **Restaurant.** *Sonnevanck* (M), 2 Rijckert Aertsweg.

ZAANSE SCHANS. Restaurant. *De Hoop op D'Swarte Walvis* (E), 13–15 Kalverringdijk, Zaandijk. First class French food. Recommended.

ZANDVOORT AAN ZEE (18 west). Popular North Sea resort. *Hoogland* (M), 5 Westerparkstraat; 02507–15541. 25 rooms. *Astoria* (M), 155 Dr. C.A. Gerkestraat; 02507–14550. 18 rooms, all with bath. *van Petegem* (I), 86 Haarlemerstraat; 02507–12076. 10 rooms, none with bath.
Restaurants. *Castell Plage* (M), summer-only restaurant in beach pavilion. *Duivenvoorden* (M), 49 Haltestraat. Fish specialties. *Stella Maris* (M), 1 Strandweg. *De Uitzichttoren* (M), in the top of the 200-ft. tower that dominates the town; offers a remarkable view even if the food is so-so.

GETTING AROUND. By Car. This is the best way of all for seeing this part of Holland. Distances are short, there are no big cities outside of Haarlem and Hilversum, and you can return to Amsterdam for the night after each excursion, if you wish. You can also stay in smaller, cheaper hotels away from the capital, where parking is also much easier. Buy a good map which will enable you to leave main roads and explore the delightful byways of the region in complete confidence that you can always find your way back at the end of the day by the most direct route. Almost every corner of this country is a delight, even the remote lanes being paved, so avoid the motorways whenever you can.

A point to remember, whatever your means of transportation, is that nearly every city and town mentioned in this chapter can be visited from Den Haag with almost as much ease as Amsterdam, thanks to the compact nature of this angle of the Netherlands. You might consider, therefore, visiting everything north of Amsterdam (excursions 1 and 2: see text) from that city and then doing the rest from Den Haag or Utrecht, so as to have a little variety.

By Train. All the key towns in this area can be reached very easily by train. On Friday mornings in July and August there are special trains, the Kaasmark (Cheesemarket) Expresses, which leave the Central Station in Amsterdam at 9.03 and 9.32, arriving in Alkmaar in good time for the market; journey takes 30 minutes. Haarlem is also easily reached by trains that leave the Central Station roughly every half hour.

Excursions. A wide variety of inclusive sightseeing tours from Amsterdam are available. Among the many on offer are: a 4-hour bus and boat tour covering

Monnickendam, Marken and Volendam, cost is around Fl. 28; an 8-hour tour around the Zuiderzee covering Urk, Hindeloopen, Makkum and Hoorn, cost is around Fl. 57.50. Most of these tours operate between June and September and are by bus starting from the area around the Central Station in Amsterdam. There are also special day excursions organized by the national railway. Ask for details of the NS *Dagtochten* which are excellent value for money. Details of these and other tours are available from the VVV in front of the Central Station.

There is also an interesting boat excursion from Harderwijk, which leaves every hour during the summer and lasts about 70 minutes. The trip covers Veluwemeer and the polder reclamation work in progress.

TOURIST INFORMATION. There are regional VVV offices at the following places: **Aalsmeer,** 8 Stationsweg (tel. 02977–25374); **Alkmaar,** 3 Waagplein (tel. 072–119841); **Bussum,** 6 Wilhelminaplantsoen (tel. 02159–30264); **Haarlem,** 1 Stationsplein (tel. 023–319059); **Den Helder,** 30 Julianaplein (tel. 02230–25544); **Hilversum,** 2 Emmastraat (tel. 035–11651); **Hoorn,** Statenpoort, Nieuwstraat 23 (tel. 02290–18342); **Texel,** 9 Groenplaats, Den Burg (tel. 02220–4741).

MUSEUMS. Among the many local museums that deal with the history of various towns in this region, there are a number of more than passing interest to the visitor from abroad.

ALKMAAR. Stedelijk Museum (Municipal Museum), in the House of National Guard. Details facets of the town's development, especially the siege of the Spanish in 1573, which was successfully resisted. Open Mon.–Fri. 10–5, Sun. 2–5. Closed Sat.

Het Hollands Kaasmuseum, Waaggebouw. Cheesemaking, ancient and modern. Open Apr.–Oct., Mon.–Sat. 10–4. Closed Sun. In winter, Fri. 9–4.

Beermuseum de Boom, Houttil. Open Mon. to Sat. 10–4, Sun. 1–5. Showing history and old methods of brewing—includes a tasting room!

BERGEN. Het Sterkenhuis, Oude Prinseweg. Small museum in house dating from 1655. Has interesting exhibits on the defeat, at Bergen, in 1799 of the Duke of York's British and Russian army by the French.

EDAM. Edam's Museum, Damplein (opposite Town Hall). Fascinating museum showing how a retired sea captain lived in the 18th century. Richly furnished with period items. Open Easter to Sept. Mon. to Sat. 10–4.30, Sun. 2–4.30.

Kaaswag (Cheese Weight House). In a building dating from 1823; interesting exhibitions on cheese. Open April to end Sept. only, daily 10–5. Closed Mon.

ENKHUIZEN. Stedelijk Waagmuseum, Kaasmarkt. Located in the old weight house; also, interesting exhibitions of contemporary art in the attic.

Wapenmuseum, located in the old prison; good collections of arms and armor through the ages.

Zuiderzee Buitenmuseum. Open-air museum, opened only in 1983; attractive and carefully-reconstructed old buildings, including a church, from around the Zuiderzee. Open Apr.–mid-Oct., daily 10–5. Adm. Fl. 9. (Entrance fee includes *Binnenmuseum,* below.)

Zuiderzee Binnenmuseum, in the Peperhuis. Located in what was once a ware house belonging to the East India Company, the museum has good exhibits on many aspects of life in Zuiderzee; fishing, costumes and furniture etc. Open Apr.–mid-Oct., Mon.–Sat. 10–5, Sun. 12–5.

HAARLEM. Frans Halsmuseum. Groot Heligland. In early 17th-century almshouse, contains marvelous collection of pictures by Hals, plus some by contemporaries. Open Mon.–Sat. 11–5, Sun. 1–5. Adm. Fl. 3.

Teylers Museum, 16 Spaarne. The oldest museum in the country, it claims, established by wealthy merchant in 1778 as museum of science and arts. Has a number of drawings by Michelangelo and Raphael. Open Tues.–Sat. 10–5, Sun. 1–5. Closed Mon. Adm. Fl. 2.50.

De Hallen, Grote Markt. Changing exhibitions of ancient and modern art, town history, sculpture and tapestries. Open Mon.–Sat. 11–5, Sun. 1–5. Adm. free.

DEN HELDER. Helders Marinemuseum (Maritime Museum), 3 Hoofdgracht. Located in attractive building dating from 1820s; traces the history of the Dutch Royal Navy since 1813. Open Jan. to Nov., Tues.–Fri. 10–5, Sat. and Sun. 1–4.30.

HOORN. Westfries Museum, Rode Steen. Located in beautiful building dating from 1632; museum traces the development of the town, especially the exploration and colonization of the Far East in which Hoorn played a leading role. Open Mon.–Fri. 11–5, Sat. and Sun. 2–5. Adm. Fl. 1.25.

Stoomtram Hoorn, Medemblik. A delightful museum railway which runs for 20 km from Hoorn to Medemblik. Trains run daily during the summer months and connect with a boat trip from Medemblik to Enkhuizen. (Tel. 02290–14862.) Open May to Sept.

KOOG AAN DER ZAAN. Molenmuseum (Windmill Museum). 18 Museumlaan. History of the windmill in Holland; models, pictures, etc. Open Tues.–Fri. 10–12, 2–5, Sat. and Sun. 2–5. Closed Mon.

LAREN. Singer Museum, 1 Oude Drift. Works of William Henry Singer Jr.; paintings of the American, French and Dutch schools, changing exhibitions. Open Tues. to Sat. 11–5, Sun. 2–5.

LELYSTAD. Informatiecentrum Nieuw Land. Oostvaardersdijk. History of the draining and reclamation of the IJsselmeer and the building of the town of Lelystad. Open Apr.–Oct. daily 10–5, Nov.–Mar., Mon.–Fri. 10–5, Sun. 1–5.

LISSE. Museum voor de Bloembollenstreek, 219 Herreweg. History and culture of bulbs. Open April to Aug. 10–5, Sept. to Mar. 1.30–5.

MUIDEN. Muiderslot. 13th-century moated castle; fascinating both inside and out. A tavern in the wine cellar is open from April to the end of August. Open Apr.–Sept., Mon.–Fri. 10–5, Sun.1–5. Oct.–Mar., Mon.–Fri. 10–4, Sun. 1–4.

NAARDEN. Vesting Museum (Fortification Museum), 6 Westwalstraat. Underground and open-air museum with casemates, cannon-cellar and collection of historical objects. Open Apr.–mid-Oct., Mon.–Fri. 10–4.30, Sat. and Sun. 12–5.

TEXEL. Nature Recreation Center, 92 Ruyslaan, De Koog. Aquarium, dioramas, slideshows. Seals' feeding time 3.30 P.M. Open Mon.–Sat. 9–5.

Marinemuseum, 21 Barendszstraat, Oudeschild. Situated in a former corn and seaweed barn; contains a fascinating collection of beachcomber discoveries, plus an exhibition of the Russian War. Open Apr.–end Oct., Tues.–Sat. 9–5.

VIJFHUIZEN. Museum de Cruquius, 32 Cruquiusdijk. Housed in historic polder pumping station built in 1849, museum provides excellent coverage of the country's battle against the sea and the draining of polders. Good models of windmills etc. Open Apr.–Sept. Mon.–Sat. 10–5, Sun. 12–5. Oct.–Nov. Mon.–Sat. 10–4, Sun. 12–4.

ZAANDAM. De Zaanse Schans, Kalverringdijk. Open-air collection of typical old wooden buildings, windmills, houses and shops, all furnished. Open daily.

 SHOPPING. Cheese is the great specialty throughout this area. It's best bought at the various colorful markets that most towns hold. All the most popular places also have shops selling the full range of the country's crafts industry. For bulb lovers, Lisse is the place to head for. Special arrangements can be made for sending bulbs home (direct importation is not generally allowed).

Moving upmarket, Haarlem is renowned for its antique shops, with prices generally lower than in Amsterdam or Den Haag.

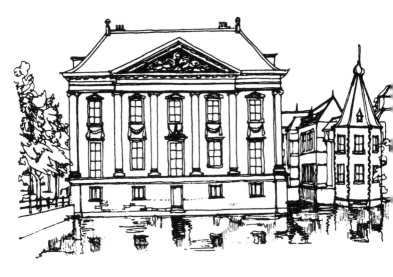

DEN HAAG AND
SCHEVENINGEN

The Count's Hedge by the North Sea

As becomes an aristocrat, Den Haag has several names. The French call it La Haye, whereas the official Dutch name is 's-Gravenhage or, literally, the Count's Hedge, while Den Haag is favored by the Dutch in conversation. In English it is known as The Hague. Its seaside resort neighbor is content with a single appellation—Scheveningen—which no foreigner can pronounce properly anyhow.

The business about the hedge recalls the early 13th century when the Counts of Holland had a hunting lodge in a small woodland village called Haag or "hedge." Then, around 1248, Count Willem II built a castle, which was subsequently enlarged and fortified. A town grew up around the castle, and gradually Den Haag became the focus of more and more governmental functions. Today, over one hundred international conferences are held here every year.

Since Den Haag is today the seat of Parliament, administrative ministries, and diplomatic missions, it is the capital of the Netherlands in everything but name, as well as being the capital of the province of South Holland. Queen Beatrix, who moved from Drakestein Palace in Lage Vuursche to Den Haag after her coronation, lives in the Huis ten

Bosch in the Haagse Bos woods. The castle, of course, is closed to the public. The palace used for official functions is the Noordeinde, situated in the street that bears its name. The royal couple's children, who also live in Huis ten Bosch, attend a government high school in Den Haag. The Queen's parents were married at this royal residence. The only circumstance that upsets Den Haag's claim as capital is the tradition of inaugurating the monarch in Amsterdam.

Prior to World War II there was a certain patrician distinction about Den Haag, a sense of detachment from the commercial pursuits that have made Amsterdam and Rotterdam larger if not wealthier. Many officials of the former Dutch colonies in the Far East used to retire to Den Haag after completing their tours of duty and heads of companies engaged in developing the East Indies found it agreeable as well as convenient to reside here.

That pattern of living has changed, however, and even the presence of the International Court of Justice, the International Institute of Social Studies, and the diplomatic colony is unable to maintain the old sense of aristocratic superiority. Instead, the mushrooming of government agencies, already launched in the 1930's, had moved at such a pace that it threatened to transform Den Haag into a community inhabited by legions of government employees. However, the government is now running a decentralization plan and moving a number of ministries, or sections of them, to other parts of the country.

For more than two decades the seaside town of Scheveningen has been under reconstruction and tremendous progress has been made to turn it into one of Europe's most modern resorts. Some of the old look is being kept because a few of the traditional buildings have been designated historic monuments, and only their interiors may be changed. But one has become a casino, others are being renovated, and new hotels face onto the Pier, still the only one in Holland. Fishing-boats chug through the enlarged harbor entrance; container and cargo ships give the port an air of bustling activity and the wide boulevard offers ample scope for breezy walking.

Exploring Den Haag and Scheveningen

The heart of Den Haag is the Ridderzaal or Knight's Hall in the center of a government complex that insulates itself from the rest of the city by the charming Vijver pond. It stands alone in the middle of the Binnenhof or Inner Court, its 13th-century towers recalling an era when architects were as much concerned with defense as shelter, its shape suggesting more a church than a castle. It has had a checkered history and served successively as a feasting hall, court of justice, market for booksellers, stables and exercise hall for soldiers, market place and archive store for the Ministry of Home Affairs.

Inside are vast beams spanning a width of 18 meters (59 feet), flags, stained glass windows, and a sense of history. It can be visited when not in use for congresses or official receptions. It is here that the two chambers of Parliament gather on the third Tuesday in September to receive Queen Beatrix and hear her speech declaring the new session open and presenting the majority program for the year ahead.

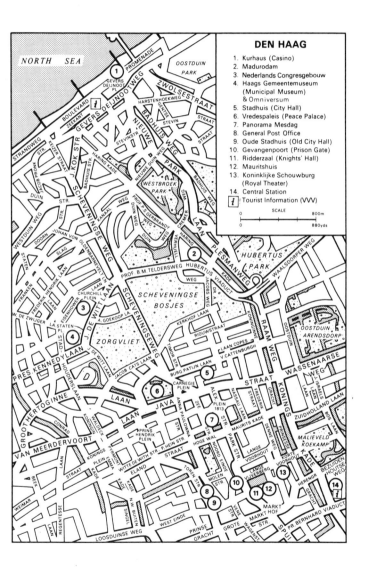

DEN HAAG

1. Kurhaus (Casino)
2. Madurodam
3. Nederlands Congresgebouw
4. Haags Gemeentemuseum
   (Municipal Museum)
   & Omniversum
5. Stadhuis (City Hall)
6. Vredespaleis (Peace Palace)
7. Panorama Mesdag
8. General Post Office
9. Oude Stadhuis (Old City Hall)
10. Gevangenpoort (Prison Gate)
11. Ridderzaal (Knights' Hall)
12. Mauritshuis
13. Koninklijke Schouwburg
    (Royal Theater)
14. Central Station
i Tourist Information (VVV)

SCALE
0   800m
0   880yds

Except on this occasion, the two chambers of Parliament sit separately in buildings on either side of the Ridderzaal. The hall of the Second Chamber, corresponding to the House of Commons or the House of Representatives, is entered from Binnenhof 1a, to the right. To the left, on the lake side of the Binnenhof at No. 21, is the entrance to the hall of the First Chamber, the House of Lords or Senate of Holland. British visitors will be amused by a 17th-century ceiling painting depicting John Bull attempting to climb out of the room so that he won't have to sign a distasteful treaty. Other government ministries occupy the remaining buildings around the Binnenhof.

The Mauritshuis

Keeping the Ridderzaal on our right, we pass through two narrow archways and emerge on the far side of the Binnenhof. The small, well-proportioned Dutch Renaissance building immediately on the left, its back bordering the Vijver pond, is the Mauritshuis, one of the greatest art museums, for its size, in the world. This superb 17th-century palace, built originally for Count Johan Maurits van Nassau, was reopened in 1987 after a five-year renovation that has fully restored its earlier splendor. Here, in a dozen rooms, is a feast of the finest in Dutch 17th-century art. Among the 15 Rembrandts are no less than four self-portraits covering a 40-year span of his life, from a smooth-cheeked adolescent to a weary, resigned old man who was about to die. Here, too, is Rembrandt's *The Anatomy Lesson,* painted when he was only 26, showing a group of eight surgeons around a cadaver. If the subject, commissioned by the Amsterdam Medical Society, is startling, the arrangement of the group into a harmonious composition represents a historic advance in 17th-century portraiture, a precursor of the vast *Night Watch* in Amsterdam's Rijksmuseum. Other of his canvases present his father, his mother, his brother Adrien, *Homer, Paul, Susanna Bathing, The Presentation in the Temple.*
Vermeer is represented in the Mauritshuis by three works, most notably his serene *View of Delft.* Jan Steen has several canvases, including the exquisite miniature, *Women Eating Oysters.* Paulus Potter's enormous *Bull*—2 by 3 meters (7 by 11 feet)—leaves nothing more to be said on the subject of beef on the hoof, and he never surpassed it during his brief 29 years of life. You'll meet Frans Hals, Carel Fabritius, Brouwer, Gerard Dou, Adriaen van Ostade, Ruysdael, Hobbema, Gabriel Metsu, and artists from other schools, such as Rubens, Hans Memlinc, Van der Weyden, Holbein, Tenier, and Van Dyck.
Beyond the Mauritshuis, but to the right, is an open square called simply the Plein (the Square). Around it are various other government departments and ministries. The statue in the middle honors Willem the Silent.
From the Mauritshuis the Korte Vijverberg and Lange Vijverberg extend along the east and north sides of the Vijver pond. They are lined with houses whose façades suggest something of the stately aspect of Den Haag during the 18th and 19th centuries.
Parallel with Korte Vijverberg, Lange Houtstraat, with its cluster of nightclubs and jazz centers, leads north from the far side of the Plein

to Toernooiveld, with, on the corner, opposite the U.S. embassy, the Koninklijke Schouwburg or Royal Theater, which occupies a former palace of Nassau-Weilburg dating from 1770. This brings us to the L-shaped Lange Voorhout, a broad avenue lined with trees that bends sharply to our left. Besides a small royal palace and the Hotel des Indes, it is the location of several embassies, two recital or concert halls, a publishing house, and several exclusive couturiers and hairdressers.

Along its right-hand long axis is the former Koninklijke Bibliotheek (Royal Library), which is being restored and redesigned as the Supreme Court. The Royal Library, which houses somewhere over a million books, is now housed in Prins Willem Alexanderhof 5 near the Central Station. The new building is striking, its modern design giving the impression of a huge ship. Beside the library is a building so narrow that tourist guides point to it as "the smallest house in Den Haag." Despite the basement doorway and the curtains at its windows, it is actually a kind of architectural plug designed to fill the gap that existed between the library and the building next door. Only about 2 meters (5 feet) wide in front, it tapers down to nothing at all towards the back where other walls converge.

At Lange Voorhout 6 is the remarkable building of the Dutch head-quarters of the Red Cross, with its skewed gable, so strangely out of place on this stately avenue. A few doors on, at the corner of Park-straat, is the Kloosterkerk, built in 1400, once used by the Black Friars and the city's oldest place of worship. On the far side of the Parkstraat crossing is the 1612 former home of the Raadspensionaris (or prime minister) Johan van Oldenbarneveld, one of Holland's greatest states-men, who was unjustly executed a few hundred yards away in front of the Ridderzaal in 1619 by order of Prince Maurits. Next to it on the left is the 1700 Kneuterdijk Palace, now used almost exclusively as government offices and record rooms.

Prison Gate and the Old Town Hall

A few steps left along the Kneuterdijk brings us to another open square, this one triangular in shape and called the Plaats. The statue memorializes Johan de Witt, another unfortunate Raadspensionaris of Holland. Hearing that his brother Cornelis was imprisoned in the Gevangenpoort or Prison Gate just opposite, he came to secure his release. A crowd gathered outside, was inflamed by factions hostile to the De Witts, and broke into the prison. The brothers were dragged out into the Plaats and literally torn apart.

Pictures of the event can be seen in the 14th-century Gevangenpoort, or Prison Gate, itself, formerly a gatehouse of the palace of the counts, which we visit next. For many centuries a prison, it is today a torture museum with enough instruments of inhumanity to satisfy any criminologist.

In 1967 the Plaats, or Place, along with the Hoogstraat and Noor-deinde running at right angles to it, was made the hub of the Palace Promenade, a pedestrians-only shopping center bright with flowers, attractive shops, show-cases and espresso coffee bars. This idea has since spread to a number of shopping streets in the area, which makes window-gazing a pleasure after 11 A.M. when the delivery vans are banned as well as other wheeled traffic.

As you leave the Gevangenpoort, a right-hand turn brings you to the Buitenhof or Outer Court, opposite the entrance to the Binnenhof and Ridderzaal, where our tour began. Around its edges are several open-air restaurants and cafés and a cinema. .

Follow the tram line right into Gravenstraat and you'll catch a glimpse of the 98-meter (321-feet) tower of the 15th-century Grote or Sint Jacobs Kerk. Between us and it, facing the Groenmarkt, is Den Haag's original Town Hall, the Oude Stadhuis, dating from the year 1565 and whose restoration was recently completed. Queen Juliana and Prince Bernhard were married in its Wedding Room in 1937. A vastly large building a few blocks from the Vredespaleis (Peace Palace) houses the present municipal administration. As a sort of annex to the old Town Hall is the Information Office of the municipality, where any questions about Den Haag are gladly answered. There is also a mini Town Hall in Javastraat used mainly for swanky civil weddings, and municipal meetings and receptions.

If you follow Schoolstraat south from the Grote Kerk through Grote Markt, and Lutherse Burgwal to Paviljoensgracht, you'll be rewarded by looking in at the doorway that breaks the long brick wall on the right. This is the Heilige-Geesthofje or Holy Ghost Almshouse, founded in 1616 and little changed in the last 300 years. Around the three sides of an interior, tree-graced courtyard is a continuous row of two-story apartments, occupied by Protestant spinsters under the terms of a centuries-old charter. A great sense of peace seems to hover over the gabled brick roofs almost as though stepping through the doorway were the first step towards a better world.

Across the street at 72/74 Paviljoensgracht is the house in which the Amsterdam-born philosopher Spinoza lived until his death in 1677. Privately owned, it can only be visited by appointment. A few steps away is his statue.

Panorama Mesdag and Peace Palace

Reversing direction, we head back across the center of Den Haag to 65b Zeestraat, a building designed specially to receive the Panorama Mesdag. You enter through a series of rooms hung with canvases by the painter and his wife, follow a narrow corridor, climb a few steps, and emerge into Scheveningen as it looked in 1880. To the west is the North Sea, and below you, pulled up on the beach, are several flat-bottomed fishing boats typical of that period. A detachment of cavalry exercises its horses near the water while fishermen repair their nets. To the east is Den Haag, detailed so perfectly that old-time residents can identify particular houses. So lifelike is the 14-meter-high (45 feet) canvas that encompasses you in its 122-meter (400-foot) circumference that it's hard to resist the temptation to step across the guard rail onto the dune and stride down to the water's edge. Perhaps even more remarkable than the panorama's fidelity is the fact that the couple, with only two assistants, completed it in four months. The transparent circle inside which Mesdag stood to make his preliminary studies has been preserved and stands in the center of the panorama.

A man of independent means, H. W. Mesdag painted as he pleased and bought the paintings of others whose work pleased him. Scheveningen, the sea, the lives of the fishermen, were his most important subjects, and he painted them a hundred times. The best of these maritime scenes are hung in the panorama building and merit more than a passing glance as you leave. The Panorama Mesdag celebrated its 100th birthday in 1981 and a permanent commemorative exhibition has been installed.

Just around the corner at 7f Laan van Meerdervoort is the painter's house, now the Rijksmuseum H. W. Mesdag. Some of his work is hung there, though few seascapes. There are canvases by Delacroix, Corot, Millet, and Rousseau. Mostly, however, it features works by the Den Haag School, which Mesdag influenced and supported. One or two rooms contain porcelain, statuettes, furniture, and other objets d'art collected by the artist. Primarily the museum is interesting as an indication of the trends of 19th-century painting.

The Vredespaleis (Peace Palace) lies just behind Laan van Meerdervoort, a monument to an ideal that still remains unrealized. Following the first peace conference at Den Haag in 1899, which was called by Queen Wilhelmina of the Netherlands at the request of Czar Nicholas II of Russia, the American millionaire Andrew Carnegie donated $1,500,000 for the construction of a building to house the proposed Permanent Court of Arbitration. The Dutch government donated the grounds, and soon many other nations offered furnishings and decorations . . . silver inkwells from Spain, iron gates from Germany, a Siberian marble urn from Russia, a tapestry from France (never finished), porcelain vases from China. When you are here, be sure to set your watch to the time on the tower clock, because this is correct to a thousandth of a second, controlled electronically from Bern.

The building itself was dedicated in 1913, its red and gray granite and brick pile rapidly becoming a local landmark. It is built in Flemish style, and as already suggested, the collection of odds and ends inside is as remarkable for its esoteric diversity as for beauty (there are daily guided tours). Today, the International Court of Justice, consisting of jurists from 15 nations, has its seat here. Summer courses on international law are presented here as well. Since the court has no compulsory jurisdiction, it can try a case only with the consent of both parties. During recent years, however, nations have chosen to settle their disputes in other ways, and comparatively few litigations have been started, a sad reflection on the ideological principle on which the Vredespaleis was founded. However, this building, with 11 halls and 83 rooms and a library of 500,000 books, is visited by over 100,000 visitors every year, with guided tours being carried out whenever the Court is not actually in session. Phone 469680 to check times.

Between the Vredespaleis and the Haags Gemeentemuseum is the super-modern Congress Center which can accommodate the largest international congresses. There are three theaters and a concert hall, the official home of the world-famed Residency Symphony Orchestra. Newest attraction in Den Haag, opened in 1984, is the Omniversum, described as Europe's first space theater and a development from the traditional planetarium. Located next to the Municipal Art Museum, the cylindrical building contains a 23-meter high dome which acts as a screen for the projection of amazingly realistic presentations, not only of outer space, but also of other "trips", such as below sea. The Omniversum is open daily, but some times for groups only. For details and reservations call 070–545454.

Madurodam, Holland's Miniature City

One of Den Haag's greatest attractions is Madurodam, a miniature city where everything is on a scale of 1/25th lifesize. It occupies one acre on the left (south) side of one of the canals connecting Den Haag with Scheveningen (follow Prinsessegracht and Koninginnegracht to Haringkade). It is named for Lt. George Maduro, who died a prisoner in the Dachau concentration camp after heroic resistance during the 1940 invasion of Holland. Profits from its operation support a number of charities, mainly connected with child welfare.

None of the details of a real city has been forgotten, from the harbor with its lighthouse, quayside cranes and ferries, to the airport with its bustle of planes about to take off. Everything works. Cars and buses stream along a four-lane highway, passenger and freight trains circulate on close schedules, merry-go-rounds and ferris wheels revolve in an amusement park, windmills turn, barges move along the canals, and music emanates from the church or opera house.

Towards dusk the lights come on inside the homes and offices of Madurodam. The lighthouse beacon begins to turn, warning lights flash from the top of the lofty radio tower, street lights are illuminated, and miniature floodlights reveal the medieval lines of the castle.

Although Madurodam represents no particular city in Holland, it is a synthesis of many, for the reason that nearly all the buildings are models of existing ones and many major new building developments in Holland are reproduced here. There is an evening sound and light show called "Moonlight Miracle".

Scheveningen, a New Lease on Life?

From Madurodam, drive west along the same canal that brought you from Den Haag. You pass through parks left and right until, about the time the canal ends, you can detect the unmistakable scent of the salt air. A block or two further and you are on Scheveningen promenade, a broad roadway nearly 3 km. (2 miles) long.

A fishing village since the 14th century, Scheveningen was developed as a seaside resort 140 years ago. At the turn of the century, the Kurhaus Hotel, built in 1885, was the rendezvous of the titled and wealthy society of Europe. But it closed down in 1973, along with its restaurants, bars and theater, as well as its neighboring postwar Grand Hotel. Various plans were put forward during 1973 to have the complex re-opened. A special organization was formed calling itself "We will never let the Kurhaus go", and one or two foreign hotel chains (mainly British) nibbled at the idea of taking it over. But most of them said that unless permission could be got to re-model the whole of Scheveningen's holiday facilities, it could never be made to pay.

The tide of opinion turned, however, in April 1973 when the Dutch Government promoted a bill in Parliament which would greatly liberalize the existing Dutch lottery and gambling legislation and enable casinos and bingo halls, for example, to be operated in any part of Holland under strict control. With the Dutch Parliament having passed the new legislation, a large property and construction combine drew up plans for the complete reconstruction of the whole Scheveningen resort area. Some of the original buildings were immediately torn down but the old Kurhaus was declared a protected monument. While retaining its original façade, the inside has been completely renovated. In 1983, the long-awaited reconstruction of this once-so-famous resort was finally completed and is again attracting visitors of all nationalities.

At its southern end are the twin fishing harbors of the herring fleets, which will be deserted or jammed according to the season. At the entrance to the harbors are arm-like breakwaters that extend into the North Sea. The harbor has now been enlarged by the addition of a freight and container terminal, and has facilities for passengers using the services operating to England's east coast.

Farther up the beach to the north is the fishing port's lighthouse, and beyond that, an obelisk marks the point opposite which King Willem I first set foot on Dutch soil in 1813 at the end of the Napoleonic wars.

The beach itself, protected from tidal erosion by stone jetties projecting out into the water, slopes gently into the North Sea in front of a high promenade whose function is to protect the boulevard and everything behind it from the fury of westerly storms. The surface of the beach is composed exclusively of fine sand, and it's possible to bicycle or walk for kilometer after kilometer to the north without fatigue by keeping just above the water's edge, especially when the tide is going out.

The Pier, completed in 1961, stretches for 366 meters (1,200 feet) into the sea. Its four circular end buildings provide (separately) an attractive sun terrace and restaurant, a 43-meter (140-foot) high observation tower, and an amusement center with a children's sector under qualified attendance, and an underwater panorama.

Part of the new design round the Kurhaus area includes the Golfbad, a "surfpool," complete with artificial waves; a shopping complex with restaurants, bars, nightclubs and a casino; plus a huge Circus Theater, just opposite the Kurhaus with performances of ballet, opera, concerts and cabaret. A bit further along is the Palace Promenade, another area of shops, discos, bowling alley, and different sorts of entertainment.

Den Haag's second resort is Kijkduin which is not quite as well-known as Scheveningen. It's a bit quieter and much more suitable for family holidays. Both Scheveningen and Kijkduin have nudist beaches.

Residential Wassenaar

Just north of Den Haag and left of the highway leading to Amsterdam is the Duindigt Renbaan, used for flat and trotting horse races from mid-March to November, on Wednesday and Sunday. There is also a dog-racing track.

Most residential areas of Den Haag consist either of varied-styled, three-storied, red brick houses set in small gardens, or large blocks of four to twelve-storied concrete apartment buildings. But Wassenaar is even more highly individualistic. Ensconced in a network of tree-shaded lanes and avenues, the inhabitants of this wealthy suburb of Den Haag have let themselves go architecturally. Here you can see an extraordinary mixture of styles. But Wassenaar has its beach, too, and the Duinrell Recreation Center, parks, camping, and sports facilities.

The *Attractionpark* here features over 50 activities such as roller-coaster, Niagara Superslide, all-season tropical wave-pool, etc. It is open daily from 10–5, during the summer till 10 P.M.

The Modern City

As with Amsterdam and Rotterdam, there have been remarkable changes in Den Haag in recent years: international headquarters, great apartment blocks and imposing government offices have been erected. Although the central sector has not been greatly changed, suburban areas are hardly recognizable to those who saw the city just a few years ago. Yet, the "green" aspect has been retained, and there are few more attractive cities in the country.

PRACTICAL INFORMATION FOR DEN HAAG AND

SCHEVENINGEN

 WHEN TO GO. Like Amsterdam, Den Haag is worth a visit any season. This is not yet true of Scheveningen, its next door, seaside neighbor, which is a typical resort in summer, a windswept fishing village in winter. An annual classical music competition is held here in March. Come as early as **April** if the bulbfields are on your list, because they begin practically around the corner (consult the previous chapter). The last day of the month is "Queen's Day", when Lange Voorhout in Den Haag's center is turned over to carnival attractions. On a Saturday in early **May,** a colorful geranium market is held at Lange Voorhout, and the end of May marks the start of the herring-fishing season: on the last Saturday all the boats in the harbor are bedecked with flags and there are special festivities. During **June** a spectacular international kite festival is held in Scheveningen and, for 10 days, an Oriental market, Pasar Malam Besar is held on Houtrust. An international equestrian show is presented annually. At the end of June is "Parkpop" in the Zuiderpark, when pop bands perform on two stages.

From May to October a curio, book and picture market is held each Thursday at the Lange Voorhout.

During the summer months (July–Sept.) some 20,000 roses in hundreds of varieties are on show in the Westbroekpark, one of the many city parks.

July and **August** are the big months at Scheveningen, especially now that the reconstruction of the resort has almost been completed. The annual North Sea

Jazz Festival is held in July. Major concerts and shows are held in the Congresgebouw, and many fringe events occur throughout the city. Every Friday sees displays of fireworks, culminating in an International Firework Festival at the end of August.

September has the greatest pageant of all, when Queen Beatrix is driven in a golden coach to the 13th-century Ridderzaal or Knights' Hall in the historic heart of Den Haag on the third Tuesday and opens the new session of Parliament in a wonderful display of color and ceremony. Den Haag's talented Residentie Orchestra presents its first concerts in September, a sign that the active music and theater season has begun. In **October** motor races are held along the beach at Scheveningen, and during October and November a ten-day international culinary festival is presented in the resort. **November** is marked by a fashion festival and New Year's Eve by spontaneous firework displays in almost every street.

TELEPHONE CODES. The telephone code for Den Haag and Scheveningen is 070. To call any number given in this chapter from outside the area, this prefix must be used, unless otherwise specified. Within either Den Haag or Scheveningen, no prefix is required.

HOTELS. Although Den Haag, Scheveningen and Kijkduin form a single metropolitan area, the differences between the three are considerable and the location of your hotel will affect the nature of your vacation greatly. Accordingly, we list hotels separately.

We have divided the hotels in our listings into four categories—Deluxe, Expensive, Moderate and Inexpensive. Price ranges for these categories are given in *Facts at Your Fingertips* (see page 17). Some hotels, particularly at the upper end of the scale, have rooms in more than one category and a consequently wide range of prices.

DEN HAAG

Deluxe

Des Indes. 54 Lange Voorhout; 469553. Old fashioned but comfortable; 77 rooms, all with bath or shower. In embassy area and popular with diplomats; attractive decor. Has fine *Le Restaurant*.

Promenade. 1 van Stolkweg; 525161. 100 rooms with all facilities; very comfortable.

Sofitel. 35 Koningin Julianaplein; 814901. Modern, overlooking Koekamp Park; 120 rooms, to shopping center. Good restaurant.

Expensive

Bel Air. 30 Johan de Wittlaan; 502021. 350 rooms half with bath. Located next to Congress Center, specially geared for conference delegates.

Corona. 41 Buitenhof; 637930. 26 rooms, all with bath or shower. Comfortable; overlooks Den Haag's central square. Old Dutch café downstairs, sidewalk terrace.

Paleishotel. 26 Molenstraat; 624621. In town center, near traffic-free shopping promenade.

Parkhotel De Zalm. 53 Molenstraat; 624371. 130 rooms, most with bath or shower. In city center, bordering the former Royal Palace.

Pullman Hotel Central. 180 Spui; 614921. 160 rooms with all facilities. Central location next to the new theater.

Moderate

Esquire. 59–65 van Aerssenstraat; 522341. 15 rooms, few with bath but very good facilities.

Petit. 42 Groot Hertoginnelaan; 465500. 20 rooms.

Savion. 86 Prinsestraat; 462560. 9 rooms, 7 with bath.

Sebel. 38 Zoutmanstraat; 608010. Good value for price.

Inexpensive

Du Commerce. 64 Stationsplein; 808511. 31 rooms, 3 with bath.

Excelsior. 133 Stationsweg; 882413. 64 rooms, 8 with bath.

Neuf. 119 Rijswijkseweg; 900748. 16 rooms, none with bathrooms.

SCHEVENINGEN

Deluxe

Steigenberger Kurhaus. 30 Gev. Deynootplein; 520052. 240 rooms. Hotel of considerable grandeur. In the center of Scheveningen close to the beach and pier with good restaurant and a casino.

Expensive

Carlton Beach. Gevers Deynootweg; 541414. 120 rooms. Right on beach; covered pool, three restaurants, bar.

Europa Crest. 2 Zwolsestraat; 512651. 170 rooms, all with bath. Pleasant, sunny location close to beach.

Flora Beach. 63 Gev. Deynootweg; 512821. 97 rooms, most with bath. Apartments, all with self-catering kitchenette.

Moderate

Badhotel. 15 Gev. Deynootweg; 512221. 96 rooms, most with bath. Modern hotel with good facilities.

Inexpensive

Aquarius. 107–110 Zeekant; 543543.

Bali. 1 Badhuisweg; 502434. 35 rooms. With excellent Indonesian restaurant.

City. 1 Renbaanstraat; 557966. 30 rooms, half with bath.

Meerbeek. 212 Dirk Hoogenraadstraat; 550884. All rooms with shower and toilet; 3 mins. from beach.

Seinduin. 15 Seinpostduin; 551971. All rooms with shower; 20 meters from beach.

Van Zanen. 39 Leuvensestraat; 554636. 30 rooms without bath.

KIJKDUIN

Expensive

Atlantic. 220 Deltaplein; 254025. 220 rooms, half with bath.

Zeehaghe. 675 Deltaplein; 256262. 100 rooms, most with bath.

 GETTING AROUND. Den Haag can be reached by train from Amsterdam in under 1 hour and there is a half-hourly service during the day. The historic heart of Den Haag is so concentrated that it is best explored on foot. From Den Haag, Scheveningen is easily reached by bus or tram. The best advice is to get a good map from the VVV offices in either city (see below). They will also be able to supply you with details of excursions in and around the area.

TOURIST INFORMATION. The main tourist information office (VVV) for **Den Haag** is adjacent to the Central Station in the Babylon Center (tel. 070–546200). In **Scheveningen,** the VVV office is on the corner of Scheveningseslag and Gev. Deijnootweg (tel. 070–546200).

USEFUL ADDRESSES. Travel Agents. *American Express,* 20 Venestraat (tel. 469515). *Wagons-Lits/Cooks,* 46 Buitenhof (tel. 656850).

Embassies. *American,* 102 Lange Voorhout (tel. 184140). *British,* 10 Lange Voorhout (tel. 645800). *Canadian,* 7 Sophialaan (tel. 614111).

Car Hire. *Avis,* 216 Theresiastraat (tel. 850698). *Hertz,* 1 Vanstolkweg (tel. 559000). *Europcar,* Sofitel Babylon, 35 Koningin Julianaplein (tel. 851708).

MUSEUMS. Haags Gemeentemuseum (Municipal Museum), 41 Stadhouderslaan. Home of the largest Mondrian collection in the world, plus interesting ceramic and musical instrument departments and a number of period rooms. Building, dating from 1935, is interesting specimen of the International Movement. Open Tues. to Fri., 10–5, Sat. and Sun. 12–5. Adm. Fl. 2.

De Gevangenpoort (Torture Museum), 33 Buitenhof. Once part of the old palace gate; presents a graphic and chilling picture of torture through the ages. Open Mon.–Fri. 10–5. During Apr.–Sept., Sun. 1–5 also. Adm. Fl. 3.50.

Huygensmuseum Hofwijck, 2 Westeinde, Voorbrug. Country seat of the poet and statesman Constantijn Huygens. Designed by Jacob van Campen, architect of the Dam Palace, and Pieter Post. Contains memorabilia of Constantijn and his son Christian, the physicist and astronomer; also portraits, books and correspondence. Open daily 2–5. Closed Mon.

Madurodam, 175 Haringkade. Magnificent model of many Dutch towns and cities—not to be missed. Open Apr.–July daily 9.30–10 P.M., July–Sept. 9.30–11 P.M., Sept.–1st Sun. in Oct. 9.30–9.30 P.M. Closed 2nd Mon. in Oct.–Apr. Adm. Fl. 8. There is a sound and light show in the evenings.

Mauritshuis, 8 Korte Vijverberg, just behind the Ridderzaal (Knight's Hall). The most important museum in Den Haag (dates from 1644). Contains no less than 15 Rembrandts and three Vermeers; plus an outstanding collection of other great Dutch and Flemish masters (Rubens, Hals, van Dyck, Holbein and many others). Open Tues. to Sat. 10–5, Sun. 11–5. Adm. Fl. 5.

Museon (Museum of Education), 41 Stadhouderslaan. Recently completely reorganized with extensive displays covering the earth, space, man, etc. The evolution of our planet and civilizations. Open Tues.–Sat. 10–5, Sun. 1–5.

Museum Voor Het Poppenspel, 8 Nassau Dillenburgstraat. Valuable and unusual collection of puppets. Open Sun. 12–2; other times by appointment. Adm. Fl.1.

Museum Swaensteijn, 101 Herenstraat, Voorburg. Formerly a notary public's house. Contains Roman archeological finds, picture books and other items from the country seats of Voorburg. Also presents temporary exhibitions. Open Tues. and Thurs. 2–5, Sat. 12–4.

Omniversum, 5 President Kennedylaan. Planetarium and space theater. Open daily, but some times only for groups. Check. Tel. 070–545454.

Panorama Mesdag, 65b Zeestraat. Remarkably life-like panorama of Scheveningen around 1880 painted by H. W. Mesdag, his wife and two assistants on a giant circular canvas 45 feet high and nearly 400 feet long. Open daily 10–5, Sun. 12–4. Adm. Fl.3.

Rijksmuseum H. W. Mesdag, 7f Laan van Meerdervoort. Paintings of the Hague School; once considered a backwater of 19th-century painting, the movement has now been promoted to a much more central position. Interesting and attractive. Open Tues.–Sat. 10–5, Sun. 1–5. Adm. Fl.3.50.

Rijksmuseum Meermanno Westreenianum, 30 Prinsessegracht. Manuscripts, books, coins and Greek and Egyptian artefacts. Open Mon.–Sat. 1–5. Closed Sun. Adm. free.

Schevenings Museum, 92 Neptunusstraat, Scheveningen. Traces history of Scheveningen and of fishing here; models, costumes, paintings and prints. Open Mon. to Sat. 10–4.30. Closed Sun. Adm. Fl.2.

Schilderijenzaal Prins Willem V, 35 Buitenhof. Exhibition of paintings belonging to Prince Willem V from 1774 to 1795, displayed as nearly as possible as they were in the time of the Prince in carefully-restored rooms—the first Dutch "museum". Works by Steen, Rembrandt, Wouwerman and Jordaens. Open daily 11–2. Adm free.

 ENTERTAINMENT. Music and Theaters. Concerts by the Residency Orchestra (The Den Haag Philharmonic) are given in the concert hall of the Congress Center, while the Amsterdam Concertgebouw Orchestra plays in the Circus Theater at Scheveningen. Popular for recitals and chamber music is Diligentia on the Lange Voorhout. Of special interest to ballet lovers is the brand new Danstheater aan't Spui which promises to be one of the country's best.

Movie Theaters. Films are screened at fixed times (generally a matinee and two evening performances), depending on the program. Saturdays and Sundays there are extra matinees. Foreign films, with American and English predominating, are shown with their original soundtracks plus Dutch subtitles.

Miscellaneous. For the young in heart, there are puppet theaters at Nassau Dillenburgstraat 8 and at Frankenstraat 66; there are circuses on the Malieveld close to the American Embassy several times a year. The Den Haag VVV office organizes a three-hour afternoon *Royal Tour,* covering points of interest connected with the House of Orange and their *Combi Tour* combines boat and bus to present highlights of Den Haag and Scheveningen. From mid-Oct. to mid-March there is a rink for figure skating and ice hockey at the Uithof skating center, 10 Jaap Edenweg; a recreation park at Soestdijksekade, open daily; Drievliet Recreation Park at Rijswijk; Duinrell Recreation Park at Wassenaar and Westbroek Park famous for its roses, and Madurodam.

Greyhound racing (nowhere else in Holland) at the Clingendael race course starts at noon every Sunday from April to October. One of Holland's finest casinos is located at the beautifully renovated Kurhaus at Scheveningen.

 SHOPPING. For those who find fun in looking out for antiques, Den Haag is just the place. There are about 150 shops selling nothing else but antiques and curios, and the local VVV has a special publication giving a tour of many of them, including the usually unexplored parts of the city. In fact, if the full route is followed, it can take anything from a long morning to a whole day. From May to October there is an openair Antique Market on the Lange Voorhout every Thursday from 9–9. On Mon., Fri., and Sat. there is a flea market at Herman Costerstraat from 8–6.

Most of the antique shops are clustered together more or less in two almost adjoining districts. One of these comprises the Noordeinde and Hoogstraat branching off from the center of the city, and the other is in the Denneweg near the Hotel des Indes.

A specially interesting shop for silver is *In den Silveren Molenbeecker,* 31 Hoogstraat. The great treasures of this establishment are its old molds, made at various times since its founding in 1868, but it is also constantly making new molds for the production of its fine handmade pieces.

 RESTAURANTS. The food in Den Haag and Scheveningen is excellent, with everything from French *haute cuisine* to exotic Indonesian dishes, from traditional Dutch to piquant Italian on offer. The choice of atmosphere is equally wide: you can dine beside a canal or beside the sea, in an early Dutch *eethuis* or a Sumatran house on stilts. With Scheveningen first and foremost a fishing port, sea food is always a good choice. Zeeland oysters come from just south of here (during the months with *r* in them), though their cost may incline you to order them one at a time. And steaks . . . Dutch beef ought to be good what with green grass almost all year round and no hills to climb. It is. For an adventurous snack, try a raw herring from a sidewalk cart.

Our restaurants listings are divided into three categories—Expensive, Moderate and Inexpensive. Price ranges for each category, per person and excluding drinks, are given in the *Facts at Your Fingertips* (see page 22). Remember that many restaurants have dishes in more than one price category, so be sure to check the menu posted outside *before* you go in. Look out too for the excellent-value Tourist Menu.

For the more expensive restaurants, it is usually necessary to book in advance.

DEN HAAG

Expensive

Auberge de Kieviet. Wassenaar; 79203. A countrified inn. Many specialties, lobster among them.

De Beukenhof. 2–4 Terweeweg, Oegstgeest; 071–173188. Out of center, but excellent French menu.

Le Bistroquet. 98 Lange Voorhout; 601170. Small, exclusive and very good. Closed Sun.

Boerderij De Hoogwerf. 20 Zijdelaan; 475514. Converted 17th-century farmhouse with delightful garden. On the border of Den Haag and Wassenaar.

Gemeste Schaap, 9 Raamstraat; 639572. Hard to find, but when you see the delightful old Dutch interior you'll be well rewarded.

In Den Kleynen Leckerbeck. 130 Prinsestraat; 461908. Reasonable, though service could be improved. Closed Mon. and Tues.

Le Relais. 35 Kon. Julianaplein; 814901. French cuisine, highly recommended.

Saur. 51 Lange Voorhout; 463344. Second-floor seafood restaurant with Edwardian atmosphere and the best food in town; highly recommended. Seafood snackbar downstairs, normally very popular. Closed Sun.

Tampat Senang. 6 Lange van Meerdervoort; 636787. Authentic Indonesian food in authentic Indonesian atmosphere; the best of its kind in town.

Moderate

Chalet Suisse. 123 Noordeinde; 463185. Good fondue dishes; tends to be crowded.

Charcoal. 130 Denneweg; 659788. As the name says, charcoal grill.

Garoeda. 18a Kneuterdijk; 465319. Good for Indonesian food.

't Goude Hooft. Groenmarkt 13; 469713. Old Dutch atmosphere, and attractive terrace in summer.

Maliehuisje (Pancakes). 10 Maliestraat; 462474. Lovely old Dutch style. In a street just off Denneweg.

Raden Ajoe. 31 Lange Poten; 644592. Excellent Indonesian food.

Wilhelm Tell. 324 Lange van Meerdervoort; 605609. Closed Wed.

Inexpensive

Buffeterie. Palace Promenade, for a good range of snacks.

Hortus. 53 Prins Hendrikstraat 53; 456736. Vegetarian.

SCHEVENINGEN

Expensive

Kandinsky. 30 Gevers Deynootplein; 520052. In the Kurhaus Hotel; good French cuisine.

Lee Towers. 155 Strandweg; 522140. Good food and nice view. Open summer only.

Raden Mas. 125 Gevers Deynootplein; 545432. Indonesian food.

Seinpost. 60 Zeekant; 555250. Also French, recommended.

Moderate

Bali. 1 Badhuisweg; 503500. Authentic Indonesian restaurant; attractive.

Caballero. 53 Strandpaviljoen; 540111. In pavilion right on beach. Open summer only.

Golden Duck. 33 Dr. Lelykade; 541095. Right by the harbor; Chinese food.

Mégot. 47 Strandweg; 522526. International menu.

NIGHTLIFE In the past year or so, the nightlife of Den Haag has become so bizarre that even the veteran police are puzzled over how to control it. There are many clubs which deal exclusively with sex and openly advertise in at least one popular local evening paper, giving addresses, telephone numbers and names of ladies offering "discreet relaxation" and "cozy friendship", by appointment. Several clubs specialize in "married couples" evenings. Your hotel porter will most likely know the safe places to recommend.

Bars and cafés normally keep open until one in the morning, while nightclubs are lively from 9 P.M. to 4 A.M. Generally there is no admission charge to the clubs nor is there a drink minimum.

Places like the *Crazy Horse* in Lange Houtstraat feature international artists, including strippers. The shows change every month or so.

There is a rash of discothèques in Den Haag, *Maliehuys*, 8 Maliestraat, being one of the best. Most of Scheveningen's discos are located around the Kurhaus Hotel.

In the city center there are several rather earthy clubs in Noordeinde. For more sophisticated tastes, *Kabouter* in the Plaats is unusual. Located there for about 100 years, it looks from the outside to be just a small and ordinary bar, but actually it rambles back to provide four intimate old Dutch-style rooms, one with a dance floor and live combo. And, almost unique in Den Haag, its restaurant is open until 2 A.M. *Mayfair,* 106 Bilderdijkstraat, is a good sex club, and *Boko,* 1 Nieuwe Schoolstraat, a gay bar.

The *Rose and Orange* is a real English pub in Westeinde.

ROTTERDAM

A Unique Delta City

There has always been great rivalry between Amsterdam and Rotterdam in the spheres of both shipping and commerce. Amsterdam has managed to retain the title of capital of the Netherlands, but Rotterdam, with a population of almost 560,000, has steadily earned the title of capital of the international shipping world, having within ten years developed from the third-largest port in the world to the largest by a big margin.

In the province of North Holland, as we've seen, a single city has become so large and influential during the last few hundred years as to sap the expansive force of its hinterland. Like some invisible magnet, Amsterdam has drawn to itself the vital energies that once animated Hoorn, Alkmaar, Enkhuizen, and even Haarlem, as if the silting of the Zuiderzee had posed so great a challenge that only one community could hope to survive with sufficient resources remaining.

The situation has been quite different in the province of South Holland. While Den Haag has prospered with the fruits of colonial administration and of government, Leiden, Delft, and particularly Rotterdam have continued to develop and grow independently. So much so, in fact, that city planners envisage the whole of South Holland becoming a single metropolitan area before the end of this century. Already Leiden stretches a hand south to Wassenaar and Den Haag, already Delft finds itself beginning to be compressed between Den Haag and Rotterdam. Happily this growth is taking the form of a strip around a central core of farmland and green spaces, instead of spreading in all directions.

Thanks to its location on the delta of two great river systems, the Rijn (Rhine) and the Maas (Meuse), and the enormous Europoort and North Sea projects, it is the largest seaport in the world. Through its harbors—there are many, and the total length of the quays is more than 37 km. (23 miles)—pass more than 30,000 vessels from some 400 shipping companies each year. New industry, attracted by cheap transportation, has already well established itself along the waterways that crisscross the delta. At Pernis, just across the Maas, the greatest oil refining complex on the Continent is still expanding. This development owes much to the vision of the Rotterdamers themselves. Not only has the main entrance been deepened to take the world's largest tankers, but the harbor itself has been extended right into the North Sea by reclaiming a site which is now a combined harbor and an industrial region. An artificial island is even being built out in the North Sea as an oil terminal and site for heavy industry.

There's more to Rotterdam than size alone, however. Gone are the days when the city fathers would commission a statue of a paint manufacturer but refuse to clear away the grim jungle of its commercial core. On May 14, 1940, the task was done for them by Nazi bombs, which swept away some 30,000 homes, shops, churches, and schools in the course of a few brief hours. The task of reconstruction, necessarily delayed not only until the end of the war but until the port itself was functioning again, was nevertheless a matter of years rather than decades, and the authorities seized the opportunity to give the city and the surrounding area a completely new look, using all modern techniques and ideas. Planning actually began only four days after the wartime bombing, with the result that a new city of concrete, steel and glass rose from the ashes. At the same time, the city designers and planners broke away from tradition; they were not hidebound believers in Dutch architecture. The new city has life, vitality, and ample growth potential. Including gleaming new suburbs set in parks and gardens, it now houses well over 1,000,000 people—and is still looking for new territory. To the dismay of some of the small adjoining municipalities, it is threatening to swallow up old-time townships and even to grab still more land from the North Sea to supplement the many acres already reclaimed for the extension of its already mammoth Europoort.

Rotterdam is modern and progressive in more than just architecture. Its citizens had the first underground railway in Holland, opened in 1968 and still expanding. While trade and commerce have made it rich, the community has not neglected culture and the arts, and the city is also a major centre for international conventions.

In 1990 Rotterdam celebrates its 650th anniversary, for which a number of special events are planned.

Exploring Rotterdam

Central Rotterdam is reached by fine motorways from Den Haag, Amsterdam, Utrecht and all the northern and central areas of Holland, while from the south, which includes arrival from Belgium and France, it is entered via either the tunnel or the new bridge, under and over the River Maas respectively. The tunnel is just over one kilometer long with twin double-lane roadways and separate paths for cyclists and pedestrians. Incidentally there is another fine tunnel linking the city with the sprawling Europoort area. This Benelux tunnel was actually paid for by the oil and transport industries headquartered in Rotterdam, on the condition that they could levy tolls on traffic until the total cost was reimbursed, when the tunnel would be handed over to the government, which it now has been and so is free.

Like Amsterdam, the name of the city is taken from a river, in this case, the Rotte, which empties into the Maas at this point. As early as 1600 Rotterdam was already the second city of the Netherlands. Its really spectacular growth dates, however, from 1872 when the Nieuwe Waterweg was completed, an 18-km.-long (11 miles) artificial channel leading directly to the sea. Just inside the entrance is Hoek van Holland from which ferries link Holland with England.

The greater part of the land to the south of the Nieuwe Waterweg is devoted to the development of the still expanding "Europoort", through which flow oil, coal, and steel to the whole of Europe. This ambitious and impressive project, stretching out into the North Sea by reclamation of the shallows, has made Rotterdam the world's largest port. All projects can be visited by regular boat services.

Sight-seeing in Rotterdam automatically divides itself into two tours: first around the city (best seen by the tram tour leaving from the Central Station, April–October), and the second around the harbors. Each is easy to tackle, because everything is arranged for you. The tram tour, which is accompanied by a multi-lingual guide, includes a brief boat tour of the harbor, or this can be taken separately, with boats leaving the Spido landing stage for a variety of water tours, lasting from 1¼ hours to a full day. Besides piers, drydocks, facilities for handling containers, wet and dry cargos, and the like, you see the radar facilities that enable ships to enter Rotterdam from the North Sea in complete safety even when visibility is reduced to zero by fog. The restored St. Laurenskerk in the center is a worthy landmark and has an imposing new organ.

The Bouwcentrum or International Building Center, directly opposite the modern Central Station, has been a major force in the development of new ideas as well as a storehouse of existing knowledge. It consists of a series of permanent and temporary exhibitions as well as an extensive library.

The Museum Boymans-Van Beuningen is the city's major art museum, a stunning building ideally designed to house the collections of painting, sculpture, ceramics, and furnishings inside. Among its Rembrandts is a portrait of his son Titus. Hieronymus Bosch's *Prodigal Son* is another masterpiece. But not only the old masters strike the eye: a

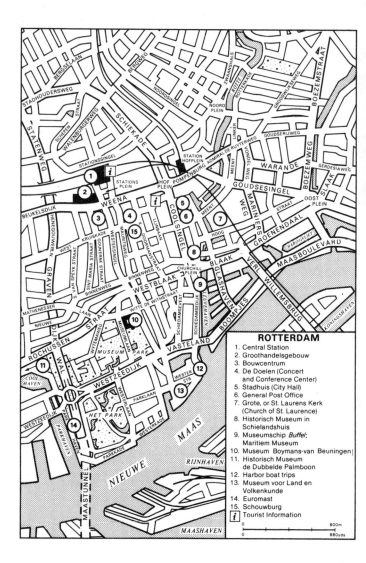

ROTTERDAM

1. Central Station
2. Groothandelsgebouw
3. Bouwcentrum
4. De Doelen (Concert
   and Conference Center)
5. Stadhuis (City Hall)
6. General Post Office
7. Grote, or St. Laurens Kerk
   (Church of St. Laurence)
8. Historisch Museum in
   Schielandshuis
9. Museumschip *Buffel*;
   Maritiem Museum
10. Museum Boymans-van Beuningen
11. Historisch Museum
    de Dubbelde Palmboon
12. Harbor boat trips
13. Museum voor Land en
    Volkenkunde
14. Euromast
15. Schouwburg
    [i] Tourist Information

0   800m
0   880yds

very fine collection of modern art is on display, with works by Dali, Kandinsky, Kokoschka and many others. There are also frequent new exhibitions of old as well as contemporary paintings.

Other museums of note include the Museumschip *de Buffel,* which is a former ironclad of the Royal Dutch Navy and dates from 1868. It has largely been restored to its original condition. There are also small displays of 19th-century maritime objects. The Museum de Dubbelde Palmboom in Delfshaven offers an insight into Rotterdam's history and an interesting collection of glass, silver and Delft tiles. There is also the Museum voor Volkenkunde, geographical and ethnographical, with an extensive collection of artifacts and an exhibition about Third World countries and the problems they face. There is even a taxation museum, Belastingmuseum Prof. Dr. van der Poel, to be found in Rotterdam. It explains taxation through the ages and has a cellar full of smugglers' tools and equipment.

The Groothandelsgebouw or Wholesale Center, ten stories high and 213 meters (700 feet) long, is one of the largest buildings of its kind in Europe. It is a city within a city with more than 360,000 square meters (1,300,000 square feet) of floor space, plus a restaurant, snackbar, shops, travel agency, barbershops, bank, demonstration rooms and post office. Nearly 4,500 people are employed within its walls. An interior network of service roads permits deliveries by truck or lorry to most of the storage area. On every floor are offices and showrooms, and among the wares displayed are textiles, cosmetics, motorcycles, cameras, machinery, furniture, jewelry, hardware, and clothing. A few foreign firms are represented, the rest being Dutch. From the roof there's a panoramic view of Rotterdam and its surroundings as far as Delft.

The main axis of Rotterdam's reconstructed core is Coolsingel, nearly all of whose buildings are postwar. An exception is the Town Hall, the largest in the country, which somehow withstood the catastrophic bombing. Erected on over 8,000 concrete piles in 1920, it has a handsome exterior plus murals in the civic reception room on the first floor. A few blocks away from the Stadshuis or Town Hall we come to the Schielandhuis, the only old building that survived the destruction of 1940. It was built originally in 1665 by J. Lois, but was destroyed by fire in 1864. The Schielandhuis housed the Museum Boymans-van Beuningen in the 19th-century and is now the home of the Historisch Museum with a wide-ranging coverage of the city's history.

A strange beehive-walled building dates from 1957. Designed by U.S. architect Marcel Breuer, it houses the Rotterdam branch of a national department store called the De Bijenkorf (or "beehive"). Completely windowless, it is a model of modern merchandising inside with gleaming escalators, indirect lighting, and muted colors.

A block or two west of Coolsingel is the Lijnbaan shopping center, a complex of four-score shops selling everything from organs to pancakes. It is organized along broad sidewalks that belong exclusively to pedestrians—no motorized traffic is allowed within the area. Close by is De Doelen, an imposing complex combining the functions of a theater, concert-hall and congress center.

By the Leuvehaven is a tortured statue called *Devastated City* by Ossip Zadkine. It depicts a despairing bronze figure whose heart has been torn out by the tragedy of war. Here, too, is the Museumschip *de Buffel* and the Maritiem Museum Prins Hendrik.

The Blijdorp Zoo on the north edge of Rotterdam is one of the most modern in Europe and is organized on the principle of allowing the animals to live in the open as much as possible in surroundings that approach those of their natural habitat.

At the corner of Parkhaven and Parkkade stands the 185-meter-high (600 feet) Euromast tower, with a glass-walled restaurant at its summit. From here there is a unique panoramic view of Rotterdam and its surroundings. The tower begins with a massive-looking pillar rising to the crow's nest 104 meters (340 feet) high, with two restaurants, one moderate in price and the other (The Rotisserie) expensive but really excellent. Then there rises the latest addition in the form of a spidery-looking mast which goes up another 81 meters (260 feet) as a sort of space tower which is climbed by a spiral lift cabin holding 32 people. The view from the top is magnificent.

In Rotterdam's western district is Delfshaven, once the harbor of Delft (despite the variant spelling) before its absorption in 1886. Here everything is on a less grandiose scale, with twisting waterways and tangled streets. In July 1620 the Pilgrims set sail in the *Speedwell* for England and the New World. Most of the port area has recently been reconstructed, many of its 110 buildings now appearing just as they were when originally built. The 1970 Tercentenary Celebrations of the Pilgrim Fathers made this one of the most popular places in Holland. The Pilgrim Fathers' Church, the Zakkendragershuisje (Sack Carriers' House) and the Crane House have been restored and are open for viewing. The Sack Carriers' House, which now contains a pewter workshop, has had a fascinating history since it was built in 1653. As the name suggests, the house was a gathering place for workers who waited patiently for hours, sometimes days, to be assigned work. Unfortunately, even in those days there was a surplus of labor. The authorities solved the problem, however, by having everyone throw a dice, the lucky winners getting the available work.

An unusual feature of Rotterdam, missed by most visitors, is the way the city has been reconstructed since its wartime destruction. Taking advantage of starting anew, the business section was separated from the residential area in a way that has become a prototype for town planners all over the world. Those interested in fine modern architecture should explore the Blaak district where there are some superb and unusual examples, including the "tree" houses and "pencil" apartment block, and the starkly modern city library. Around the Oude Haven (Old Harbor) area there are ultra-modern cube houses (Paalwoningen), and many cafés, pubs, restaurants and shops.

Schiedam and Vlaardingen

Adjoining Rotterdam to the west along this waterway is Schiedam, once the greatest gin-producing city of Europe. On the banks of the Schie River, there used to be over 300 gin distilleries. Now there are just over 50, which still pour out stupendous rivers of *jenever* (pronounced yahnaver), as Dutch gin should be called. The world-famed firm of Bols and the almost equally well-known Melchers firm, whose brand-mark Locomotive honors George Stephenson, have their main distilleries here. It is surely good for the nose and the eyes to go round these works and see the giant vats in the peaty soil in which the gin is stored for seven years to give it that "Zeer Oude" (Very Old) flavor the Dutch insist on.

On your visit to Schiedam, visit the Nationale Gedistilleerd Museum, with its huge collection of miniature bottles and objects used in the distillation of jenever. Here more than five thousand specimens tell the romantic story of liquor and liqueurs through the ages. The De Jongh collection, the largest and most valuable in the world, took more than 50 years to accumulate and represents the popular, and unusual, beverages (excluding wines and whiskies) of more than 50 countries.

Almost next door to Schiedam and only 11 km. (7 miles) from Rotterdam is Vlaardingen, an old town of some 77,000 inhabitants and Holland's most important center of cod and herring fishing. There is Visserijmuseum, a sea-fishing museum at Westhavenkade 53 with models and pictures of Dutch fishing vessels and marine fish. It also has period rooms, a diorama and an aquarium. From the year 1400 Dutch trawlers have been sailing to and from this waterland center, rising to a mammoth fleet of over 3,000 boats in the 1600s. Unfortunately the curious old-style fishing auction has succumbed to more speedy methods of salesmanship. But there still remain not only many architectural reminders of the early days of this historic town but also, as a permanent memorial of its hey-day, a hooker, or herring boat, sailing into the wind up on the top of the Great Church tower. However, fishing now takes second place in Vlaardingen since it developed into a thriving industrial town as well as a dormitory-suburb for Rotterdam. To recapture something of this salty spirit, drop in at the ultramodern Delta Hotel, which literally overhangs the Maas. From its glass-walled restaurant or crow's nest bar you can watch the constant traffic of ships. The Benelux Tunnel under the waterway starts from Vlaardingen and provides a quick connection with the Pernis refineries and Europoort, before continuing to Zeeland.

PRACTICAL INFORMATION FOR ROTTERDAM

GETTING TO TOWN FROM THE AIRPORT. Though Rotterdam has its own airport, the large majority of visitors fly in via Amsterdam's Schiphol airport, from where there are excellent train links with Rotterdam. There are four trains an hour; journey time is around 50 minutes.

TELEPHONE CODES. The telephone code for Rotterdam is 010. To call any number in this chapter, unless otherwise specified, this prefix must be used. Within the city, no prefix is required.

HOTELS. Rotterdam is well supplied with hotels in all categories, though only one truly luxurious spot. But standards are high and all hotels are comfortable and well run. Most also provide excellent food.

We have divided the hotels in our listings into four categories—Deluxe, Expensive, Moderate and Inexpensive. Price ranges for these categories are given in the *Facts at Your Fingertips* chapter (see page 20). Some hotels, particularly at the upper end of the scale, have rooms in more than one category and a consequently wide range of prices.

For anyone arriving in the city without reservations, the VVV in the Central Station provides a free hotel list and operates an accommodations service; a small fee is charged for this.

Deluxe

Hilton. 10 Weena; 4144044. 250 rooms, all with bath and all convertible into two- or three-unit suites. The only luxury hotel in the city; among its several restaurants perhaps the best is *Le Restaurant* for very elegant dining. Also features an all-night disco, *Le Bateau,* every night but Mon. and a casino.

Expensive

Atlanta. 4 Aert Van Nesstraat; 4110420. 164 rooms, all with bath or shower. Excellent location.

Central. 12 Kruiskade; 4140744. 64 rooms, all with bath or shower. Comfortable; near Central Station and handy for Lijnbaan shopping.

Delta Crest Hotel. 15 Maasboulevard, Vlaardingen; 4345477. 78 rooms, all with bath or shower. Very new and modern, with all facilities, including indoor pool. Out of center.

Parkhotel. 70 Westersingel; 4363611. 157 rooms, all with bath. Opposite canal minutes from Lijnbaan and Coolsingel; parking.

Rijnhotel. 1 Schouwburgplein; 4333800. 140 rooms, all with bath or shower. Has good restaurant (*Falstaff*).

Moderate

Baan. 345 Rochussenstraat; 4770555. 15 rooms, 9 with bath. Pleasant.

Commerce. 56–62 Henegouwerplein; 4774564. 39 rooms, most with bath. Friendly atmosphere; near Central Station.

Novotel. 2 Hargalaan, Schiedam; 4713322. 138 rooms, all with bath or shower. Modern and comfortable, with many facilities.

Savoy. 81 Hoogstraat; 4139280. 100 rooms, all with bath or shower.

Van Walsum. 199 Mathenessaerlaan; 4363275. 30 rooms, most with bath. Good restaurant.

Inexpensive

Bienvenue. 24 Spoorsingel; 4677475. Good value.

Floris. 68–70 Graaf Florisstraat; 4259113. 32 rooms, most with bath; good value for the price.

Gare du Nord. 7 Villapark; 4227273. 13 rooms, most with bath or shower.

Holland. 7 Provenierssinge; 4653100. 22 rooms, no private baths.

Pax. 658 Schiekade; 4663344. 45 rooms, most with bath. Ask for a quiet room.

Youth Hostel. There is a Youth Hostel at 107 Rochussenstraat; 4365763; just out of the city center by the Boymans Van Beuningen Museum.

GETTING AROUND. By Metro and Bus. The city has a good metro system, running partly underground and partly overhead, the latter sections giving a unique view of the city. Public buses are easy to use and inexpensive. The VVV can help with route maps and details of special day tickets, essential if you plan to see a lot of the city.

By Taxi. Very expensive, but readily available at ranks throughout the city.

City Tours. The VVV organizes daily sightseeing tours Apr.–Oct. by tram and boat which leave from in front of the Central Station and take in all the principal sights in Rotterdam. There are also a range of tours of the harbor and surrounding river and sea areas, which leave from Spido Pier at the edge of Willemsplein. These take from 1¼ to 7 hours. The shorter harbor tours run every ½ hour during summer. There are also excursions available to all the more popular and interesting areas outside the city either by bus or train. Details of all these trips are available from the VVV.

TOURIST INFORMATION. The tourist information offices (VVV) are located at Stadhuisplein 19 (tel. 010–4136000) in the center of town and in Central Station. They operate an accommodations service, for which there is a small charge, and can supply information on restaurants, places to visit in and around Rotterdam and excursions. They can also provide maps of the city.

USEFUL ADDRESSES. Travel Agents. *American Express*, 92 Meent (tel. 4330300). *Wagon-Lits/Cooks*, 19–21 Meent (tel. 4116200).

Car Hire. *Avis*, 21 Kruisplein (tel. 4332233). *Hertz*, 64 Heer Vrankestraat (tel. 4651144). *Europcar*, 646 Pompenburg (tel. 4114860). All the major companies also have car hire desks at Rotterdam airport.

MUSEUMS. Belastingmuseum Professor Van Der Poel (Tax Museum). 14 Parklaan. An historical collection detailing taxes and taxation throughout the ages—exactly what most people come on holiday to forget! But also features smuggling. Open Mon.–Fri. 9–5.

Boymans-VanBeuningen, 20 Mathenesserlaan. Splendid and wide ranging collection of paintings by Dutch and Flemish 16th- and 17th-century painters (Rembrandt, Rubens, Bosch, Hals, Steen, van Goyen etc.). There is also a good modern collection, principally of the Barbizon and Hague schools. Other wings house pewter, etchings, glass, ceramics, silver and sculpture. There are also regular exhibitions of modern—sometimes very modern—works, international as well as Dutch. This is one of the biggest, best and most important museums in the country and should not be missed. Open Tues.–Sat. 10–5, Sun. 11–5. Adm. Fl. 2.50.

Historisch Museum de Dubbelde Palmboom, 12 Voorhaven. Large museum detailing the history of the town through crafts, fragments of buildings, silver, glass, prints etc. Top floor has good tea room and bar. Open Tues.–Sat. 10–5, Sun. 11–5. Adm. Fl. 2.50.

Historisch Museum Schielandhuis, 31 Korte Hoogstraat. Housed in a unique 17th-century building is this large collection of material relating to the city's history. Also numerous drawings and prints. Open Tues.–Sat. 10–5, Sun. 11–5.

Maritiem Museum Prins Hendrik. Splendid collection of things naval including ships' logs, charts, navigation instruments, models, etc. The Museumschip *"Buffel"* at Leuvehaven is a restored ironclad warship of 1868 and admission is included as part of Maritiem Museum. Open Tues. to Sat. 10–5, Sun. 11–5. Adm. Fl. 2.50

Museum Hendrik Chabot, 12 Berglustlaan. Etchings, drawings and sculptures by Chabot, a Dutch Expressionist of the early to mid 20th century. Visits by appointment only (tel. 4224274). Adm. free.

Museum Stoomdepot (Steam Museum), 82 Giessenweg. Collection of steam locomotives and industrial engines. Open Sat. only 10–5.

Museum Voor Volkenkunde (Ethnographical Museum), 25 Willemskade. Extensive collection of weapons, sculptures, textiles, musical instruments, puppets, masks etc. from China, Tibet, Nepal, Java, New Guinea and many other countries around the world. Open Tues.–Sat. 10–5, Sun. 11–5. Adm. Fl. 2.50.

Toy-Toy, 41 Groene Wetering. Delightful collection of antique dolls, miniatures and mechanical toys from 1700 to 1940, in private house. Open Sun.– Thurs. 11–4. Closed July and Aug. Adm. Fl. 5.

SHOPPING. For the best of the shopping streets, head down the Lijnbaan, an arcaded quadrangle closed to traffic and flanked by expensive shops. Other roofed-over shopping centers include the Winkelcentrum Zuidplein with 140 shops, and the Winkelcentrum Oosterhof with 110, on the outskirts of the city.

There is a flea market, for antiques and curios, on Tuesday and Saturday 9–5 at Binnenrotte, and a secondhand book market on Tuesday and Saturday 9–5 at Grotekerkplein in front of the St. Laurens church.

RESTAURANTS. Rotterdam has a good array of restaurants in all price categories offering a wide choice of international and traditional Dutch food. Prices are generally similar to those in Amsterdam (see page 19). Remember that many of the more expensive spots have dishes in more than one price category, so be sure to check the menu posted outside before you go in. Similarly, watch out for the excellent value Tourist Menu.

Expensive

Boris. 936 Diergaardesingel; 4110831. Excellent Balkan specialties; well worth trying.

Coq d'Or. 25 Vollenhovenstraat; 4366405. Excellent French restaurant; best food in town. Upstairs for more formal dining, downstairs for good value snacks. 5 minutes from Coolsingel.

La Duchesse. 9 Maasboulevard; 4264625. Excellent French cuisine.

Euromast. 4364811. The view is probably better than the food, but the grill is good, the snack bar fair.

Gasterij De Kleine Visser. 26 Lange Haven, Schiedam; 4263898. Good restaurant in 18th-century house.

The Old Dutch. 20 Rochussenstraat; 4360344. Traditional and atmospheric Dutch restaurant (as the name suggests) and one of the best places in town. Terrace in summer.

La Vilette. 160 Westblaak; 4148692. One of the best. French dishes, popular meeting place for business community. Closed Sun.

De Zwetheul. 480 Rotterdamseweg, Zweth; 4704814. International cuisine to high standard; book ahead. On the road to Delft.

Moderate

Beef Eater Carvery and Steakhouse. 45 Stationsplein; 4119550. One of a complex of restaurants right by the station, this one's an English-style pub restaurant.

In de Bernisse Molen. 1 Spuikade Geervliet; 01887–1292. First class food in genuine old mill 20 km. outside the city; well worth the drive.

Chalet Suisse. 31 Kievitslaan; 4365062. Excellent food in delightful park; the restaurant is attractively sited by a lake.

Falstaff. 1 Schouwburgplein; 4333800. Good food in rather quiet and attractive spot.

Hong Kong. 15 Westersingel; 4366463. Excellent Chinese food.

De Lange Muur. 1 West Kruiskade; 4125622. Good Indonesian dishes.

Napoli. 81a Meent; 4148467. Italian specialties; reasonably good.

De Pijp. 90 Gaffelstraat; 4366896. Good international cuisine; recommended.

In Den Rust Wat. 96 Honingerdijk; 4134110. To the east of the city; attractive restaurant in delightful 16th-century house.

La Toscana. 135 Schiekade; 4661411. Good Italian food.

Inexpensive

De Big. 20 Kralingsweg; 4526874. Excellent for traditional and inexpensive Dutch pancakes of all kinds.

Bongers. 20 Meent; 4128668. This is the place to come for *poffertjes,* another traditional Dutch specialty (a delicious sort of waffle).

De Nachtegaal. 11 Prinses Beatrixlaan; 4527361. Pancakes galore; easy on your purse and very tasty.

Scala Bodega. 28 Kruiskade; 4143273. Snacks, mainly wine and cheese; good.

 NIGHTLIFE. The nightclubs of Rotterdam have not yet become as numerous and as daring as those of Amsterdam, or Den Haag. There are, of course, a few which go in for striptease, while there are two or three quarters in which ladies of all nations and ages seek to attract the seamen who always have a few hours to spare in large ports.

Your hotel porter or the VVV will give you the best advice on nightclubs to suit your particular taste or fancy, especially as new ones occasionally appear. The list, however, will probably include *The Ambassador,* 151 's Gravendijkwal, which has cabaret and dancing as well as hostesses.

SOUTH HOLLAND PROVINCE

Historic Leiden, Delft and Gouda

Apart from the attractions of cities like Amsterdam and Rotterdam, the South Holland Province has a great deal to offer the tourist.

As will be seen from the map, the network of roads gives easy access to a number of historic towns, no matter whether the visitor has made Amsterdam, Den Haag or Rotterdam his headquarters. Most of these roads, in spite of transformation into modern motorways, still run through a storybook Holland of green fields, windmills, brimming canals and rosy-cheeked children. Cows graze in the meadows nearly all year round, even though in the colder months they have special waterproof coats on, and only the distant spires, with a steadily increasing forest of factory chimneys, destroy the illusion of a flat infinity. In many of the districts, too, each house has it own private bridge across a ditch.

Exploring South Holland

If you decide to make Leiden your first port of call, then you will see it burst upon you as a maze of twisting streets and tempting vistas. Leiden has been famous over the centuries for its courage and learning, so you will want to see its university, the Lakenhal Museum with its reminiscences of cloth-weaving days, the Pieterskerk with its memories of the Pilgrim Fathers and their spiritual leader John Robinson who is buried inside, the delightful Rapenburg Canal, and the fine Arms Museum with its interesting exhibits, through which you can have a guided tour. Nor should you miss the windmill museum "De Valk" on Lammerlnmarkt.

Leiden's historical center is marked very clearly by the Burcht, an 11th-century mound of earth with a fortification on top to control the confluence of the Old and New Rhine, which almost encircle it. Here there may have been a Roman colony, Lugdunum Batavorum, though no one knows for sure. The history of the town and its 104,000 citizens has been full enough without insisting on classical origins. Their finest hour was in the 16th century when the Spanish laid siege after the mayor, in a fashion typical of the age, rejected the surrender terms with a verse from Cato. The siege lasted for five terrible months, claiming the lives of 6,000 Dutchmen through fighting, starvation, and disease. So desperate did the situation become that the mayor, Van der Werff, offered his own body as food for the famished population. The city honored him with a statue in the park that bears his name.

Relief came, incredibly, by sea. The Dutch fleet sailed inland from lake to lake, breaking another dike every night so that its advance could continue in the morning. On October 3, 1574, the ordeal was over, and the day has been marked by the distribution of loaves of white bread and herring (*haring en witte brood*) on that anniversary ever since. As a reward for its courage and steadfastness, Willem the Silent offered Leiden the choice between relief from taxes and the establishment of a university. With a sense of realism that has perhaps been overidealized, the rejoicing citizens concluded that tax relief would be only temporary at best, whereas a university, the first in the country, would never cease to be an asset.

Leiden's professors were soon renowned all over Europe for their learning, their integrity, and their independence. So much so, indeed, that James Boswell, the fun-loving biographer of Dr. Johnson, protested when his father proposed sending him here to study law. He went to Utrecht instead, which he found more to his taste. The university still leads all others in the Netherlands, especially its faculties of law and medicine. The classical tradition is still strong—it wasn't long ago that landladies with rooms to let ceased posting their notices in Latin. Queen Juliana was a graduate, and her eldest daughter, now Queen Beatrix, also studied here.

Stop at the VVV tourist information office at 210 Stationsplein, and request their detailed folders. Like so many other Dutch towns, Leiden is best seen by a walking tour. A VVV leaflet will guide you, taking in many of the more important sights, or, from May to September, there is a guided tour every Saturday leaving the VVV at 10.30 A.M.

Sightseeing can begin at the Lakenhal on the Oude Singel. Built in 1639 for the city's cloth merchants, it carries decorative motifs alluding to the various processes involved in the manufacture of textiles. Inside are various art masterpieces, including the first great triptych of the Dutch Renaissance by Lucas van Leyden, who, as his name suggests, was born here. (So were Rembrandt and Jan Steen.) Other rooms tell much about the technique of making cloth in the 17th century and, most particularly, guaranteeing its quality. Indeed, perhaps the most important function of the guild was to certify the value of the goods produced by its members, or refuse to certify them if they were not up to par. You will see a collection of what are, in effect, trademarks, used corporately instead of competitively.

A display honors the pilgrims who in 1609 were granted permission to move to Leiden from Amsterdam, which they found "torn by the spirit of controversy". A decade later a city magistrate commented that "these English people have now lived amongst us these ten years and never any complaint or accusation has been brought against any of them".

Proceed next up the Breestraat, the narrow bustling street that forms the backbone of the old city. You'll note the glorious 17th-century façade of the Town Hall. It is all that remains of the original building, destroyed by fire in 1929. A left turn down the street beyond gives you a glimpse of the Korenbeursbrug (Cornmarket Bridge), an unusual covered affair from which there are magnificent views, beyond which are the Burcht fortification, the 14th-century Hooglandse or St. Pancras Church, built in 1315 as a wooden church. The present building dates from about 1500. Then proceed to the delightful St. Anna Almshouse, the oldest and one of the most beautiful in town. In the chapel of the St. Annahofje—and it is rare for an almshouse to have its own chapel—is one of the only altars in Leiden to have survived the iconoclasts of 1566.

A right-hand turn from the Breestraat leads uphill to the imposing mass of the Sint Pieterskerk, the site of Thanksgiving Day services by Americans each November in honor of the Pilgrims, who worshiped here. Plaques inside and out refer to the death of their spiritual leader, the Rev. John Robinson, who was prevented by poor health from accompanying the group that set sail for the New World in 1620. Five years later he was buried in the church. In the Kloksteeg opposite the outdoor plaque is the Persijnhofje, an almshouse founded in 1683 by a Delano ancestor of the late President Franklin Roosevelt, some years after Robinson had lived there.

The narrow street that continues downhill from the entrance to the Persijnhofje (which can be visited), leads across the charming Rapenburg Canal to the university, behind which are the Hortus Botanicus gardens. A left turn as you leave the university takes you along the Rapenburg past the Museum van Oudheden (Museum of Antiquities) on the other side, and back to Breestraat.

Another stroll from the Pieterskerk leads down Herensteeg past the house (there is a plaque) where William Brewster and his Pilgrim Press published the theological writings that clashed so strongly with the dogmas of the Church of England. Proceeding across the Rapenburg Canal along Doezastraat to the Witte Singel, you may visit the tiny Documentatiecentrum (Pilgrim Fathers' House museum).

If you have a little extra time to spare, the Rijksmuseum voor Volkenkunde (Ethnographical Museum) and the Museum Boerhaave (History of Science Museum) are both on Steenstraat. Not far away is the 17th-century Morschpoort, an old town gate and the Rembrandt bridge. The Weddesteeg, a small street across this bridge, is where

Rembrandt was born in 1606. At the intersection of Breestraat and Pieterkerkchoorsteeg is a blue stone set into the pavement where executions once took place.

Leiden's Interesting Neighbors

The district north and west of Leiden is a vacationer's delight. The Oude Rijn or Old Rhine River flows from Leiden towards the North Sea, which it enters at the beach resort of Katwijk aan Zee, where the Romans erected a lighthouse centuries ago and which is still in use as a coastguard post. More cosmopolitan is the next resort up the coast, Noordwijk aan Zee, which is mostly a string of hotels stretched along some 13 km. of beach dunes. Besides swimming, speedboating, and the like, it offers tennis, golf, horseback riding, and walks through the heath.

Just north of Leiden are the famous bulb fields, magnificent in spring, and the Kaag Lakes. The town of Warmond at its southern end is a forest of masts during the week, a tumult of activity weekends when everyone races to get his boat out on the water first. At the northern end is the village of De Kaag, reached by ferry from a dike that encloses the Haarlemmermeer Polder. Both are fun to visit, and you can even rent a boat of your own at Warmond.

Avifauna, the International Bird Park

We turn east, however, and follow the Oude Rijn upstream for 16 km. (10 miles) to Alphen aan de Rijn. Here, amid the idyllic surroundings is the Avifauna International Bird and Recreation Park where some 10,000 birds of 420 different species are housed in gardens of unusual beauty. Started as a private aviary, Avifauna attracted so many visitors during its first year that it has been open to the public ever since. From all parts of the world the feathered creatures have come, from the tropics and the polar regions, and all of them have been put in what are literally natural conditions. The tropic birds live in heated glass houses full of orchids and exotic plants against a background painted by some of Holland's best mural artists. The polar birds splash about in cold water in huge houses cleverly camouflaged to resemble icy caves. The ostriches and the emus stroll about unconcernedly on lovely lawns, and all are housed in conditions as close as possible to their natural habitats. The gardens are open daily, from 9 A.M. to 9 P.M. during April to September, and from 9 A.M. to 6 P.M. October to March. Admission is Fl. 4.

Trips can be made daily by boat from Den Haag, Rotterdam, Amsterdam and Gouda/Leiden, not only to Avifauna but through the chain of lakes surrounding it. Some of the larger sightseeing craft offer a hot or cold buffet.

About 3 km. (2 miles) east of Alphen a country road branches right and leads south towards Boskoop and Waddinxveen, a district that specializes in growing flowering plants, shrubs, and small trees, many of the latter trained and trimmed into a fantasy of shapes: animals, baskets, churches, jewels. Lovers of rhododendrons, azaleas, hydrangeas, all kinds of conifers, cyclamens, flowering cypresses, camellias, cherry trees, and pigmy rose trees will find them all here in gorgeous profusion. The first nurseries were established here in the 1870s. In Boskoop you may wish to visit the rosarium and the botanical gardens.

Delightful Delft

From Vlaardingen (or Rotterdam, or Den Haag) it's a short run north (south from Den Haag) to Delft on the main highway to Den Haag and Amsterdam. There is probably no spot in the Netherlands that is more intimate, more attractive, and more traditional than this little town whose famous blue and white earthenware has gone round the world. A few hours spent here put you in the company of Vermeer who lived and painted in Delft, of the scions of the House of Orange who are buried here, of the historian Grotius and the great naturalist, Van Leeuwenhoek, who were born here, and of the mysterious Karl Naundorf, whose remains lying here are declared to be those of Louis XVII, Dauphin of France.

Compact and easy to traverse, despite its web of canals, Delft is best explored on foot, although water-taxis are available in the summer to give you an armchair ride through the heart of the town. During the summer (Easter–Sept.) on Tuesday, Wednesday, Friday and Saturday, you can also enjoy a ride on a horse-drawn bus that leaves from the market place. Every street is lined with medieval Gothic and Renaissance houses that have lost neither charm nor beauty through the centuries. And at every corner you see a small bridge or façade that looks as lovely as Delftware itself.

Almost every square centimeter of Delft is a living masterpiece. In the market place, the only lively spot in this tranquil town, is the Nieuwe Kerk (though built in the 14th century) with its piercing Gothic spire, 300 ft. high and with a magnificent carillon of 48 bells which are played several times a week. One hundred years of Dutch craftsmanship went into its erection, as though its founders knew it would one day be the last resting-place of the builder of the Netherlands into a nation, Willem the Silent, and his descendants of the House of Orange. Hendrik de Keyser designed and started the heroic monument to Willem but did not live to see it completed, a task finished by his son. No less than 22 columns surround the tomb, which is further adorned with allegorical figures of Justice, Liberty, Religion, and Valor. At Willem's feet lies his faithful dog, which is said to have refused to eat after his master's death and thus soon starved.

Beneath this grandiose sarcophagus is a crypt in which rest the remains of nearly 40 members of the Orange-Nassau line, including the entire royal family since King Willem I ascended the throne.

While in Delft, visitors will certainly want to see the famous local specialty—Delftware. The history of this distinctive blue and white porcelain goes back to its country of origin, China. Decorated porcelain was brought to Holland from China on East India Company ships and was so much in demand that potters of the time felt their existence to be threatened, as sales of their own products dropped dramatically. So they set about the creation of a pottery to rival the Chinese porcelain,

at least in outward appearance. Imitating the multi-colored Chinese
and Japanese varieties, Delftware was produced not only in blue but
also in other colors. In the middle of the 17th-century, Delft alone had
more than 30 potteries. Some of those that still carry on the old trade
are: *De Porceleyne Fles,* 196 Rotterdamseweg; *De Delftse Pauw,* 133
Delftweg; and *Atelier de Candelaer,* 13 Kerkstraat.

On the other side of the market place is the Town Hall with a
collection of paintings by Delft artists. Take a look inside, and then
emerge to spend some minutes feasting your eyes on the lovely façades
of the houses and shops which line this historic square, one of the most
romantic in Holland.

Let's walk around the right-hand side of the New Church, then left
at the back and along the Vrouwenregt canal for a few steps before
another left-hand turn into the Voldersgracht, a name that recalls the
guild of the fullers, who cleaned and thickened cloth before it was dyed.
On our left, the backs of the houses rise straight from the water as we
stroll to the end of the street, marked by the sculptured animal heads
and outdoor stairs of the Meat Market on the right. The meat market
does not take place here any longer, but there is a general market on
Thursdays and a fruit and vegetable market on Saturdays from the end
of April till the end of September. We cross the Wijnhaven and turn
left along its far side to the Koornmarkt, a stately canal spanned by the
high arching bridges that are the hallmark of Delft.

At No. 67 is the Paul Tetar van Elven Museum, an artist's house
with 19th-century furnishings downstairs and an upstairs studio that
seems to have been asleep since the time of Vermeer. Everything is
complete, from the massive easel to the mortar and pestle for grinding
pigments.

Just before you reach the end of the Koornmarkt the Wapenhuis van
Holland, or Arsenal, comes into view. Completed in 1692, it was filled
with the powder, muskets, and cannon needed to defend the liberty of
the young Dutch Republic. We turn right to the Oude Delft canal and
right again along its far side. This is the city's oldest waterway, as the
name suggests, and dates back to about the year 1000.

In a few blocks you will suddenly come upon the incredible Gothic
façade of the Gemeenlandshuis, built as a private residence in 1520
with a flamboyant display of painted coats of arms from 1652. The
oldest dwelling in town, it was used on occasion by the Counts of
Holland during their visits.

The Prinsenhof

A few doors on is the Prinsenhof, formerly the Convent of St. Aga-
tha, founded in 1400. The chapel inside dates from 1471, its interior
being remarkable for the wooden statues under the vaulting ribs. Willem the Silent made this gracious building his headquarters, and it was
here that he was murdered in 1584 by an assassin in the pay of the Duke
of Alva. Near the bottom step of a winding staircase you can see the
holes made in the plaster by the bullets. The murderer ran out into
Schoolstraat, tripped over a pile of straw, and was immediately cap-
tured. Here, too, is the famous chest, of which there seem to be several

in Holland, in which Grotius is said to have escaped from confinement in Loevestein Castle near Gorinchem.

Today the Prinsenhof is regarded as the cradle of Dutch liberty. Part of it is used to house a museum telling the story of the Liberation of the Netherlands from 1568 to 1648 (80 years of Spanish occupation) depicting both the maritime and the martial epics of those years of tireless struggle. Another section is used for temporary exhibits, most notably the annual Art and Antique Dealers' Fair.

Across the Oude Delft canal is the Oude Kerk or Old Church, a vast Gothic monument of the 13th century. Its beautiful tower surmounted by a brick spire leans somewhat alarmingly to the west, although the experts say this was deliberate and therefore quite safe. High in the belfry is a huge bell rung only on momentous occasions, for fear of damaging it or the tower. Inside are the tombs of two Dutch admirals, Piet Heyn, whose birthplace we visited in Rotterdam, and Maaerten Harpertzoon Tromp, who, after defeating Blake in the Strait of Dover, sailed up the Channel with a broom at his masthead, to denote that he had swept the English off the seas. Here also are monuments honoring the microscopist Van Leeuwenhoek and the poet Hubert Poot.

Beyond the Prinsenhof on the same side of the Oude Delft canal is the Lambert van Meerten Museum, a mansion whose timbered rooms are filled with the country's most complete collection of old Dutch tiles as well as early Delft pottery.

In a nutshell, mention of Delft to the average tourist conjures up displays of distinctive hand-painted blue and white porcelain: to the art lover, the quaint town of the great 17th-century Dutch master, Johannes Vermeer: to the experienced engineer, one of Europe's greatest universities. Delft is certainly all of these, but to all visitors there remain memories of having walked through fascinating pages of European history.

Gouda, Stained Glass and Pipes

Another old Dutch city well worth visiting, lying on the main motorway running from Den Haag (and another from Rotterdam) to Utrecht is Gouda, pronounced "How-dah". It has its own weekly cheese market, during July and August, a factory turning out clay pipes and another making luxury candles, and the priceless stained glass windows in a lovely old church. Moreover, a visit here can be combined with a call at Oudewater with its scales for weighing witches (you can test yourself in this connection if you wish), and then on to the quiet village of Schoonhoven on the River Lek, a renowned silver center. The Netherlands Goud-, Zilver- en Klokkenmuseum, with its beautiful collection of Dutch and French clocks and display of silver from the 17th to the 20th centuries, is well worth a visit. If you still have time, complete the day's outing by passing by Kinderdijk with a greater concentration of windmills than anywhere else in Holland today.

Thursday mornings from mid-June to mid-August there is a lively cheese market, quite different from its rival at Alkmaar. Instead of porters wearing colored hats, there are brightly painted farm wagons loaded high with orange cheeses. While the bargaining is going on, you can sample the cheese by stepping into the back of the Town Hall, where a color film explains how it is manufactured.

After you've had a look at the 1668 Waag, or Weigh House, built by Pieter Post who did Leiden's, stroll around to the front of the Town Hall itself, one of the quaintest and oldest in all the Netherlands. Parts of it date back as far as 1449, the Gothic façade, for example. The Renaissance staircase was added two centuries later. Happily it stands free and unencumbered so that we can view it with the same perspective the builders intended.

The towers of the 15th-century Sint Janskerk attract us next. Some of the stained glass inside this, the country's longest church, with a 400 ft. nave, approaches that of Chartres in delicacy of color and boldness of design. Fifteen of the windows are attributed to Wouter and Dirk Crabeth, most of the others being executed by their pupils. The first ones were begun in 1555, the last ones were completed in 1603. Willem the Silent, who is represented in #25 depicting the relief of Leiden, donated a window (#22, the driving of the money-changers from the temple). So did his archrival Philip II of Spain (#7, the dedication of the temple by Solomon, and the Last Supper, in which he appears with his consort, Mary Tudor). Even Erasmus is pictured—Gouda claims he was conceived within its limits even though he was born in Rotterdam. Altogether there are 70 windows, whose 2,412 panels form a surface of nearly half an acre. No glazier's work like this is being done in Holland today, for it is a craft whose secrets seem to have been lost, a point you can confirm by looking at window #28a which represents the occupation and liberation of the Netherlands during 1940-5.

In the Catharina Gasthuis adjoining Sint Jans is the municipal museum with many quaint exhibits. One of them is one of the finest gold chalices in existence, given to the Society of Archers in 1465 by Countess Jacqueline of Bavaria, lost for a century or more, and then recovered. Another item is a terracotta plaque claiming Erasmus as Gouda's own. You can also see a fearsome collection of medieval surgical instruments more suggestive of a torture chamber than a means of restoring health.

Close by in the Spieringstraat is the façade of an old orphanage. At 29 Westhaven is a 17th-century merchant's house called De Moriaan containing a collection of the clay pipes for which Gouda has long been noted. More of them can be seen in the Goedewaagen factory, which also makes Delftware pottery. One of their more interesting products is a so-called mystery pipe. When new it is pure white, but as it turns brown through use a pattern appears on the bowl. Just what the design will be the buyer never knows in advance.

Oudewater's Witches and Schoonhoven's Silver

From Gouda our route lies east about 13 km. (8 miles) to the charming village of Oudewater, an old rope-making town that achieved great fame during the 16th-century witchcraft mania. Because the district around Oudewater was one of the worst persecutors of witches and because the resulting reputation was hurting business, the people of the town, who were also regarded as being among the most honest merchants in Europe with the most accurate weights and scales, passed an ordinance requiring that all alleged witches be brought to the Weigh House. Dressed only in a witch's costume of paper, complete with a paper broom, the accused person was placed on the scales in the ceremonial presence of the mayor, the alderman, the weighmaster, and (for a reason now unknown) the chief local midwife. After careful adjustments of weights and scales, the weighmaster solemnly declared that the suspect was too heavy to ride safely on a broomstick. A certificate to this effect was then issued, which shortly became so valuable that people came from as far away as Germany to get it.

It is still possible, between May and September, to present yourself at Oudewater's Weigh House, step on the scales, and receive the diploma. This valuable service is offered from April 1 to October 31, on Tuesday–Saturday 10–5, Sunday 12–5. Admission a modest Fl.1. It is worthwhile exploring afterwards. Oudewater went up in flames twice (witchcraft?), most recently in 1575, with the result that many buildings show the pleasing lines and stately proportions of the Dutch Renaissance. The Town Hall is one of these, and on its roof you'll note the nests of storks who have returned here faithfully every March for nearly 350 years.

From Oudewater we retrace our steps west for 8 km. (5 miles) to Haastrecht, turn left, and follow a delightful country road south along the Vlist River to the town of Schoonhoven. Here, if you are interested in watching silver filigree jewelry being made, are a host of small workshops where visitors are welcome. The technique used is unusual and requires a high degree of skill. Unfortunately most of the output consists of souvenir gewgaws featuring windmills, wooden shoes, and tulips. To see more ambitious silverware, pay a visit to the Edelambachtshuis on the main canal, where there are demonstrations of silver flatware, candlesticks, salt-and-pepper shakers, and the like, which are for sale. The Town Hall, a few doors away, is a Gothic jewel that dates back to 1452. Its bells were cast from ships' cannon, and a circle of stones in front recalls the spot where a witch was burned.

A must for anyone interested in gold, silver or old clocks is the Nederlands Goud-, Zilver- en Klokkenmuseum just behind the Waag (Weigh House). The specialized collections are among the finest in Holland, covering the 17th-century Golden Age of Dutch craftsmanship. There is also a reconstruction of an old silversmith's workshop.

The broad Lek River flows past Schoonhoven's southern edge. We cross it on a ferry and turn west along the river dike that protects the polderland from inundation when tidal waters back up from Rotterdam. The dike twists and turns around every bend in the river as we look into the upper stories of farm buildings alongside. Farther downstream towards Kinderdijk the houses are built on top of the dike itself and are actually a part of it. If you look closely you'll note vertical slots on either side of every door and passageway. These hold wooden boards in times when there is danger of flooding, thus giving the dike an extra meter or so of effective height up to the level of the windowsills.

More and more windmills come into view until just before Kinderdijk, where no less than 19 can be seen. On Saturday afternoons in July and August they are put into operation.

Dordrecht and Gorinchem

Claiming to be the oldest town in Holland, Dordrecht lies just east of the main road leading south to Antwerp and Brussels. Thanks to its location in the midst of a tangle of waterways, the Noord, Merwede and Oude Maas, it was once among the most important towns in the Netherlands. Fortified in 1271, its surrounding lands were badly damaged by the St. Elizabeth flood of 1421, when whole villages were drowned, an event recalled by a stained glass window in the town's Grote Kerk. Here the Protestant synod met in 1618 to settle the controversy that had arisen between Arminius and Gomarus, two professors of theology at Leiden. Arminius proposed a relaxing of the strict Calvinist teachings, a viewpoint espoused by Oldenbarneveldt, whereas Gomarus believed in no compromise. His doctrine, supported by Prince Maurits, prevailed at the synod, which condemned all Arminians as heretics. The political consequences of this religious debate troubled the Netherlands for many years afterwards and were responsible, in part, for the execution of Oldenbarneveldt and the murder of the De Witt brothers, who were born in Dordrecht.

Today the city is a major shipbuilding and yachting center with a strange mixture of new and old. The oldest section of Dordrecht lies along the riverfront—indeed, the best view of the city is from the opposite (north) bank—and in the streets leading back inland to the Voorstraat. Dominating the scene is the imposing mass of the 15th-century Grote Kerk, whose tower is a good 2 meters (6 feet) off the vertical. A window pictures the 1421 disaster, and the huge 3,600-pipe organ has a 10-second echo. The interior is astonishing because it is gleaming white. Its white marble pulpit with a mahogany sounding-board weighing more than a ton contrasts strikingly with the great bronze screen. The carving on the choir stalls depicts the history of the world from the Garden of Eden to Charles V (1542).

From the church follow the Voorstraat (on the far side of the canal), with old houses at every turn, to the Groenmarkt, where you will find one of the city's most fascinating houses. At No. 105 you'll find another historic building, dating from 1562 and called De Sleutel. No. 43 has a late Gothic façade. From the Groenmarkt follow Wijnstraat to the delightful early-17th-century Groothoofdspoort gate at the end. Here the rivers Oude Maas, Noord and Beneden Merwede join; the view here is said to have no equal in the Netherlands.

The Dordrecht Museum has a large collection of paintings by artists who were born here—the so-called Dordrecht School—including Aelbert Cuyp, Ary Scheffer, Nicolaas Maes, and Samuel van Hoogstraten. There are also a number of modern works. Worth a visit, too, is the Museum Simon van Gijn in an old patrician house. There is a collection of dolls, furniture and kitchen utensils, as well as a toy museum in the garden which will be of special interest to children since the dolls move and are rather exceptional.

Don't miss De Hof or "the court," so-called because it was here that the history of the Netherlands began when representatives of Prince Willem the Silent and of the 12 largest towns (with the exception of

Amsterdam) met in 1572 to organize opposition to their Spanish over-lords and to proclaim Willem the Silent as the sole Stadholder of the Free States.

About 27 km. (17 miles) east of Dordrecht is Gorinchem (pro-nounced "Gorkum"), a tiny fortified town dating back to the 13th century. Its Gasthuispoortje gate is amongst the oldest in the Nether-lands, and at 25 Gasthuisstraat is the Dit is Bethlehem house (1566). It has been made into a museum and shows the development of the town as well as paintings, dolls, historical clothes and a collection of coins.

Two or three kilometers southeast of Gorinchem, in the angle formed by the Maas and Waal rivers, is the 14th-century castle of Loevestein, which has had a dramatic history. Grotius, the great jurist, was imprisoned here in 1619 but escaped two years later, appropriately enough in a chest supposed to contain books.

PRACTICAL INFORMATION FOR SOUTH HOLLAND

TELEPHONE CODES. We have given telephone codes for all the towns and villages in this chapter in the hotel and restaurant lists that follow. These codes need only be used when calling from outside the town or village concerned.

HOTELS AND RESTAURANTS. Outside the main cities, South Holland offers only modest accommodations, the reason being that visitors tend to concentrate in the cities and use them as touring bases. However, most of the places mentioned below have good, mostly small hotels at much more reasonable prices than in the cities.

The situation is rather different as regards restaurants: there is an abundance of good eating places, indeed there are few areas in Holland where there are more to the square mile than in South Holland. However, prices do reflect quality and even the smaller, rural restaurants tend to be fairly expensive.

We have divided the hotels and restaurants in our listings into three catego-ries—Expensive (E), Moderate (M) and Inexpensive (I). Price ranges for these categories for both hotels and restaurants are given in the *Facts at Your Finger-tips* (see pp. 17–18). Some hotels, particularly at the upper end of the scale, have rooms in more than one category. Similarly, many restaurants have dishes in more than one category, so be sure to check the menu outside before you go in. Look out too for the excellent value Tourist Menu.

ALBLASSERDAM. *Het Wapen van Alblasserdam* (M), 24 Dam; 01859–14711. 30 rooms.

ALPHEN AAN DE RIJN. *Toor* (M), 2 Stationsplein; 01720–72118. 29 rooms, 16 with bath or shower. Right by the station.

Restaurants. *Avifauna* (M), 65 Hoorn; 01720–31087. In the Avifauna park. *'s Molenaarsbrug* (M), 2 Molenaarsweg; 01720–32087. Good restaurant in hotel of the same name.

BOSKOOP. *De Landbouw* (M), 26 Koninginneweg; 01722–3223. *Neuf* (M), 10 Barendstraat; 01727–2031.

BRIELLE. *De Zalm* (E), 6–8 Voorstraat; 01810–13388. 30 rooms, good restaurant.

DELFT. *De Ark* (E), 65 Koornmarkt; 015–140552. *Juliana* (M), 33 Maarten Trompstraat; 015–567612. *Leeuwenbrug* (E), 16 Koornmarkt; 015–123062. *'t Raethuijs* (M), 38 Markt; 015–125115. *De Vlaming* (M), 52 Vlamingstraat; 015–132127.
Restaurants. *Le Chevalier* (E), 125 Oude Delft; 015–124621. French restaurant; best in town. *Prinsenkelder* (E), 11 Schoolstraat; 015–121860. Impressive hall in the Prinsenhof museum, with good food and service. *De Dis* (M), 36 Beestenmarkt; 015–131782. For good Dutch cooking. *Stadsherberg De Mol* (M), 48a Molslaan; 015–121343. Food served in medieval style.

DORDRECHT. *Bellevue* (M), 37 Boomstraat; 078–137900. 20 rooms, 9 with bath. Has remarkable view over the four-arm junction of the Maas. *Dordrecht* (M), 12 Achterhakkers; 078–136011. 22 rooms and restaurant. *Klarenbeek* (M), 35 Joh. de Wittstraat; 078–144133. 22 rooms. Thoroughly recommended. *Postiljon Dordrecht 's Gravendeel* (M), 30 Rijksstraatweg; 078–184444. On the road to Breda. 96 rooms.
Restaurants. *Au Bon Coin* (E), 1 Groenmarkt; 078–138230. Good French cuisine. *Camelot* (E), 389 A. Cuypsingel; 078–144929. Highly recommended. *Herberg de Hellebaard* (M), 37 Boomstraat; 078–137900. Dutch specialties.

GOEDEREEDE. *Motel Koningspleisterplaats* (M), 18 Provinciaalweg; 01879 –1223. 16 rooms; heated pool.

GORINCHEM. *Metropole* (M), 3 Melkpad; 01830–30778. Only 9 rooms but pleasant. *Motel Gorinchem* (M), 8 van Hogendorpweg; 01830–22400.

GOUDA. *Het Blauwe Kruis* (M), 4 Westhaven; 01820–12677. 22 rooms, none with bath. *L'Empereur* (M), 11 Keizerstraat; 01820–28096. Small hotel with restaurant. *De Utrechtse Dom* (M), 6 Grenzenstraat; 01820–27984. Pleasant and small. *De Zalm* (M), 34 Markt; 01820–12344. Claims to be the oldest hotel in Holland. 25 rooms with bath.
Restaurants. *Mallemolen* (E), 72 Oosthaven; 01820–15430. Atmospheric and traditional French dishes. *Rôtisserie l'Etoile* (E), 1 Blekerssingel; 01820–12253. Exclusive; French cuisine. *Centraal* (M), 23 Markt; 01820–12576. Dutch dishes. *Old Dutch* (M), 25 Markt; 01820–21347.

HOEK VAN HOLLAND. *America* (M), 96 Rietdijkstraat; 01747–2290. 25 rooms; close to ferry.
Restaurant. *Koetshuis* (M), 108 Rietdijkstraat; 01747–2817. Typical Dutch atmosphere, 5 mins. from ferry port.

182   HOLLAND

KATWIJK AAN ZEE. *Noordzee* (M), 72 Boulevard; 01718–13450. *Zee en Duin* (M), 5 Boulevard; 01718–13320. *Lindehof* (M), 67 Boulevard; 01718–13134. All rooms with balcony, facing the sea.

LEIDEN. *Holiday Inn* (E), 10 Haagse Schouweg; 071–769310. 200 rooms with bath. All the expected Holiday Inn comforts, plus indoor pool, tropical garden, sauna and good restaurant *Dutch Mill. Mayflower* (M), 5 St. Aagtenstraat; 071–142641. 15 rooms. Near Ethnological Museum; no restaurant. *Nieuw Minerva* (M), 23 Boommarkt; 071–126358. 40 rooms, all with bath. *Pension Bik* (I), 92 Witte Singel; 071–122602. 10 rooms. *Pension Witte* (I), 80 Witte Singel; 071–124592. 10 rooms.
    Restaurants. *Rôtisserie Oudt Leyden* (E), 51 Steenstraat; 071–133144. Traditional Dutch restaurant near the Lakenhal on the street from the station; best in town. *Bernsen* (M), 157 Breestraat; 071–124563. Good tourist menus. *Bistro de la Cloche* (M), 3 Kloksteeg; 071–123053. *De Doelen* (M), 2 Rapenburg; 071–120527. Pleasant, on the atmospheric Rapenburg canal. *Het Koetshuis* (M); 071–121688. At foot of Burchthill. *Pannekoekenhuis* (I), Steenstraat. Wide range of inexpensive pancakes and beers.

LEIDSCHENDAM. Restaurant. *Chagall* (E), 20 Weigelia, Leidschenhage; 070–276910. Elegant atmosphere with lovely views, one of the best. Also excellent with fine French food is *Villa Rozenrust* (E), 104 Veursestraatweg; 070–277460.

LISSE. *De Nachtegaal van Lisse* (E), 10 Heereweg; 02512–14447. 130 rooms. A mile or so out of town on the road to Hillegom. Golden Tulip hotel. *De Duif* (M), 17 Westerdreef; 02521–10076. 21 rooms.
    Restaurant. *De Engel* (M), 386 Hereweg.

MIDDELHARNIS. Restaurant. *De Hooge Heerlijkheid* (E), 21 Voorstraat; 01870–3264. Excellent traditional Dutch restaurant; highly recommended.

NOORDWIJK AAN ZEE. (Most hotels close for the winter). *Noordzee* (E), 8 Kon. Wilhelminaboulevard; 01719–19205. 85 rooms, all with bath. Near the sea and probably the best hotel in town. *Astoria* (M), 13 Emmaweg; 01719–13484. 26 rooms. *Fiantema* (M), 32 Juliananstraat; 01719–13684. 30 rooms. Good value for the price. *Marie Rose* (M), 25 Emmaweg; 01719–12697. 25 rooms. *Noordwijk* (M), 7 Parallelboulevard; 01719–19231. 92 rooms, most with bath. Golden Tulip hotel.
    Restaurants. *Badhotel Zeerust* (E), 103 Quarles van Uffordstraat; 01719–12723. Best restaurant in town by a mile. Delicious seafood specialties. *De Graaf van het Hoogveen* (E), 103 Q. van Uffordstraat; 01719–14323. Excellent.

OEGSTGEEST. Restaurant. *De Beukenhof* (E), 2 Terweeweg; 071–173188. Attractive inn in a delightful garden; the best dining you'll find in this corner of Holland.

ROCKANJE. *Badhotel Rockanje* (M), 1 Tweede Slag; 01814–1755. 60 rooms. Near the beach; heated pool. *De Dreef* (M), 1 Swinsdreef; 01814–1100. 14 rooms.

SASSENHEIM. *Motel Sassenheim* (M), 8 Warmonderweg; 02522–19019. 60 rooms. A mile or so out of town on the road to Den Haag.

SCHIEDAM. *Novotel Rotterdam-Schiedam* (M), 2 Hargalaan; 010–4713322. 140 rooms. Heated pool. On the Rotterdam–Vlaardingen road a little out of town. *Rijnmond* (M), 12 Nieuwelandplein; 010–738666.

VIANEN. *Motel Vianen* (M), 75 Pr. Bernhardstraat; 03473–72484. 54 rooms. A little out of town on the Utrecht–'s-Hertogenbosch road. *Het Zwijnshoofd* (M), 6 Prinses Julianastraat; 03473–71286. 14 rooms only.

VLAARDINGEN. *Delta* (E), 15 Maasboulevard; 010–4345477. 80 rooms, most with bath. Overhangs the river on a bold cantilever; fine view and restaurant. Also has pool and sauna. A Crest hotel.

WASSENAAR. **Hotel/restaurant.** *Auberge de Kievit* (E), 27 Stueplaan; 01751–19232. In woods, 11 km. from Den Haag. Only 6 rooms but truly superb restaurant.

TOURIST INFORMATION. The most important regional VVV offices are at the following places: **Delft,** 85 Markt (tel. 015–126100); **Dordrecht,** 1 Stationsweg (tel. 078–132800); **Gouda,** 27 Markt (tel. 01820–13666); **Hoek van Holland,** 23 Hoekse Brink (tel. 01747–2446); **Leiden,** 210 Stationsplein (tel. 071–146846); **Noordwijk,** 8 de Grent (tel. 01719–19321); **Schiedam,** 9 Buitenshavenweg (tel. 010–733000).

MUSEUMS. South Holland, rich in historic towns and cities, is similarly rich in museums. A visit to some of the more prominent should be a must for any visitor. Below, we list some of the best.

DELFT. Koninklijk Nederlands Leger—en Wapenmuseum "General Hoefer". Situated in the Armamentarium, Korte Geer, illustrates the development of weapons and the armed forces of Dutch territories. Open Tues. to Sat. 10–5, Sun. 1–5.

Museum Huis Lambert van Meerten, 199 Oude Delft. Imposing 19th-century mansion with excellent collections of Delftware, plus much 16th-, 17th- and 18th-century furniture. Open Tues.–Sat. 10–5, Sun. 1–5. Adm. Fl. 3.50 (includes adm. to Prinsenhof).

Museum Paul Tetar van Elven, 67 Koornmarkt. Home of the 19th-century painter with original furnishings and furniture, plus a 17th-century style studio. Open mid-Apr.–mid-Oct, Tues.–Sat. 11–5. Adm. Fl. 2.

Museum Het Prinsenhof, 185 Oude Delft. Built in the early 16th-century as a convent, this subsequently became the residence of Willem the Silent, and it was here that he was assassinated in 1584. The museum has been carefully restored to resemble its appearance during Willem's time. Besides temporary exhibits, it records the Dutch struggle against the Spanish in the 16th century. Open Tues.–Sat. 10–5, Sun. 1–5. Adm. Fl. 3.50.

Nusantara (Ethnological Museum), 4 Agathaplein. Masks, weapons, artifacts from the Indonesian cultural area. Tickets combined with Prinsenhof Museum. Open Tues.–Sat. 10–5, Sun. 1–5. Closed Mon.

DORDRECHT. Dordrechts Museum, 40 Museumstraat. Good picture gallery with representative collections of Dutch 16th- and 17th-century painters and Den Haag school. Open Tues.–Sat. 10–5, Sun. 1–5. Adm. Fl. 2.

Museum Simon van Gijn, 29 Nieuwe Haven. Attractive early 18th-century merchant's house, good collections of ceramics, model ships, toys, medals and coins. Open Tues.–Sat. 10–5, Sun. 1–5. Adm. Fl. 1.50.

GOUDA. Stedelijk Museum Het Catharina Gasthuis, 10 Oosthaven. Mansion dating from 1665 housing, among its many treasures, guild relics, furniture, a triptych by Dirck Barendtsz and a solid gold Gothic chalice dating from the 15th century; there is also a terra cotta plaque of Erasmus with an inscription in Latin claiming that the great humanist was conceived in Gouda (though born in Rotterdam). Open Mon. to Sat. 10–5, Sun. 12–5. Adm. Fl. 2.

Stedelijk Museum De Moriaan, 29 Westhaven. 17th-century merchant's home containing extensive collection of pipes and ceramics. Open Mon.–Sat. 10–12.30, 1.30–5. Sun. 12–5. Adm. Fl.2.

LEIDEN. Stedelijk Molenmuseum de Valk (Windmill Museum), 2 Binnenvestgracht. Small museum, located in a windmill, appropriately enough. Open daily 10–5, Sun. 1–5. Closed Mon. Adm. Fl. 2.50.

Museum Boerhaave (National Science Museum), 1 Steenstraat. Splendid museum containing many important and historic Dutch scientific instruments: two globes that belonged to the cartographer Blaeu, microscopes made by Van Leeuwenhoek, thermometers made by Farenheit, an early planetarium, and a room devoted to the physician and astronomer Huygens; plus sections on biology, astronomy, chemistry etc. Open Tues.–Sat. 10–5, Sun. 1–5. Closed Mon. Adm. Fl. 3.50.

Leids Pilgrim Documentatie Centrum (Pilgrim Fathers' Museum), 45 Vliet, near Vliet River. A tiny museum housing photocopies of documents and maps etc. relating to the Pilgrim Fathers during their stay in Leiden, from where they left to go to Delftshaven on the first stage of their arduous voyage to the New World. Open Mon.–Fri. 9.30–4.30. Closed Sat. and Sun. Adm. free.

Rijksmuseum van Geologie en Mineralogie (National Geological and Mineralogy Museum), 17 Hooglandse Kerkgracht. Excellently displayed museum in series of 17th- and 18th-century buildings; minerals, jewels, meteorites galore. Open Mon.–Fri. 10–5, Sun. 2–5. Adm. Fl.3.

Rijksmuseum Van Oudheden (National Museum of Antiquities), 28 Rapenburg. Outstanding collection of antiquities; one of the leading European museums of its type. Greek pottery, Egyptian items, including several mummies. Other displays on Dutch prehistoric finds, plus Roman, Frankish and Saxon treasures. Open Tues.–Sat. 10–5, Sun. 1–5. Closed Mon. Adm. Fl. 3.50.

Rijksmuseum voor Volkenkunde (National Ethnological Museum), 1 Steenstraat. Has an unusually rich collection of objects from the Far East, Africa and the Americas. Open Tues.–Sat. 10–5, Sun. 1–5. Closed Mon. Adm. Fl. 3.50.

Stedelijk Museum De Lakenhal, 28 Oude Singel. Housed in the early 17th-century cloth merchants' guild hall. Pride of place here goes to the collection of Dutch 16th- and 17th-century pictures, with works by Steen, Dou, Rembrandt and, above all, a triptych by Lucas van Leyden, certainly his masterpiece and the first great Dutch Renaissance painting. Other rooms are devoted to furniture, the history of the cloth guild and to the Pilgrim Fathers. Open Tues.–Sat. 10–5, Sun. 1–5. Closed Mon. Adm. Fl. 2.50.

SCHOONHOVEN. Nederlands Goud, Zilver en Klokkenmuseum (Dutch Gold, Silver and Clock Museum), 7 Oude Haven. As the name says, gold, silver and clocks; interesting and attractive. Open Tues.–Sat. 10–5, Sun. 1–5. Closed Mon. Adm. Fl. 3.

Het Zilverhof (The Silver House), 13 Haven. Silver, pottery and glassware. Demonstrations by silversmiths on application. Open Tues.–Sat. 10–5, Sun. 1–5. Adm. Fl.2.50.

VLAARDINGEN. Museum voor de Nederlandse Visserij (Fishing Museum), 53 Westhavenkade. Models and pictures documenting Dutch fishing through the ages; plus period rooms, diorama and aquarium. Open daily 10–5, Sun. 2–5.

SHOPPING. Every visitor to Holland scurries off to Delft, often called the loveliest little city in the Netherlands. Its heart is the charming Prinsenhof, about which cluster a few curio shops.

The place for genuine blue Delftware is Reynders, 45 Markt, where you will also find the products of the Royal Delftware Manufactury, De Porceleyne Fles, 196 Rotterdamseweg. The purchasable pieces here, of course, are completely new and not antique. However, they are made in the traditional manner, still hand-painted by craftsmen.

If your interest lies in antiques, plot to coincide with the annual Antique Dealers' Fair, housed in the enchanting Prinsenhof palace. Here, noted Dutch experts gather their treasures for the benefit of buyers who come from all over the world. Gouda is a city of ceramics, pipes and cheeses, all of which are on sale in great profusion.

Handpainted Royal Gouda pottery can be found in many forms, such as vases, plates, ashtrays, and beakers. The predominant colors are beige and red, though modern adaptations of Delft blue in big floral patterns are fairly prevalent. Gouda is also famous for its thick, heavy white candles whose clear flame burns for a long time. For guided tours of Delft blue in Gouda visit De Drietand B.V., 5 Stavorenweg.

At Moordrecht, near Gouda, the Royal Netherlands Carpet Factory makes unusual hand-knotted rugs. If you have the time and inclination for a visit, you will be a welcome guest.

Schoonhoven is the Dutch silver center for both factory-made and hand-wrought trinkets.

CENTRAL HOLLAND

Utrecht, Gelderland and Overijssel

The central area of the Netherlands—covering the three Provinces of Utrecht, Gelderland and Overijssel and the former Zuyder Zee (Zuiderzee), now the IJsselmeer—is considered by many Dutch people to be the most beautiful in the country. Probably this is because when approaching the region from the west, south or north the landscape suddenly bursts into lovely old trees amidst which are fairylike castles, attractive hotels and beautiful mansions.

Utrecht, with a population of 450,000 living in an area of 1,382 square kilometers (535 square miles) is the smallest province in the Netherlands. But it has such a variety of features for the visitor that it is often called "Holland in a Nutshell." It is an area that combines many features seen to be "typically Dutch," and, being small and compact, it is easy to arrange a touring plan that covers many of the major attractions in a relatively short time.

Next to Utrecht is the park-strewn province of Gelderland, stretching across to the German border. Although as steeped in history as any Dutch province, Gelderland seems to put the emphasis on the beauties of outdoor life. For within its boundaries it has Holland's largest national park, its largest open-air exhibition, and a great variety of beautiful parks.

Overijssel, third of these lovely provinces, is not visited by foreign tourists as much as it should be. It has its own character, and accommodation and food are less expensive than in the major cities.

Exploring Central Holland

The capital of Utrecht Province is the city of Utrecht, Holland's fourth-largest city, with a population of some 234,000, and known all over the world for its regular industrial and trade fairs, which continue to expand in size and importance.

Utrecht has so many curiosities and antiquities to offer with its high-gabled houses, picturesque water-gates, and winding canals that it is well worth spending a night or two here. Especially worth visiting are the wharves and cellars along the main canals, which have been extensively reconstructed and are believed to be unique. Every Sunday from June to August, a walking tour leaves from the VVV office at 10.30 A.M. which covers many of the city's most interesting features.

Until very recently Utrecht was dominated by the 111-meter (365-foot) tower of the Cathedral, known as the Dom. But the tall Holiday Inn and the modern Hoog Catherijne complex have now joined the Dom in the skies, and this combination of two contrasting worlds at such close quarters in one town sums up the contrasts to be seen everywhere in Holland.

The Domkerk was built during the period 1254 to 1517 on the site of the earlier 7th-century St. Martin's Cathedral which had been destroyed by fire in 1253. Misfortune dogged its life story however, because in 1674 the nave of the present building collapsed during a storm. The sturdy tower remained undamaged, apart from some projecting decorations. The remains of the nave were not cleared away until 1826 when the church was given a new front, a new Gothic door and the tower became self-standing. Thus the so-called cathedral, although still traditionally revered, now consists of a large church with several chapels, the tomb of the Holy Sepulchre, monumental tombs, and a series of fine modern stained-glass windows, separated from its tower by a large square.

The Dom Tower has 465 steps, and can be climbed by those whose legs feel fit for the task. If in doubt, remember you can rest at the 14th-century St. Michael's Chapel halfway up. On the way you pass the heavy church bells, 13 in number and weighing over 13,000 kg., as they were in 1506, and the cathedral's carillon. Thirty-five of the 50 bells were cast in 1663–4 by the Hemony brothers, and the chimes make up the largest musical instrument of its kind and the highest set of bells in the Netherlands. But if you want to hear these at their best, sit quietly in the cloisters between the cathedral and the university. In the latter is the famous Treaty of Utrecht Hall.

For many centuries the present-day Domplein or Cathedral Square was the site of a Roman fortification. This lasted until the Anglo-Saxon priest Willibrord formed the two churches of St. Salvator and St. Martin there in 690 and converted this region of the Netherlands to Christianity. Their destruction was followed by the construction of the huge Dom, the country's largest medieval church, its tower being the highest of its kind in the Netherlands. The cloisters now connect with the former Hall of the Chapter, where the Union of Utrecht was signed in 1579 to lay the foundations of the later Kingdom of the Netherlands.

But do not linger here too long, as Utrecht has much to show you. Apart from the unusually large number of churches grouped around the cathedral, there is Rijks Museum Het Catharijneconvent (St. Catherine's Convent) with its collection of paintings, carvings, vestments, and religious relics, all beautifully showing the evolution of Christianity in the Netherlands from the 8th to the 20th centuries. The display is highly recommended but very large, so be sure to have time: the lovely Bruntenhofje Almshouses for old ladies in Lepelenburg; the Bartholomei Gasthuis (Bartholomew Guesthouse) for old men in Lange Smeetstraat—which unfortunately cannot be visited—with its magnificent Gobelin tapestries of 1644 around the four walls of the Regent's room; the Butchers' Guildhall of 1673 in Lange Nieuwstraat; the Cracknel House in Keistraat with its extraordinary decorations; and the chained "Devil's Stone" on the Oude Gracht.

Due west of Utrecht lies Woerden, about 18 km. (11 miles) by road, full of historic buildings, with a castle and a museum thrown in.

The second-largest city in Utrecht Province is Amersfoort. Although today it is a town of industrial importance, Amersfoort has never completely lost its medieval character. Amersfoort's charter was granted in 1259 and it is the only European city with a center enclosed by a double ring of canals.

To the sightseer it presents the graceful and imposing 15th-century 107-meter (350-foot) Gothic Tower of Our Lady, Onze Lieve Vrouwetoren, with its lovely carillon which can be heard every Friday between 10 and 11 A.M.; the splendid Koppelpoort of 1440, a magnificent watergate bridging the River Eem, which dominates the approach by land and water; the St. Pieters-en-Bloklands Gasthuis, a hospice of 1390; the Museum Flehite, with its unusual medieval collections; and several other gateways, old buildings, and historic sites. But above all, Amersfoort has a special Dutch atmosphere that gives it a peculiar charm. Local trumpeters appear occasionally in the city center on Saturdays during the summer.

Amersfoort is very conveniently located as a center for day-trips in this region. In the immediate vicinity are Spakenburg, Bunschoten and Hilversum (described in earlier chapters); Loosdrecht (yachting); River Vecht area (old mansions); Hoge Veluwe National Park and Kröller-Müller Art Gallery of Van Goghs and outside sculptures; Zuyder Zee works; outdoor bathing pools, woods and zoos. There are many beauty spots in the area, including estates and parks; Treek-Henschoten, 21 square kilometers (8 square miles) with walking paths; Nimmerdor; Randenbroek; and Birkhoven with lake and pinetum.

The Eemland region of meadows, polders and woods on each side of the River Eem was for centuries a miniature battlefield as the Bishops of Utrecht, the Counts of Holland and the Dukes of Geldern contended for it.

Het Gooi

Draw an imaginary line from Utrecht to Amersfoort, and the land north of it, with the River Vecht as its western boundary, extending to the IJsselmeer, once known as the Zuyder Zee, is the lovely region known as Het Gooi, which we first visited during an excursion from Amsterdam (see earlier chapter). Part of its beauty is due to the fact that this land has always been above sea level and has therefore had time to grow the great trees that are absent from the polders.

Part of this region is in Noord Holland, and has already been described. But the rest of it is in the province of Utrecht, and from that city you can explore it to the northeast or northwest.

If you take the first direction, with the intention of going through Baarn to the IJsselmeer costume towns of Bunschoten and Spakenburg, you will see some of the loveliest homes in Holland. Many of them, though of modern construction, have thatched roofs of intriguing shapes, inspired by the older farmhouses of the country. If you drive, pass through Bilthoven to see some fine examples of the domestic architecture of Gooiland.

At Soestdijk, near Baarn, is the Palace of the Queen Mother, modernized and furnished as a wedding present from the Dutch people. Here, in the heart of Holland, are the four "Soest" villages—Soest, Soestdijk, Soestduinen, and Soesterberg. Quiet hotels are hidden in the woods, and although successive wars have wiped out practically all historic buildings and relics, the district caters for modern needs with its bathing pools, open-air theater, lakes, and magnificent woods. Het Militaire Luchtvaart Museum (Royal Dutch Air Force Museum) at the Soesterberg Air Base is open to the public.

A few kilometers west of Soest, near the village of Lage Vuursche, lies the delightful, small, octagonal 17th-century castle of Drakestein, property of Queen Beatrix and her former residence where, before her coronation, she lived with her husband Prince Claus of the Netherlands and their three sons.

For idyllic scenery, a drive along the River Vecht west of Utrecht will introduce you to a chain of villages that have retained a beauty as attractive as their names: Zuilen, Maarssen, Breukelen, Nieuwersluis, Loenen, and Nigtevecht. Here is a real tourist playground with old-fashioned inns, medieval buildings, and the magnificent Vecht mansions with their garden tea-houses along the river.

Yachting enthusiasts visiting Utrecht Province will be enticed on to the wide stretches of the Loosdrecht Lakes. (Loosdrecht is the headquarters of the Royal Water Sports Club.) The extensive waters are lined with villages and inns, and from any of them as a center, sailing, fishing, swimming, motorboat trips, and journeys up and down the River Vecht can fill up a week of wonderful outdoor life.

Regional Castles

Lovers of castles, from authentic 12th-century ruins to contemporary restorations, are well served in this province. A few which can be visited are Haarzuilens and Zuylen, near Utrecht; Zuilenstein near Amerongen; and Guntherstein near Breukelen. The ruins of the 13th-century castle Wijk-bij-Duurstede are the essence of the romantic.

Some 6 km. (4 miles) west of Utrecht, at Haarzuilens, is the imposing 15th-century castle De Haar, with gardens reminiscent of Versailles. Gutted by fire during the last century, a fortuitous marriage with one of the Rothschild family provided the money for its restoration. Although still occupied by the owners, it can be visited from mid-March to mid-August, and from mid-October to mid-November between Tuesday and Friday. The medieval Gobelins, French furniture, Oriental treasures and Spanish primitives are well worth a visit. The gardens are open all year, except from August 15 to October 15.

Sypesteyn Castle, near Nieuw Loosdrecht, started in 1288, destroyed during Charles V's time, and restored according to the original ground-plans, is now a museum that concentrates on furniture, porcelain, silver, glassware and paintings.

About 18 km. (11 miles) east of Utrecht is Doorn, exile home of the ex-Kaiser of Germany from 1920 to 1941. The manor castle, which lies hidden in a belt of woods, is now a museum. It contains an extensive collection of odds and ends connected with the history of the former German Royal House, and shows that ex-Kaiser Wilhelm did his best to keep his illusion of emperorship alive at least in his own tiny domain. His remarkable personality is indelibly stamped inside the castle, from the rusty horseshoes he hung over the doorway of each room for luck to the incredible gallery of photos and paintings and statues of himself he scattered incongruously everywhere. Strict in discipline both for himself and his staff, his study still contains the full-size riding saddle mounted on stilts on which he did every scrap of his writing. Here, too, are the unique collections of Wedgwood and snuff-boxes, tapestries and silver, all belonging to Frederick the Great of Prussia which the Kaiser brought with him from Germany. The park contains a collection of conifers from all over the world.

Between Doorn and Utrecht lies Driebergen, in the center of several lovely villages. Just outside on one of the heights is an earth pyramid surmounted by a sandstone obelisk, erected in 1805 by French soldiers to celebrate the victory of Austerlitz.

Vianen, 14 km. (9 miles) south of Utrecht, is seldom visited by tourists, but has a most attractive collection of medieval buildings. These include two 15th-century gateways known as Lekpoort and Hofpoort, a 15th-century Town Hall, and other memories of the famous Counts of Brederode.

By the River Vecht between Utrecht and Maarssen is Slot Zuylen. Built before 1300, this is one of the most characteristically medieval castles in the Netherlands. For generations it was in the hands of the van Tuyll van Serooskerken family and was modernized by J. Marot for Diederik Jacob van Zuylen in the 18th century. His daughter, the well-known writer, Belle van Zuylen, spent a large part of her youth here. The castle was turned into a museum in 1952 and most of the rooms are in the same state as when they were inhabited. In addition there is a collection of old charters, with letters written by the Duke of Alva and Willem the Silent among others.

On now to the southeast corner of the province for Rhenen, poetically called the Pleasure Grounds of the Bishopric. But whether you feel like a bishop or not, you can be sure of having a good time here. Heavily damaged during the last battles of World War II, it has been completely restored, with all its objects of pride bursting to show themselves to the visitor. There is the 15th-century Sint Cunerakerk and Tower; the most attractive cageless and fenceless zoo in Europe in the Ouwehand park and dolphinarium; and the well-stocked Streekmuseum, the district museum at 25 Molenstraat. In Rhenen are the last resting places of many fallen soldiers of the Allied Forces and their graves have been "adopted" and cared for by the locals.

Gelderland, Province of Beauty

Here you are in the Dutch Rhine district, which has welcomed visitors for hundreds of years. The first "tourists" were foreign tribes who came here about 100 B.C. on their rafts and made the Veluwe (as the region is also called) one of their early stopping-places. Some liked it so well that they stayed here.

Tucked away in the woods along the Rhine today is accommodation to suit every taste and purse. It ranges from luxury hotels to well-equipped camping-grounds. The restaurants specialize, too, in game in season as well as in juicy steaks.

Reaching this district is easy and convenient. You can still sail down the Rhine from Germany to Rhenen, like the Batavians, by taking the river boat at Emmerik. If, on the other hand, you arrive at Amsterdam or Rotterdam, you are just about two hours away from this peaceful country. By train, head for Arnhem, Oosterbeek or Wolfheze. By car, drive through Doorn and Amerongen to Rhenen, move up the Rhine to Arnhem, or turn off at Arnhem and double back.

Getting around Gelderland is also easy without a car, as you can choose between using the efficient bus services, hiring a horse, renting a bicycle or a yacht, or just walking down by the rivers or through the woods. After enjoying the varied scenery, you can explore the robber barons' castle of Doorwerth, visit the oldest church in Western Europe and the Airborne Museum in the old Hotel Hartenstein at Oosterbeek, and drop in at the little hilltop church at Heelsum, all of which are remnants of early Dutch history. There are museums to visit, and those who are brave can wait under the trees near Renkum at midnight for the white-dressed ghost of the "Woman of Grunsfoort."

Arnhem and Its Parks

Arnhem, a city which, with Nijmegen, is probably as well-known around the world as any other Dutch town because of its wartime drama, with the mammoth airborne attack on the Germans, is the capital of the province of Gelderland. It has been growing very quickly in the past few years and now has about 128,000 inhabitants, and more than ever proudly carries its honor of capital, perhaps because it believes it was once the district that Tacitus called Arenacum. Today, Arnhem's attractions are not only its battlefields, which have become places of pilgrimage, but also its modern city center and surroundings rich in scenic beauty.

In the heart of the capital are several magnificent parks, notably the 30-hectare (75-acre) Netherlands Open-Air Museum, which reveals Holland's national culture through the centuries in farms, windmills, ancient customs, medieval crafts, traditional costumes, thatched cottages, forgotten means of transport, colorful flowerbeds, and rural architecture drawn from every province. Then there is Sonsbeek Park, with its stately avenues and peaceful lakes, forming a popular park.

In Rozendaal, a suburb of Arnhem, is Castle Rosendael, headquarters of the International Castles Institute, where you can find out all you want to know about castles anywhere in the world.

The Hoge Veluwe National Park, 57 square kilometers (22 square miles) of moors, dense woods and open plains, lies inside the triangle formed by Arnhem, Apeldoorn, and Ede. It is a real national park, with abundant natural life. But it is even more, for it has two unique features. One is the Hunting Lodge of St. Hubert, a delightful private museum which you should visit; the other is the Rijksmuseum Kröller-Müller at Otterlo, one of the major art collections in the Netherlands. There are roughly 1,500 paintings, 275 pieces of sculpture, outstanding Chinese porcelain, and many hundreds of Delftware items, plus a library. Mainstay of the paintings are more than 300 works by Van Gogh. Artists from the 16th and 17th centuries are also represented—Cranach, Van Goyen, Jan Steen, Van Ostade, etc.—plus the Impressionists and men such as Mondriaan, Braque, Juan Gris, and Picasso. In a private bungalow in the park is the finest collection of old Dutch tiles in existence, going back to the 14th century. The museum gardens feature Europe's largest and most famous collection of outdoor sculpture with works by Moore, Rodin and Lipchitz, among others.

Northeast of Arnhem is the Zuidelijke Veluwezoom National Park, which, with adjoining woods, covers thousands of hectares and provides magnificent views from the Posbank and Zijpenberg.

Oosterbeek, adjoining Arnhem, was once a flourishing Roman settlement. In the 19th century it exercised considerable influence on the romantic school of European painting. Its ancient Catholic church, spared from the battle, contains the famous *Fourteen Stations of the Cross* by Jan Toorop. The 13th-century Castle Doorwerth, rebuilt after heavy damage during the airborne landings of 1944, again shows the characteristic architecture of the stronghold of a robber-baron of the Rhine in the Middle Ages, and now houses a hunting and wildlife museum, the Netherlands Jachtmuseum. The Airborne Museum is now housed in the Hotel Hartenstein, the former British Command Center during the war. Buses leave Arnhem center every hour for the Hoge Velulwe National Park and other places of interest.

Athletics and Safaris

Sports lovers will enjoy a visit to the National Sports Center Papendal in Arnhem, where there are maximum facilities for both the training and coaching not only of Dutch athletes and competitors but also of a number of foreign groups coming here to train for forthcoming important events. It has sleeping capacity for 120, very well-equipped demonstration and lecture rooms, a large sports hall, a massage center, an international-size athletic track, and a power training room. Every form of sport can be taken advantage of in this training complex, and coaches and trainers find it an ideal place to blend theory with practice and concentrate on new methods and techniques.

Visitors to Arnhem are also fortunate in having a choice of two "safari" opportunities. The first is at Burgers' Zoo, entrance in Schelmseweg, which started as a lions' park in 1968 and has now grown into a 20-hectare (50-acre) safari park used as a home for African wildlife. In this savanna there are over 300 animals, so selected as to preserve the balance of nature, through which visitors can drive slowly, while on the safe side of a 5-meter-high (16 feet) fence are three families totalling 20 lions which seem to beg to be photographed.

At de Grebbeberg in Rhenen, not far from Arnhem, is Ouwehand's Zoo. Reindeer, crocodiles, chimpanzees, lions, giraffes, elephants, wild boar, polar bears, reptiles of all kinds, birds of all colors, and even royal Bengal tigers are there to be snapped. The zoo also has its own dolphinarium, with daily shows. When tired of animal-gazing, you can go sunbathing or swimming, or sit on a terrace for a drink or lunch. Both these safari zoos are open all year round and every day. There are also some ruins of a 12th-century church and an Old Dutch restaurant in the former watchtower.

Daily boat trips in this area run from April to August and give a restful view of Holland and neighboring countries. Starting almost every hour, there is a choice of 12 trips a day from Arnhem into the Rhine region, including a stop at Kleve in Germany. Full details are available at the VVV or from the boat owners, Rederij E. Heijmen & Zn, Rijnkade, Arnhem.

Nijmegen and the Holy Land Foundation

Gelderland's largest town (though not the capital, which is Arnhem) is Nijmegen, with a population of 150,000 that includes 15,000 students at the university. Together with Maastricht in the south, it is one of the two oldest cities in the Netherlands. Nijmegen, its name deriving from Novio Magus (new market), was established in A.D. 105 by Trajan who needed a frontier town and fortress for the Batavian provinces against Frankish intrusion. The town was extremely valuable to the Romans, subsequently became a favorite residence of Charlemagne, and later it was a member of the Hanseatic League.

Upon arrival in Nijmegen, make your way as soon as possible to the Valkhof. From here there is a magnificent view over the Waal towards Arnhem and you can well understand, remembering basic military strategy, why the following words are inscribed in one corner: "Here Claudius Civilis (leader of the Batavian and Frisian revolt againt Rome) ground his teeth at the sight of the advancing enemy legions."

On this site nowadays you can see the remains of St. Martin's Chapel or the so-called Barbarossa ruin, the origins of which go back as far as the 12th century when it was built by Frederic Barbarossa. Nearby you will notice a little chapel, built in 1030, that was thought until not long ago to have been founded by Charlemagne, hence its name—the Caro-lingian Chapel. In fact it was built by Conraad II.

Nijmegen has some rather dainty hills standing guard over it. One of them, Berg en Dal (Mountain and Valley) can be reached by taking the city bus No. 5 and you might like to make the popular climb to the 106-meter (350-foot) summit.

As far as museums are concerned, Nijmegen follows the general Dutch rule. The Municipal Museum, or Commanderie van St. Jan Historie en beeldende Kunst as it is in Dutch, contains beautiful old masters and local historical material. The Rijksmuseum G. M. Kam in Kamstraat contains Roman antiquities found in the district, includ-ing a fine collection of coins. The Nijmeegs Volkenkundig Museum van de Katholieke Universiteit has permanent and temporary exhibitions showing the ethnological development of different peoples.

The Town Hall, founded in the 14th century but more or less rebuilt in 1553, is a strange mixture of Gothic and Renaissance styles. Its facade is decorated with statues of all those emperors who were bene-factors of the town. The building was badly damaged in 1944 and most of the contents lost. Just outside the city is the fine Goffert Park with a stadium and charming openair theater. Near Nijmegen, too, are a British War Cemetery, close to the Goffert stadium, and where 1,300 officers and men are laid to rest; a Canadian War Cemetery at Groes-beek 9.5 km. (6 miles) south, where 2,600 are buried on a hill overlook-ing the ground on which they fought so relentlessly and successfully; one at Mook with 300 British war dead; and another at Middelaar.

But back to Nijmegen where yet another magnificent view will make this historic place unforgettable. The Belvedere, a watch tower dating from the 15th century but rebuilt in the 17th century, reaches above the low-lying plain of the Lower Waal. During the Restoration win-dows were installed and the building was used as a meeting place for the city's patricians. Nowadays you can enjoy the view while having a good meal.

The most picturesque part of Nijmegen is the Grote Markt with the Weigh House, or Waag, of 1612; and the Kerkboog, a vaulted passage from 1545 with an elaborate gable (1606). The Laekenhall, a bit further away, used to be an open gallery where cloth merchants assembled for negotiations and business. Near it is the well-known statue of Mariken van Nieumeghen who, so the legend goes, was seduced by the devil and lived with him for seven years until her conversion to Christianity.

Behind the archway is the restored St. Stevenskerk. It was built between 1254 and 1550 and this explains the great variety of styles, from Romanesque to late Gothic. The beautiful spire dates from the Renaissance and behind it you'll find the Latin school used over the centuries for various purposes. Around this church a typical Dutch flea market is held every Monday morning and there are usually some quaint souvenirs and curios to be picked up.

A mile or two southeast of Nijmegen on the road to Groesbeek on a 48-hectare (120-acre) plot, you'll find the Heilig Land Stichting, or "Holy Land", a unique openair biblical museum. Making everything lifesize, the Holy Land Foundation has reproduced the surroundings and atmosphere of the period and the country in which Jesus lived.

Buildings and furniture, clothes and household articles, temple and synagogue, tent and manger, husbandman and nomad, all are there "to let visitors see Christ as a man, who grew up amid normal surroundings, and whom divinity did not prevent from being entirely human", as the founder of the museum put it. The grounds are in three sections. One deals with the antecedents and private life of Jesus; the second displays His public life; and the third shows the Passion and Resurrection.

Apeldoorn and Wageningen

Glorying in the title of "The Largest Garden City in the Netherlands", Apeldoorn, 27 km. (17 miles) north of Arnhem, attracts about 1,000,000 visitors a year. Lavishly endowed with everything nature could provide, the city likes to call itself "Royal" Apeldoorn. The late Queen Wilhelmina, when abdicating from rulership in 1948, chose its 1685 Palace of Het Loo in which to spend her years of retirement. The palace was originally built for Willem III in 1685 and completed in 1692 by J. Roman. It was used as a summer palace by Louis Napoleon in 1809–10, during which time the extensive formal gardens were created. It remained a royal palace until comparatively recently; ex-Queen Wilhelmina died here in 1962, and the house was subsequently occupied by Princess Margriet until 1971. After extensive restoration, Het Loo was opened fully to the public in 1984 as a museum covering the history of the House of Orange. Called Rijksmuseum Paleis Het Loo, it contains collections of paintings, silver, ceramics, glass, furniture and Royal memorabilia, plus a splendid collection of veteran cars. The superb formal gardens have also been restored to their full glory.

Among the many parks provided by Apeldoorn for its residents and visitors the best is probably the Berg en Bos, covering two and a half square kilometers of what appears to be natural woods and ponds aglow with luxuriant gardens and sparkling with bubbling springs. Interestingly, the whole of this rich parkland is entirely artificial.

Apeldoorn's encircling villages, which are really its suburbs, have their own diminutive magnetism. At Beekbergen is the 12th-century church sheltering the tomb of the first Dutch papermaker, who gave Apeldoorn one of its greatest industries. At Loenen, in the woods, you will find the ruined 1557 Castle Ter Horst, as well as the largest waterfall in the Netherlands. Hoenderlo is best known as the nearest village to the Hoge Veluwe National Park of which we have already written. Ugchelen has many lovely springs and fine stretches of moorland, while somewhere in the village lies buried—so the legend says—a huge golden bell from an 8th-century monastery.

Wageningen, about 17 km. (11 miles) west of Arnhem, is doubly famous. It was here, in the appropriately named *De Wereld* restaurant, that the Germans surrendered to General Foulkes on May 5, 1945. But this ancient town is also the seat of Holland's great agricultural university with its arboretum, 21 laboratories, 22 institutes, and 10 large associations all connected with agriculture, horticulture, and husbandry. Hundreds of vital experiments are carried out here. Here are Holland's ship-testing basins, where small-scale models of new ships are buffeted in manmade gales and simulated weather conditions to prove their ultimate seaworthiness—even the new mammoth tankers. The Euratom Research Laboratory for the peaceful use of isotopes and other nuclear products to improve plant growth is also located here.

Orchard Country

Southwest of Wageningen is the heart of the Betuwe, or orchard-land. In April and May, as far as one can see, the cherry, apple, and pear trees are covered with a foam of blossom, and with Tiel as head-quarters a trip in any direction is a ride through a land of delight. Tiel, dating back to the middle of the 5th century, tells through its buildings a tale of wars and destruction, a record that was epitomized, as it were, during the last war, when it was shelled continuously every day from October 1944 to May 1945. Reminiscent of its glory is its ring of guardian castles: Ophemert to the south, Waardenburg to the south-west, and Zoelen to the west.

Southwest from Tiel lies Zaltbommel, the ancient stronghold that defied the Spaniards for so long. It was here, the story goes, that Dr. Faustus made his contract with the devil. We know that many towns in Europe claim to have been the original abode of the man who sold himself to the devil, but whereas they all admit that only Faustus signed the contract, these hard-headed Dutchmen of Zaltbommel declare that both the devil and the doctor signed, thus giving it legal status.

Northeast from Arnhem, about 29 km. (18 miles) is Zutphen. Lying peacefully on the banks of the IJssel, it is a happy maze of gables, gateways, twisting streets and old houses. But its chief attraction to visitors is the chained medieval library of the Grote or Walburgiskerk, whose magnificently proportioned interior has many interesting works of art. The outstanding collection of rare books, manuscripts and *incunabula,* all neatly chained to reading desks, is still in use.

It was here at Zutphen that the gallant Englishman Sir Philip Sidney died when helping the Dutch against the Spaniards in 1586. And it was in one of the fields of this lovely old town that, although mortally wounded himself, he handed a cup of water to a dying soldier with the words: "Thy need is greater than mine."

From Vorden, 10 km. (6 miles) southeast of Zutphen, you can make the Eight Castles Tour, details of which are available at the local VVV Office. But some can only be viewed from the outside.

Here and There Around the Province

Epe, 18 km. (11 miles) north of Apeldoorn, is another delightful haven of peace in the Veluwe, and nearby are the attractive villages of Vaassen and Heerde. In Vaassen don't miss the Kasteel Cannenburgh which was built in the 14th century and, after restoration in the 16th century, was the home of Maarten van Rossum, a nobleman of the region. The style of that period, with original furniture and artifacts, has been maintained.

West of Epe lie Nunspeet at 14 km. (9 miles) and then Harderwijk, a further 13 km. (8 miles). Both are happy old towns that are very popular holiday resorts with the Dutch but are seldom visited by foreigners. Each has its usual array of churches and old buildings. Eight kilometers (five miles) north of Nunspeet is Elburg, a small harbor town with a lovely old gateway (1392), an unusually large 15th-century church, crude mosaic sidewalks, and two interesting almshouses, the Weduwenhof from 1650 (first right-hand turn inside gate) and the Feithenhof from 1740 (first left-hand turn inside gate). The former Town Hall, dating from 1300, is one of the oldest buildings in Holland.

Harderwijk is the home of one of Europe's largest dolphinariums and several shows a day are given here. There is also important research work carried out into the life and habits of dolphins, including a study of the way they talk to one another. The Oceanarium, 1 Strandboulevard, is open from March to October, daily from 10 to 7 P.M.

On the eastern edge of Harderwijk is a sign pointing northwest to Lelystad. Follow this road for about 29 km. (18 miles) and you will reach a blossoming town which has sprung up as the main center of the new polder. The 96-km.-long (60 miles) dike which was closed in the fall of 1956 enabled this section of the old Zuiderzee (now called the IJsselmeer) to be pumped dry, so that it could provide about 52,000 hectares (130,000 acres) of new land. Here, in fact, there is the unique sight of a new town being built on new territory snatched from the waters. The cost of all this to the government, incidentally, was computed at about $1,300 for half a hectare, without roads or other improvements.

The eastern portion of the province has a number of very well-known resorts. Twello, 10 km. (6 miles) east of Apeldoorn, is a straggling rural village and a walker's paradise. Its municipal park will do for the less energetic, but for those who really like hiking in beautiful surroundings there are a dozen country manors to be seen, including De Groote Noordijk, Het Kleine Noordijk, De Parkeler, Kruisvoorde, Hunderen, and De Pol.

Zelhem, 21 km. (13 miles) southeast of Zutphen, is another noted hiking and cycling center. In its surrounding woods and moors are over 320 km. (200 miles) of paths winding through a lovely nature reserve. It has few hotels, but many pensions and campsites.

Winterswijk, 43 km. (27 miles) east and south of Zutphen, is another township that serves as the center of a national park even though it is a textile-making area and the home of the largest knitwear factory in the Netherlands. It has a fine open-air theater, one of the best natural history museums in the country, and parks and woods with abundant wildlife.

Gelderland province is, above all, a walking or cycling province. Here the Dutch people, young and old, gather in many thousands to enjoy themselves without thought of motors or buses. Cycling specials are run by the railways on which every passenger takes a bicycle.

It is from Nijmegen, too, that the annual four-day walk (de Vierdaagse) is held. Some 20,000 people, singly or in groups, come from all over the world to participate in this hiking marathon, while many thousands come to watch along the route. There are various categories,

with assignments varying from 30–55 km. (20–35 miles) a day, depending on age and sex.

Overijssel, a Province of Contrasts

A close neighbor (but very different in every way) of Gelderland is
the quaint province of Overijssel, usually neglected by foreign visitors
and therefore offering the adventurous tourist something which most
others miss. It is a particularly rewarding area to explore because it
offers several completely distinct areas in which the population as well
as the scenery differ widely. In the northwest is the Noordoostpolder,
most recently snatched from the former Zuiderzee, where you can
study the latest Dutch ideas on agriculture, architecture, town planning
and social organization. Over the east is Twente, a contrasting region
that has been inhabited since the dawn of history. The Salland district,
between the IJssel and Vecht rivers, presents yet another landscape,
with areas still unexplored even by Dutch holidaymakers, and with
three of Holland's most ancient cities rejuvenated into prosperous activity.

Let us visit first its capital, Zwolle, with 87,000 inhabitants, which
stands at the crossroads from north to south and from east to west.
Unpretentious except in its prosperity, it is a charming town in which,
with commendable practicality, the city fathers have leveled the old
ramparts into a girdle of lovely parks, lawns, and flowerbeds, and
turned the moat into a graceful canal that still winds beneath the
former bastions.

Points of special interest in this town of many facets are the Gothic
Aldermen's Room, or Schepenzaal, of 1448 in the Town Hall, the
Pepperpot Tower of the 15th-century Church of Our Lady, the lovely
Sassenpoort gateway (1408) flanked by a quartet of octagonal towers,
and the Provinciaal Overijssel Museum (Provincial Overijssels Museum) in the Melkmarkt, with its collection of French furniture, a room
dedicated to the history of Zwolle and a restored 16th-century kitchen.
The Grote or St. Michaelskerk built between 1406 and 1446 is a Gothic
triangular hall church. It used to have a 125-meter-high (400 feet)
tower—once the highest in the country—but, regrettably, it was destroyed by fire in 1669 and never rebuilt. The church houses the world-
famous Schnitger organ with 4,000 pipes. During the summer, concerts
by famous international organists are regularly presented here.

Roughly 32 km. (20 miles) south of the capital is Deventer, an
11th-century town that has developed into an industrial center manufacturing metal goods, Smyrna carpets, and its own famous spiced
gingerbread called *Deventer Koek*. This is an intimate place, easy to
explore but full of such surprises as the Weigh House with its gigantic
cauldron, the Municipal Museum with its splendid collection of costumes and furniture, the exceptionally large library of 16th-century
books and manuscripts in the Town Hall, and four fine historic churches.

Kampen, 14 km. (9 miles) west of Zwolle, is located on the southwest
side of the River IJssel and has a population of some 32,000. Tied to
its wharves are seagoing ships, bound generally for Britain or the

Baltic. Along the quays is a wide boulevard lined with tall, proud houses and warehouses, many built during the golden age, for Kampen was a Hanseatic League city. In the Middle Ages it was an important shipping and trade center, and its prosperity is reflected in its many fine buildings.

There are many historic buildings to be seen: the 16th-century Town Hall, or Oude Raadhuis, with its Schepenzaal (Aldermen's Room) lined with panelling dated 1544–1545 and a richly carved fireplace of the same date; south of the Town Hall, the "New" Tower, dated 1664; the Bovenkerk, or Sint Nicolaaskerk, dated 1369. Kampen has also several old and interesting gateways.

Not far from Kampen, just opposite Elburg in the East Flevoland Polder on the bed of the former salty Zuiderzee is the unique Flevohof where it is possible to spend a real day in the country. This is a 140-hectare (350-acre) farm where you can milk a cow, make cheese or butter and go completely agricultural and experience farming life first hand. Apart from modern buildings for demonstrations and exhibitions, there is a wide variety of recreational facilities, with promenades, horse-drawn trains, several restaurants, sunny terraces and a Red Indian village for the youngsters. It is open all the year round every day and has ample parking space. This is a real day in the country in which modern farming can be watched at first hand. It actually has two different farms on its 140 hectares (350 acres): a 66-hectare (165-acre) agricultural farm where corn, wheat, potatoes and other crops are grown, and a 35-hectare (88-acre) cattle farm where pigs and chickens are also raised. It is open daily from April to October.

Holland's Quaintest Villages

North of Zwolle and west of Meppel is one of the most-talked-of places in Holland—for the picturesque village of Giethoorn has no streets. The baker, the postman, and the courting swain all have to travel by canal or narrow paths. Every house set amidst trees is an island reached only over its own high-arched bridge or along its own off-shooting stream. The only apology for a street is the rough path by the side of the main canal leading from the main highway, and from which you board the motorboat or punt that runs you round the village, gliding past enticing little cottages and slipping under graceful bridges.

While in this district, make for Staphorst, just north of Zwolle on the road to Meppel, the other very-much-discussed village of Overijssel. Primarily noted for its costumes (and what costumes they can be!), it has also come to be regarded with a mixture of awe and incredulity. On weekdays, Staphorst is a more or less normal Dutch-picture village of 10,000 inhabitants, where the people, gay in dress but serious in face, look on the foreign visitor (and this means anyone from more than 15 kilometers away) as an unavoidable necessity, or perhaps at times as a tolerated guest. But on Sundays visitors are not so welcome. Indeed, they are resentfully unwelcome. For on that day the village is flooded with solemnity and piety. The locals will not ride bicycles, and visiting cars are stopped on the outskirts. In two separate files the men and the women foot their silent and sober way to church. With downbent heads and eyes fixed on the ground, the slow processions of Calvinists fill the Sabbath with awe, revealing a regimentation both in walk and dress that is undoubtedly unique in Europe. If you want to see this quaint spectacle, keep out of sight as much as possible. Sunday to the Staphorsters is no day of peep-show or festival. They would prefer you to ignore their village and let them concentrate their thoughts on more godly matters than inquisitive foreigners.

Yet another example of the extreme conservatism in this village was the refusal of the people, supported by the local parson, to allow their children to be inoculated or vaccinated against a threatened epidemic. Even though they were all told that the Dutch law laid down compulsory protection of this kind, only three or four mothers reluctantly (and secretly) took their children along to the dispensary.

Although many of the more extreme attitudes are becoming softened by modern education, this is still one of the most conservative areas of Holland.

Here, as in many communities in Holland, it is still the custom that even adult children contribute their labor or wages to the head of the family. The theory is that the children are investing in their inheritance. The more ambitious sons and daughters, however, are often unwilling to postpone their own careers for an uncertain number of years, so they are tending to emigrate to the cities (or even abroad) where they can earn—and keep—a cash income, and develop their own lives more independently.

Whilst in this district visits might be made to the old towns of Blokzijl and Vollenhove, now turned from former Zuiderzee ports into small inland industrial centers; Hasselt, with its many medieval buildings; and the lake region of Beulakerwijde and Belterwijde where water sports abound.

Coming to the heart of the province we reach an area well worth exploring, as it is among the earliest inhabited districts of Western Europe. Its center is the town of Ommen, 29 km. (18 miles) due east of Zwolle, a popular camping place with many attractive buildings and corners, which shares its beauties with the adjoining castle of Eerde and the woods of Junne at the foot of the Lemelerberg Hill. To the west is the extremely picturesque Dalfsen with its Gothic church and old castle, and the wooded areas of Raalte and Heino, both of them villages with many ancient relics. East of Ommen are the rarely-toured areas of Hardenberg and Gramsbergen, easy of access and unusual in historical charm. To the south of Ommen are the lively little rural town of Rijssen; the contrasting villages of Hellendoorn and Nijverdal in the "Golden Mountain" area; the towns of Goor, Markelo, and Diepenheim, nestling among the hills; and many other havens of peace and unexpected scenery, including the charming village of Holten where a Canadian war cemetery is carefully and proudly tended by the Dutch inhabitants.

Textile Triangle

The group of towns of Almelo, Enschede, and Oldenzaal form a triangle within which lies one of Holland's most important textile-making areas, although all around are fertile fields and shady woods, traditional farms and imposing castles, picturesque villages and reminders of centuries past. Old customs die hard here. At Ootmarsum, 21 km. (13 miles) northeast of Almelo, is the singing procession at Easter when the inhabitants walk in a hand-in-hand chain through the 12th-century church and most of the old houses. Incidentally, when looking at this church, glance up at one of the inside pillars to see how a proud stone-mason left his own picture, complete with rouged cheeks, for future visitors to admire. It is at Easter, too, that the farmers distribute bread to the poor in accordance with an ancient vow, and burn the traditional bonfires.

Enschede, an ultramodern city that is surprising in its progressiveness, is the chief Dutch cotton-spinning and weaving center. It produces some astoundingly rich materials reminiscent of the best and most entrancing French brocades and velvets, and as a city is the very opposite of what one would expect from a textile-making center. Its 140,000 inhabitants pride themselves not only on their industrial activity but on their determination to be modern but attractive. The rail station is one of the best in the country and the city's range of museums is in strange contrast to its canal harbor, which serves as a link with all Holland and Germany. Of all Dutch cities, Enschede can be regarded as a model of progress against a background of solidity.

Hengelo, a center of metal industries and an important cattle market, is another example of enterprise and tradition. Situated in an area of scattered moors, its 70,000 inhabitants have learned to be practical despite their conservatism. But Castle Twickel (1347), just north of Delden and 5 km. (3 miles) west of Hengelo, provides the best scenic attraction, with its orangery, Versailles-style gardens, and centuries-old woods. The castle itself, however, is not open to the public.

Almelo is a great Dutch weaving center. It has also been called the City of Friendship, because it began the popular plan by which Dutch cities have established close civic contact with other cities of many countries. It has its own attractions, however, for it is an old city with interesting surroundings.

Oldenzaal, the oldest town of Twente, lies 13 km. (8 miles) north of Enschede, and is a fine center for day or half-day trips. Its lovely 12th-century Basilica of St. Plechelmus has a massive tower with the largest belfry in Europe and an exceptionally fine carillon. If you enjoy unraveling mysteries, try to find out from local experts why the walls of the church have so many arrow-shaped markings carved on them, like an inverted V-for-victory sign of the type Winston Churchill made famous.

Perhaps the last recommendation in Overijssel should be Boekelo, famed for its saltwater lake (many kilometers from the North Sea), which has been turned into a unique beach resort amidst an area of rolling heathland. The land all around is thick with salt, thus enabling a thriving salt industry to grow up under the imposing title of the Royal Dutch Salt Works Limited. The prevalence of the salt made the lake like seawater, and so with typical Dutch enterprise and imagination the Enschede town leaders decided to turn it into a real seaside resort.

Realizing that a seaside, no matter how briny, was tame without waves, they installed a large machine to produce vigorous surf.

The Wonders of the Polders

Around the old Zuiderzee—now called the IJsselmeer—are several polders which have been reclaimed from that huge basin which was once part of the North Sea. For centuries the Dutch had been battling against the vagaries and the tumult of the Zuiderzee, for although it gave access for world shipping to ports like Amsterdam which laid the foundation of Holland's maritime and trading greatness, it also caused disasters as a result of storms. Its bottom is, indeed, still a graveyard of ships of all ages which were lost there, but that same sea bed has provided Holland with thousands of acres of good land now being used not only for agriculture but also for dwellings, industry and recreation. There are few more fascinating stories than that of the Zuiderzee and its reclamation.

The North Sea launched its assault on Holland's coast around the end of the Roman occupation, A.D. 200–300. It broke through the Frisian dunes and left them a chain of islands: Texel, Vlieland, Terschelling, Ameland, and others. It flooded great marshes with salt water and in the 13th century, aided by terrific storms, broke through in strength and joined an inland lake called Flevo to create the Southern Sea or Zuiderzee. That was the end of its invasion; since then Dutch engineers have fought back, snipping off a bit of land here, another there, for seven centuries. They lost some disastrous battles: on December 14, 1287, floods killed 80,000 people in one night; on November 18–19, 1421, about 8,000 were drowned in the south. But security against such major disasters was finally achieved in the 17th century, and land-grabbing was made easier in 1932 with the completion of the enclosing dike.

Now, just a few more dates and figures. As early as the 17th century there were plans to reclaim the Zuiderzee, all of them financially or technically impractical. Finally engineer Lely's plan was approved by parliament in 1919, with work starting during a time of high unemployment a few years later. In 1927–1930 the Wieringermeer Polder was seized back from Neptune. This gave an instalment of 20,000 hectares (50,000 acres) of new land, and was the smallest of the five proposed polders. It was here that the first experiments were made to solve the great problem of converting the salty bottom of the former sea into fertile land for agriculture. The solution was lowering the groundwater level in the polder to about 1.5 meters (5 feet) below the lowest surface and then taking the water from the soil. While this was being done, about 600 farmhouses and three townships were built, along with 19 km. (12 miles) of canals, 60 bridges and two pumping-stations.

All went well until World War II, when in the closing weeks the Germans inundated the polder in an attempt to stop the advance of the Allied troops. No one was drowned, but the whole polder—houses and farms and shops and churches—was covered to a depth of anything from 4–12 meters (12–40 feet). In some places only church steeples were showing.

One of the early postwar tasks, therefore, was to pump the water away. This was done in four months, and within a year of the German defeat crops were being sown and half the houses had again been made habitable. At this time work had already made good progress on the reclaiming of the second section, the Northeast Polder of 48,000 hectares (119,000 acres); in fact, much of the work was continued during the war. Here more than a million million liters (250,000 million gallons) of water had to be pumped out by three monster stations before the land was dry so that about 1,600 farms and 400 market gardens could be started. Today 10 villages are grouped around the township of Emmeloord, which is now a thriving center for the 40,000 inhabitants of this second polder.

Work on the third East Flevoland Polder of 53,000 hectares (133,000 acres) began in 1950, with a 92-km. (57-mile) dike being simultaneously built in four places, as well as three pumping-stations and four locks. Although the great flood of 1953 meant that some of the equipment had to be transferred to the new protective project of the Delta Works in Zeeland, this polder was reclaimed by 1957.

While the development work on the East Flevoland Polder was in full swing, work was started on building the dikes of the last two polders: the South Flevoland Polder and the Markerwaard Polder. South Flevoland became dry in 1968, and the final dikes of the Markerwaard have been finished, increasing the land area of the Netherlands by some 97,000 hectares.

The final draining of the Markermeer is still a subject of controversy, however, as the people of such former port towns as Hoorn and Volendam are convinced that the draining of this lake will greatly harm their local economies. This problem has still to be finally resolved.

Yet another fascinating hydraulics scheme still under consideration is the building of a dike joining together the necklace of islands off the Groningen and Friesland coasts: Texel, Vlieland, Terschelling, Ameland, Schiermonnikoog, and Rottum. This would be followed by the reclamation of a great deal of land from the present Wadden Sea which would be enclosed: such a mammoth work is admittedly for a future generation.

Knowing this background of the Zuiderzee miracle, a tourist can have few more fascinating and inspiring trips than through these manmade polders. It has other special characteristics also. Most visitors will be struck at once by the fact that the broad roads have none of the sharp curves so typical of older farmland where highways were constructed after the lots were divided up, instead of before. Here they are as straight as the enclosing dike itself, broken only by clusters of farmhouses, usually four together, surrounded by trees that seem remarkably tall already for a region that lay at the bottom of the IJsselmeer until 1942.

Broad fields, perhaps of yellow mustard, bronze flax, green alfalfa, and brown barley stretch far out in a harmonious color scheme, with here and there the red-orange tile of huge barn roofs. Down the canals, which are as straight as the roads, barges sweep along and houseboats are anchored to the shore.

Here and there along the road you may see temporary hutments and groups of men called *polderjongens* trained specially for polder work, who mostly come from Sliedrecht in South Holland. They travel from place to place where trained services are needed. The great Dikemaster Andries Vierlingh praised them in 1570, and Dr. van Veen describes them as "the workers of willow mattresses, who can handle the unwieldly dredging machines with unerring skill . . . who can strangle wild streams . . . those heavy-handed slow-speaking workers in long boots, who have traveled over the whole world to do their mud and mattress work . . . "

The Netherlands government retains title to the polder land, renting it out to able farmers at low rates. Farms here are of 16 hectares (40 acres) or more; anything smaller is considered inefficient. In order to win priority for a farm lease, young Hollanders go to work on polder land a long time, maybe five years, before the area is suitable for food production. Then they move in, after their title has been confirmed. Many farmers from Walcheren in Zeeland, made homeless by a postwar division of the land, are here in the polders making new homes.

Practically in the geometric center of the Northeast Polder is the booming young city of Emmeloord, and we should note that its location was no accident. With the aid of a detailed map you'll see how a system of waterways radiates out from Emmeloord, paralleling the road system. At the end of each canal is a community, more or less equidistant from Emmeloord and the edge of the polder. This arrangement, if a trifle regular, has the merit of making it possible for Emmeloord to service the entire region with schools, medical facilities, specialty shops, banks and the like. It was at first intended to have five or six different municipalities in the polder, but now the whole area is combined in the Emmeloord Municipality, with one Burgemeester administering the whole area.

At the same time that practical considerations were being taken into account, the planners recognized that variety has an important function, too. Thus, an effort has been made to make every settlement just a little different from the others. You will be particularly aware of this as you explore Emmeloord itself. There is no dreary uniformity, no oppressive sense of everything having been cast in the same mould. However you do sense another characteristic; the community hasn't quite jelled yet because there hasn't been time to put down human roots, and everyone, by definition, is an outsider. Barriers are slow to fall in the Netherlands, and it may well be several decades before these new citizens cease to think of themselves as settlers from another region, despite all the skill—and art—displayed by those who have planned so impressively.

Old Towns and New

One of the features of a trip through the Zuiderzee polders is the variety of buildings and layouts. The new towns like Emmeloord and Lelystad are still very much in the making, and show many signs of new ideas of civic life. When the polders were first conceived it was felt that the future inhabitants would want to live in much the same way as they have been doing for centuries in more or less watertight compartments belonging to the different religious groupings. But it has been found that even the former conservative communities have now gone modern, and that it is no longer practical or advisable to give each sectarian community its own schools, libraries and recreation centers. The result has been a decrease in the number of separate villages.

Lelystad is a good example of a town near the beginning of its growth, while Emmeloord has, as it were, come of age but is nowhere near maturity. Both are well worth visiting, especiallly as the areas surrounding them provide good illustrations of the way even the polder layout and use has changed as a result of the greater emphasis put on small industries and much more ample recreational facilities. In fact, a good proportion of the newly-reclaimed polderland is now being taken over to provide more outdoor recreation.

When at Emmeloord the visitor should not leave out a trip to Urk, about 16 km. (10 miles) to the west, as this is considered by many as one of the most interesting spots in Holland. For 700 years or more Urk was an island in the Zuiderzee, well isolated from other communities, with its own way of life, traditions and costumes. In 1942 the polder crept up and joined it to the mainland; it remained a seaport but its isolation was ended. The road to Urk was only completed in 1948 and in the summer of 1951 the Urk town council decided they would have none of those new-fangled gadgets, automobiles, in the streets of their town. Unfortunately, the decision didn't stick, and the town is now as full of cars as any—especially in the height of the tourist season.

At the harbor's long piers are dozens of stubby, tough-looking fishing boats, moored quietly in the protected water when the weather is too cold for eel fishing. On Sundays, cold or warm, the boats also stay home as the people are careful not to let anyone, or anything, work on that day. The religious scruples of these devout Protestant townsfolk are so strong, in fact, that they will not ride their bicycles on a Sunday.

Entering the village, the visitor finds that Urk is quite tourist-minded. For sale in small booths or carts are postcards and varied souvenirs, ice cream, and the town's specialty—smoked eel. When tempted to buy some, ignore the fat eels as they usually are not as nice as the thin ones. The houses are small, the streets paved with bricks.

Urk's costumes may be less prominent with the coming of "civilization," but there are still some to be seen. Women's corsets are of light-blue material, on which chamois leather is sewn to prevent wear, the whole garment being stiffened with whalebone or, more likely today, plastic! A broad yoke of flowered silk is worn over it. Urk women usually wear necklaces of garnets, with a square gold fastener. A white bonnet is worn around the back of the head, and gold ear ornaments press into the cheeks.

Men of Urk generally wear dark costumes: black wooden shoes, thick black socks, black pantaloons above the knees, and a round black hat or black skull cap. Silver buckles may flash from the belt, and sometimes gay red-and-white striped shirts brighten the whole effect.

The people of Urk are cordial to strangers, but not many of them speak English. From May to September, the men go out after eels whenever the weather is propitious. Then for a few weeks, they have a season of catching a large fish called *snoekbaars,* which are "pike-perch"—or *stizostedion americanum* to you. Personally we prefer any one of the other three names it is known by: glass-eyed, goggle-eyed, or wall-eyed pike. Visitors are taken eel fishing on summer nights if they wish. Determined to be independent despite being joined to the mainland, Urk fishermen formed a cooperative: the whole catch of all kinds of fish is "pooled", sent to a large new factory to be canned, dried, deep-frozen or made up into ready-to-cook dishes, then exported to many parts of Europe. The whole installation is a cooperative invest-ment, the profits being distributed according to the amount of fish caught by each boat's crew.

From Urk, take the road that runs due east through Nagele to Ens. Between these two villages you'll come upon a tiny ridge, perhaps 6 meters (20 feet) above the vast flatland that stretches without a break toward the horizon. It is all that is left of Schokland, once an island of fisher-folk, constantly cut down through the centuries by encroach-ing water and later practically swallowed by the new polder. On it now is a church building, a few anchors and a cannon, dated 1537. The cannon—a *hoogwaterkanon* (high-water cannon)—was fired to warn the people of the coming of a very high tide. The church has now been converted into a museum, displaying objects found on the bottom of the Zuiderzee.

The museum exhibits throw light on the dim past, prehistoric days and those more recent, before and after the North Sea claimed most of the area. Among them are: Bronze Age tools, bone of a mid-Euro-pean mammoth, jaw of a wolf, and teeth of a bison. Objects of a different category are: pottery (900–1200) and stone coffins (1100) from Germany. Anyone interested in historic ships should certainly visit the Museum voor Sheepsarcheologie (marine archaeology) in Ketelhaven which lies north of the road between Lelystad and Kampen. Here have been assembled many of the remains of wrecked ships uncovered by the draining of the Zuider Zee, some dating back as far as Roman times.

All around the shores of the IJsselmeer there have sprung up attrac-tive yacht harbors and beach resorts in the different provinces border-ing the region. In fact, in recent years the hydraulic engineers learned that the polderland itself would be improved if there were a strip of water separating the new land from the old. This strip of water has in many places been turned into aquatic sports and recreation centers, with ample accommodation ranging from bungalow parks to camping sites.

PRACTICAL INFORMATION FOR CENTRAL HOLLAND

TELEPHONE CODES. We have given telephone codes for all the towns and villages in the hotel and restaurant lists that follow. These codes need only be used when calling from outside the town or village concerned.

CENTRAL HOLLAND 207

HOTELS AND RESTAURANTS. Utrecht, Overijssel and Gelderland have ample and comfortable accommodations, but the popularity of Central Holland as a vacation area means that rooms can be hard to find during July and August, so it's prudent to call ahead to your next stop a few days in advance if you haven't already made reservations. VVV offices can normally help, however, should you be stuck.

We have divided the hotels and restaurants in our listings into three categories—Expensive (E), Moderate (M) and Inexpensive (I). Price ranges for these categories for both hotels and restaurants are given in the *Facts at Your Fingertips* (see pp. 17–18). Some hotels, particularly at the upper end of the scale, have rooms in more than one category and a consequently wide range of prices. Similarly, many restaurants have dishes in more than one category, so be sure to check the menu outside before you go in. Look out too for the excellent value Tourist Menu.

AALTEN (Gelderland). *De Kroon* (M), 62 Dijkstraat; 05437–3051. 15 rooms.

ALMELO (Overijssel). Attractive manufacturing city 30 miles east of Zwolle. *Postiljon Almelo* (M), 2 Aalderinkssingel; 05490–26655. 50 rooms with shower.
    Restaurant. *Oude Verkeershuis* (I), 80 Grotestraat; 05490–15775. Reasonable Dutch cuisine.

ALMEN (Gelderland). *De Hoofdige Boer* (M), 38 Dorpsstraat; 05751–744. 20 rooms with shower.

AMERSFOORT (Utrecht). Charming old city 14 miles east of Utrecht. *Berghotel* (E), 225 Utrechtseweg; 033–620444. 40 rooms, all with bath or shower. On edge of town, with fine view, tennis and mini golf. *De Witte* (M), 2 Utrechtseweg; 033–14142. 15 rooms with bath or shower. Stylish restaurant with seasonal dishes.
    Restaurants. *De Enhoorn* (E), 26 Stationsplein. International food. *Floryntje* (M), Krommestraat. Dutch dishes.

APELDOORN (Gelderland). Garden city 17 miles north of Arnhem. *De Keizerskroon* (E), 7 Koningstraat; 055–217744. 70 rooms, all with bath or shower. Near the Het Loo Palace. Very comfortable, and with fine restaurant (see below). *Berg en Bos* (M), 58 Aquamarijnstraat; 055–552352. 17 rooms. Reasonable restaurant. *Bloemink* (M), 56 Loolaan; 055–214141. 90 rooms, all with bath or shower. Comfortable hotel, good restaurant. *Nieland* (M), 73 Soerensweg; 055–554555. 45 rooms, most with bath or shower.
    Restaurants. *De Echoput* (E), 86 Amersfoortseweg; 05769–248. Excellent restaurant, certainly the best in town, though a little out of the center. *'T Koetshuis* (E), 10 kms. south of Apeldoorn in Vaasen, beside the 14th-century castle of Cannenburgh; 05788–1501. Specializes in game and French cuisine, lovely interior. *Le Petit Prince* (E), 7 Koningstraat; 055–217744. Excellent restaurant of De Keizerskroon hotel (see above). *De Woeste Hoeve* (E), 792 Arnhemsweg; 05766–1580. Traditional spot some three miles out of town at Beekbergen, building dates from 1771.

ARNHEM (Gelderland). Provincial capital. *Groot Warnsborn* (E), 277 Bakenbergseweg; 085–455751. 30 rooms, all with bath. Located a mile east of the Amsterdam highway, three miles from town, in own grounds. *Golden Tulip Rijn Hotel* (E), 10 Onderlangs; 085–434642. 23 rooms with shower. By the river with good views and restaurant. *Haarhuis* (M), 1 Stationsplein; 085–427441. 99 rooms with bath or shower. Opposite station, with good restaurant. *De Leeren Doedel* (M), 467 Amsterdamweg; 085–332344. Small hotel about three miles out of town with good restaurant. *Postiljon* (M), 25 Europaweg; 085–453741. On the E36 a couple of miles out of town. 30 rooms with shower.

Restaurants. *Rijzenburg* (E), 17 Koningsweg; 085–436733. Excellent if expensive spot at the entrance to the Hoge Veluwe park, seven miles out of town. *De Steenen Tafel* (E), 1 Weg achter het Bosch; 085–435313. *Boerderij* (M), 2 Parkweg; 085–424396. Attractive 19th-century farm in Sonsbeek park.

BAARN (Utrecht). *Prom* (M), 1 Amalianlaan; 02154–12913. 30 rooms.

BERG EN DAL (Gelderland). *Erica* (M), 17 Molenbosweg; 08895–3514. 60 rooms, most with bath or shower; restaurant. *Val Monte* (M), 5 Oude Holleweg; 08895–1704. 90 rooms, most with bath. Situated in own grounds with good view of the Rhine; good restaurant. Golden Tulip hotel.

BLOKZIJL. (Overijssel). **Restaurant.** *Kaatje bij de Sluis* (E), 10 Browerstraat; 05272–577. Lovely situation, 12 kms. from Emmeloord; excellent French and Dutch dishes.

BOEKELO (Overijssel). *Boekelo* (E), 203 Oude Deldenerweg; 05428–1444. 78 rooms, all with shower. Situated in extensive grounds, with pool, tennis and many other facilities.

BREUKELEN (Utrecht). *Hofstede Slangevegt* (M), 40 Straatweg; 03462–1525. 5 rooms with shower. Country hotel right by river; exclusive restaurant.

BUNNIK (Utrecht). *Postiljon Utrecht-Bunnik* (M), 8 Koterijland; 03405–69222. 85 rooms. On Utrecht–Arnhem expressway. Good restaurant.

DELDEN (Overijssel). Market town 48 miles southeast of Zwolle. *Carelshaven* (E), 30 Hengelosestraat; 05407–61305. 20 rooms. In attractive grounds and with excellent restaurant. *De Zwaan* (M), 2 Langestraat; 05407–61206. 15 rooms, about half with bath. Near Twickel Castle.

DENEKAMP (Overijssel). *Van Blanken* (M), 10 Grotestraat; 05413–1308. *Dinkeloord* (M), 48 Denekampstraat; 05413–1387. 40 rooms with bath or shower.

Restaurant. *de Watermolen* (M), 4 Schiphorstdijk; 05413–1372. Lovely location, Dutch specialties.

DEVENTER (Overijssel). *Postiljon Deventer* (M), 121 Deventerweg; 05700–24022. Just out of town. 100 rooms with shower. *Royal* (M), 94 Brink; 05700–11880. 28 rooms with shower; central location.

DOESBURG (Gelderland). Charming town on the IJssel 12 miles east of Arnhem. **Restaurant.** *De Waag* (M), 2 Koepoortstraat; 08334–2462. Delightful restaurant in weigh house dating from 1540s.

DOETINCHEM (Gelderland). Small market town. *De Graafschap* (M), 10 Markt; 08340–24541. 30 rooms, most with bath. Excellent restaurant.

EDE (Gelderland). *De Paasberg* (M), 20 Arnhemsweg; 08380–19021. *Mon Reve* (I), 2 Oude Bennekomseweg; 08380–33901.

ENSCHEDE (Overijssel). *DISH Hotel Schermerhovn Hall* (M), 2 Boulevard 1945; 053–866666. Central location. 371 rooms with shower. *Atlanta* (M), 12 Markt; 053–316766. 27 rooms. *Memphis* (M), 55 M. H. Tromplaan; 053–318244.

Restaurants. *Het Koetshuis* (E), 48 Walstraat; 053–322866. Bistro-style in old coachhouse, lovingly decorated. French dishes. *Raedthuys* (M), 12 Raadhuis-straat; 053–312200.

EPE (Gelderland). *Dellenhove* (M), 115 Dellenweg; 05780–12814. 120 rooms with shower. *Dennenheuvel* (M), 27 Heerderweg; 05780–12326. 17 rooms.

Restaurant. *'t Soerel* (E), 22 Soerelseweg; 05780–88276. Rustic restaurant in forest; has charm of a hunting lodge. Game specialties. *De Veldhoeve* (E), 1 Dellenweg; 057–15000.

GARDEREN (Gelderland). *Het Speulderbos* (E), 54 Speulderbosweg; 05776–1541. 83 rooms and all comforts. Attractive woodland setting.

GIETHOORN (Overijssel). Village with canals instead of streets. *Jachthaven Giethoorn* (M), 128 Beulakerweg; 05216–1216. 20 rooms.

GROESBEEK (Gelderland). *Sionshof* (E), 53 Nijmeegsebaan; 080–227727. 22 rooms. Very comfortable and attractive hotel; on the road to Nijmegen, couple of miles out of town. Good restaurant. *De Wolfsberg* (M), 12 Mooksebaan; 08891–1327. 20 rooms. Quiet hotel in attractive woodland setting.

HARDERWIJK (Gelderland). IJsselmeer port and gateway to Oostelijk Flevoland Polder. *Baars* (M), 52 Smeepoortstraat; 03410–12007. 20 rooms, half with bath. *De Stadsdennen* (M), 7 Leuvenumsseweg; 03410–12003. 18 rooms.

Restaurant. *Zwaluwenhoeve* (M), 108 Zuiderzeestraat; 03413–1993. Attractive 18th-century farm housing good restaurant at Hierden, a mile north.

HEELSUM (Gelderland). *Hotel Klein Zwitserland* (E), 5 Klein Zwitserlandl-aan; 08373–19104. With excellent restaurant in attractive farm buildings. Highly recommended.

Restaurant. *De Kromme Dissel* (E), 5 Klein Zwitserlandlaan; 08373–13118. Adjacent to above hotel, specializes in game.

HENGELO (Overijssel). Industrial center 39 miles southeast of Zwolle. *'t Lansink* (M), 18 C. T. Storkstraat; 074–910066. 25 rooms, all with bath.

HOLTEN (Overijssel). **Restaurant.** *'t Losse Hoes* (M), 14 Holterbergweg; 05483–1353. Attractive small restaurant in hotel of the same name.

KAMPEN (Overijssel). Former Hanseatic port 10 miles west of Zwolle. *De Stadsherberg* (M), 48 IJsselkade; 05202–12645. 16 rooms. Good view of river. *Van Dijk* (M), 30 IJsselkade; 05202–14925. 22 rooms. By the river.

LELYSTAD (Gelderland). *Hotel Lelystad* (M), 1 Agoraweg; 03200-42444.

LEUSDEN (Utrecht). *Huize Den Treek* (M), 23 Trekerweg; 03498–1425. 20 rooms. In quiet woodland setting.

LOCHEM (Gelderland). Holiday town 30 miles east of Arnhem. *Alpha* (M), 2 Paaschberg; 05730–4751. 40 rooms. *'t Hof van Gelre* (M), 38 Nieuweweg; 05730–3351. 60 rooms. Comfortable with indoor pool, solarium, etc. *De Scheperskamp* (M), 3 Paaschberg; 05730–4051. 35 rooms. *Vijverhof* (M), 11 Mar. Naefflaan; 05730–1024. 23 rooms.

LOOSDRECHT (Utrecht). *Hotel Jachthaven 't Kompas* (E), 203 Oud-Loosdrechtsedijk; 02158–3200. Small, but with good restaurant.

LUNTEREN (Gelderland). *Hostellerie de Lunterse Boer* (M), 87 Boslaan; 08388–3657. 16 rooms. Attractive hotel in woodland; good restaurant.

MARKELO (Overijssel). Resort town 28 miles southeast of Zwolle. *De Haverkamp* (M), 28 Stationsstraat; 05476–1292.
Restaurant. *In de Kop'ren Smoore* (M), 20 Holterweg; 05476–1344. Old farmhouse with authentic tiled walls; atmospheric and good. 8 rooms.

NIJMEGEN (Gelderland). Largest city in the province, 10 miles south of Arnhem. *Belvoir* (E), 101 Graat v. Roggestraat; 080–232344 75 rooms, all facilities, including heated pool. *Altea-Etap* (M), 29 Stationsplein; 080–238888. 80 rooms. *Apollo* (M), 14 Bisschops Hamerstraat; 080–223594. 20 rooms. *Atlanta* (M), 38 Grote Markt; 080–240128. 17 rooms, centrally located.
Restaurants. *De Belvedere* (E), 28 Kelfkensbos; 080–226861. International menu. *Het Poortwachtershuys* (E), 57 Kelfkensbos; 080–235024. Closed Sun. *In de Boterwaag* (M), 26 Grote Markt; 080–226736. In an old Weigh House; Dutch dishes. *In d'Oude Laeckenhal* (M), 23 Markt; 080–229113. Interesting and atmospheric old restaurant next door.

OOSTERBEEK (Gelderland). *De Bilderberg* (E), 261 Utrechtseweg; 085–340843. 150 rooms, most with bath or shower. Attractive and quiet woodland setting. *Dreijeroord* (M), 12 Graaf van Rechterenweg; 085–333169. 30 rooms. Attractive garden. *Strijland* (M), 6 Stationsweg; 085–343034.

OOTMARSUM (Overijssel). In the woods, about 15 miles northeast of Almelo. *Kuiperberg* (E), 63 Almelosestraat; 05419–1331. 16 rooms. Attractive old hotel with pool and good restaurant. *de Wiemsel* (E), 2 Winhofflaan; 05419–2155. 48 rooms and suites. Very attractive grounds; pool, tennis and riding, excellent restaurant. *Van der Maas* (M), 7 Grotestraat; 05419–1281. 24 rooms. Comfortable.
Restaurant. *De Wanne* (E), 2 Stoldesenkamp; 05419–1270. Excellent and recommended.

OTTERLOO (Gelderland). *Jagersrust* (M), 19 Dorpsstraat; 08382–1231. 20 rooms, near entrance to National Park.

RHENEN (Utrecht). Garden town on the Rhine, 17 miles west of Arnhem. *De Koerheuvel* (M), 5 Koerheuvelweg; 08376–6532. 20 rooms. Excellent view from the tower of seven provinces! *'t Paviljoen* (M), 105 Grebbeweg; 08376–9003. Excellent restaurant.

CENTRAL HOLLAND

Restaurant. *Chez Jacques,* in Hotel de Eekhoorn, 3 Utrechtsestraatweg; 08376–2276. Lovely view over the park.

RUURLO (Gelderland). Attractive little village between Zutphen and Winterswijk. *Avenarius* (M), 2 Droopstraat; 05735–1403. 18 rooms, all with bath.

SOEST (Utrecht). 12 miles east of Utrecht. **Restaurant.** *Het Zwaantje* (M), 2 Rademakerstraat; 03463–1423. Good restaurant at Soesterberg by Utrecht–Amserfoort highway.

UTRECHT. Provincial capital, 26 miles southeast of Amsterdam. *Holiday Inn* (E), 24 Jaarbeursplein; 030–910555. 250 rooms, all with bath and TV. Pool, sauna and extensive conference facilities among all the many expected comforts; adjacent to the Exhibition and Congress Halls. *Des Pays-Bas* (E), 10 Janskerkhof; 030–333321. 50 rooms, all with bath. *Smits* (M), 14 Vredenburg; 030–331232. 45 rooms, most with bath. *Hotel Hes* (M), 2–4 Maliestraat; 030–316424. 20 rooms, most with bath; quiet location.
Restaurants. *Cafe de Paris* (E), 16 Drieharingstraat; 030–317503. French, highly recommended. *Jean d'Hubert* (E), 228 Vleutenseweg; 030–945952. French, seasonal specialties. A bit out of the center. Closed Sun. and Mon. *Codninck van Portugal* (M), Voorstraat; 030–322775. Dutch dishes. *Hoog Brabant* (M), 23 Radboudkwartier; 030–331525. Good grill. *Juliana* (M), 464 Amsterdamsestraatweg; 030–440032.

VEIRHOUTEN (Gelderland). Village in middle of Veluwe, 31 miles north of Arnhem. *De Mallejan* (E), 70 Nunspeterweg; 05771–241. 45 rooms, all with bath or shower. Attractive woodland setting, plus tennis and riding.
Restaurant. *Le Gueridon* (M), 5 Elspeterbosweg; 05771–200. Woodland inn; game specialties.

VINKEVEEN (Utrecht). *Vinkeveen* (E), 1 Groenlandsekade; 02949–3066. 60 rooms, all with bath or shower. Superior hotel located right by the lakes, with water sports facilities; very good restaurant.
Restaurant. *Le Canard Sauvage* (E), 1 Groenlandskade; 02949–3066. French, highly recommended.

WAGENINGEN (Gelderland). 11 miles west of Arnhem; German forces surrendered here in 1945. *Nol in t'Bosch* (M), 60 Hartenseweg; 08373–19101. 30 rooms, most with bath; attractive woodland setting.

WIJK BIJ DUURSTEDE (Utrecht). Attractive old village 11 miles southeast of Utrecht with 13th-century ruins. *De Oude Lantaarn* (M), 1 Markt; 03435–71372.
Restaurant. *Duurstede* (E), 7 Maleborduurstraat; 03435–72946. Dinner only; highly recommended.

WINTERSWIJK (Gelderland). Attractive city near German border, 41 miles east of Arnhem. *Centraal* (M), 68 Misterstraat; 05430–12229. 14 rooms. Centrally located.

WOLFHEZE (Gelderland). *Buunderkamp* (E), 8 Buunderkamp; 08308–1166. 55 rooms, 25 apartments. Many facilities; attractive woodland setting.

Wolfheze (E), 17 Wolfhezeerweg; 085–337852. 70 rooms. Quiet hotel in wood-land setting.

ZEDDAM (Gelderland). *Aaldering* (M), 1 s'Heerenbergseweg; 08345–1273. *Montferland* (M), 1 Montferland; 08245–1444. 12 rooms; very quiet.

ZEIST (Utrecht). 6 miles east of Utrecht. *Kasteel 't Kerkebosch* (E), 31 Arnhemse Bovenweg; 03404–14734. Historic building in quiet woodland set-ting. *Figi* (M), 3 Het Rond; 03404–27411. 40 rooms, all with bath or shower. A Golden Tulip Hotel. Excellent restaurant. *Hermitage* (M), 7 Het Rond; 03404–24414. 10 rooms; excellent restaurant.

Restaurant. *Het Slot Zeist* (E), 1 Zinzendorflaan; 03404–27528. In castle dating from 1686. *Hoefslag* (E), 28 Vossenlaan; 030–784395. Splendid seafood restaurant, 2 miles north of Zeist in Bosch en Duin; very expensive and grand.

ZUTPHEN (Gelderland). Delightful city 18 miles northeast of Arnhem. *'s Gravenhof* (M), 11 Kuiperstraat; 05750–18222. 14 rooms. Very attractive 16th-century building in center of town; pretty garden, excellent restaurant.

ZWOLLE (Overijssel). Capital of province, 73 miles east of Arnhem. *Golden Tulip Hotel Wientjes* (E), 7 Stationsweg; 038–211200. 50 rooms, most with bath or shower. Considerable character. *Postiljon Zwolle* (M), 1 Hertsenbergweg; 038–216031. 72 rooms.

Restaurants. *De Handschoen* (E), 103 Nieuwe Deventerweg; 05200–650437. In attractive 18th-century farm buildings, a mile out of town on the Deventer road. *De Toerist* (M), 10 Kranenburgweg; 038–31064.

 GETTING AROUND. By Train and Bus. Transporta-tion is no problem in the provinces of Utrecht, Gelder-land and Overijssel. The roads are excellent, buses convenient and trains fast and comfortable. However, if you plan to use public transport you may well find that though trains are the fastest way of getting around, buses take more scenic routes. Details of good-value special rate tourist tickets are available from any VVV office.

Around Utrecht, there is so much to see within a short radius of the city that the best way to get around is by inter-city bus. Similarly, within Gelderland, buses are the best way to get around. Arnhem is the most logical base from which to explore the province, but Apeldoorn is rather more beautiful, and is almost as convenient.

For Overijssel province, it is a good idea to use Zwolle as your central point for exploring the western part and then go to Hengelo or Almelo for trips into the eastern area.

By Car. The VVV have details of a number of special tourist routes, marked with special signposts, such as the Erica Road, some 120 miles of varied land-scapes in the Arnhem region. Otherwise, the whole of Central Holland is easily explored by car as distances, as ever in Holland, are not great and roads are good. You will also find it easy to get off the beaten track.

Excursions. All the VVV offices in Central Holland have details of excursions in and around the region. To mention just two; try a trip along the Utrecht canals on a summer's evening; or there is the "Eight Castles Tour," a popular excursion from Vorden.

TOURIST INFORMATION. There are regional VVV offices at the following places: **Almelo,** 1 De Werf (tel. 05490–18765); **Amersfoort,** 28 Stationsplein (tel. 033–635151); **Apeldoorn,** 6 Stationsplein (tel. 055–788421); **Arnhem,** 45 Stationsplein (tel. 085–420330); **Nijmegen,** 72 St. Jorisstraat (tel. 080–225440); **Utrecht,** 90 Vredenburg, in the Music Center (tel. 030–314132); **Zeist,** 19a Steynlaan (tel. 03404–19164); **Zutphen,** 40 Wijnhuis/Markt (tel. 05750–19355).

MUSEUMS. The three provinces of Central Holland are particularly well endowed with musuems, many of which are worth more than a merely cursory visit. The following are among the more interesting.

AMERSFOORT (Utrecht). **Museum Flehite,** 50 Westingel. Extensive collection illustrating history of the city. Open Tues.–Fri. 10–5, Sat. and Sun. 2–5.

APELDOORN (Gelderland). **Rijksmuseum Paleis Het Loo,** Het Loo Palace and Park. Late 17th-century palace, built for Willem III and beautifully restored to illustrate the domestic surroundings of members of the House of Orange over three centuries.The museum is in the stables and consists of an interesting collection of royal memorabilia, including cars and carriages. Open daily except Mon. 10–5. Adm. Fl. 7.

ARNHEM (Gelderland). **Nederlands Openlucht Museum** (Dutch Openair Museum), 89 Schelmseweg. Splendid museum illustrating everyday life of the Dutch through the ages, though the emphasis is on the last century. Over 70 original buildings, transported here and rebuilt, from various parts of the country and many costumes, artefacts, furniture, etc. Open April 1–Nov. 1, Tues.–Fri. 9–5, Sat., Sun. 10–5. Adm. Fl.5.
Museum Bronbeek Arnhem, 147 Velperweg (tel. 085–426441). Interesting collections on the Dutch East Indies. Admission by appointment only.

NIJMEGEN (Gelderland). **Heilig Land Stichting** (Holy Land Foundation), on Groesbeek road, a mile or so from town center. Large open air museum that recreates areas of the Holy Land as illustration of Biblical stories. Open daily from Easter–Nov. 1, 9–5.30. Adm. Fl. 7.50.
Museum Kam, 45 Museum Kamstraat. Prehistoric, Roman and Frankish finds from the area, donated to the city by archeologist of the same name. Open Tues.–Sat. 10–5, Sun. 1–5. Closed Mon. Adm. Fl.3.
Stedelijk Museum (Municipal Museum), 3 Franseplaats. Housed in the Commanderie van St. Jan the museum details the history of Nijmegen and also presents good temporary exhibitions. Open Mon.–Sat. 10–5, Sun. 1–5.

OOSTERBEEK (Gelderland). **Airborne Museum Hartenstein,** 232 Utrechtseweg. Good exhibits on the battle of Arnhem, the doomed Allied attempt to outflank and isolate the German forces in Holland in September 1944. The building, dating from the 18th century, was the headquarters of the British Commander during the battle. Open Mon. to Sat. 11–5, Sun. 12–5. Adm. Fl. 2.75.

OTTERLOO (Gelderland). **Rijksmuseum Kröller-Müller,** in De Hoge Veluwe park. Magnificent collections of Van Goghs, plus many other excellent

19th-century works and some 17th-century paintings. Superb sculpture garden. One of the finest galleries in the country. Open April 1 to Oct. 31, daily 11–5. Adm. Fl. 6.

SCHOKLAND (Overijssel). **IJsselmeer Poldermuseum.** Interesting museum exhibiting material found after the draining of the polders—includes mammoth bones. Open daily 10–5. Adm. Fl. 1.50.

SOEST (Utrecht). **Het Militaire Luchvaart Museum** (Aviation Museum). Charts the history of the Royal Netherlands Air Force, with good displays of engines, planes, models and other flying paraphernalia. Open April–Dec. 1, Mon.–Fri. 10–4. Sun. 1–5. Closed Sat.

UTRECHT. Centraal Museum, 1 Agnietenstraat. Houses the city collections; good picture galleries and exhibits on the city. The latter includes a ship unearthed in 1930 and believed to date from the ninth century. Open Tues.–Sat. 10–5, Sun. 2–5. Closed Mon. Adm. free.

Hedendaagse Kunst-Utrecht (Museum of Contemporary Art), 14 Achter de Dom. Reasonably interesting exhibitions of modern art. Open Tues.–Sun. 1–5. Closed Mon. Adm. free.

Nationaal Museum van Speelklok tot Pierement (From Musical Box to Barrel Organ), 10 Buurkerkhof. Interesting and rather unusual collection of mechanical musical instruments and street organs. Open Tues.–Sat. 10–4, Sun. 1–4. Closed Mon. Daily guided tours available. Adm. Fl.4.50.

Nederlands Spoorwegmuseum (Dutch Rail Museum), 6 Johan van Oldenbarneveltlaan. Excellent museum with many steam engines (including copy of one built in 1839) and many other rail mementoes. A must for all train buffs; housed in a former station. Open Tues.–Sat. 10–5, Sun. 1–5. Closed Mon. Adm. Fl.1.50.

Pijpenkamer en Koffie en Theekabinet (Pipe, Coffee and Tea Museum), 143 Keulskade (tel. 030–979111). Unusual museum. Visits by appointment only.

Rijksmuseum Het Catharijneconvent, 63 Nieuwe Gracht. Offers survey of Dutch Christianity; many of the exhibits are very sumptuous, all are excellently displayed. Open Tues.–Fri. 10–5, Sat. and Sun. 11–5. Closed Mon. Adm. Fl.3.50.

Universiteitsmuseum, 166 Biltstraat. Documents the history of the museum founded in the mid-17th century. Open during summer Mon.–Fri. 10–5. Sun. 1–5. Adm. free.

 CASTLES. This area is rich in splendid castles, many of which are open to the public. The following is a selection of some of the more famous.

Kasteel Sypesteyn, 150 Nieuw Loosdrechtsedijk. With a collection of art and handicrafts, 16th-18th-century, especially porcelain. Open May–mid-Sept., Tues.–Sat. Tours at 10.15, 11.15, 2, 3 and 4; on Sundays at 2, 3, and 4. Adm. Fl. 4.50.

Kasteel de Cannenburg, Vaassen, 1 Maarken u. Rossumplein. Antiques arranged as in a nobleman's house. Open April to Oct., Tues. to Sat. 10–5, Sun. 1–5. Adm. Fl. 5.

Kasteel de Haar, Haarzuilens. A good collection of paintings. Open Mar.–mid-Aug., Oct. 10 to Nov. 15, Mon. to Fri., tours hourly 11–4, Sun. 1–6. Adm. Fl. 6.75.

Huis Doorn, 10 Langbroekerweg, Doorn. Collections of furniture, silverware, snuffboxes. Open mid-Mar.–mid-Nov. Mon.–Sat. 9.30–5, Sun. 1–5. Adm. Fl. 4.50.

Slot Zuylen, Zuilenselaan, Maarsen. Collection of furniture, paintings, tapestries. Open mid-Mar.–Oct. 1, Tues.–Sat. for tours at 10, 11, 2, 3 and 4, Sun. at 2, 3, 4 P.M.; Oct. 2–Nov. 15, Sat. and Sun. only. Adm. Fl. 4.50.

 SHOPPING. In Gelderland province, visit Zwollow Shop and 9 Cronieweg in Oosterbeek, near Arnhem: this small firm is building up a fine export business, hammering out metal vases—go to the source and take home a handbeaten Dutch work of art. Cigars are a product of Overijssel province. Hoog Catherijne, Utrecht, is the largest covered shopping complex in Holland, adjoining the central railway station.

ZEELAND

The Land That Invades the Sea

One of Holland's most popular holiday regions is Zeeland, the cluster of islands in the southwest corner of the country that is rapidly being joined up to form one of Europe's most attractive water-sports areas.

For centuries the people of Zeeland preferred to live a more or less isolated life, quite content with their fishing and agriculture, and basking in their historical glamor. They were rather rudely awakened to the facts of modern life when Walcheren Island was bombed by Allied planes during World War II as part of the strategy to drive the Germans out of Holland. Although this was a calamity to many of them, most Zeelanders accepted it calmly and were, in fact, not really surprised when one of the first postwar activities of the Dutch was to repair the breached dikes of Walcheren by using the surplus caissons left over from the Normandy D-day landings. But there was worse to come.

Zeeland Province is, as the name suggests, the land of the sea. In most Dutch provinces the sea presses in to the land constantly striving to win a foothold; Zeeland to the contrary pushes out into the water, invading the invader's territory, looking for trouble. On February 1, 1953, it got it.

A southwest storm of terrific velocity hit the coast simultaneously with the spring flood tide. The wind drove the high waters over the dikes, and these barriers, undermined by water on both sides, gave way. The sea poured in over virtually the entire province of Zeeland and flooded tremendous areas of North Brabant and South Holland as well, killing almost 2,000 people. It was the worst disaster Holland had suffered in its unending battle against the sea since the St. Elizabeth Flood in 1421. Water stood in the streets of Rotterdam and in the cathedral of Dordrecht it lapped against the walls under the stained glass window depicting the ravages of the flood that had invaded that same building five hundred years earlier.

A less indomitable people than the Dutch might have resigned themselves to returning to the sea, for a matter of a few years at least, the territory that had originally been won from the ocean over the centuries and which the ocean had now reclaimed overnight. But the Dutch are used to fighting the sea. Their counter attack was launched immediately. At the end of four months, all the tourist attractions of Zeeland and the two neighboring provinces, also badly hit, were again on view, with one exception—Zierikzee, on the island of Schouwen-Duiveland, which, dry again (it stands on land a little above the level of the surrounding country) was still surrounded by water; but by July Zierikzee also was once more accessible. By then the last remaining impediment to travel into this region had likewise been eliminated. The flood cut across the neck of the narrow isthmus leading from the mainland to the South Beveland peninsula. For some months afterwards, traffic had to cross in improvised fashion.

But out of that calamity Zeeland is now profiting. Within a few weeks of the flood a special commission was studying the best ways to prevent a recurrence, and the result was the implementation of the Fl. 10 billion Delta Works, a 25-year plan to close up all of the sea-arms on the southwest coast, entailing the construction of 32 km. (20 miles) of new dikes in the North Sea. Most of the dikes carry modern highways and are linked by great bridges, giving Zeeland shorter and quicker connections with the Dutch mainland. One of these is the Zeeland Bridge, which is the longest bridge in Holland, forming a 5-km. (3-mile) span across the river.

The Delta Expo

Realizing that the Delta project is even greater than the reclamation of the Zuiderzee, and that many visitors to Holland would like to see just what it has entailed and how the sea-arms are being closed, a special Delta Expo has been constructed by the authorities, which shows the whole undertaking in model form. As the works have recently been completed, this model exhibition is a fascinating opportunity to learn just how the Dutch use not only their long experience but also all the technical aids provided by modern science. All the planned dams are now closed including the most daring of them all—the one across the Eastern Schelde (Scheldt) River between Schouwen-Duiveland and North Beveland which was completed in 1986. As a result of changes in environmental and technological thought, this final element in the Delta Project has not been built as a closed dam, but as an expensive barrier, which will close only when storms threaten. The building of this barrier has taken almost 30 years and employed some 10,000 construction workers.

The Delta Expo is located in Stellendam, near the Haringvliet sluices, which stretch out along the dam. They not only function as a means of holding back the sea and protecting the northern delta area with its dense population and industry, but also as the "stop-cock" for the freshwater management of almost the whole of the Netherlands. The Delta Expo is a permanent exhibition. It is easy to reach from any direction, and has a wealth of working models, a good restaurant and a car park. A special path will take you to, and under, the enormous sluices. You can even buy Delta postage stamps with the "Nabla" postmark.

Exploring Zeeland

Zeeland consists mainly of three strips of land, like the fingers of a right hand, pointing westward toward the North Sea. The southern-most, across the River Schelde (Scheldt), is a bit of the Belgian coastline called Zeeuwsch-Vlaanderen or Zeeland Flanders. The middle finger is South Beveland and Walcheren, with North Beveland just off the northern shore. The northernmost strip, beyond the East Schelde, consists of the island of Schouwen-Duiveland, St. Philipsland, a penin-sula, and Tholen, another island.

These fingers are either islands, or peninsulas made from islands. As inlets between islands are continuously being blotted up to form more land, it is difficult at any time to state with certainty where a peninsula begins and an island ends, or vice versa. For example, Walcheren is always called an "Isle", and it is so designated on maps; actually it is linked by land to the South Beveland peninsula. The connection was formed when the channel between the two, Het Sloe, was filled in, resulting in 480 hectares (1,200 acres) of new land.

At the moment there is plenty of water separating the three strips of land, but in a couple of decades the picture will be quite different. As part of the ambitious Delta Plan to prevent the recurrence of disasters like the one in 1953, dikes are connecting the western tips of these islands, shutting out the ocean and vastly shortening the total length of the sea walls. The first of these, the Veerse Gat connecting Walcheren and North Beveland, was completed in 1961, and new dikes are appearing almost every year as rapid progress is made.

Interesting water trips covering half a day or a day can be made to the Delta Works from Rotterdam or Hellevoetsluis, with multilingual guides explaining everything.

Zeeland is a quiet, charming region, with ancient buildings and a romantic history and most of the land is below high-tide sea level. Many of its 290,000 people are still farmers, although tourism is be-coming of major importance to the local economy. As in other parts of Holland, its farms and gardens are neat, its flowers delightful. At Vlissingen, Zoutelande, and Koudekerke are the only Netherlands beaches with a southern exposure. Off Schouwen-Duiveland are large areas of beach and dunes with few houses, fine for vacationers who dislike crowds. This region has also been developed into one of Holland's finest boating and camping centers.

In South Beveland there is a distinction between the costumes worn by Protestant and Roman Catholic women. This difference centers on the rich white lace headgear. The first-named have bonnets shaped like conch shells, while the Catholics' bonnet takes the form of a trapezium through which can be seen the light-blue under-bonnet now discarded by the Protestant women. In the center of this elaborate headwear is the ever-present ear-iron, which for the beauties of South Beveland takes the form of a narrow band with small rectangular disks of highly polished gold. A five-row necklace of large coral beads is fastened with a gold filigree clasp.

In the South Beveland women's costume, breast and back are covered with a combination yoke and *beuk,* made of gaily flowered silk. Catholic women decorate their beuks with what is called "bead-lace", black tulle on which beads are sewn. Until about 1900 a jacket was worn above these garments, but it has been discarded.

The golden ear-iron worn by the Walcheren women and girls has cylindrical curls hung with gold plates. The bonnet has in recent years been growing smaller and receding backwards, so that the under-bonnet, made of an embroidered linen called *feston,* becomes prominent and hugs the head in a semicircle. The low-cut neck of the jacket displays a small yoke. A striking part of this costume is the blood-coral or garnet necklace which fastens in the front with a large golden clasp.

Formerly all Zeeland men wore shirts of colored damask or gay cotton, fastened by silver buttons, knee-breeches and light-colored woolen stockings. Now their costume is all black, except for a scarf around the neck, gold throat buttons, and silver buttons at the belt.

Zeeland people are hard-working and, being removed from the stream of world events, are interested largely in local matters. The new plan for a north—south canal being cut through their land to link Antwerp and Rotterdam roused them far more than, say, the Common Market, the Council of Europe, or events in the Far East. The people have been dominantly Protestant or "neutral" since the Spaniards were thrown out and the Reformation came in around 1572, but today there are many Catholics, too. Coloring of face and hair is darker than in more northern provinces, owing to Spanish occupation. Names of many towns still end in "kerke" (church): Biggekerke, Serooskerke and Grijpskerke.

Walcheren, Tourist Center

A tidy-minded tourist would probably look at the map of Zeeland, list its islands in order from north to south, and then start a systematic trip through as many of them as attracted him. But that is not the way to explore this province, and as it is so small it doesn't matter where the exploration starts or the route it takes. Remember that it can also be done by water as well as by road.

However, Walcheren is probably the best place to make for as a center, because this is the island with the most history and most surprises. Before you start sightseeing, you should know a little about what has happened there through the centuries, or at least this century.

Walcheren was, in fact, the scene of one of the most dramatic episodes of World War II. The Germans occupied it completely in 1940 and fortified it strongly as part of the Atlantic Wall. The Allies, after the Normandy landings, needed Antwerp as a place to unload supplies. German guns at Walcheren covered the Schelde, preventing any ships from entering or leaving the Belgian port. Drastic action was needed.

The island, or peninsula tip, is shaped like a saucer, with dunes and dikes forming the outer rim. It lies at mean tide level: when the tide is high the land is below sea level, when low it is above: breaking the saucer's rim would let the ocean in. So the Allies bombed the dikes to wash the Germans out. There followed Commando landings and after bitter fighting the last German soldier surrendered.

The flooding, with the ebb and flow of the tides, brought swift currents that swept away the topsoil and left salt brine in its place. For a time it seemed that most of Walcheren would have to be abandoned, but Dutch courage and ingenuity, with Allied help, repaired the dikes and drove out the water. Reclamation was a tremendous task. In early May, 1945, the entire Dutch dredging fleet, 312 units strong, arrived to begin the work. By that time the width of the four breaches was 2,700 meters (3,000 yards). Strong tides prevented the success of ordinary methods for closing the gaps, so 70 concrete landing craft and other vessels were sunk in the waters. New and heroic methods were used, with ultimate success. So, true to its motto *Luctor et Emergo,* Walcheren emerged from the sea and has again become the "Garden of Zeeland".

Reminders of the war, such as anti-personnel fences, tank traps, cement blockhouses and gun emplacements, some battered by shells from British warships, are still seen at Westkapelle facing the Schelde. Here, too, on the bleak shore is a stone tablet inscribed in English and Dutch: "The 4th Commando Brigade, British Liberation Army, landed here Nov. 1, 1944, to liberate the island". Sunk into the sides of the high dunes are little cement rooms, only their windows visible, which were formerly used by German soldiers but which now serve the Dutch as vacation cottages. New dikes have been constructed to replace the bombed barriers.

So much for the recent past. But the Dutch—or at least the Zeelanders—are so proud of their postwar recovery that they have prepared a miniature Walcheren panorama at Molenwater, Middelburg. It is a gigantic maquette covering about 7,000 square meters (8,500 square yards), with roads, harbors, dikes, dunes, villages and towns all to one-twentieth size. Over 200 buildings are there, along with cranes, dredgers and ships all in operation. This bustling activity is set admist about 120,000 dwarf trees and shrubs, while at night it is turned into fairyland by thousands of lights. Middelburg, the capital of the province, is as proud of this miniature representation as it is of the lovely historic buildings scattered all over the island. And, of course, the Miniature Walcheren dramatically shows the epic flooding of the island by the Allies and its subsequent resurrection.

Walcheren is one of the most popular— and oldest—holiday areas of Holland, because in addition to its fine architecture and folklore it has miles of clean beaches and wide stretches of woodland. Apart from its own great attractions, Walcheren is so located that it is easy for the holidaymaker to make excursions not only to other parts of the province but also to the attractive art cities of Belgium.

Middelburg and Veere

One of the most fascinating Dutch cities to explore is Middelburg, not only because it is the provincial capital but also because its lovely buildings still tell the story of a rich past. It is a busy city of about 40,000 people, now showing little sign of its bombing in 1940 when 500 houses were destroyed. Even the old (1123) Abijkerken, with its 88-meter (289-foot) belfry nicknamed Lange Jan (Long John) and visible all over the island, has had its massive damage restored. The Town Hall, dating from 1452, decorated with 25 statues of Counts and Countesses of Holland and Zeeland, is regarded as one of the finest in the country. The tower and the former meat hall, sometimes used for exhibitions, were added in 1506. Other additions have been made to the façade over the centuries.

The only way to enjoy this city is to walk around it quietly. Hidden away in the old stronghold called the Inner Town are many treasures of old architecture and placid canals reflecting past glory. Every Thursday, too, is market day, attended by people from all over the province, a few of them wearing the attractive Zeeland costumes. Make certain that your tour includes the Blauwpoort (Blue Gateway), the Kuiperspoort (Cooper's Gate), the Koepoort (Cow Gate), and Fish Market in a picturesque square, the Doric columns and the auctioneer's little house; in June, July and August the square features an art market every Thursday.

About 6 km. (4 miles) from Middelburg is the show-place of the island, Veere, which, strangely enough, was only slightly damaged in the war. A village of less than 2,000 now as against 15,500 to 20,000 in the 16th century, it is today, as an early result of the Delta Works, a leading yacht harbor and water-sports center.

Veere's best-known attraction is probably the house where Hendrik Willem van Loon lived and wrote *De Houttuin* (The Wood Garden), built in 1572. But another building, the huge 15th-century church Grote Kerk bears the mark of a more famous man, Napoleon. In 1811 the Emperor chose Veere as a safe last stronghold for his 1,400 sick and wounded soldiers. He made the church into a hospital, building four new floors. To keep out the chill North Sea winds he used gravestones from the church floors as window sills.

The history of the church is wrapped up with Veere's story of greatness. The town was the port of entrance of raw wool from Scotland, which was transshipped to Flemish merchants in Bruges, Belgium, to be made into fine cloth. As late as 1805 Scotland sent an ambassador to Veere, but by that time its prosperity was on the decline.

Veere's power was at its height in the 15th and 16th centuries with the Van Borselen family, who were linked by marriage to the Scottish

Stuarts and who also received English aid when needed—there is still a Warwick Street in town. The Van Borselens, who had exclusive rights to the Scottish wool trade, built Veere's Town Hall in 1474, decorating its exterior with seven statues of themselves. About the same time they began the church, planning to make it a Dom Kerk, or seat of a bishop. For this distinction, they had to have 24 chapels, each dedicated to a saint. Each chapel required its own official and he had to possess farms, cattle, and money to spend on religious matters. Rich though they were, the Van Borselens could not make it, and had to give up. Soon after came the Reformation and the Protestant faith, and the big church was no longer needed. Today, no longer used for worship, it is used for exhibitions. Its restoration is continuing.

Veere also has a small museum called De Schotse Huizen (The Scottish Houses) once used by the Guild of Scottish Merchants. It was established when a Van Borselen, Wolfaert, married Mary Stuart, a daughter of James I of Scotland. In it are busts of the Lords of Veere, the Van Borselens, of Philip of Burgundy, old maps, costumes, wrought iron and Ming china.

The people of Veere, however, have eyes for the future as well as the past, and are making the most of its new importance as a yachting center. When the dam between Walcheren and North Beveland was finished in 1961, the "Zandkreek" was separated from the sea. So Veere is now situated on the shore of the Veerse Meer, 26 km. (16 miles) long and one of the largest lakes in Holland. In the past few years this lake has developed into a splendid water sports center in which every form of aquatic activity is practiced, and with small boarding-houses, camp-sites, summer cottages and furnished rooms available in various price categories.

The Zeeland Riviera

It is only a short drive from either Middelburg or Veere to the western part of the island, sometimes called the Zeeland Riviera. It must be remembered that Walcheren is only 21 km. (13 miles) in diameter, but on this side you will find more than 10 km. (6 miles) of uniquely located southern beaches. They all have clean white sand, all carry spotless bills of health, bathing is free and safe, there are comfort-able beach cabins to be rented for the day or the week, there is a choice of well-provided beach pavilions for refreshments, and the region offers ideal possibilities for inland or sea angling.

The stretch runs from Westkapelle to Dishoek, just northwest of Vlissingen, but is also within easy reach of delightful little places like Domburg, Biggekerke and Kouderkerke. Nor need it be so quiet as to become boring after a day or so. Domburg, for example, has mini-golf, tennis, a golf course, lovely countryside dotted with windmills, and attractive woods. This is why it is a very popular family resort for the Dutch, Germans, British and Belgians.

At Westkapelle the attractions are more simple, and the youngsters at least will find the war reminders interesting. Viewing the thickness of the bunkers battered by the 15-cm. (6-inch) shells of the British warship *Rodney* in 1944, you can judge the bitterness of the fight in which the commandos lost 60 to 70 percent of their strength.

Vlissingen is a summer resort, fishing and shipbuilding center. As a port, it has been strategically important since the Middle Ages.

Facing the Schelde River and high above the water is Vlissingen's magnificent boulevard, successively called De Ruyter, Bankert and Evertsen, after famous Dutch sea captains. At the north end of this walk on the sea wall is a dike, constructed since 1944; at the south end is a wide terrace called the Rotonde, and inland from the Rotonde is Bellamy Park, a large square with flowerbeds and a bust of J. Bellamy, native poet. Nearby is the Stedelijk Museum with local antiquities, the Oude Markt (old market), and the 14th-century Grote Kerk or St. Jacobskerk.

Vlissingen is a pleasant place, quiet and picturesque. Newcomers, the story goes, "wake up unconscious", for the air is heavy and soft and the sea air most conducive to sleep. The many ships that pass here *en route* to Antwerp are not asleep, however, for it is here that the sea pilots hand over control to river pilots. You can watch this happening from the Boulevard de Ruyter, named after the 17th-century Admiral who has his statue here.

Down into East Flanders

From Vlissingen it is an easy trip by ferry south across the Schelde to Breskens, to explore the 64-km. (40-mile) stretch of Zeeland Flanders. This region has been called "oasis of peace": the peace of polders guarded by massive dikes, the peace of wide fields and creeks weaving a ruff of reeds, the peace of the local inhabitants and their ways. Yet at the same time you are very close to the art treasures and historic buildings of the Belgian cities of Brussels, Ghent, Antwerp and Bruges, and the Belgian bathing resorts of Knokke and Ostend, the port town noted for its casino.

Of course, Eastern Zeeland Flanders itself has much to offer: the little fortified town of Hulst, industrialized Terneuzen, Axel with its shops and Saturday market, the "Drowned Land of Saeftinge" with its saltings and marshes, the creeks of the Schelde simply begging you to fish in them.

Hulst is a medieval city still completely surrounded by moats and ramparts. In the market place is the monumental St. Willibrordus-basiliek, the basilica, which was founded about 1200 and enlarged between 1462 and 1531. After 1807 its choir and transept were used by Roman Catholics, while the nave was the worshipping place of members of the Dutch Reformed Church. After 1929, when the nave was bought by the Catholics, the whole church was restored and converted back into a basilica in 1935.

Other old buildings in the city are the refuge of the Abbey Ter Duinen dating back to the 15th century, and the Abbey of Baudeloo built in the 16th century. There are some lovely old façades in the market place, while in the Oudheidkamer (Museum of Antiquities) is an interesting collection of old costumes, maps and folklore items. This city also boasts one of the loveliest cornmills in Holland, built in 1792 on the city ramparts. Finally, Hulst is called the city of Reynard the Fox, because the writer of the fable of that name lived here.

Terneuzen is of interest because it is a blending of the past and the present. It is intersected by a canal leading to Ghent the locks of which are among the most modern in Europe, accommodating ships of up to 60,000 tons.

Here, also, are several small villages named Biervliet, Hoek, Sluiskil and Zaamslag. In Biervliet, for example, the little market square houses the statue of Willem Beukelszoon: the man who discovered the technique of curing herrings, which is still used in Holland. The stained glass windows of the church, dating from 1660, are in sharp contrast to the modern scene of the huge lock for sea-going ships, the chemical plants and the busy shipping on the Western Schelde.

But there is much more in this extreme southwest corner of the Netherlands. You can enjoy a 16-km. (10-mile) stretch of coast with its seaside resorts of Breskens, Nieuwvliet, Cadzand and Retranchement, with their many facilities for boating, swimming and sunbathing, while all around are areas of great natural charm. Further inland are a number of interesting villages and small towns: Aardenburg, celebrated for its Roman excavations and basilica; Sas van Gent, famed for its mussels, and the Braakman region offering every form of outdoor recreation under ideal conditions.

South Beveland

A tour of South Beveland logically starts with Goes, the largest city (population 29,000) and center of a rich fruit-growing region. In the big central square are most of its picturesque historic buildings, the most spectacular being the Gothic Grote Kerk (1427) with a beautiful interior and a famous organ, the 15th-century Town Hall, and the Museum van Noord en Zuid Beveland, the Municipal Museum.

On the square are several good hotels, the best-known being the Hotel de Korenbeurs (Corn Exchange). It is a tourist sight in itself, noted for its interior decorations, tiles, and mottos, as well as for its food and service.

Goes has traditions, one in particular connected with Jacqueline of Bavaria, who had a castle here. Her story, one of Holland's great tales, is more tragic than romantic. She was born (1401) Countess of Holland, and for that reason was the target of intrigue all through her short life.

Jacqueline, or Jacoba, was betrothed at 5 years of age to the Dauphin of France, was widowed, orphaned, and re-married by the time she was seventeen. She left her second husband after two years, disavowing the marriage, and fled to England in 1421. A year later she married Humphrey of Gloucester, brother of Henry V. Together they returned to Holland where she was defeated in battle and imprisoned by her old enemy Philip of Burgundy. Escaping in 1425, she continued fighting for her rightful heritage until 1428 when, deserted by Gloucester and her marriage to him dissolved by Papal decree, she finally came to terms with Philip. She retired to her castle of Teilingen where, in 1432, she contracted a secret marriage with Frank van Borselen of the old Veere family, and died of consumption at the age of 35.

Jacoba had a hunting seat, as well as a castle, near Goes. Legend has it that she won an archery contest there and was made Queen of the Day. Doubtless she had few such happy days. In her last years she took up pottery-making and her mugs or jugs were noted as "Vrouw Jacoba's kannetjes". It is claimed she introduced a new work—"porcelain" derived from "Borselen".

South Beveland has many small but interesting towns. To name a few near Goes: Kloetinge, with a 14th-century church; Kwadendam, named after the "evil dike"; Baarland with its "two stones of disgrace" which quarreling women were forced to carry; Nisse, with its 13th-century church, Heinkenszand, and Borssele.

In the northeast corner of South Beveland is Yerseke, long renowned for its production of the succulent Zeeland oyster (30 million in good years). But during the long, hard winter of 1962-63, havoc was wreaked in the oyster beds. And a further threat was posed by the proposed damming of the Eastern Schelde, which was to have taken place in 1978 and would have cut off Yerseke from the sea. Trials were carried out by transferring the oyster culture to the eastern part of the Eastern Schelde, but these attempts failed. However, in 1976 it was decided not to close off the Schelde completely, but to build a barrier that will only close when storms arise. So the Eastern Schelde will remain a salt-water tidal estuary and the Yerseke oyster culture will be spared.

The grading of oysters is unusual. Some say that once the best were labeled No. 1, and that as grading developed the numbering started *downward* to "0", six zeros representing today's best; others claim that each "0" indicates the age of the oyster from one year old up. In fact, the number of zeros indicates the weight, it taking 1,000 oysters weighing 70 kilos (154 lb.) to merit one zero, and a 10-kilo increase per thousand molluscs for each extra zero.

To sum up this particular area of Zeeland, it can be said that South Beveland is an El Dorado for the angler, the yachtsman and the lover of every other kind of aquatic sport. Skin divers are already talking of the underwater gardens of the "Goese Sas", while for those who prefer landscapes it provides a changing panorama of tiny villages, rich orchards and rural landscapes.

Calling in at Schouwen-Duiveland

The last sector of the province to be explored is the former island of Schouwen-Duiveland, reached from the south by passing through the Wilhelmina Polder, comprising the largest farm cooperative society in Holland. Owned by six farming families, it consists of 2,400 hectares (6,000 acres) centering in Wilhelminadorp. The owners, "gentlemen farmers" all, have their own hunting-grounds, and although by standards elsewhere their joint farm is not large, the idea that they have pooled their lands (and their profits) is an interesting one.

The old ferry service to this region was discontinued once the fine 5-km. (3-mile) Zeeland Bridge was opened in 1966 as part of the Delta Works. It cost 75 million guilders to build, has 52 spans, and at places rests on concrete piers sunk into more than 30 meters (100 feet) of water. It opened up many new holiday possibilities, as it gives a direct link between the mainland and the Zeeland islands and enables motorists (including coach parties) to get to this comparatively unknown area quickly and easily.

The focal point of Schouwen-Duiveland is Zierikzee, the entrance to which now runs along a wide canal, and is well worth spending a day or so in exploration. Most of its historic monuments have been restored; its Thursday market is a feast of color and surprises; and it is noted for its hospitality. It stands, too, in the midst of typical Dutch scenery: busy tillers of the soil, black-and-white cattle, distant windmills, broad green fields, and neat rows of plants and flowers. Ahead, at the harbor end of the canal, are high sea walls and rising above them is the four-spired tower of one of Zierikzee's medieval gateways.

Zierikzee, founded in 849, is reputed to be the best-preserved town in The Netherlands. With a population of 10,000, it is the chief town of Schouwen-Duiveland. Its most spectacular attraction is the great tower of the cathedral, Sint Lievens Monstertoren, begun in 1454 but never completed. It was to have been 204 meters (680 feet) high, but when it reached 60 meters (199 feet) the townspeople ran out of money. The Town Hall (1554) has a wooden steeple with a statue of Neptune. The oldest part, originally the meat hall, dates from the end of the 14th century, but was rebuilt in 1554 and again in 1779. It now houses the Gemeentemuseum, which traces the city's history. It includes the will of Peter Mogge, made in 1580. Mogge was a Zeeland member of the Dutch government, and through his will Zierikzee still derives revenues. Mogge was imprisoned for two years for alleged aid to the Spaniards, then he was found not guilty and released. He died soon after, and left 200,000 florins to found a university for Zierikzee. But other provinces objected—Leiden University was just getting started—so the fund remained on the town's books.

Also in the museum are details for making "royal purple", the color "fit only for Kings", by crushing tiny crabs to powder.

Zierikzee's streets are narrow and cobblestoned. Its three gateways are old but solid. One of them, the Nobelpoort (15th century) has two towers, each guarding roads along both sides of a canal. The two others are the Noordhavenpoort, its façade dating from 1559 and the Zuidhavenpoort, from the 15th-century.

The wide open beaches and wooded sand dunes of western Schouwen, already mentioned, are about 64 km. (40 miles) across the island. Bird-lovers find the beaches delightful because of the many species found there. They are ideal for a quiet vacation.

A village of unusual type is Dreischor, a few kilometers northeast of Zierikzee. Built on three mud flats, it is all contained in a circle. In the center is a large building, combining Town Hall, church, school, and firehouse. Around it is a small canal stream, bright with yellow and red water-lilies.

Leaving Schouwen-Duiveland, the tourist can take a short ferry ride from Zijpe on the eastern tip of the island to Anna Jacoba in St. Philipsland. From here it is a short drive east and then south, over a bridge across the Eendracht to the island of Tholen, the last stop in Zeeland.

Recently, interest has been aroused in Oud Vossemeer (population 2,200), for it is reported to have been the family seat of the ancestors of the late President Franklin D. Roosevelt. This belief is due to the fact that the name "Van Roosevelt" was discovered on one of the coats-of-arms found in an old court room.

The people of the island of Tholen are farmers, and workers in the oyster and mussel fisheries. They are, like other Zeelanders, conservative in politics and devout in religion.

Zeeland Progress

This short survey of Zeeland Province would be incomplete without another look at the world-famed Delta Works which have closed up the sea-arms. As mentioned earlier, the project is now complete, and visitors to Zeeland should not miss the opportunity of visiting the area to see how the Dutch hydraulic engineers used ultramodern methods to build the world's largest open-sea dams and dikes. Using cable railways and helicopters to drop mammoth concrete blocks, as well as radar, computers, electronic devices and nylon sheeting, the work was speeded up to an almost unbelievable extent. It is still regarded in the realm of hydraulic engineering as one of the modern wonders of the world, so it is not surprising that among the hundreds of thousands who go there every year are many engineers who regard a visit as a crash course on dike construction. But even non-engineering visitors find it a fascinating experience.

Last but not least, we'd like to stress the attractiveness of Zeeland Province for a boating holiday. Indeed, it is in many ways ideal for this, with its dozens of yacht harbors sheltering many thousands of boats. As a result of strong tides and a high tidal range, however, the estuaries of Southwest Holland should only be sailed by experienced crews. But at the same time, the new inland lakes being formed by the closing up of almost all the sea-arms are providing abundant opportunities for ordinary boating and all kinds of water sports. Major yacht harbors include Veere, Breskens, Zierikzee, Yerseke, St. Annaland and Bruinisse, as well as others along the banks of the newly created Brielse Meer southwest of Rotterdam, the Veerse Meer between Walcheren, North and South Beveland, and the Braakman in Zeeland Flanders. Except for this last lake, all the lakes and waters are accessible through canals and other waterways.

These lakes are particularly suitable for small boats, sailing, windsurfing and waterskiing. The many new facilities have turned this region into a complete water-sports haven with varied accommodations, boating and recreations. This means that, apart from its original historical and romantic attractions, the region has become one of the most popular areas in the country for a holiday afloat.

PRACTICAL INFORMATION FOR ZEELAND

 TELEPHONE CODES. We have given telephone codes for all the towns and villages in this chapter in the hotel and restaurant listings that follow. These codes need only be used when calling from outside the town or village concerned.

 HOTELS AND RESTAURANTS. Zeeland's extensive nature reserves, bird sanctuaries, campsites, and excellent beaches and sailing amenities attract hordes of German, Belgian, French—and of course Dutch—tourists in search of a simple, inexpensive summer holiday in agreeable surroundings. Except for such centers as Middelburg, Vlissingen and Domburg, hotel accommodations are not extensive. Good restaurants are few and you will fare best in hotels. However, with the development of the water-sports centers, it is worth calling in at any of the VVV offices and asking for details of the campsites and bungalow villages. Hotels are relatively inexpensive in this part of Holland.

We have divided the hotels and restaurants in our listings into three categories—Expensive (E), Moderate (M) and Inexpensive (I). Price ranges for these categories for both hotels and restaurants are given in the *Facts at Your Fingertips* (see pp. 17–18). Some hotels, particularly at the upper end of the scale, have rooms in more than one category and a consequently wide range of prices. Similarly, many restaurants have dishes in more than one category, so be sure to check the menu outside before you go in. Look out too for the excellent value Tourist Menu.

BRESKENS. Family resort on Zeeland Flanders opposite Vlissingen. *De Milliano* (E), 4 Promenade; 01172–1855. 50 rooms. *Scaldis* (M), 3 Langeweg; 01172–2420. *'t Wapen van Breskens* (M), 33 Grote Kade; 01172–1401. 16 rooms, 6 with bath.

CADZAND. Seaside resort near Belgian border. *De Blanke Top* (E), 1 Blvd. de Wielingen; 01179–2040. *Badhotel* (M), 57 Blvd. de Wielingen; 01179–1920. 17 rooms.

DOMBURG. Seaside resort on Walcheren. *De Burg* (M), 5 Ooststraat; 01188 –1337. 22 rooms. *Duinheuvel* (M), 2 Badhuisweg; 01188–1282. 17 rooms 11 with bath. *The Wigwam* (M), 12 Herenstraat; 01188–1275. Family hotel.
Restaurants. *De Burg* (M), see above. *Eetsaal den Roemer* (M), 11 Stationsstraat; 01188–2948. Closed Tues. *Juliana* (M), 9 Ooststraat; 01188–1309.

GOES. Fruit-growing center on South Beveland and main city of the region. *Terminus* (M), 37 Frans den Hollanderlaan; 01100–30085. 25 rooms. Opposite rail station and bus terminal.
Restaurant. *Slot Ostende* (M), 5 Singelstraat; 01100–15362. Specializes in seafood.

HULST. Inland provincial center in Zeeland Flanders. *De Korenbeurs* (M), 10 Grote Markt; 01140–12213. Small hotel. *De Kroon* (I), 2 Wilhelminastraat; 01140–14468.

KOUDERKERKE. Quiet resort on Walcheren. *De Wijde Landen* (M), 13 Verlengde Dishoekseweg; 01185–1275.

MIDDELBURG. Large, interesting island center on Walcheren. *Du Commerce* (M), 1 Loskade; 01180–36051. 53 rooms with bath or shower. *De Huifkar* (M), 19 Markt; 01180-12998. 5 rooms. Good restaurant. *Nieuwe Doelen* (M), 3–7 Loskade; 01180–12121. 27 rooms. *Court Oxhooft* (I), 14 Singelstraat; 01180 –26823.
  Restaurants. *Den Gespleten Arent* (E), 25 Vlasmarkt; 01180–36122. In an old Patrician house. *Rotisserie Michel* (E), 19 Korte Geere; 01180–11596. Fish specialties. *Schouwburg* (M), Molenwater. *Stationsrestauratie* (M), Kanaalweg. *Visrestaurant Bij Het Stadhuis* (M), 8 Lange Noordstraat; 01180–27058. For fish dishes.

OOSTKAPELLE. Small resort on Walcheren. *Zeelandia* (M), 39 Dorpsstraat; 01188–1366. 19 rooms, 10 with bath.

RENESSE. Small resort on Schouwen Diuveland. *Apollo Hotel Renesse* (E), 2–4 Laone; 01116–2500. 32 rooms with bath or shower. Pool. *Motel de Zeeuwse Stromen* (E), 5 Duinwekken; 01116–2040.
  Restaurants. *De Horizon* (M), Hoogeboomlaan. *Rietnisse* (M), Oude Moolweg.

SAS VAN GENT. *De la Bourse* (M), 67 Westkade; 01158–2420. *Royal* (M), 12 Gentsestraat; 01158–1853.

SCHUDDEBEURS. *Hostellerie Schuddebeurs* (M), 35 Donkereweg; 01110–5651. 3 km. outside Zierikzee. 24 rooms; excellent restaurant. In the woods.

SLUIS. Inland Zeeland Flanders town, near Belgian border. *Sanders de Pauw* (M), 44 Kade; 01178–1224. *Ter Kade* (M), 13 Meerminnestraat; 01178–1437.

TERNEUZEN. Major town and ferry terminus in Zeeland Flanders. *Churchill* (E), 700 Churchillaan; 01150–21120. 54 rooms. Pool. *'l Escaut* (M), 65 Scheldekade; 01150–94855. 10 rooms. *de Post* (M), 60 Nieuwstraat; 01150–12427.
  Restaurant. *de Milliano* (M-E), 28 Noteneeweg; 01150–20817. Good food in attractive waterside setting.

VEERE. Delightful old town on Walcheren. *De Campveerse Toren* (M), 2 Kade; 01181–291. 19 rooms, 9 with bath. Restaurant. Panoramic location in medieval powder magazine at entrance to harbor. *'t Waepen van Veere* (M), 23 Markt; 01181–231. 14 rooms.
  Restaurant. *d'Ouwe Werf,* by the harbor.

VLISSINGEN (FLUSHING). Walcheren seaport and largest city in Zeeland. *Maritiem Hotel Britannia* (E), 244 Blvd. Evertsen; 01184–13255. 35 rooms with bath, all facing the sea. A Golden Tulip hotel and the best in town. *Strandhotel*

Golden Tulip (E), 4 Blvd. Evertsen; 01184–12297. 43 rooms, good facilities. By the sea. *Piccard* (M), 178 Badhuisstraat; 01184–13551. 36 rooms, 17 with bath.

Restaurants. *Rôtisserie La Mer* (E), in Strandhotel, see above. Very good cooking. *De Beurs* (M), 11 Beurplein. Situated in the former stock exchange. *Boulevard* (M), 4 Bellamypark. *Gevangentoren* (M), 1 Boulevard de Ruyter; 01184–17076. International and fish dishes.

WESTKAPELLE. Westernmost point of Walcheren and of Holland. *Badhotel Westkapelle* (M), 2 Grindweg; 01187–1358. *De Valk* (M), 97 Zuidstraat; 01187–1294. 15 rooms.

YERSEKE. *Restaurant Hotel Reymerswall* (E), 5 Jachthaven; 01131–1642. By the harbor, excellent food. Closed Tues. and Wed.

ZIERIKZEE. Largest town of Schouwen–Duiveland and ferry terminus. *Mondragon* (M), 21 Havenpark; 01110–3051. 9 rooms. *Monique* (M), 7 Driekoningenlaan; 01110–2323. *van Oppen* (M), 11 Verrenieuwstraat; 01110–2288. Good Chinese restaurant.

Restaurants. *De Beuze* (M), 7 Havenplein; 01110–7194. Fish specialties. *Bistro 't Schuitje* (M), 6 Schuithaven; 01110–3015. French.

ZOUTELAND. Seaside resort on south of Walcheren. *Zuiderduin* (E), 2 de Bucksweg; 01186–1810. Golden Tulip hotel. 110 rooms; pool, tennis. *Willebrord* (M), 175 Smidsstraat.

GETTING AROUND. By Car. Zeeland is another of the rural areas of Holland that is best toured by car. From Rotterdam and points north, two roads lead to Zeeland. The 160-km. (100-mile) inland route bypasses Dordrecht to the east, crosses the broad Holands Diep, and then swings west just outside Breda. From there it's a straight run via Roosendaal to Bergen-op-Zoom —the name means "mountains on the riverbank" though there is little flatter than this part of the Netherlands—where you turn either north for, say, Zierikzee, or south for Goes, Middelburg and Vlissingen. The 97-km. (60-mile) route across the islands takes you west and south from Rotterdam on secondary roads to Voorne where you cross the Haringvliet bridge to Goeree, then south, again, to Schouwen, turning inland to Zierikzee, then across the Oosterschelde to Goes, via the 5-km. (3-mile) toll bridge.

In touring Zeeland, the best plan is to establish a central headquarters, then branch out on day trips to the neighboring districts. Goes, on South Beveland, or beyond on Walcheren, Middelburg or Vlissingen, are your best choices for this purpose. Thus, after exploring South Beveland and Walcheren, you would ferry across the Scheldt River for a look at Zeeland Flanders, returning to headquarters at the end of the day. Then you would pack up, go north to Zierikzee on Schouwen-Duiveland, look around, and motor back to Rotterdam or Den Haag.

Different considerations apply, of course, if a seaside holiday is your main objective. In this case you would choose among (from north to south) Cadzand in Zeeland Flanders; Vlissingen, Koudekerke, Zouteland, Westkapelle, and Domburg on Walcheren; or Haamstede or Renesse on Schouwen-Duiveland. Of these, Vlissingen is the most important, the most central and has the advantage of facing south.

By Train and Bus. Goes, Middelburg, and Vlissingen are the only cities in Zeeland to be served by trains because at the time the railways were built most of the region was either a net of islands or still under water! The bus network is excellent with many routes running along the modern dykes and across the mouth of the Rhine delta connecting the formerly isolated communities.

TOURIST INFORMATION. There are about 40 VVV offices in Zeeland, the most important of which are: **Axel,** Stadhuis, 1 Markt (tel. 01155–2220); **Cadzand,** 17a Boulevard de Wielingen (tel. 01179–1298); **Domburg,** 32 Schuitvlotstraat (tel. 01188–1342); **Hulst,** Stadhuis, 21 Grote Markt (tel. 01140–13755). **Middelburg,** 65 Markt (tel. 01180-16851); **Terneuzen,** 2 Burg. Geillstraat (tel. 01150–95976); **Veere,** 28 Oudestr. (tel. 01181–365); **Vlissingen,** 15 Nieuwendyk (tel. 01184–12345); **Zierikzee,** 29 Havenpark (tel. 01110–2450); **Zouteland,** 19 Ooststraat (tel. 01186–1364).

CAMPING. There are many campsites in Zeeland, as well as good camping houses at Haamstede on Schouwen-Duiveland and at Oudeland on South Beveland. There are youth hostels at Domburg (Walcheren), and Bruinisse.

MUSEUMS. Museums in the province of Zeeland provide a good coverage of the archeological and cultural history of the land and the sea, as well as of the region's prolonged battle against the elements.

AARDENBURG. Gemeentelijk Archeologisch Museum (Municipal Archaeological Museum), 18 Marktstraat. Archaeological finds include objects used in Stone Age, Roman and Medieval times. Open June to Aug. daily 1–5.

GOES. Museum van Noord en Zuid Beveland, 13 Singelstraat. Exhibition of costumes, guild silver, medals, utensils, toys, and the archeology of South and North Beveland. Open Tues.–Fri. 10–5, Sat. 11–4, from Easter to the end of summer.

HAAMSTEDE. Kasteel Haamstede, Noordstraat. Knights Hall. Audio-visual presentation about the history of the early 15th-century castle. Open mid-June–mid-Aug. Thurs. Reservations via VVV, 45a Noordstraat.

HULST. Speelgoedmuseum, St. Jansteen, 25 Hoofdstraat. Toys from the last 100 years. Open May–Sept. Fri., Sat. and Sun. 12–5.
   Streekmuseum, 28 Steenstraat, the district museum, with archeological and historical material and costumes.

MIDDELBURG. Zeeland Museum, 3 Abdij. An exhibition of objects relating to the culture and history of Zeeland, including costumes, jewels, archeological finds, 16th-century tapestries and a paleontological collection. Open May–Sept. Mon.–Fri. 10–5; June–Aug. also Sat. and Sun. 1.30–5.

STELLENDAM. Delta Expo, describes the Delta Plan in detail and covers water control in general in Holland. Open daily 10–5 from Easter to the end of October. Adm. Fl. 8. From Nov. to March, Wed. to Sun. 10–5, adm. Fl. 6.

VEERE. De Schotse Huizen, 25 Kade. Museum with topographical material on Veere, furniture, costumes, jewelry, and popular art of Zeeland. Open April–Sept., Tue.–Sat. 10–5.

VLISSINGEN. Stedelijk Museum (Municipal Museum), 19 Bellamy Park. History of town, the room dedicated to Admiral de Ruyter. Open June–Sept. daily 10–5 Sat. and Sun. 1–5 Sept.–June weekdays only 10–12.30, 1.30–5.

ZIERIKZEE. Gemeentemuseum (Municipal Museum), 8 Meelstraat. On exhibition are objects relating to the history of the town. There are also archeological finds, silver and porcelain, pottery and paintings. Open from May 1–Sept., Mon.–Fri. 10–12 and 1.30–4.30.

Maritiem Museum, 23 Mol. Everything from ship models to fishing equipment reflecting maritime history. Open May–Sept. Mon.–Sat. 10–5.

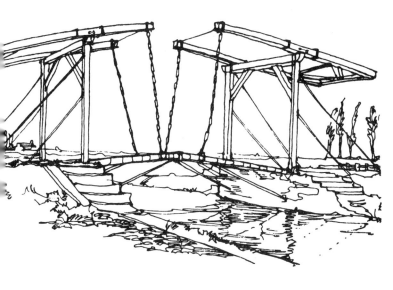

THE SOUTHERNMOST
PROVINCES

Scenic Brabant and Polyglot Limburg

Many visitors to the Netherlands pass through the two provinces of
North Brabant and Limburg on their way to Belgium and Luxembourg, or to Germany, but few pause along the way for any length of
time. This is unfortunate, because both have special attractions that are
well worth seeing.

North Brabant has been described by experts as being Dutch
through and through, yet with subtle differences from the other provinces. Scenically, it certainly has much to offer in woods, streams,
pools, forests, moors, parks, and farmsteads with reed-thatched roofs.
But it is the people who give it its real atmosphere, for the inhabitants
of North Brabant have that happiness, optimism and sincerity that
come from being deeply religious.

Limburg, the southernmost province, can be variously described.
Perhaps it is hanging on to the Netherlands like a reluctant child to its
mother's skirt, anxious to go its own way. Maybe it is like a waggling
finger pointing to the rolling Ardennes and the warmer sun farther
south. It could even be called the mark of Dutch stubbornness deter-

mined to separate Germany and Belgium, no matter at what inconvenience or danger to itself.

But whatever you think of this straggling strip of Holland, it is worth visiting, if only because of its ancient Roman flavor or because of its attractive, atypical landscapes. From its topmost point down to the southern border there are traces of ancient, even prehistoric life, such as the caves of unknown antiquity at Valkenburg, the catacombs outside Maastricht, the Roman bath at Heerlen, or the quaint farm-buildings huddled around a courtyard based on the Roman villa layout.

Sandwiched between countries that have been war's cockpit for centuries, Limburg has a polyglot charm. The earliest Dutch culture began here 2,000 years ago, and ever since then contrasting cultures from north, south, east and west have left their visiting cards, as seen in the language, architecture, folklore and art. Even the scenery seems to portray this fusion of cultures, for here you find a greater variety than in any other province.

Exploring the Southernmost Provinces

While we explore North Brabant province, let's make 's-Hertogenbosch, the capital, our headquarters. If you cannot pronounce this intricate name, copy the local people and call it Den Bosch (the Woods). Formerly a powerful fortress, it is now mainly noted as a cathedral town with a resident Roman Catholic Bishop and a growing industrial importance. In 1985 the city celebrated its 800th anniversary.

Like most Dutch cities it has seen its share of wars, and has often been in foreign hands. It was even the capital of a French district in the beginning of the 19th century.

Its most interesting sights today are the 16th-century Town Hall in the market place (which, however, is not particularly outstanding), and Sint Janskathedraal, undoubtedly the finest example of late Gothic architecture in Holland. Rebuilt between 1380 and 1530 on the site of a church almost wholly destroyed by fire in 1240, it is noteworthy not only for its fine proportions and rich decoration, but also for its army of little stone mannikins swarming over the flying buttresses and up the steep copings in a frantic effort either to escape the grasp of the demon-gargoyles or to reach heaven as quickly as possible. If you want a good local souvenir, buy one of the carved or cast miniature copies of these delightful figures.

If you are lucky you might hear the wonderful carillon (only about 60 years old), but in any case do not miss going inside to walk through the impressive corridor of 150 columns under the 33-meter-high (110 feet) nave. The pulpit, copper baptismal font, 17th-century organ case of 400 pipes, and altar screen are all exceptionally fine.

The statue in the market square honors Hieronymus Bosch, who was born here in 1450. At 94 Hinthamerstraat, is the magnificent building of the Illustrious Brotherhood of Our Lady, Het Zwanenbroedershuis Lieve Vrouwebroederschap, the oldest (1318) religious brotherhood in the Netherlands, having since 1642 Protestant as well as Catholic members. It is now a museum showing monastic life in the

Middle Ages. The Noordbrabants Museum, currently at 4 Bethanies-traat, has a large collection of coins, weapons, maps, manuscripts, and the like, representative of the region. Note that the museum is due to be moved to Government House.

Den Bosch is the focal point of one of the most attractive districts of the North Brabant Province. It is called the Meierij, and consists mainly of a quiet rustic countryside. The nature lover can stroll through woodland and moorland, or through polders with thousands of poplars and small farm houses hidden in trees or leaning against a dike. There are, however, a few places regularly frequented by holiday-makers, the most popular of which are the fen-lake De Ijzeren Man, near Vught, which is a recreation park in a forest, with a natural swimming pool, children's playgrounds and sailing facilities. Kienehoef near St. Oedenrode has quiet walks through its huge forest area. It is from these rural areas that up to 10,000 cattle are taken into Den Bosch every Wednesday for the famed Cattle Fair.

Some 20 km. (12 miles) from Den Bosch is Drunen, which houses the Autotron. Its display of vintage cars runs from 1892 to 1932, and its 230 old vehicles that have made automobile history include a 1910 Stanley Steamer Tourer, a 1926 Bugatti Brescia, and a 1922 Citroën Torpedo Cabriolet. The collection is in an old Brabant-style barn, and there are two rustic-style restaurants accommodating about 250 people, as well as facilities for hiring out certain veteran cars, complete with an Autotron chauffeur.

North Brabant

A glance at the map will show that 's-Hertogenbosch is an ideal springboard for other chief centers of North Brabant. Suppose we first go 22.5 km. (14 miles) southwest to Tilburg, with its 153,000 inhabi-tants, once a thriving woolen-textile center. Though industrial, it is also a major university town and center of the wine trade. Its fine modern theater, the Stadsschouwburg, presents plays, revues and opera. The Town Hall is a real palace, once the home of Willem II; its parks are a delight and its educational facilities the envy of many other cities. The modern mills and leather factories help to provide prosperity for the community. Town planning has been both aesthetic and scientific, building for an expected future population of 250,000; and its textile school is a model industrial and cultural center. The nearby Beekse Bergen Safari Park, at Hilvarenbeek, together with the very large Beekse Bergen Recreation Park and Campsite, is worth a visit and might inspire you to stay for a couple of days, enjoying not only the animals and the walks through the forest, but also the pleasure of swimming in the lake. In the Safari Park there are 40 different kinds of wild animals living free, among them elephants, rhinoceroses, giraffes, lions, cheetahs, camels and zebras. The best time to see all this is probably in spring or autumn, in the mating season and when the young animals arrive. Beekse Bergen Park is open daily from Easter until mid-October, 10–6, and the Safari Park from January to March and October to November, 10–4. Admission Fl. 12.50 with safari bus to Safari Park, only Fl. 8.75 with your own car.

About 10 km. (6 miles) east of Tilburg is Oisterwijk, the center of the Land of Fens and Woods. Amidst this unexpected Dutch scenery, with nature reserves and many quiet retreats are a bird sanctuary, monkey park, and a special children's playground.

If when in the village you see a happy couple in full wedding array walking up the long avenue of lime trees that form the main street, do not think there is a taxi or carriage strike. You will just be witnessing a popular custom of certain parts of the Netherlands by which (no matter what the weather) the betrothed walk to the registrar's office at the Town Hall and from there to the church.

Known as the Pearl of Brabant, Oisterwijk has another great attraction, the Eurobird Park. This is nothing like a zoo, but is a huge collection of birds in a park with fen-pools, with many tropical and foreign species. It is open from Easter until late September.

Just 11 km. (7 miles) north of Tilburg, on the left-hand side of the road before you reach the town of Kaatsheuvel, is one of the most unusual recreation parks in Europe. Called De Efteling, it is a 280-hectare (700-acre) complex of playgrounds, pony rides, puppet theaters, restaurants, and lakes for swimming and boating, plus a miniature city, an enchanted tower complete with Sleeping Beauty, a train that children can ride in and operate, a steam-drive merry-go-round, and much more. This remarkable park is, in fact, a Disneyland of the Fairytale World, in which every childhood hero, heroine, ogre and giant lives in its fabled surroundings. It is open from the end of March to mid-October, 10–6; admission Fl.16.50.

Breda the Besieged

A 24-km. (15-mile) run west of Tilburg brings you to the city of Breda, at the junction of several railway lines and on the main road from Rotterdam to Antwerp. Sightseeing should perhaps be divided between the old castle, now the Royal Military Academy, and the Great Church.

The Grote of Onze Lieve Vrouwekerk, or Great Church of Our Lady, is regarded as a splendid example of 15th-century Gothic-Brabantine style. Its beautiful tower, 97 meters (318 feet) high, was finished in 1509 and it has a remarkable carillon with 45 bells ranging in weight from 5 kg. (10 lb.) to 3 tonnes. The most striking tomb is the mausoleum of Count Engelbert II and his wife. This Renaissance monument of white marble is thought to be by Tomaso Vincidor of Bologna.

The Begijnhof in Catherinastraat, in which "beguines" (lay sisters) still lived until very recently, was founded in 1267. It was transfered to its present site in 1531. The Kasteel (castle) was begun in 1536 by the Polanan family on the site of earlier (1198) fortifications. It was subsequently greatly enlarged by Willem III in 1696. It has been a military academy since the beginning of the last century and is not open to visitors.

The town's cultural sights include, first, the Volkenkundig Museum Justinus van Nassau, named after the illegitimate son of Willem de Zwijger. It was here that Napoleon held audiences when he visited the town. It is now the Ethnographic Museum. The Stedelijk en Bisschoppelijk Museum, the municipal museum, is in the market square, housed in the exceptionally beautiful 17th-century building Het Lam, where the meat hall used to be. Finally, an innovation in Breda is the flea market held every Wednesday at the Grote Markt.

But the main emphasis in this progressive town is on its open-air spaces. You can take your choice of the Valkenberg Park, the Wilhelmina Park, the Brabant Park, the Sonsbeek Park, or the Trekpot. In addition there is a splendid chain of woods and nature-reserves branching out verdantly in every direction.

Breda, historically known as the "Baronie," lies in the area between the Biesbosch. It is a 3,840-hectare (9,600-acre) region of creeks, sandbanks, reed marshes and osier beds. It forms one of the most fascinating nature parks in the Netherlands, and is a sanctuary for many rare water-birds. Boat trips can be made through this unusual water region from Drimmelen.

Every village and township you pass through has something special. At Oosterhout is the 15th-century nunnery Catharinadal where ancient books and manuscripts are still carefully repaired, as well as St. Paul's Abbey where earthenware articles are still made in the old way. At Oudenbosch there is a Renaissance basilica, a replica of St. Peter's in Rome, but only one-twentieth of its size.

All around Breda are landed estates, many of which are open to the public, and some containing delightful swimming pools set in lovely parks, with play-gardens and restaurants galore. The landscape is dominated by many woods, prominent among which are the Mastbos and the Liesbosch with oak trees more than 180 years old.

Where Everybody Breaks the Law

While we are here, it is well worth taking time for the 23-km. (14-mile) trip down to one of the most remarkable villages in Holland, Baarle-Nassau/Baarle Hertog. Here you will find the strangest mixture of nationalities, for inexplicably tangled together are Dutch and Belgian citizens. On the map it is just a tiny speck of Belgian territory which has somehow got geographically lost in Holland since 1830. But in real life it is a fantastic civic jumble. The Nassau part, with 4,500 people, is Dutch and under Dutch law, whilst the Hertog part, with 2,000 residents, is Belgian and subject to King Baudouin's government. The main square is Dutch, except for the local pub and church, which are Belgian. Going to the Belgian frontier, you will see Belgian houses on one side, Dutch on the other, then vice versa. Some of the houses are partly in Holland and partly in Belgium: this can, and does, lead to the bizarre situation where husband and wife sleep in different countries! To help distracted tax-collectors, there are colored number plates: figures in blue are Dutch; the Belgians have white plates with black figures, and a black, yellow and red vertical stripe. In these bureaucratic times, every citizen inevitably breaks the law of both countries every day. But as there is no jail in the twin villages, no one seems to bother. Most of the inhabitants apparently pay taxes to both Holland and Belgium, and then recoup themselves by devious means that should not be blazoned abroad. There is no imaginable shopping or living puzzle that does not show itself here, for with a wandering boundary line zig-zagging through a grocery store, you can pay more on one side of the shop than on the other for the same article.

Still farther west from Breda, on the banks of an estuary of the Schelde, is the ancient fortified town of Bergen-op-Zoom. Renowned for its wealth during the Middle Ages, it is still an important center for asparagus, strawberries and oysters, but otherwise retains little of its oldtime glory except through its romantic atmosphere, which mysteriously lingers on. The town still whispers of its early importance through the impressive Town Hall, the Markiezenhof or Court of the Marquis, the Grote Kerk or Great Church and the last remaining 14th-century gateway.

The local VVV organizes guided city walks, including visits to the synagogue, Town Hall and the museum in the Markiezenhof.

Eindhoven, City of Light

We go now to "The Town that Anton Built." Its name is Eindhoven, and its founder was that great Dutch industrialist and visionary, Anton Philips, who died in 1951. Even though Eindhoven gained its city charter in 1232, until 80 years ago it was still a town of only 6,500 people who thought it a real advantage to journey to any of the neighboring villages. Today all those villages have been merged into a mushrooming development (the fifth-largest town in the Netherlands) which sustains 200,000 inhabitants, and the center of an industry that has literally illuminated the world. Philips is now an international name, known in most homes. It has factories and branches in almost every country, worldwide, all of which have sprouted from that small electric bulb factory started in 1891 with 26 workers. The various workshops of the company now cover some 2,400,000 square meters (3,000,000 square yards) and its social system for its workers has been equally as pioneering and successful as its research and manufacture. Hundreds of different varieties of electric bulbs, every kind of radio, TV and video, industrial ceramics and novel plastics, new and secret radar devices, commercial communications equipment, transmitters and receivers, scores of intricate medical and surgical devices, uncanny artificial hearts and mechanical kidneys—these are some of the products of this huge concern, which has not yet failed to solve a scientific or production problem. Present research enters such fascinating scientific worlds as speeding up plant growth, and developing nuclear reactors and alternative fuel sources.

From these factories, too, have come intricate components (some actually invented or developed here) which enabled America's astronauts to reach the moon, and from here, also, the NATO countries are being given new eyes and ears in the form of electronic devices which make gunnery more accurate even in the dark. Philips is today one of the great multi-national companies. Its annual turnover is vast and it employs well over 400,000 throughout the world; and it is growing in size and importance every year.

Appropriately, Philips celebrated its 75th anniversary in 1966 by inaugurating the Evoluon, erected to man in relation to technology.

Shaped like a discus and resting on 12 V-shaped columns, it is a permanent exhibition giving a comprehensive picture of what science has done and can do for man. The elements of its main theme are relayed to the visitor through visual aids and electronic devices.

At Westerhoven, a few miles southwest of Eindhoven, is the 50-hectare (125-acre) Kempervennen Bungalow recreation center. It has silver sands, shallow and deep bathing waters, rowing lake, waterskiing, sunbathing fields, modern camping accommodation, including fully equipped bungalows, several restaurants, trampolines and many other recreational facilities.

Museum of Mechanized Warfare

About 56 km. (35 miles) southeast of 's-Hertogenbosch lies the village of Overloon with the largest Oorlogsmuseum or War Museum in the Netherlands. At this spot one of the fiercest tank battles of World War II was fought in September and October, 1944. The village was first pulverized by a 100,000-shell barrage, and when the mechanized attack was ended, more than 300 tanks of both sides lay wrecked.

As a permanent memorial of the ordeal the war museum was established in a 14-hectare (35-acre) park. Every conceivable type of armored and mechanized vehicle and tank is on display, together with what is probably the most comprehensive collection in existence of anti-tank devices, grenades, machine guns, shells, and other weapons. Boobytraps have a room to themselves, while historical documents and pictures tell the story of the German occupation of the Netherlands. The Park is open daily from 10 A.M. to 5 P.M.

Aarle-Rixtel, 19 km. (12 miles) northeast of Eindhoven, is Holland's bellmaking center. The chief factory here is that of Petit and Fritsen, and there is always a guide ready to show you round and roll off all kinds of figures to show how great and exclusive an art this is. In half an hour he will go round the globe with you, pointing out where carillons from this little town have been installed during the centuries, and will probably surprise you by saying that more than one-third of all the carillons in the world are in the Netherlands. Gemert, 8 km. (5 miles) beyond, is one of the most beautiful villages in this part of the country.

Another Dutch art, that of clog-making, can be seen at Best, about 11 km. (7 miles) northwest of Eindhoven. You never saw so many wooden shoes in your life as are always piled up in the yards of the small factories here. Sometimes there is an accumulation of several months' work, totaling 100,000 pairs. It is interesting to note that the Dutch clog was used as the model for the U.S. astronauts' moon-walking shoes.

Between Eindhoven and 's-Hertogenbosch you will see a profusion of windmills along the River Dommel. The medieval dues that the millers still have to pay are reserved for charity, being administered with solemn ceremony by a foundation in 's-Hertogenbosch aptly called Godshuizen, or God's Houses.

Other tips for trips in scenic Brabant include: The Simon Stevin Observatory at Hoeven (between Breda and Bergen-op-Zoom), which is really a permanent exhibition of everything connected with astronomy and contains the Copernicus Planetarium, the only one in Europe. The recreation center of Hoeven with its rich natural attractions and a four-fold series of water basins for swimming or water cycling. The Windmill Museum at Nieuw Vossemeer (in the extreme west of the province), a windmill 'museum', with one full-size mill and working models of others.

In and Around Limburg

Limburg is a region of great natural beauty mixed with a wealth of cultural monuments and treasures. Its people clearly show a Latin strain, marked by love of music and of good living, with their whole outlook reminiscent of the Mediterranean countries. This is obviously due to their Roman heritage, for this area was part of the Roman Empire for four centuries, during which both Maastricht and Heerlen were thriving Roman settlements and the whole countryside was dotted with Roman buildings ranging from castles to villas and from farm houses to fortresses. The famous Via Appia (Appian Way) leading from Cologne to the Channel ports passed through both Heerlen and Maastricht, and Bishop Servatius, who played such an important part in converting this region to Christianity when the Romans were in full power, was buried near Maastricht in A.D. 384.

So here in this attractive province you can enjoy the product of the heyday of Romanesque art, the majesty of Gothic art, the delights of Renaissance and Baroque culture, the reorientation of an era born in Napoleonic times, and finally the results of that new era as seen in modern Dutch art which flourishes in this province. So steeped is the region in the art and culture of the centuries that today more than 300 artists live here, producing a remarkable variety of work.

Limburg, therefore, is a region in which to linger, and as it has some good hotels and a surprising number of excellent restaurants, all producing a lively atmosphere, the temptation is strong to stay for a few days and explore its many attractions.

Traveling down from the north through pleasant farming land, the first stop might be Venlo, a city of 63,000 inhabitants. Formerly an important fortress, it was still a fortified town 100 years ago. Venlo received its city rights in 1343 and became a member of the Hanseatic League in 1364. Over the centuries it has gone sadly through the battle-mill, but has now developed into an attractive industrial and commercial center. However, it is still proud of its past very important history, and is still famous for its annual carnival in February or March. More tangible relics of earlier days are the 16th-century Town Hall, a beautiful Renaissance building with its council room completely covered with gilded Cordova leather, and the Church of St. Martinus, built at the beginning of the 15th century and with a carillon of 48 bells. It was heavily damaged in 1944 but has now been completely restored.

The history of Venlo and North Limburg can easily be traced in the Goltzius Museum. The exhibits include an important collection of coins and medals and various beautiful period rooms. The Van Bommel-Van Dam Art Gallery displays contemporary paintings.

Tegelen and the Passion Play

Three kilometers (two miles) south of Venlo is Tegelen, where a Passion Play is presented every five years, the next being in 1990. Recent performances, more often than not, depict Christ as a modern social reformer. The actors are all local people who really live the part; the play was written and produced by locals, and is staged in a marvelous open-air theater designed and made by the villagers. Altogether 525 players take part. They get neither wages nor expenses, and they rehearse for two years. As in Oberammergau, they are all ordinary folk such as the house painter, the poultry-farmer, the rent-collector and the schoolteacher. A total of up to 25 performances are given, usually during June, July, and August.

Roermond and Heerlen

Near Tegelen in Steyl is Jochum Hof with its Botanical Garden in which cacti, orchids, and citrus, coffee and banana plants are to be admired. Continuing south into the small richly wooded section in the center of the province, with its medieval towns, we come to Roermond, whose beautiful Norman cathedral dominates the scene. With 38,000 inhabitants, Roermond is the seat of a Roman Catholic Bishop. The early Gothic Minster of Our Lady, or Munsterkerk, was consecrated in 1224, and the Kathedraal was begun in 1410, almost destroyed during World War II, and is now completely restored. As for the remainder of the town, it will speak for itself as you stroll round. But do not miss going along that superb avenue, the Kapellaan, leading to the Chapel of the Redemptionists, the Kapel m't Zand, ending at the famous pilgrimage shrine of Our Lady.

About 16 km. (10 miles) west and slightly south of Roermond on the opposite side of the Maas is the tiny village of Thorn, called *Witte Stadje* (White Village), as the little old houses around the church are mostly painted white. The huge stone church, the Abdijkerk, with its beautiful Baroque interior, originated as an abbey, founded about 995. The church was rebuilt in Gothic style at the end of the 13th century and enlarged in the 15th century. Finally, it was restored by the famous architect Cuypers at the end of the 19th century. A beautiful Renaissance altar and a magnificent Baroque High Altar, as well as a little church museum, make the church well worth a visit.

Another 26 km. (16 miles) south from Roermond bring you to Sittard, an old Limburg gem, quite content to remain with about 45,000 residents. Its 13th-century parish church is in unusual contrast to the lovely Church of the Sacred Heart, built in 1875. And if you want to learn a little about the history and customs of this part of the province, spend an hour at the Regional Museum in the Old Jesuit Seminary.

Another few kilometers leads to Heerlen, until recently the heart of the coalmining area but now developing into a light industrial district due to the closing of the mines. The surroundings here are not typically Dutch, for it is a hilly district without polders, dikes, or tulips. The many traces of Roman occupation, including the ruins of the bath houses near the Town Hall, show that Heerlen has had an exciting history emphasized by the chain of erratically modernized ducal castles dotted over the surrounding hills.

The Heerlen of today is eminently progressive. It keeps alive its memories of the past in the fine Museum Thermen, but has concentrated on being the headquarters of the mining industry and the educational center of the area. This was once an important center for coal mining, but when the mines became exhausted they were closed down, with new and lighter industries being attracted to the area to take their place.

In contrast to the industrial scene, visitors could visit the 14th-century Kasteel Hoensbroek near Heerlen, with its collections of archaeological and geological finds, archery museum, and extensive displays of African and Asian art and artifacts. It is open daily from 10 to 5.30. On the main road from Heerlen to Sittard, about 3 km. from Heerlen's center, you will see a huge stone elephant on the left, marking the entrance to the Droomkasteel (Dream Castle). It presents fanciful stone creations in a garden, with a watch tower from which there is a fine view.

Maastricht and Valkenburg

The second leg from Sittard stretches 24 km. (15 miles) southwest to Maastricht, the oldest fortified city of Holland and capital of Limburg, lying in the center of hilly country cut by deep valleys and swift streams. An excellent tourist center and gateway to Holland from the south, it has a fine range of hotels.

Wedged somewhat hesitatingly between Belgium and Germany, this Dutch town is a queer mixture of three languages, times, currencies, and customs. It is a miracle that it has remained Dutch—probably because the dignity of its capitalship has weighed heavily upon its hoary head. There is a wide range of sights to see. The twin relics of St. Servatius, for example, are unique. One is the cyclopean cathedral St. Servaaskerk, begun in its present form about 950, whose porch (1225) is the earliest example of Gothic sculpture in Holland. The other is St. Servaasbasiliek or Oude Maasbrug, built in the 13th century to replace an earlier bridge dating back to at least the 4th century.

Lovers of old places of worship can visit the 14th-century St. Jan-skerk, or Church of St. John (Protestant since 1632), in Gothic style, with its 69-meter (230-foot) tower, square at the base and becoming octagonal higher up; the very impressive 11th-century Romanesque Basilica of Onze Lieve Vrouwebasiliek, the oldest place of worship in Maastricht, parts of which date back to the 10th century; the Baroque Augustijnerkerk (1661); the small Gothic Church of St. Mathias with its lovely 15th-century Pietà; the 13th-century Dominican Church (now a concert and exhibition hall).

The Town Hall in the center of the Market is moderately interesting, dating from 1664. Near the post office is the Oudheden (Antiquities) Museum, also known as Bonnefantenmuseum, housing relics and works of art found in Limburg. To the east is the picturesque Helpoort gate (1229) with crenelated towers and pepper-box turrets.

A scant 3 km. (2 miles) south of the capital is a real world wonder, the tunneled Hill of St. Pietersberg (indicated also as Grotten Noord on road signs). Quarried since primitive times for a chalky stone that gets hard in the air, this 108-meter (360-foot) hill was once laced with over 320 km. (200 miles) of tunnels through galleries up to 15 meters (50 feet) high. This remarkable manmade labyrinth is well worth exploring, but do not try to do it behind the backs of the guides. Others have tried and have never come out. The guides will show you the huge art gallery of pictures painted on the white walls by scores of artists. They will tell you the story of the fossils dating back to prehistoric times. They will point out the great autograph book of history, with names written in charcoal on the pillars, starting in 1037 and including Napoleon, the Duke of Alva, Voltaire, Sir Walter Scott, and even the Princes of Orange. Every tourist, out of courtesy, is invited to add to the great chalky record. The VVV office in Maastricht will advise on sections to be visited and times of tours. Entrance fee Fl. 3.50.

During the war these caves, through which runs the Dutch-Belgian border, were used by the people of Maastricht as a shelter and refuge. Wounded were nursed here, and many an airman and resistance worker was hidden here while waiting for transfer to England. Fearing the worst in the last days of the war, the ingenious citizens planned to turn part of the caves into a modern town to house 20,000 people, complete with bakery, hospital, chapel, recreation room, and library.

In 1973, however, a great problem suddenly arose. An adjoining large cement works—which incidently is very important for the economy of this region—found it necessary to expand, and the only direction in which it could do so, it was thought, was towards the St. Pietersberg maze of tunnels. The young people of the district got to work in real earnest on the gigantic task of photographing and otherwise copying the mural paintings and the huge autographic pages of this stone book, so that at least the historic side of the unique show would be saved. The task is still in progress though there is no longer a threat to the tunnels.

Those who think that Holland is monotonously flat should visit Valkenburg, 13 km. (8 miles) east of Maastricht in the direction of Heerlen. This district is known as the Dutch Alps, and even though imagination is needed to agree, its steep, 300-meter-high (1,000 feet) hills are some justification.

Hiking, riding, motoring, and climbing are all available in and around this small ancient fortified town of 17,000 people in the center of the picturesque valley of the Geul. It also offers surprises for the botanist, geologist, or archeologist, while the needs of the gambler are also served by a small casino.

Valkenburg Grotto

There are several grottos in Valkenburg, but the most famous is the Gemeentegrot Valkenburg, where for an hour you can make a well-guided trip into the underground to see the lake, galleries, sculpture and collection of mural paintings and drawings. In another of the grottos, also covered by guided tours, is a scale-model of a coal mine.

This labyrinth is not so spectacular as the tunneled mount of St. Pietersberg at Maastricht, but it is undoubtedly a sight to be included.

At the Open-Air Theater in Rotspark, modern and classical drama is presented during the summer, and farther along is an exact reproduction of the catacombs of Rome, with a tiny museum of artifacts found during the local excavations.

Climbers will marvel at the panoramic view over the frontiers from the top of the Heunsberg, and you need not be afraid of making the trip because there is an attractive little restaurant to give refreshment.

Margraten Military Cemetery is about 5 km. (3 miles) south of Valkenburg on the main Maastricht-Aachen highway. In it lie all the American dead who fell in Holland, with the exception of those who have since been removed to their home cemeteries. At times there have been as many as 17,750 buried there, and it has come to be regarded as the most hallowed American spot in Holland. Dutch families have "adopted" many of the graves and bring wreaths and flowers.

A trip up-river from Valkenburg reveals a bevy of ancient castles. On the left is the Oost Castle, and on the right are the castles of Schaloen and Genhoes near Oud Valkenburg which dates back 1,000 years. Further to the east lies Schaesberg with its two castles, and on the other side of the valley is the Keutenberg.

To the east of Valkenburg, en route to Gulpen, you can add to your snapshot album of old Dutch castles, because here you will see good specimens at Schin and Wittem (the latter, where in 1568 Willem the Silent readied his band of patriots to attack the powerful Duke of Alva, has been converted into a hotel).

Asselt, a small riverside village just north of Roermond, has a small Romanesque church dating from the 11th century.

A few kilometers from here is Swalmen, site of Kasteel Hillenraad, a really fine baronial castle. The owners do not allow visitors inside, although they let the Roermond tourist association make special arrangements for seeing the lovely grounds.

At Kerkrade, 35 km. (22 miles) east of Maastricht on the German border, is one of the few abbeys left in Holland, the Abdij van Rolduc, or Abbey of Rolduc. Founded in 1104, it is a splendid Romanesque church with a crypt that today forms part of a Roman Catholic Boy's College. A mining museum, which is well worth a visit, is housed in part of Rolduc Abbey. It is open from May to October, Tuesday to Saturday.

Kerkrade's Music Festival

But the reputation of Kerkrade largely rests nowadays on the international music contest it organizes every four years. The last one to be held proved to be the largest and most ambitious contest yet with four main sections: marching bands, concert programs, show performances, and conductors' skill. More than 320 bands from all over the world take part and it is restricted to amateur musicians. Standards are surprisingly high.

Yet visitors are not treated only to amateur musical ability. As a background to the festival, world-famous professional orchestras and companies give gala concerts, chamber musical programs and popular evenings.

Meerssen, the last on our random list, is 6 km. (4 miles) northeast of Maastricht and was the favorite residence of the Frankish kings in the 9th century. Its 14th-century cloister church was built by the Champagne monks of St. Remy, in Rheims, and contains a magnificent late Gothic tabernacle.

It will have been seen from this lightning tour of Limburg that this is a province which can offer almost everything. The visitor is, therefore, specially urged to drop in at one of the many VVV's to collect some brochures which give many ideas of where to go for a little exploration. For example, there is the Windmill Tour through the western part of South Limburg. Its total length is about 80 km. (50 miles), starting and ending at Maastricht, and it includes calls at about 10 mills of all types. For those especially interested, details can also be obtained of 15 other mills in the province. There are also regular folkloristic displays in different areas, old-style shooting competitions, horse markets, and exciting archery championships.

PRACTICAL INFORMATION FOR THE
SOUTHERNMOST PROVINCES

TELEPHONE CODES. We have given telephone codes for all the towns and villages in this chapter in the hotel and restaurant lists that follow. These codes need only be used when calling from outside the town or village concerned.

HOTELS AND RESTAURANTS. Because there are more cities of importance, standards of accommodations and restaurants are higher in these provinces than in Zeeland. Especially in the Limburg district, hotel space is extremely limited during the peak season, most notably Easter and August.

We have divided the hotels and restaurants in our listings into three categories—Expensive (E), Moderate (M) and Inexpensive (I). Price ranges for these categories for both hotels and restaurants are given in the *Facts at Your Fingertips* (see pp. 17–18). Some hotels, particularly at the upper end of the scale, have rooms in more than one category. Similarly, many restaurants have a wide range of prices, so be sure to check the menu outside before you go in. Look out too for the excellent value Tourist Menu.

ARCEN (Limburg). Beside Maas River, 14 km. (9 miles) north of Venlo. *Maashotel* (M), 18 Schans; 04703–1556. 20 rooms, 9 with bath. *De Oude Hoeve* (M), 6 Radhuisplein; 04703–2098. Small but comfortable.

Restaurants. *De Hamet* (E), on the road to Nijmegen (N271). *Maas* (M), see above, is the place to try *vlaai,* a fruit tart that is a Limburg specialty.

BAARLE-NAASAU (Brabant). Belgian enclave border town 23 km. (14 miles) south of Tilburg. *De Engel* (M), 3 Singel; 04257–9330. 7 rooms. *Den Bonten Os* (I), 23 Past. de Katerstraat; 04257–9075.

BEEK (Limburg). 8 km. (5 miles) from Maastricht, by airfield. *Euromotel Limburg* (M), 19 Vliegveldweg; 04402–72462. 62 rooms with bath. *Kempener* (M), 22 Prins Mauritslaan; 04402–71319.
    Restaurant. *La Diligence* (E), 29 Maastrichtlaan; 04402–71425. Elegant Dutch setting, light and tasty French dishes. Highly recommended.

BERGEN OP ZOOM (Brabant). Old city beside Schelde estuary. *De Draak* (M), 36–38 Grote Markt; 01640–33661. 28 rooms. Good restaurant. *De Gouden Leeuw* (M), 14 Fortuinstraat; 01640–35000. 22 rooms. Both central.
    Restaurants. *De Bloembool* (M), 146 Wouwsestraatweg; 01640–33045. *De Moyses* (M), 1 Moolstraat; 01640–34340.

BORN (Limburg). Industrial center. *Crest Hotel Bern* (E), 21 Langereweg; 04498–51666. On E9 Highway. 50 rooms with bath or shower; restaurant.

BREDA (Brabant). 50 km. (31 miles) south of Rotterdam. *Motel Breda* (E), 20 Roskam; 076–222177. Over 100 rooms, many with bath or shower. Restaurant, snackbar and indoor pool. *Mastbosch* (E), 20 Burg. Kerstenslaan; 076–650050. 47 rooms, all with bath. Opposite woods on the edge of town. *Bel Air* (M), 45 Boschstraat; 076–226949. *Motel Brabant* (M), 4 Heerbaan; 076–224666. 85 rooms with bath. *De Klok* (M), 24 Grote Markt; 076–214082. Family-run, small, right in center.
    Restaurants. *Arent* (M). In a 17th-century building in main square. *Het Voske* (M), in the market square. Old Brabant style. *De Boschwachter Liesbosch* (M), Nieuwe Dreef; and *'t Valken* (M), Stationsplein, are all also good.
    At Princehage, 4 km. (2½ miles) southwest of Breda, try the *Mirabelle,* 76 Dr. Batenburglaan, or the *Princeville,* 57 Liesboschlaan. Both are (M) and good.
    At Dorst, near Breda, is *Surae,* a recreation center in the middle of the national forest. Pool, playgrounds, sports facilities, and (I) restaurant.

DRUNEN (Brabant). *Royal* (M), 13 Raadhuisplein; tel. 04163–72381.
    Restaurant. *Duinrand* (E), 2 Steegerf; 04163–72498. Excellent French food.

EINDHOVEN (Brabant). *De Cocagne* (E), 47 Vestdijk; 040–444755. 207 rooms with bath. Cinema, good Dutch-style restaurant, garage. *Golden Tulip Geldrop* (E), 219 Bogardeind; 040–867510, at Geldrop on the outskirts of Eindhoven, on E13 Hwy. 141 rooms with bath. Pool, sauna. *Holiday Inn* (E), 1 Veldm. Montgomerylaan; 040–433222. 215 rooms, swimming pool. *The Mandarin* (E), 17 Geldropseweg; 040–125055. 60 rooms. Chinese restaurant. *De Bijenkorf* (M), 35 Markt; 040–454545. 50 rooms. Central; Mexican restaurant. *Motel Eindhoven* (M), 322 Aalsterweg; 040–116033, on the A67. 180 rooms with bath. *Parkhotel* (M), 18 Alb. Thijmlaan; 040–114100. *Mulders* (M), 35 Guido Gezellestraat; 040–445506. Breakfast only. *Eikenburg* (I), 281 Aalsterweg; 040–110957.
    Restaurants. *Bruegel* (E), in Cocagne Hotel, 47 Vestdijk; 040–444755; *L'Etoile,* same address and phone, for Dutch and French cuisine. *De Karpendonske Hoeve* (E), 3 Sumatralaan; 040–813663. Superb quality, recommended. *Mei Ling* (E), 17 Geldropseweg; 040–125055. In Mandarin Hotel. Choice of 300 genuine Chinese/Indonesian dishes. *L'Aubergade* (M), 9 Wilhelminaplein; 040–446709. *Grillbar De Bus* (M), 9 Nieuwstraat; 040–449070. *La Fontana* (M), 50

Stratumseind; 040–444617. Excellent Italian food. *Trocadero* (M), 15 Stationsplein; 040–449016.

GULPEN (Limburg). Village 18 km. (11 miles) east of Maastricht on the road
to Aachen, Germany. *Kasteel Neubourg* (E), 1 Riehagarvoetpad; 04450–1222.
26 rooms, 16 with bath. Open Mar. through Dec. A 17th-century castle with
moat, drawbridge, and gardens; just south of village in Gulp Valley. Unusual,
attractive. *Bettina* (I), 43 Rijksweg; 04450–1581.
Restaurant. *De Blaasbalg* (E), 37 Einderstraat; 04450–1364. Superb French
cuisine.

HEERLEN (Limburg). City in the midst of the "Dutch Alps", 23 km. (14
miles) east of Maastricht. *Grand* (E), 23 Groene Boord; 045–713846. City
center. 100 rooms, most with bath or shower. *Motel Heerlen* (M), 10 Terworm;
045–719450. 76 rooms. 3 km. (2 miles) out on A76.
Restaurants. *Bon Appetit* (M), 56 Geleenstraat; 045–717086. *De la Station*
(M), 16 Stationsstraat; 045–719001. *De blaue Schuit* (I), 6 Wilhelminaplein;
045–717499. *Heerlen* (I), 8 Homeruspassage. *Jugoslavija* (I), 21 Dautzenberg-
straat. Small, cozy.

HEEZE (Brabant). *Hostellerie du Château* (E), 48 Kapelstraat; 04907–3515.
12 rooms and highly recommended restaurant in attractive setting.

HELMOND (Brabant). Attractive textile center 38 km. (24 miles) southeast
of 's-Hertogenbosch. *Sint Lambert* (M), 2 Markt; 04920–25562. 21 rooms. *West
Ende* (M), 1 Steenweg; 04920–24151. 43 rooms most with bath or shower.
Restaurant. *De Hoefslang* (E), 2–4 Waranda; 04920–36361. Not to be missed,
tasteful French cuisine.

's HERTOGENBOSCH (Brabant). Provincial capital and cathedral city 79
km. (49 miles) southeast of Rotterdam. *Golden Tulip Central* (E), 98 Burg.
Loeffplein; 073–125151. 124 rooms with bath. Central. *Eurohotel* (M), 63 Hinthamerstraat; 073–137777. 46 rooms with bath. *Nuland Motel* (M), 25 Rijksweg; 04102–2231. 15 km. (9 miles) eastwards. 85 rooms with shower.
Restaurants. *Chalet Royal* (E), Wilhelminaplein; 073–135771. Superb international menu. *De Pettelaar* (E), 1 Pettelaarseschans; 073–137351. Excellent
international cuisine. *'t Misverstant* (E), 28 Snellestraat; 073–134281. Also superb, recommended. *De Leeuwenborgh* (E), in the Central Hotel. *De Gotische
Raadskelder* (M), la Markt; 04102–136913. In the cellar of the town hall.
Metropole (M), 60 Orthensweg; 073–133533.

KERKRADE. *Hotel-Restaurant Kasteel Erenstein* (E), 6 Oud Erensteiner-
weg; 045–461333. 45 rooms. In lovely park. Comfortable, with excellent French
restaurant. Sauna and fitness center.

LEENDE (Brabant). Village 13 km. (8 miles) southwest of Eindhoven. *De
Schammert* (M), 2 Kerkstraat; 04906–1590. *Kempenland* (I), 34 Dorpsstraat;
04906–2161.

MAASTRICHT (Limburg). Provincial capital on Maas River. *Du Casque*
(E), 52 Helmstraat; 043–214343. 43 rooms, 30 with bath. Between market
square and the cathedral. *Maastricht* (E), 1 De Ruiterij; 043–254171. Deluxe.
134 rooms; beside river. Golden Tulip hotel. *Beaumont* (M), Stationsstraat;

043-254433. *Du Chêne* (M), 104 Boschstraat; 043-213523. *De l'Empereur* (M), 2 Stationsstraat; 043-213838. 30 rooms with bath. *Old Hickory* (M), 372 Meerssennerweg; 043-2620548. *Stijns* (M), 40 Stationsstraat; 043-214973. *In den Hoof* (I), 218 Akersteenweg; 043-2610600. 30 rooms. 2 km. out of town.

Restaurants. *Au Coin des bons Enfants* (E), 4 Ezelmarkt; 043-212359. Excellent, recommended. *Grand-Mère* (E), 16 Helmstraat; 043-252325. Lovely setting, superb cuisine. *'t Klaoske* (E), 20 Plankstraat; 043-218118. Lovely atmosphere, many specialties. *'t Plenkske* (E), 6 Plankstraat; 043-218456. *Taverne Jean* (M), 6 Spoorweglaan; 043-212591. *'t Gevelke* (M), 2 Achter de Molens; 043-250401. Rustic setting.

Five kilometers (3 miles) south of Maastricht on the road to Canne is the expensive but outstanding *Château Neer-Canne* (E), 800 Cannerweg; 043-251359. Attractive views of the river, elegant.

MEERSEN (Limburg). *Koningen Gerberga* (M), 31 Volderstraat; 043-642080. *De Witte Hoek* (M), 2 Maastrichterweg; 043-642741.

MOOK (Limburg). Village 8 km. (5 miles) south of Nijmegen. On its outskirts, set in lovely scenery, are three hotels, the best of which is *De Plasmolen* (E), 170 Rijksweg; 08896-1444. 24 rooms with bath or shower. Set in private park with swimming lake, fish pond, tennis courts. Ideal for children. *De Schans* (M), 95 Rijksweg; 08896-1209; with 10 rooms; and *'t Zwaantje* (M), 106 Groesbeeksweg; 08896-1434; both comfortable.

OISTERWIJK (Brabant). Town on the edge of attractive hills, 14 km. (9 miles) southwest of 's-Hertogenbosch. *De Swaen* (E), 47 De Lind; 04242-19006. 19 rooms; excellent. *De Blauwe Kei* (M), 4 Rosepdreef; 04242-82314. *Bosrand* (M), 127 Gemullenhoekenweg; 04242-19015. *Hotel de Twee Stromen* (M), 93 Gemullenhoekenweg; 04242-82574. Small but good value. *'t Vennenland* (M), 8 Burg. Vogelslaan; 04242-82609.

Restaurant. *De Swaen* (E), 47 De Lind; 04242-19006. One of the region's best; superb and recommended. *Kleyn Speyck* (M), 140 Bosweg; 04242-82263.

ROERMOND (Limburg). Old city at the confluence of the Maas and Roer rivers, 48 km. (30 miles) north of Maastricht. *Cox* (M), 102 Maalbroek; 04750-21154. *Füserhof* (M), 1 Raadhuisstraat; 04750-29298. *Graeterhof* (M), 23 Graeterweg; 04750-1340. *De la Station* (M), 9 Stationsplein; 04750-16548. 28 rooms.

Restaurants. *Kasteeltje Hattem* (M), 25 Maastrichterweg. *Old Dutch* (M), 22 Wilhelminaplein. *de Pollepel* (M), 13 Zwartbroekstraat.

ROOSENDAAL (Brabant). Rail junction near Belgian border, 26 km. (16 miles) southwest of Breda. *Central* (M), 9 Stationsplein; 01650-35657. *Goderie* (M), 5 Stationsplein; 01650-55400. 22 rooms. *Merks* (M), 57 Brugstraat; 01650-33169. *Poort van Kleef* (M), 70 Molenstraat; 01650-34713. Central, old tavern.

Restaurant. *De Hoefslag* (M), 3 Bloemenmarkt; 01650-33755.

SITTARD (Limburg). Medieval town with many interesting old buildings, 26 km. (16 miles) north of Maastricht. *de Limbourg* (M), 22 Markt; 04490-18151. 12 rooms. *Oranjehotel* (M), 23 Rijksweg Zuid; 04490-13673. *De Prins* (M), 25 Rijksweg Zuid; 04490-15041. 25 rooms, near station.

Restaurants. *Le Caribou* (M), 56 Maenweg; 04490-10365. In an old watermill. *Rôtisserie Si-Tard* (M), 20 Wilhelminastraat. Good food.

STEENSEL (Brabant). *Motel Steensel* (M), 43a Eindhovensweg; 04970–2316. 39 rooms.

THORN (Limburg). *Golden Tulip Hotel Thorn* (M), 2 Hoogstraat; 04756–2341. 18 rooms with bath or shower; good restaurant.

TILBURG (Brabant). Modern textile town 23 km. (14 miles) southwest of 's-Hertogenbosch. *Hotel Heuvelpoort* (E), 300 Heuvelpoort; 013–354675. *Ibis* (M), 105 Dr. Hub. van Doorneweg; 013–636465. *De Lindenboom* (M), 126 Heuvel; 013–351355. Good value. *De Postelse Hoeve* (M), 10 Dr. Deelenlaan; 013–636335. 20 rooms. Out of center near ringroad spaghetti junction.

VALKENBURG (Limburg). Attractive town, 11 km. (7 miles) east of Maastricht. *Prinses Juliana* (E), 11 Broekhem; 04406–12244. 27 rooms with bath. Excellent, recommended restaurant. *Grand Hotel Voncken* (M), 1 Walramplein; 04406–12841. 50 rooms. *Parkhotel Rooding* (M), 68 Neerhem; 04406–13241. 95 rooms, most with bath. *Atlanta* (M), 20 Neerhem; 04406–12193. 20 rooms. *Brouwers* (M), 76 Plenkerstraat; 04406–13631. *Hermens* (M), 61 Neeerhem; 04406–13020. *De Toerist* (M), 3 Hovetstraat; 04406–12484. *Tummers* (M), 21 Stationsstraat; 04406–13741.

Restaurants. *Lindenhorst* (E), 130 Broekhem; 04406–13444. Another highly recommended French restaurant. *La Brasserie* (M), Passage. *De Fransche Molen* (M), Lindenlaan; 04406–12797. Both French menus.

VENLO (Limburg). Border town 72 km. (45 miles) northeast of Maastricht. *De Bovenste Molen* (E), 12 Bovenste Molenweg; 077–541045. 65 rooms with bath or shower. Outside town; tennis and swimming. *Venlo Novotel* (M), 90 Nijmeegseweg; 077–544141. 88 rooms; restaurant. *Wilhelmina* (M), 1 Kaldenkerkerweg; 077–516251. 40 rooms, 10 with bath.

Restaurants. *Valuas* (E), 9 Urbanusweg; 077–541141. Excellent French cuisine. *De Watermeule* (E), 3 Molenkampweg; 077–525214. Game dishes.

VUGHT (Brabant). Attractive old village in wooded countryside 5 km. (3 miles) south of 's-Hertogenbosch. *Heidelust* (M), 80 Kampdijklaan; 073–560593.

Restaurants. *De Beukenhof* (M), Stationsstraat. *Kasteel Maurick* (M), 3 Dijk v. Maurick; 073–579108. Excellent food in very attractive setting. On the A2.

WITTEM (Limburg). *Kasteel Wittem* (E), 3 Wittemer Alle; 04450–1208. 12 rooms with bath. 15th-century castle with restaurant noted for fine French cuisine. *In den Rooden Leeuw van Limburg* (M), 28 Wittemer Alle; 04450–1274.

 GETTING AROUND. Taken together, North Brabant and Limburg cover the entire southern strip of the Netherlands plus the tail that hangs down to the east along the German frontier. Although distances are not great, they are relatively much more than in the provinces of North Holland and South Holland. To try to explore this region in detail except by car would consume time better spent in the western part of the country. While 's-Hertogenbosch, Breda, Tilburg, and Eindhoven are readily reached by rail, some of the smaller centers are not. This is particularly true of Limburg, much of whose charm is derived from the countryside. Thus, non-motorists will likely prefer to select those localities that interest them most and then assemble them into an itinerary leading to or from another, more important region of the Netherlands. Or, they can set up headquarters at 's-Hertogenbosch and then Maastricht, making day trips by rail and bus to the surrounding communities.

TOURIST INFORMATION. The most important VVV offices are: **Bergen op Zoom**, 2 Hoogstraat (tel. 01657–66000); **Breda**, 17 Willemstraat (tel. 076–222444); **Eindhoven**, 17 Stationsplein (tel. 040–449231); **Heerlen**, 4 Stationsplein (tel. 045–716200); **Helmond**, 211 Markt (tel. 04920–43155); **Maastricht**, 1 Kleine Straat (tel. 043–252121); **Roermond**, 24 Markt (tel. 04750–33205); **Sittard**, 16 Wilhelminastraat (tel. 04490–24144); **Tilburg**, 416A Spoorlaan (tel. 013–351135); **Valkenburg**, 5 Th. Dorrenplein (tel. 04406–13364); **Venlo**, 2 Koninginneplein (tel. 077–543800). **'s Hertogenbosch**, 77 Markt (tel. 073–123071).

MUSEUMS. Holland's southernmost provinces offer a wide choice of subjects and many fascinating as well as unusual collections and exhibitions in museums across the region. Some of the most important are listed below.

ASTEN. Asten Museum, 23 Ostadestraat. This is a museum in two parts: the *Jan Vriends Museum* is a nature study center with a very good collection of butterflies and birds, as well as outdoor biotopes and aquaria. The *Nationaal Beiaardsmuseum* has bells and chimes, tower clocks, musical boxes, keyboards, and bell founder's tools. Open Tues.–Sun., 10–5. Closed Mon.

BERGEN OP ZOOM. Gemeente Museum Markiezenhof (Municipal Museum). Collection of local pottery, history of town, guild objects. Open Tues.–Sun. 2–5, mid-June–mid-Aug. Tues.–Fri. 10–5, Sat. and Sun. 2–5.

BREDA. Stedelijk en Bisschoppelijk Museum, 19 Grote Markt. Contains a collection of ecclesiastical art and objects relating to the history of Breda. It includes a collection of coins and prints. Open Wed.–Sat. 10.30–5; Tues., Sun. and holidays 1–5.
Volkenkundig Museum Justinus Van Nassau, 15 Kasteelplein. Ethnographic collection from Indonesia and other Third World countries. Changing exhibition. Open Mon.–Sat., 10–5; Sun. and public holidays 1–5.

CADIER EN KEER. Museum Africa-Centrum, 3 Rijksweg. Art and ethnographic collection from West Africa. Material from 13th century to the present day; includes all aspects of tribal life and culture. Open Mon.–Fri. 10–12 and 2–5; Sat., Sun. and public holidays 2–5.

DRUNEN. Themapark Vervoer Autotron, 100 Museumslaan. The biggest car museum in Europe with more than 400 cars including famous old-timers such as the Mercedes of the last German Emperor. Open Oct.–Apr. Sat. and Sun. 11–5; June–Oct. Mon.–Fri. 10–5, Sat. and Sun. 11–5. Adm. Fl. 8.

EINDHOVEN. Stedelijk Van Abbemmuseum, 10 Bilderdijklaan. The municipal museum; changing exhibitions of 20th-century visual arts. Open Tues.–Sat. 10–5, Sun. 1–5.

Evoluon, la Noord Brabantlaan. The evolution of science and technology and their influence on society. Very imaginative displays and lots of opportunities for the visitor to work various pieces of apparatus. Open Mon.–Fri. 9.30–5.30, Sat. and Sun. 10.30–5. Adm. Fl. 12.50.

HEERLEN. Kasteel Hoensbroek. 14th-century castle with local archeological finds, archery museum, African and Asian art and artifacts. Open daily from May to Sept. 10–6; rest of year 10–12, 1.30–5.30. Adm. Fl. 4. **Museum van het Geologisch Bureau,** 131 Voskuilenweg. Collections of fossils from the carboniferous region of South Limburg, other regions of Holland and various foreign parts. Also rocks and fossils from Cretaceous and Tertiary regions of Limburg, as well as models and maps on the geology of Limburg and a collection of minerals. Open Mon.–Fri. 9–12, 2–4. Closed Sat. and Sun. Adm. free.

Museum Thermen, 9 Coriovalumstraat. Local Roman remains including baths; also charts the development of Heerlen from 11th century. Open Tues.–Fri. 10–5, Sat and Sun. 2–5. Closed Mon. Adm. Fl. 1.50.

's-HERTOGENBOSCH. Het Noordbrabants Museum, 4 Bethaniestraat. All aspects of the region's history. Includes archeological finds, paintings, pewter, silver, copper, coins and medals, prints, religious art: changing exhibitions. Open. Tues.–Fri. 10–5, Sat. and Sun. and public holidays 1–5. Fl. 2.50.

Het Zwanenbroedershuis, 94 Hinthamerstraat, 15th- and 16th-century psalm books, and a collection of pewter, crystal and antique tiles. Open Fri. 11–3 (closed in Aug.); and by appointment. Adm. free.

Museum Slager, 16 Choorstraat. The gallery exhibits the versatile work of the artistic Slager family. Open Tues.–Fri. 2–5, each first Sat. and Sun. of month 2–5.

MAASTRICHT. Limburgs Museum voor Kunst en Oudheden (Bonnefanten), 5 Dominicanerplein. Exhibitions on archeology, sculpture, paintings, ecclesiastical art, the history of Maastricht, silver and glass. Open Mon.–Fri. 10–5, Sat. and Sun. 2–5. Adm. free.

Natuur Historisch Museum, 6–7 Bosquetplein. Geological, paleontological and biological collection, including garden of region's flowers. Open Mon.–Fri. 10–12.30, 1.30–5, Sun. 2–5.

NIEUW VOSSEMEER. Assumburg Windmill Museum, 1 Veerweg. Miniatures of Dutch windmills, as well as photographs and documents. Open approx. mid-May to mid-Sept., Sat. and Sun. 2–5.

OVERLOON. Nederlands Nationaal Oorlogs en Verzetsmuseum (Dutch National War and Resistance Museum), 1 Museumpark. History of World War II. Includes photographs and documents, charts and models, tanks, armored cars and other vehicles. Open daily, June to Aug. 9.30–6; Sept. to May 10–5. Adm. Fl. 6.

TILBURG. Maison du Vin, Geminiwegg. Wine museum and typical French street scene with bistro and bar. Open Tues.–Sat. 10–5.

Nederlands Textielmuseum, 96 Goickestraat. Old tools and apparatus for spinning, weaving, and finishing textiles. Collection of antique and exotic textiles, and a library. Daily demonstrations of spinning and weaving. Open Mon. to Fri. 10–5, Sat., Sun. and public holidays 2–5.

Het Noordbrabants Natuurmusuem, 434 Spoorlaan. All aspects of the region's natural history. Open Tues.–Fri. 10–5, Sat. and Sun 1–5.

Schrijften en Schrijfmachinen Museum (Writing and Typewriter Museum), 3 Philips Vingboonstraat. Calligraphic art, old writing styles and techniques, antique writing materials. Over 500 different typewriters, adding machines and calculators. Open first Sat. of each month 2–5. Group visits by previous arrangement.

Volkenkundigmuseum, 434a Spoorlaan. Ethnic displays and changing exhibitions of many lands. Open Tues.–Fri. 10–5, Sat. and Sun. 1–5.

VENLO. Goltzius Museum, 21 Goltziusstraat. Urban and regional history. Various period rooms and valuable porcelain. Open Mon.–Fri. 10–12 and 2–5, Sat., Sun. and public holidays 2–5.

Museum Van Bommel-van Dam, art gallery with changing exhibitions mostly displaying works of contemporary artists. Open Mon.–Fri. 10–5, Sat. and Sun. 2–5.

WAALWIJK. Nederlands Museum voor Schoenen, Leder en Lederwaren (Netherland's Museum of Shoes, Leather and Leatherwork), 48 Grotestraat. History of shoes from 15th century onwards and exotic footwear. Also leatherwork from 30 countries and an old cobbler's room from *c.* 1900. Prize-winning shoes from an international shoe design contest in 1967 to the present day. Open Tues.–Fri. 10–5. Sat. and Sun. 12–4.

 SHOPPING. The main cities of Brabant and Limburg provinces have branches of the stores found in Amsterdam, but for unusual objects we suggest the following: at Beesel, about 5 km. (8 miles) southwest of Venlo, the Atelier St. Joris bakes ceramic vases of a unique character.

Breda has an art and antique market on Saturdays in summer, where bargains can sometimes be picked up.

At Deurne, about 40 km. (25 miles) southeast of 's-Hertogenbosch, P. Wiegersma, in the Klein Kasteel, has revived the old Dutch art of beautiful stained glass work: you can order anything from the costliest memorial window to the tiniest glass ornament and have the thrill of watching a particular artist design it for you.

IN AND AROUND THE NORTH

Drenthe, Groningen and Friesland

In this chapter we introduce visitors to a very attractive holiday region composed of the three Dutch provinces which form the northeast corner of the Netherlands. Between them this trio offers a wide range of interests: from the simple to the deluxe, from leisure to activity, from woodlands to seaside, from modern cities to rural peace. What is the difference between the three? In one way, this is an easy question to answer, because each province has its own atmosphere, tradition and scenery.

Drenthe is an area of great natural beauty, with woods alternating with green fields and moors dotted with hundreds of small lakes, flocks of sheep and picturesque villages with age-old tree-bordered greens. This is why visitors here are always told that the bicycle is the best means of becoming acquainted with the heart of the province. More than 320 km. (200 miles) of cycle tracks wind their way through the region, leading the tourist to idyllic spots where many prehistoric graves can be discovered among huge boulders known as "hunebedden". And, of course, there are numerous holiday centers, camping sites, comfortable country hotels and restaurants.

Now for Groningen, steeped in history and culture, and full of surprises. The province is dominated by the city whose name it bears, which is also the capital, a university center, and an ideal excursion starting-point. Up in the north, Uithuizen has a notable castle, Menkemaborg, one of Holland's oldest and best preserved, built as a fortified manorhouse in the 15th century and restored in the early 18th century, with period furnishings and gardens. Over to the east Heiligerlee makes both bells and strawboard. Ter Apel features a medieval convent; Zoutkamp has shrimp-fishing and a fish auction; in Leens you will find the Verhildersum fortress with its agricultural history displays and old fashioned gardens of flowers and herbs. Appingedam is particularly picturesque with a church dating from 1255 and a Town Hall from 1630; Delfzijl is a fast-growing port and ocean terminal, the third largest in Holland; and Loppersum has a large medieval church with vault paintings and a massive 14th-century tower.

On a more mundane note, there is Slochteren where the huge underground natural gas reserves found in 1959 have proved to be one of the largest sources in the world, and have resulted in this almost forgotten village becoming an industrial center.

As for our third province in this group, Friesland, this will prove a real tour of exploration. It has, for instance, been called the Scotland of Holland, because it is inhabited by a fiercely independent people, proud of their separate history, language and traditions. This is the area in which Rembrandt found his wife Saskia, and where Pieter Stuyvesant, the man who founded New York, was born. Its borders contain the Wadden Islands, the unique birdland of Western Europe; a very extensive lake district; large woods and moors; old towns and charming villages; and a varied choice of recreation.

Exploring the Northern Provinces

Drenthe province, named first in this trio only for geographical reasons, is the only one in the Netherlands that has no direct association with either the sea or a major river. Once a vast swamp, it is now a quiet land of wide moors, full of character, peace, and beauty. It has comparatively few large towns—even the capital, Assen has only 46,000 inhabitants—and shows few indications of modern growth. This apparent conservatism may be misleading, however, because something close to a miracle has happened here. Just as the age-old supplies of peat, the poor man's fuel, were beginning to peter out, almost unlimited supplies of oil and natural gas were discovered, bringing with them a new prosperity that was timely. Even so, the prevailing atmosphere is still such that the Dutch themselves often speak of *mooi Drenthe* . . . beautiful Drenthe.

Assen shows little sign of modern growth: long just a small hamlet, it has successfully withstood both time and progress. The Provincial Hall, Provinciehuis, was originally the chapel of a Cistercian nunnery, founded in the 13th century but used in its present capacity since 1885. It now houses the Provinciaal Museum van Drenthe. Now normally, few tourists are interested in spending their holidays looking at rocks and stones but here we have something very different, something that must be seen, for Drenthe is the region of the *hunebedden* which abound in this part of the country. These consist of groups of enormous smooth boulders carried here by the ice-age glaciers many thousand years ago and then buried by the sand until the early inhabitants unearthed them and thought they would make good readymade monuments for their tombs. It is believed that most of these originated in Scandinavia, but no matter when or whence they came, they are certainly the only relics left by the earliest prehistoric dwellers of Holland who were buried there with their stone axes and wooden vessels. In the museum there is a very interesting archeological section on the *Hunebedden,* with documentation of prehistoric times, an exhibition of urns found in these early graves, as well as pottery and weapons of that time and Celtic and Merovingian jewelry.

Local legends say these *hunebedden* were the homes of a race of giants. Maybe, or maybe not. But there are at least 50 of these beds, the most easy of access being at Rolde (6 km., or 4 miles, east of Assen), Anloo, Borger (the largest), Emmen, Sleen, Vries, and Havelte. The last-mentioned place, 10 km. (6 miles) north of Meppel, had a rougher time from the Nazis during the last war than it had in thousands of years of time's buffetings, for all the huge rocks were scooped up and dumped in a hole during the making of an airfield. Fortunately a local archeologist had made a scale model of the place before the war, so that it has now been fully restored as a unique form of war monument.

Apart from relics of the giants, the Assen museum exhibits remarkable things found in the peat-bogs (such as Roman sarcophagi) and traditional local costumes.

In the southeast corner of the province, 37 km. (23 miles) from Assen, is Emmen, lying in the heart of woodland and having on its doorstep a beautiful nature reserve with a profusion of wild life that justifies its reputation of being a free-and-easy zoo. Here also is a small Museum of Antiquities, called the Hondsrug Museum, specializing somewhat expectedly in memories of the days of the giants and of the Ice and Iron Ages.

Emmen was once the center of huge dreary peatfields, which formed the basis of its economy. With the peat nearing exhaustion, the town's already high unemployment roll was steadily being increased. The farseeing burgomaster promptly decided there was no reason why his little town, though hidden in Drenthe, should not get at least its share of the help being doled out under the Development and Incentive Funds, and Emmen is now thriving again. Its conservative peat workers have been enlisted in the large metal, textile and other factories which have sprung up in the new industrial area.

Southeast of Emmen, the peat moors of Barger-Compascuum unfold before you. In neighboring villages of Weerdinger and Zuidbarge handsome Saxon farmhouses attract many visitors. But it is the peat-producing museum-village 't Aole Compas that is the main focus of interest. Here, the village of Barger Compascuum has been recreated.

The Best-Dressed Oilfield in the World

To Drenthe has gone the honor of really striking oil. One of the largest European oilfields has been drilled and opened up in the region of Coevorden, with the center at Schoonebeek, a lovely old village south of Emmen, famous for its old farmsteads, whose beauty has been generously but relentlessly sacrificed on the altar of necessity.

Drilling in the Netherlands started in 1932. In 1947 the Nederlandse Aardolie Maatschappij, in which Royal Dutch Shell and Standard Oil of New Jersey each have a 50 percent interest, was set up. This company now carries out most of the operations in the field of oil and natural gas prospecting and production in the Netherlands. Esso and Caltex are exploring the South. Prospecting is gradually extending over the whole of the country, including certain offshore areas, notably in the North Sea continental shelf and among the Wadden islands with positive results.

At Schoonebeek the crude oil output provides about one-third of Holland's total oil production, which now covers a little more than one-quarter of home requirements.

Portable derricks are used for drilling, with a portable rig for servicing the wells. Visitors will also notice, probably with surprise, that once the well has been completed and the derrick removed, the pumping installation is prevented from being an ugly blot by a hedge of rapidly growing trees. Indeed, Schoonebeek has been called by experts, "the best-dressed oilfield in the world".

For a change from the gush and rush of Holland's oilfields, try a trip to Hoogeveen, 32 km. (20 miles) south of Assen. Situated in a beautiful belt of countryside strangely contrasting with the rather bare stretches of heathland round it, here is an industrial town that carefully blends piety and enjoyment. Strictly Protestant, the bulk of its 43,000 inhabitants are comparatively stern and strait-laced, although by force of economic circumstances they do not have the antipathy towards foreign visitors that the Staphorsters have. Yet for many of them their lives are run on an unusually strict basis. They will stick, for example, to the medieval custom of being summoned to church three times on Sunday by beat of drum. And with the drum patriotically painted in the national colors of red, white, and blue, no one dares disobey the throbbing call, or plead deafness, or claim forgetfulness. The drum, by the way, is part of the church equipment, and is kept in the vestry behind the pulpit.

Drenthe's Lakes

Situated about 19 km. (12 miles) northeast of Assen, right on the border of the neighboring province of Groningen, is Paterswolde, with both a village and a lake of the same name. Sailing is particularly good here, and so are the seasonal programs of aquatic sports against a wonderful background of woods and gardens. Slightly southeast is another water center named Zuidlaren, built round a village green, and leading to a small lake called after the village. One of Holland's largest horse fairs is held here every October, also a weekly sale that attracts a magnificent collection of animals. The greater part of the two lakes, Paterswoldermeer and Zuidlaardermeer, is already in the province of Groningen.

"Groningen, Scholastic, Rural and Maritime Province"

Without a doubt, a visit to this province is best made by making the capital (which has the same name) the focal point, although there are several places in which it is well worth spending a night rather than rushing a sightseeing visit.

Groningen city is the fourth-largest commercially important Dutch city, is eighth in terms of population, 165,000, has the second-largest university enrolment, and is the most important business, cultural and industrial center of the north. Moreover, within the next few years it will have improved its status still more, as several government departments, with their full office staffs, are being moved here as part of a comprehensive decentralization scheme. Some idea of its importance since early times can be seen from the record that it joined Bremen in the 12th century in arming a fleet to take part in the Crusades. It increased in prestige as the centuries rolled on, and when a university was established within its walls in 1614, it became recognized far and wide as a seat of learning.

Architecturally Groningen is considered one of the finest cities in the Netherlands, being unusually well designed with two central squares from which all main streets start. It suffered badly during the last war, but still possesses many fine old buildings. St. Martin, the patron saint of all tourists, is also the holy guardian of this city, and the 97-meter (315-foot) five-storied spire of the 15th-century St. Martinikerk is only a little less tall than the mighty Dom Tower of Utrecht, the highest in the country. The church's history dates back to 1230, but it was reconstructed in the 15th century. The tower, or, as the Dutch call it, the Martinitoren, has a carillon by the famous Hemony brothers. It is open only from April to October, Tuesday to Saturday, 12–4.30. Adm. Fl. 1.50). The Goudkantoor (Gold office) near the town hall is a delightful Renaissance edifice dating from 1635. It used to be the tax office but changed its role during the 19th century when it was used for the weighing of precious metals. You can admire it only from the outside.

Groningen is as much a water-town as Delft, Amsterdam, or Dordrecht, but it does not depend on its canals for its picturesqueness. The city's beauty has long been expressed in color and art, and in the 18th and 19th centuries the walls of its great houses were often hung with rich, almost flamboyant, canvases, producing Holland's most lavish schemes of decoration as masterpieces of the applied arts. There are very few of these left in Groningen now, although occasionally they are to be found in patrician mansions. The best examples of such canvases are now in a small house off the Princessehof in Leeuwarden, the capital of the neighboring province of Friesland, fortunately taken there before the war from a house in Oude Ebbingestraat, in Groningen, later destroyed by the Nazis.

Groningen has a quiverful of museums to attract you. There is the Museum voor Stad en Lande (Municipal Museum) full of antiquities, porcelain, and paintings by Dutch masters born here, not to mention a room devoted to regional costumes. Or you can visit the Noordelijk Scheepvaart en Tabacologisch Museum (Shipping and Tobacco Mu-

seums), the Natuurhistorisch Museum near the Prinsenhof, the Volkenkundig Museum Gerardus van der Leeuw, or the Botanical Gardens
in Haren. And do not miss the magnificent gardens in the Prinsenhof
where 250 years of topiary, lawn-making, and hedge-growing have
produced a masterpiece. The Prinsenhof was originally built for the
Brotherhood of the Common Life, but in 1568 it became the seat of the
Bishops of Groningen.

The university is, of course, a sight in itself. It has about 18,000
students, of whom many are foreigners. Its buildings are comparatively
modern, and contain some of the best modern Dutch window glass to
be seen anywhere. And as a sort of echo of the more colorful days of
Groningen art, the graduates still wear colored caps. It is an interesting
pastime trying to figure out from the appearance of the student and the
color of his cap to which faculty he belongs. Try it for an hour or so,
then check as follows: pink for chemistry, blue for theology, red for
medicine, white for law, and yellow for mathematics.

A detour to the nearby village of Leek will bring you to the Rijtuigmuseum, the National Carriage Museum Nienoord: among the coaches
on display are several belonging to the last German Kaiser.

Historic Towns and Modern Industries

About 32 km. (20 miles) north of Groningen is Uithuizen, famous
mainly for its 15th-century Castle of Menkemaborg, a manor house of
the local "jonkers" or land owners. One part dates from the 14th
century and two more wings were added in the 17th and 18th centuries.
It is especially well-preserved and is furnished mainly from the period.
The park, protected by a double moat, provides a lovely setting.

Those who like water-sports can, as usual in Dutch touring, easily
find a good lake within reach. This time it is once more the Zuidlaardermeer, on the borderline with Drenthe. Or, of course, there is Paterswolde Lake, a few kilometers to the west, which Groningers share
most amicably with their neighbors of Drenthe.

Delfzijl, the largest port of the province, is on the Eems, the estuary
of which forms the Dollard Gulf, which is about 19 km. (12 miles) long
and 8 (5) wide. The town has about 50,000 inhabitants, and in the past
few years has developed into a busy industrial center, with many factories supplementing its former salt and soda production, while its harbor
has expanded sixfold. There is also a thriving shipbuilding industry,
mainly of coasters. Large ships reach Groningen from here by following the Eems canal.

Slochteren, halfway between Groningen and Winschoten, is a small
town with a long history. It sprang into postwar prominence as the
largest known deposit of natural gas in the world. Its enormous gas
output, supplemented by gas deposits elsewhere in Holland, has greatly
changed the country's fuel situation, as it now supplies over one-third
of all power and heat requirements as well as producing enough to sell
huge quantities to neighboring countries. There is also some fascinating
architecture.

Now for a little town with the musical name of Heiligerlee, 34 km.
(21 miles) east of Groningen, next door to Winschoten. It is famous as

being the scene of one of the first (and successful) battles against the Spaniards for Dutch independence. Economically it is today noted as the center of a thriving industry of agricultural products, including, believe it or not, cardboard. When the local peateries were being worked, it was found that the soil under the peat had remained fertile and was particularly good for the growing of potatoes. To meet the rising demand for potato flour, large factories were soon built, which later engaged in making such byproducts as glucose and dextrin. From this the manufacture of coarse strawboard was developed, and grew so rapidly that this district became a major producer.

Here in Heiligerlee, too, is another of Holland's world-famous bell factories. In long rows, bells of all sizes hang in bold relief against the sky awaiting either tuning or transport to a score of countries. This factory makes any form of bell, right up to a carillon of 50 bells weighing many tonnes.

Exploring the Province

For those who like to explore into the uttermost parts of a province Groningen offers something special. Away down in the southeast corner is the Westerwolde area, with the strange-sounding village of Ter Apel, excellent for walks into the surrounding forest. Snugly hidden in a magnificent beech forest is a medieval monastery with a 14th-century cloister, where visitors are welcome. Other villages that welcome either your camera or your easel are Sellingen, Wallinghuizen, Onstwedde, and Vlagtwedde.

When you are touring through Groningen, keep an eye open for tall poles surmounted by huge wheels on which, perhaps, is a collection of sticks and leaves. This is a stork's nest. The pole and the wheel are permanent, having probably been there for years. The nest is made every year when the storks return to the same nest in the summer.

Unfortunately, storks are at present giving Holland the go-by for their summer vacation. Barely two dozen nests are now in regular seasonal occupation, compared with several hundred half a century ago. One theory is that as they feed on frogs, which are disappearing due to the changes in the local ecology, the storks have moved on to other, better feeding grounds. Yet each pole-plus-wheel is still carefully protected, and at least one Groningen municipality (that of Haren near Paterswolde) maintains on the pay-roll a special storks'-nest inspector.

To see what a really modern port is like, specially built to meet the ocean shipping demands of Holland up to the year 2000, visit the new harbor of Eemshaven near Delfzijl. Opened in 1973, it can receive vessels of up to 80,000 tonnes, and although its attached industrial area of 200 hectares (500 acres) is already attracting foreign as well as Dutch firms, the strict anti-pollution rules ensure that it will be the cleanest and safest manufacturing region in Western Europe.

If your exploratory desire is still not quenched, then try a visit to the charming village of Bourtange in the southeastern part of the province. 300 years ago it was one of the main strongholds in the north, but in 1851 its walls and fortifications were completely demolished. With an eye to the tourist, perhaps, as well as history, the stronghold has been reconstructed on plans of 1750. Or, go to Haren to see the Groningen University's Botanical Garden and Tropical Paradise (Hortus Botanicus de Wolf), in which alpine flowers, desert cacti, banana trees and pineapple plants grow side by side with coffee bushes and many exotic plants. At Middelstum is a perfectly restored 18th-century bakery, while for a change you can go to the Het Hoogeland, the Highland Museum at Warffum where mound relics, medieval costumes and other old-time village treasures are on show. Warffum is an outstanding *terp* village, with houses built on artificial mounds to be above water level. Numerous historical monuments, a 19th-century town center, and unique *kerkpaadjes,* tiny footpaths radiating out from the church, make this an interesting little village to explore.

Even after seeing all, or many, of these attractions, you will probably agree that Groningen Province is difficult to describe succinctly. It has so few large cities and so many medium-sized towns and overlarge villages. But you will also have seen why it is often called the rampart of the Netherlands, because it wraps its fertile curve in intimate protection around Drenthe, and at the same time seems always on the alert to protect its western neighbor, Friesland. Its fertile land literally has been dug from under the peat fields and has made the province today one of the most important agricultural centers of the country.

Friesland, the Individual Province

The last of the trio of northerly provinces is Friesland, unique in so many ways and so full of surprises. The average Netherlander does not take too kindly to the Frisian insistence on keeping its own identity and its own language. Yet a visitor from abroad can probably understand why this individuality is so important to the people of Friesland: they have won their province by courage, work and imagination; they have battled through the centuries, often alone, against human and natural enemies. So they see every reason why they should continue to have their own significant characteristics. They have, in fact, now become a sort of mixture of the Scots and the Welsh in demanding the retention of their independence and of their own language (observe that the names of towns on the road signs are sometimes in both languages).

If, as seems likely, the Dutch trekked in from Central Europe, it is doubtful whether they were accompanied by the Frisians who settled in the north. These people seem to be a different breed. Their origin is obscure; perhaps they came from south Sweden, perhaps they are Celts and allied with the Scots, as their language and customs seem to indicate. When the Romans first came in about 50 BC, the Frisians had been established for three or four centuries. Caesar's legions found them hard to digest; they beat them in battle but when it came to collecting taxes the Frisians rose in wrath and threw the conquerors back to the Rhine. Later aggressive visitors came that way, the Vikings, Franks under Charlemagne, Normans, Spaniards, French under Napoleon, and the Counts of Holland. All found the Frisians very tough.

In early days the Frisians occupied a great stretch of land all along the northern coast of what is now the Netherlands and extending well into northeast Germany. It was divided into West, Main, and East

Friesland. When the water broke in to form the Zuiderzee, it also began the breakup of the little Frisian empire by isolating West Friesland, which, as we've seen, was gradually absorbed into the province of North Holland. German tribes took over East Friesland. Today only Main Friesland remains, although the Frisian language is still spoken on the islands of East and North Friesland in Germany.

The early Frisians did not have things easy. Their number one enemy was the North Sea. They were the Marsh Dutch, and historians like Homer and Pliny refer to their country as the "land of eternal fog", near which were the "gates of Hell". It was called by the Greek explorer Pytheas "Coast of Awe" as far back as 325 B.C. So much mud, tidal rivers, salt water, and storms and fog. Survival was difficult, a never-ending battle. An ancient Frisian oath—according to Dr. van Veen—runs as follows: "With five weapons shall we keep our land, with sword and with shield, with spade and with fork and with the spear, out with the ebb, up with the flood, to fight day and night against the North-king (the sea?) and against the wild Viking, that all Frisians may be free, the born and the unborn, so long as the wind from the clouds shall blow and the world shall stand".

In this oath are a few Frisian words that show much resemblance to English roots: *uth mitha ebbe, up mitha flood* (out with the ebb, up with the flood). The distinctive Frisian language seems closer to English than to Dutch.

When peaceful days came and some control over tides and floods was obtained, the Frisians set up a profitable trade with Hanseatic League cities, such as Lübeck, Danzig and Visby. Bolsward and Stavoren in Friesland were Hansa members. Through the years they remained stubbornly self-sufficient; for three centuries during and after the struggle with Spain—the Eighty Years' War—Friesland kept its separate identity. The present royal family of Holland numbers among its lines the descendant of a doughty Frisian Stadholder.

Strong Ties and Traditions

Today's Frisians cling to their native arts, music, little theaters, customs, and traditions. Their language is taught only in some of the schools, but the majority of Frisians speak it. There is a well-defined Frisian Movement aimed at retaining the language and customs, and at winning more States' Rights. While recognizing and valuing the economic advantage of centralization most Frisians resent the power of the centralized Netherlands government, forgetting the very considerable influence they have always had, and still have, on that body.

Friesland is the great dairy province of Holland. Its butter, cheese, milk, and famous black-and-white cattle are shipped to far ports. Its people are mostly Protestant, some are strict Calvinists. The men are tall and strong, the women blue-eyed and blonde.

Although Friesland's traditional costume is dying out, an effort is being made to revive it—for the women anyway. But Frisian pride of heritage and tradition is far from dead—on the contrary. The province has a national anthem, a very old tuneful song titled, "Frisian Blood, Rise Up and Boil!"—and when Frisians sing it they rise up and stand straight, pull out all the stops and shake the rafters. Friesland also has its own flag, blue and white, dotted with the red leaves of the water lily. The Frisians still call their fellow-countrymen "Hollanders," and even issue their own "passport" to tourists, which you can obtain through the VVV office.

Exploring Friesland and the IJsselmeer

It is almost impossible to tour Friesland without including a number of places on the IJsselmeer (or old Zuiderzee) which are on the borders of that huge lake but are administratively parts of other Dutch provinces. So in this chapter we are taking a few geographical liberties and including some non-Frisian towns and villages which are easily reached when exploring the Friesland Province.

As we approach Friesland from the south across the enclosing dike that leads east from the province of Noord Holland, the road divides almost as soon as we touch the mainland. Since we shall first explore the interior of the province and then return to follow the shore of the former Zuiderzee, we take the left-hand fork, which leads under the shadow of a high seawall into Harlingen, one of the province's chief seaports. From here the rich Frisian dairy products are shipped to Britain and elsewhere in small but sturdy ocean-going steamers such as those you'll see lining the harbor. On the dike you'll also notice a monument called the Steenen Man (Stone Man) dedicated to the Spanish Governor Caspar di Robles. The stone base bears a double-faced bronze head, said to turn when the clock strikes midnight. And "when you go round its foot three times you may be surprised with a little brother or sister".

From Harlingen it's a 2-hour ferry ride to the islands of Vlieland and Terschelling, part of the chain that begins with Texel, which we visited during our second excursion from Amsterdam. Terschelling, the more important of the two, has a population of only 3,700, and most of the men are either fishermen earning their families' livelihood on the sea, or are training at the Merchant Marine Academy. Dutch visitors know the island well, but very few foreign tourists make their way in this direction. A trip is well worth while, for here is one of the few tourist spots left in Europe that has not lost its original beauty and simplicity. We asked a retired Dutch sea captain why he had retired there. He replied with a droll smile, "If Terschelling could be taken from the North Sea and dumped into the South Pacific, it would be one of those islands men dream about but never seem to find".

But if you wish to visit Terschelling, or Texel for that matter, while each is still an island you must hurry. For a start has already been made, coincident with the Delta Works project in Zeeland, on damming up large areas of the Wadden Sea between these islands and the mainland. This is the last of the mammoth hydraulic schemes to protect Holland against the sea, to ensure fresh water, to prevent costly salt infiltration, and to provide new recreation areas. The Wadden Plan will take about 25 years to complete, but the dikes closing off the Lauwerszee part of the plan were finished in 1969.

Back on the mainland again, Franeker, a town of 9,500, is a scant 10-km. (6-mile) drive east of Harlingen. It once boasted a famous university (1585–1811), which was suppressed by Napoleon. Of its attractions, probably the most unusual is the Planetarium, opposite the handsome Dutch Renaissance Town Hall, begun in 1775 by a local wool comber named Eise Eisinga. For seven years he spent his evenings, working by candlelight, on its construction. All the planets and other celestial bodies are seen on the ceiling, in correct position over the years. Iron wheels in the garret operate the stars.

Where the USA Was First Recognized

Nineteen kilometers (12 miles) farther eastward is Leeuwarden, capital of Friesland, population 85,000—the province itself has 516,000 inhabitants. Leeuwarden has much to recommend it to Americans. It was the people of this city who, in 1782, first voted for Holland's recognition of the new United States, in connection with which action a Dutch loan of $30,000,000 helped the young nation to get on its feet economically. In Leeuwarden's Provincial House, Tweebaksmarkt 52, is a bronze tablet with the inscription: "Memorial of Gratitude. At Leeuwarden, In the States of Friesland, February 1782, The First Vote Was Taken Which Led To The Recognition Of The Independence Of The United States Of America By The Republic Of The United Netherlands. Erected By The De Witt Historical Society Of Tompkins County At Ithaca, NY, A.D. 1909."

Also on display in the Provincial House is a document relating to a Petrus Stuiffsandt, born in Scherpenzeel in Friesland in 1592, known to us as Peter Stuyvesant. A letter from an early "roving Ambassador", John Adams, dated from Paris May 10, 1783, pays tribute to the Leeuwarden citizens who so helped America at a critical time.

Perhaps the city's most spectacular building is the massive Oldehove Tower (1529), the unfinished steeple of a church which was pulled down in 1595. Leeuwarden has four museums: The Museum Het Princessehof (Grote Kerkstraat 11) with an outstanding collection of Eastern art, the Fries Natuurhistorisch Museum, or Natural History Museum (2 Schoenmarkersperk), the Verzetsmuseum Friesland (Frisian Resistance Museum) (Zuiderplein) and the extensive Fries Museum, or Frisian Museum (Turfmarkt 24), renowned for its antiquities. The latter is worth a long visit. It pictures Frisian life from earliest times. Shown, for example, are the 1397 drinking-horn of the St. Anthony Guild of Stavoren, a chalice from Bozum, 1505, and the immense sword of the Great Pier, the Frisian champion who in 1515–20 drove the Saxons out of Friesland. There are also medieval costumes, silver, porcelain, and paintings.

From Leeuwarden the visitor would do well to head north to get a quick look at some of the rich farms for which the province is noted. The farmhouses are usually set in clusters of trees and consist of three parts: the "head" where the family lives, the "neck" used as a kitchen, and the "frame" which is a huge barn for the animals. Friesland was the first Dutch province to develop centralization of milk, butter, and cheese production, and its cooperatives are famous. With less than 5 percent of the Dutch population, it claims production of 55 percent of the cheese, 17 percent of milk and butter, and 75 percent of the export of cattle.

Some 32 km. (20 miles) northeast of the capital lies Dokkum, a small walled town believed to have been founded about the 3rd century. St. Boniface was murdered here in 754 when he was trying to convert the Frisians to Christianity. The Town Hall (1762) has a Louis XIV council room well worth visiting.

A few kilometers north at the tiny village of Hantumhuizen is a Romanesque church of modern appearance. It has a curious history. It looks brand new, yet its bricks are over 600 years old. The Roman Catholics built it about 1300. The Protestants took over with the Reformation, rearranged and whitewashed the interior. By 1940, it had almost fallen apart, so a job of restoration was done. The old bricks, well scrubbed, were used; only the cement to bind them was new. Whitewash was cleaned off the interior, revealing dainty color decorations painted by the Catholics. Tiles from bombed Rotterdam were sunk in the floors, as were ancient gravestones of around 1561–1616, bearing old coats-of-arms.

Drive up to the coast from here, and you can see how, through the centuries, the Dutch have built their country. We have made such a trip, though farther to the east, with a farmer-guide whose family had been there for several generations. We started several kilometers from the sea, along a raised road. "We're riding on a dead dike", the guide said: "this was built in 1600". Farther on, and we rode on a "Sleeper" dike, dated 1800. Then came a "Dreamer" or "Dozer", year 1867, and at last a "Watcher" of 1945. The Watcher is the first line of defense, backed by the Dreamer and then the Sleeper. As time goes on the Sleeper dies, the Dreamer becomes the Sleeper and the Watcher the Dreamer.

Getting to the water's edge, we could see the process of stealing land still under way. Next to the water was a vast expanse of mud, with little channels to let the water out, and little clumps of stones and brush to catch the silt from the receding waves and thus build up the land. This is the first or *slikken* stage. In the second, tough *kwelder* grass is grown, and sheep graze on it at low tide. The third stage is the polder, which must be built up and fertilized over a period of several years before the soil is suitable for ordinary agriculture.

Following the Shores of the IJsselmeer

Having had a glimpse of the northern portions of Friesland, let's turn our attention to the villages and towns to the south, including the vast new Noordoostpolder. From Leeuwarden we have merely to drive down the 24 km. (15 miles) that separate us from Sneek, then swing west to Bolsward. If you do come this way, the village of Wieuwerd, about 16 km. (10 miles) south of Leeuwarden on a side road, has a rather gruesome attraction in its mummies in the church's crypt. There are four now, put here about 1600, which logically should be nothing but bones and powder but instead are leathery mummies. It is believed that an unusual cross-ventilation accounted for this freak.

However, we'll assume that you have just crossed the enclosing dike from the province of Noord Holland and, instead of selecting the lefthand fork for Harlingen and the cities already described, are turning right (east) for Bolsward.

Although only 15,000 people live here now, Bolsward is one of Friesland's oldest towns and was once a member of the Hanseatic League. It has two noted churches, the St. Martinikerk (1446–66) and the Broerekerk (1270), the latter badly damaged by fire some years ago. Its Town Hall (1613–17), one of the treasures of the region, is Dutch Renaissance in style, with a striking tower and beautiful sculpture. Since this is the heart of a rich milk and cheese producing area, it is only appropriate that Bolsward is the home of the National Dairy School.

Only 11 km. (7 miles) east of Bolsward is Sneek (pronounced "snake"), the center of one of Holland's favorite sports—sailing. Friesland calls itself, justifiably, a "paradise for yachting enthusiasts". Hundreds of lakes dot the province, and there is usually a good wind. A small harbor leads right into the center of Sneek, where dozens of boats, large and small, are tied up at night. On weekends, and evenings, youths and adults climb aboard and steam or sail out of a channel into the broad Sneekermeer or Sneek Lake, to live on board for days, or weeks. From here they can travel over most of Holland. The first Saturday in August is Race Week, with national competitions in which boats from all over the country compete.

Sneek, population 31,000, has its share of tourist attractions. Most spectacular is perhaps the Hoogeindster Waterpoort, a watergate built above a bridge over the little River Geeuw. Its narrow arch was once closed by a portcullis. Dating from 1613, it is supported by two arcades and flanked by two octagonal towers. Sneek's Scheepvaart Museum en Oudheidkamer (Frisian Shipping Museum) is worth visiting too.

If you are in Sneek during the evening you may be lucky enough to hear the women's chorus from a nearby village sing Frisian songs in the street outside the Town Hall. They wear the new, or revived, Frisian costume. Later you can sit in one of the hotels on the square and join in a song-fest of the old melodies of Europe and America, to the lusty accompaniment of a small orchestra of piano, violin, and accordion. This is generally climaxed by a vigorous rendering of the Frisian "national anthem". On Tuesdays during July and August there are also colorful folk dance performances here.

Returning from Bolsward from Sneek, we turn south along a picturesque country road for Workum (the names of many towns end in "um"—Blessum, Swichum, Rottum, etc.) which supplied London from the time of the Restoration (1660) until the outbreak of World War I (1914) with some 20,000 pounds of eels each year. In its church are some remarkable hand biers dating from as early as 1756. Each was made and owned by a guild—blacksmiths, carpenters, farmers, doctors, sea captains—and carries painted emblems of the trade plus appropriate quotations from the psalms. Except for one, entirely black, which was reserved for suicides. The 18th-century Town Hall and 17th-century Waag or Weigh House are also of interest.

Makkum lies too far back up the coast to merit the detour, but it's interesting to note that it has long been known for its pottery, including a blue variety, which the local residents claim is superior to the better-known Delftware. During an occupation by French troops the potters were ordered to make cooking pots for the military. Having no choice, they did so, but the pots they delivered were the kind more commonly used after meals than before, at least in those days.

Hindeloopen, a few kilometers south of Workum, lies directly on the IJsselmeer and is known for its gaily painted and carved furniture fashioned after the style once in vogue in Visby, Sweden. Originally, a hunting lodge (729) of the Kings of Friesland, it was raised to town status in 1255 and was a prosperous seaport during the Golden Age. Today it seems asleep, except perhaps for the men who gather around the "gossip bench" (1619) on the sea wall, which enfolds the town on three sides. Take time to stop and stroll about, and if you have a few more moments to spare, drop in for a visit to its tiny museum, the Hidde Nijland Stichting, across from the church. Hindeloopen is an utterly charming place, one of the jewels of the region.

Stavoren, next seaport to the south, is not, however, and you will do well to bypass it entirely and follow the road on through Koudum, Hemelum, Rijs, Oudemirdum, and Sondel to Sloten, unless you are taking the ferry that shuttles from here over to Enkhuizen in the province of Noord Holland. Though not an attractive city today, Stavoren has a long history and was once the chief port of the region. It was destroyed by Vikings in 991, but rebuilt. Legend has it that the *Vrouwtje van Stavoren,* the "little lady of Stavoren", ruled the city despotically and for a long time kept it prosperous. Finally, when her sailors brought back grain instead of gold one day, she furiously dumped it into the water. Disasters followed. The harbor became clogged with mud, a fire destroyed much of the city, and Stavoren's day was done.

Sloten, on the other hand, merits the word delightful. It is the smallest "town" in the country—most small places without special historical distinction are merely "villages". A star-shaped community built in the sixteenth century, its narrow streets, walls and houses have changed little since.

Eels as Mosquito Killers

Our last stop in Friesland as we head southeast for the Noordoost-polder is Lemmer, back on the IJsselmeer again. Its chief interest is the powerful pumping station, one of three used to pump the polder dry. Its capacity is a fantastic 1,620,000 liters (360,000 gallons) per *minute.* Lemmer and Vollenhove, about 32 km. (20 miles) southeast, once were the two big eel-catching centers on the IJsselmeer, but have been largely displaced by Volendam, Enkhuizen and Urk.

When the enclosing dike was built, fishermen feared it would keep the eels out of the new IJsselmeer, but the young wrigglers swarm in through the sluices and business is still good. These young eels did an extraordinary job in the first days of the IJsselmeer, according to Dr. van Veen. At first, as the dike was completed, the fish seemed to disappear and in their place came a real plague of mosquitoes, so terrible that they covered houses, fields, and humans, slowing traffic to a crawl by their dense clouds. To get rid of them, the locks in the dike were opened at night, and baby eels, having come all the way from the Florida deeps and hungry for freshwater food, devoured the mosquito larvae. Thus the plague was beaten, and the eels fattened. Besides providing a larger catch than for many decades past, today's eels are said to be tastier than living memory can recall.

If you are still reluctant to leave Friesland, a few more tips might help. Of course, there are always the "Islands": Terschelling, Ameland, Schiermonnikoog and Vlieland. These can be a holiday in themselves. Dunes, woods, bird sanctuaries, interesting architecture, sandy beaches and, especially, peace and quietness.

Or there is Heerenveen, with its Museum Willem van Haren, which covers the town's history and its important peat industry. Perhaps Bakkeveen will be of special interest to Americans, because still preserved from 1593, halfway to the village of Een, are the defense works which served Peter Stuyvesant as an example for construction of the fort of Nieuw Amsterdam (now, of course, New York). And if you want one last remembrance of your visit to Friesland go to Joure, where you can get a modern replica of the famous Frisian clocks first made here (the originals are now worth fortunes).

Tucked away in these northern provinces, therefore, are probably as many places of interest as in any other part of Holland. Most of the places mentioned here are still well off the beaten track for most visitors, and are accordingly fitting attractions with which to end our Guide to Holland.

PRACTICAL INFORMATION FOR THE NORTH

TELEPHONE CODES. We have given telephone codes for all the towns and villages in this chapter in the hotel and restaurant listings that follow. These codes need only be used when calling from outside the town or village concerned.

HOTELS AND RESTAURANTS. Until recently hotel accommodations were fairly limited because Dutch tourists who came to this region spent all their time on yachts and other water craft, or went camping. Nevertheless, there are now some good hotels and motels scattered around the three provinces; of course the better ones are in the large cities, or close to them. But the VVV's can provide very useful lists of camping-sites, bungalows to rent, yachts to be hired, and caravan centers. Hotel and motel lists are also available.

There are few restaurants in the area, so best dine at the hotels, many of which offer excellent food.

We have divided the hotels and restaurants in our listings into three categories—Expensive (E), Moderate (M) and Inexpensive (I). Price ranges for these categories for both hotels and restaurants are given in the *Facts at Your Fingertips* (see pp. 17–18). Some hotels, particularly at the upper end of the scale, have rooms in more than one category and a consequently wide range of prices. Similarly, many restaurants have dishes in more than one category, so be sure to check the menu outside before you go in. Look out too for the excellent value Tourist Menu.

ASSEN (Drenthe). Provincial capital, 193 km. (120 miles) from Amsterdam. *De Jonge* (M), 85 Brinkstraat; 05920–12023. 19 rooms. *De Nieuwe Brink* (M), 13 Brink; 05920–10046. 16 rooms; also good restaurant. *Overcingel* (M), 10 Stationsplein; 05920–11333. 40 rooms, 22 with bath. Opposite the station.
   Restaurants. *La Belle Époque* (M), 6 Markt; 05920–15818. *De Ponderosa* (M), 1 Rode Heklaan. *Stadsherberg* (M), 39 Molenstraat.

BEETSTERZWAAG (Friesland). 5 km. (3 miles) south of Drachten, set in picturesque countryside. *Lauswolt* (E), 10 van Harinxmaweg; 05126–1245. 34 rooms. Rather special; fine building in spacious grounds. Tennis, golf, pool, sauna. Probably the best restaurant in the region.
   Restaurant. *Vogelpark Boschlust* (M), Beesterweg; 05126–1334. Game restaurant.

BOLSWARD (Friesland). Former Hanseatic city 34 km. (21 miles) southwest of Leeuwarden. *De Wijnberg* (M), 5 Marktplein; 05157–2220. 34 rooms, most with bath. Attractive restaurant.
   Restaurant. *'t Wapen van Wonseradeel,* 64 Harlingerstraat; 05157–2506.

BOURTANGE (close to German border, near Vlagtwedde). *De Staakenborgh* (M), 33 Vlagtwedderstraat; 05993–54216. Delightful small inn, converted from 17th-century farmhouse.

COEVORDEN (Drenthe). Oilfield town 58 km. (36 miles) south of Assen. *Markzicht* (M), 3 Markt; 05240–3573. 8 rooms. *Talens* (M), 51 Sallandsestraat; 05240–16251. 17 rooms.
   Restaurant. *Gasterie Kasteel* (M), 30 Kasteel; 05240–2170. Cellar restaurant with good food.

DELFZIJL (Groningen). Easternmost seaport of the Netherlands, 32 km. (20 miles) east of Groningen. *Du Bastion* (M), 78 Waterstraat; 05960–18771. 18 rooms.

DOKKUM (Friesland). Old town with St. Boniface associations, 27 km. (17 miles) northeast of Leeuwarden. *de Granaet* (M), 35 Koningstraat; 05190–2598. *De Posthoorn* (M), 21 Diepswal; 05190–2301. 25 rooms.

DRACHTEN (Friesland). 32 km. (20 miles) southeast of Leeuwarden. *Crest Hotel Drachten* (E), 1 Zonnedauw; 05120–20705, on the A7 highway. 48 rooms. *Servotel* (E), 75 Haverstuk; 05120–16555. 20 rooms with bath or shower.
   Restaurant. *de Wilgenhoeve* (M), 2 de Warren; 05120–12510. Rustic spot on the edge of town. Good food.

EERNEWOUDE (Friesland). Tiny village 19 km. (12 miles) southwest of Leeuwarden. Water-sports center on Prinsenhof lake. *Princenhof* (M), 15 P. Miedemaweg; 05117–9206. 48 rooms, 39 with bath.

EMMEN (Drenthe). 37 km. (23 miles) southwest of Assen. *Boshuis* (M), 138 Boslaan; 05910–12592. 12 rooms. *Ten Cate* (M), 44 Noordbargerstraat; 05910–17600. On the outskirts.

FRANEKER (Friesland). Former university town 19 km. (12 miles) west of Leeuwarden. *De Doelen* (M), 6 Breedeplaats; 05170–2261. 9 rooms. *Motel de Valk* (M), 78 H. V. Saxenlaan; 05170–8000. Good value.

GIETEN (Drenthe). Village 14 km. (9 miles) east of Assen. *Braams* (M), 7 Brink; 05926–1241. 40 rooms, all with bath. First class superior; good restaurant.

GRONINGEN (capital of Groningen province). *Inter Hotel Groningen* (E), 156 Donderslaan; 050–252040. 60 rooms with bath or shower. *Euromotel* (E), 7 Expositielaan; 050–258400. 140 rooms with bath. Next to Martini Congress Center. *De Doelen* (M), 36 Grote Markt; 050–127041. 40 rooms. Very central. *Weeva* (M), 8 Gedempte Zuiderdiep; 050–129919. 70 rooms.
Restaurants. *Rôtisserie le Meijno d'Or* (E), 1A-Straat; 050–137770. Excellent French cuisine; recommended. *De Stadtlander* (M), 35 Poelestraat; 050–127191. *'t Wad* (M), 27 A-Kerkhof; 050–130383. Fish restaurant.

GROUW (Friesland), lakeside village 18 km. (11 miles) south of Leeuwarden. *Oostergoo* (M), 1 Nieuwe Kade; 05662–1309. 25 rooms, all with bath. Pleasant rustic setting, with view over harbor.

HAREN (Groningen). *Postiljon Motel* (M), 33 Emmalaan; 050–347041, 2 km. (1 mile) out on A28. 97 rooms.
Restaurant. *Herberg de Rietschans* (M), 221 Meerweg; 05907–1365. Attractive setting on the edge of a lake 2 km. (1 mile) towards Paterswolde. Closed Sun. and Mon.

HARLINGEN (Friesland). Seaport and gateway to Vlieland and Terschelling islands, 29 km. (18 miles) west of Leeuwarden. *Anna Casparii* (M), 67–69 Noorderhaven; 05178–2065. 14 rooms, 3 with bath. *Heerenlogement* (M), 23–25 Franekereind, 05178–5846. 25 rooms.

HEERENVEEN (Friesland). Attractive rural town. *Postiljon Motel Heerenveen* (M), 65 Schans; 05130–24041. 61 rooms. Good restaurants.

HOOGEVEEN (Drenthe). 35 km. (22 miles) south of Assen. *Homan* (M), 3 Stationsstraat; 05280–62012. 25 rooms, 10 with bath or shower. *Motel Hoogeveen* (M), 1 Mathijssenstraat; 05280–63303, on the A28. 39 modern rooms.
Restaurant. *van 't Hooge* (M), Hoofdstraat 71.

LEEUWARDEN (capital of Friesland). *Eurohotel* (M), 19 Europaplein; 058–131113. 50 rooms, all with bath. *Oranje* (E), 4 Stationsweg; 058–126241. 70 rooms, most with bath. Golden Tulip hotel. *Hardegarijp* (M), 36 Rijksstraatweg; 05110–5846. Motel with 28 rooms in the village of Hardegarijp, 7 km. (4 miles) along the N41. *'t Anker* (I), 71 Eewal; 058–12516. Breakfast only.
Restaurants. *Onder de Luifel* (M), Stationsweg. *La Spunta* (M), 50 Eewal; 058–138372. *De Stadhouder* (M), 75 Nieuwstad.

MEPPEL (Drenthe). Agricultural city 48 km. (30 miles) south of Assen. *Gruppen* (M), Parallelweg; 05220–51080. 10 rooms with bath. *Kwint* (I), 15 Kerkplein; 05220–52410. 10 rooms, 4 with bath.

Restaurants. *Drentse Heerlijkheid* (M), 1 Prisengracht; 05220–51630. *De Munnik* (M), 88 Hoodstraat. *De Putstoel* (M), 1 Putstoel.

PATERSWOLDE (Drenthe). Resort village 19 km. (12 miles) north of Assen. *'t Familiehotel Paterswolde* (E), 19 Groningerweg; 0597–1831. A Golden Tulip hotel; 45 rooms. Tennis. Good restaurant.

SNEEK (Friesland). Old city and yachting center 24 km. (15 miles) south of Leeuwarden. *Hanenburg* (M), 2 Wijde Noorderhorne; 05150–12570. 13 rooms, 12 with bath, good restaurant. *De Wijnberg* (M), 23 Marktstraat; 05150–12421. 25 rooms with bath or shower.

Restaurants. *Hindelooper Kames* (M), 10 Oosterdijk; 05153–12756. Local specialties. *De Kriel* (M), 20 Pr. Hendrikkade; 05153–14874. *Onder de Linden* (M), 28 Marktstraat; 05150–12654.

TER APEL (Groningen). Village 58 km. (36 miles) southeast of Groningen. *Boschhuis* (M), 6 Boslaan; 05995–1208. 11 rooms.

TERSCHELLING. Island, reached from Harlingen; ferry docks at West Terschelling, where the establishments listed below are located. Other hotels are available at the towns of Hoorn, Midsland, and Oosterend. *Europa* (M), 35 Europalaan; 05620–2241. 84 rooms, most with bath. *Oepkes* (M), 3 de Ruyterstraat; 01031–2005. 12 rooms with bath.

VLIELAND (Wadden Islands). *Seeduyn* (E), 63 Doorpstraat; 05621–1560. Amid the dunes; pool, sauna. *Badhotel Bruin* (M), 88 Doorpstraat; 05621–1301. 35 rooms; good restaurant.

DE WIJK (Drenthe). *Havesathe de Havixhorst* (E), 34 Schiphorsterweg; 05224–1487. 9 rooms in converted farm, 6 km. east of Meppel; fine restaurant.

WINSCHOTEN (Groningen). 37 km. (23 miles) east of Groningen, near the German border. *Royal York* (M), 21 Stationsweg; 05970–14300. 25 rooms. Good for its class.

GETTING AROUND. Although these northern provinces are at the moment comparatively underpopulated, road, bus and rail communications are remarkably good. Moreover, the policy of the Government to spread its administrative services and civil servants more in the north to relieve the congestion in and around Den Haag is resulting in a rapid opening-up of the area, with many millions of guilders being spent every year on motorways, public utilities and recreational facilities. Visitors will find it convenient to make one of the large towns their center and radiate out from there throughout the provinces.

TOURIST INFORMATION. The main VVV tourist information offices are located in the following places: **Assen,** 42 Brink (tel. 05920–14324); **Delfzijl,** 10 Landstraat (tel. 05960–18104); **Emmen,** 2 Raadhuisplein (tel. 05910–13000); **Groningen,** 3 Naberpassage (near Grote Markt) (tel. 050–

139700); **Leeuwarden,** 1 Stationsplein (tel. 058–132224); **Sneek,** 21 Leeuwen-
burg (tel. 05150–14096); **Terschelling,** 19a Willem Barentzkade (tel. 05620–
2289); **Winschoten,** 26 Torenstraat (tel. 05970–12255).

 MUSEUMS. The towns of Holland's northern provinces
are the home of several interesting museums that, with
their historical and cultural collections and exhibitions,
reveal the individual character of each province.

ASSEN. Provinciaal Museum van Drenthe, 5 Brink. Collection of objects
telling the history of Drenthe, including material on *hunebedden*. It is housed
in the former Receiver's House which is furnished in 18th-century style and in
the Bormer Provincial Hall, formerly a Cistercian chapel. Open Tues.–Fri.
9.30–5, Sat. and Sun. 1–5; July and Aug. open Mon. also.

APPINGEDAM. Gewestelijk Historisch Museum, 17 Wijkstraat. Has exhibitions on the history, work, and life of the district.

BARGER-COMPASCUUM. Openlucht Museum 't Aole Compas, 4 Berken-
rode. Open-air museum showing the lives and work of the first pioneers who
came to live in the peat colonies. There is a model, actual size, of the colony,
and demonstrations of peat-digging and the operation of various pieces of
machinery. Open Easter to end of Oct. daily 9–6.

BORGER. Hunebedden Museum, 3 Hoofstraat. Exhibition on *hunebedden*
in Drenthe. Open Tues.–Sat. 10–12 and 2–5, Sun. 2–4.30.
Natuurmuseum, 9 St. Walburgstraat. Features flora and fauna of Holland.
Open Thurs.–Fri. 10–5, Sat. and Sun. 2–5.

EMMEN. Hondsrug Museum, contains prehistoric and historic material connected with the *hunebedden* found in this region.

FRANEKER. Planetarium of Eise Eisinga, 3 Eise Eisingastraat. Original
house of woolcomber Eise Eisinga, who from 1774–81, built a replica of the
planetary system, as it was then known. Open Tues.–Sat. 10–12 and 1.30–5.

GRONINGEN. Groninger Museum Voor Stad En Lande, 59 Praediniussin-
gel. Objects relating to the history and culture of the town and province. Open
Tues.–Sat. 10–5, Sun. 1–5. Adm. Fl. 2.
Noordelijk Scheepvaart en Tabacologisch Museum (Shipping and Tobacco
Museums), 24–26 Brugstraat. Objects relating to the history of shipping, mainly
with reference to the northern provinces, and to the history of tobacco. Open
Tues.–Sat. 10–5, Sun. and public holidays 1–5. Adm. Fl. 2.50.
Volkenkundig museum Gerardus van der Leeuw (Ethnological Museum).
104 Nieuwe Kijk in 't Jatstraat. Objects from Indonesia, Pacific and West
Africa. Open Tues.–Fri. 10–4, Sat. and Sun. 1–5.

HEERENVEEN. Willem van Haren Museum, 50–52 van Harenspad. In an
old patrician house, it shows the history of local peat industry. Open Mon.–Fri.
10–5, Sat. 11–5.

HINDELOOPEN. Hidde Nijland Stichting (Municipal Museum), 1 Dijkweg. Town history, costumes, Hindeloopen-painted furniture and interiors. Open Mar. 15–Oct. 14, Mon.–Sat. 10–5, Sun. and public holidays 1–5.

LEENS. Borg Verhildersum, 40 Wierde. French furniture and exhibition on the history of Marshes and Land. Open Easter to Oct. Tues.–Sun. 10.30–5.30. Adm. Fl. 1.75.

LEEUWARDEN. Fries Museum, 24 Turfmarkt. Art, costumes, silver, finds from refuge mounds. Open Tues.–Sat. 10–5, Sun. and public holidays 1–5.

Museum Het Princessehof, 9–15 Grote Kerkstraat. General ceramic study center. Chinese and Japanese porcelain, workshop, period room, exhibition garden, and the world's largest collection of tiles. Open Tues. to Sat. 10–5, Sun. and public holidays 2–5.

MARSSUM. Heringa State (or Popta Slot), 1 Slotlaan. Furniture, porcelain and silverware in period rooms. Open Apr.–Sept., Mon.–Fri. For appointment call 05107–1231.

NIENOORD/LEEK. Rijtuigmuseum (Nienoord National Carriage Museum), Nienoord Estate, Bosweg. Antique carriages, horse sleighs, uniforms and accessories, paintings and prints. Open Easter to Sept. 30, daily 9–5.

ORVELTE. Old Saxon village with handicraft demonstrations.

RODEN. Nederlands Museum Kinderwereld (Dutch Child's World Museum), 31 Brink. Collection of old children's games, toys, dolls' houses, miniature cooking stoves, dolls. Open Mon.–Sat. 10–12 and 2–5 (Sept. 1–Mar. closed on Mon.). Sun. and public holidays 2–5. Adm. Fl. 3.

SCHOONOORD. Openlucht Museum De Zeven Marken (Open-Air Museum), 73 Tramstraat. Traces the way of life in Drenthe at the turn of the century by means of turf huts, houses and barns, one of which houses a smithy, clog-maker's shop, bee-farm and sawmill. Open daily from Sun. before Easter to Oct. 31, 9–5.

SLOCHTEREN. Fraeylemaborg, 32 Hoofdweg. Portraits of the House of Orange, paintings, porcelain in an old manor house. Open Tues.–Sun. 10–12, 1–4 during summer; closed Jan. and Feb. Adm. Fl. 2.50.

SNEEK. Fries Scheepvaart Museum en Oudheidkamer (Marine History and Antiquities), 14 Kleinzand. Exhibition of all aspects of Frisian marine activities over the years, including models of ships. Mon.–Sat. 10–12 and 1.30–5.

UITHUIZEN. Menkemaborg, 2 Menkemaweg. Interesting example of an inhabited Groningen fortified manorhouse with authentic furniture, paintings, porcelain, glass, silver, etc. Open Tues.–Sun. 10–12 and 1–5. Adm. Fl. 2.50.

WARFFUM. Het Hogeland, with cottages and stables showing the country life of the region. Open March–Oct., Tues.–Sat. 10–4. Adm Fl. 2.50.

SHOPPING. Sneek, 24 km. (15 miles) southwest of Leeuwarden, is one of the chief centers for the manufacture of the silver souvenir articles that sell all over the country. Here, if you have time, you may have your own special design made at Schijfsma, Grootzand 48. Friesland is noted also for its brightly painted Hindeloopen furniture from the coastal town of that name.

Local shops in this region sell replicas of the famous Frisian clocks. The town of Makkum produces beautiful hand decorated pottery that many consider to be superior to Delft ware.

ENGLISH-DUTCH
VOCABULARY

ENGLISH-DUTCH VOCABULARY

USEFUL EXPRESSIONS

English	Dutch
Please	Alstublieft
Thank you very much	Dank U zeer
Good morning, sir	Dag, Mijnheer
Good evening, madam	Goedenavond, Mevrouw
Good night	Goede nacht
Goodbye	Tot ziens
Excuse me	Neem me niet kwalijk
I understand, I don't understand	Dat begrijp ik, dat begrijp ik niet
Hunger, thirst	Honger, dorst
I am hungry, thirsty	Ik heb honger, dorst
Yes, no	Ja, nee
Yesterday, today, tomorrow	Gisteren, vandaag, morgen
This evening, this morning	Vanavond, vanmorgen
How much?	Hoeveel?
Expensive, cheap	Duur, goedkoop
Where? Where is? Where are?	Waar? Waar is? Waar zijn?
Is this the right way to . . . ?	Is dit de goede weg naar . . . ?
Can you direct me to the nearest . . . ?	Kunt u mij . . . dichtsbyzynde . . . bijzijnde . . . wijzen?
doctor	de . . . dokter
hotel/restaurant	het . . . hotel/restaurant
garage	de . . . garage
post office	het . . . postkantoor
police station	het . . . politiebureau
telephone	de . . . telefoon
Left, right	Links, rechts
To the left/right	Naar links/rechts
Bus/trolley stop	Bus/tram halte
Church	Kerk
Theater	Theater
Movie theater (cinema)	Bioscoop
Entrance	Ingang
Exit	Uitgang
Admission free	Vrije toegang
Open from . . . to . . .	Geopend van . . . tot . . .
No smoking	Verboden te roken
Gentlemen	Heren
Ladies	Dames
Town Hall	Stadhuis
Art Gallery	Schilderijenmuseum
Cathedral	Kathedraal (domkerk)

RESTAURANTS AND DINING

Please give us the menu	Kag ik het menu zien?
What do you recommend?	Wat kunt U aanbevelen?
Please give us the table d'hôte	Wij nemen table d'hôte
Please serve us as quickly as possible	Bedien ons zo vlug mogelijk, alstublieft
Please give me the check (bill)	Ober, kan ik betalen?
Have you included the tip?	Is dit inclusief?
Waiter! Waitress!	Ober! Juffrouw!
Please give us some . . .	Geeft u ons wat . . .
Bread and butter	Boterham
Toast	Geroostered brood
buttered	warm gesmeerd
dry	zonder boter
Jam	Jam
Marmalade	Marmelade
Cheese	Kaas
Sugar	Suiker
Salt	Zout
Pepper	Peper
Mustard	Mosterd

Eggs

Bacon and eggs	Eieren met spek
Fried eggs	Spiegeleieren
Boiled egg	Gekookt ei
soft-boiled	zachgekookt
medium	halfzacht
hard-boiled	hardgekookt
scrambled	roerei

Fish

Cod	Kabeljauw
Flounder	Bot
Eel	Paling
Halibut	Heilbot
Herring	Haring
Mackerel	Makreel
Plaice	Schol
Salmon	Zalm
Trout	Forel
Crab	Krab
Crayfish	Rivierkreeft
Lobster	Kreeft
Oysters	Oesters
Shrimp	Garnalen

Meat

Spring chicken	Piepkuiken
Chicken	Kip

Duck	Eend
Wild duck	Wilde eend
Goose	Gans
Partridge	Patrijs
Rabbit	Konijn
Hare	Haas
Pork Chops	Varkenskotelet
Roast lamb	Gebraden lamsvlees
Roast mutton	Gebraden schapenvlees
Roast veal	Gebraden kalfsvlees
Roast beef	Rosbief
Fried	Gebakken
Roasted	Gebraden
Smoked	Gerookt
Stewed	Gestoofd
Rare	Bloedrood
Medium	Half gaar
Well done	Goed gaar

Vegetables

Asparagus	Asperges
Beans	Bonen
String beans	Snijbonen
Green beans (French beans)	Sperciebonen
Brussels sprouts	Brusselse spruitjes
Cabbage	Kool
Carrots	Worteltjes
Cauliflower	Bloemkool
Cucumber	Komkommer
Mushrooms	Champignons
Onions	Uien
Peas	Doperwten
Potatoes	Aardappelen
boiled	gekookte
fried	gebakken
French-fried	Pommes frites
mashed	Aardappelpuree
Rice	Rijst
Sauerkraut	Zuurkool
Spinach	Spinazie
Tomatoes	Tomaten
Turnips	Koolraap
Lettuce, salad	Sla

Fruit

Apple	Appel
Cherries	Kersen
Grapes	Druiven
Lemon	Citroen
Orange	Sinaasappel
Pears	Peren
Fruit salad	Vruchtensla

Drinks

A bottle of . . .	Een fles . . .
A pot of . . .	Een potje . . .
A glass of . . .	Een glas . . .
A cup of . . .	Een kop . . .

Water	Water
Iced water	IJswater
Mineral water	Mineraalwater
Milk	Melk
Coffee	Koffie
Coffee with hot milk/cream	Koffie met hete melk/room
Tea, iced tea	Thee, thé glacé
Hot chocolate	Warme chocolade
Beer	Bier
Wine (red, white)	Wijn (rode, witte)

AT THE HOTEL

Can you recommend a good hotel?	Kunt u me een goed hotel aanbevelen?
Which is the best hotel?	Wat is het best hotel?
Have you anything cheaper?	Hebt u iets goedkoper?
What is the price including breakfast?	Wat is de prijs met ontbijt?
Does the price include service?	Geldt de prijs inclusief bediening?
At what time is . . .	Hoe laat is . . .
breakfast?	het ontbijt?
lunch?	het middageten?
dinner?	het avondeten?
Please wake me at . . . o'clock	Ik wil graag om . . . uur gewekt worden
I want this dry-cleaned	Kunt U dit laten stomen?
I want these clothes washed	Wilt U alstublieft deze kleren in de was doen
I would like to have a . . .	Ik zou . . . willen hebben
single room	een eenpersoonskamer
double room with	een kamer met
twin beds	twee bedden
double bed	een tweepersoonsbed
with bath	met bad
Another pillow	Nog een kussen
Another blanket	Nog een deken
Soap, towel	Zeep, handdoek
Coat-hangers	Klerenhangers

TRAVELING BY TRAIN

Timetable	Dienstregeling
Through train	Doorgaande trein
Slow train	Stoptrein
Fast train	Sneltrein
Express train	Exprestrein
Weekdays only	Alleen werkdagen

Sundays and holidays only	Alleen zon- en feestdagen
Return ticket	Retour
One-way ticket	Enkele reis
Fare	Prijs van het biljet
Compartment	Coupé
Dining car	Restauratiewagen
Sleeping compartment	Slaapcoupé
First class	Eerste class
Second class	Tweede klas
Delay	Vertraging
Connection	Aansluiting
All aboard	Instappen

AT THE POST OFFICE

Air mail	Luchtpost
Ordinary mail	Gewone post
Special delivery	Expresse
Cable	Telegram
Stamp	Postzegel
Registered	Aangetekend
Insured	Verzekerd

MOTORING

How many kilometers is it to . . . ?	Hoeveel kilometers is het naar . . . ?
I want . . . liters of gasoline	Ik wens . . . liter benzine
Fill it up, please	Bijvullen, alstublieft
Will you . . .	Wilt U . . .
grease the car	de wagen doorsmeren
change the oil	de olie vernieuwen
check the oil	de olie controleren
wash the car	de wagen wassen
clean the windscreen (windshield)	de voorruit schoonmaken
top up the battery with distilled water	de accu met gedistilleerd water bijvullen
change this wheel	dit wiel verwisselen
test the tyre (tire) pressures	de spanning van de banden controleren
fill the radiator	de radiateur bijvullen
There is something wrong with . . .	Er mankeert iets aan . . .
I will come for the car at . . . o'clock	Ik zal de wagen om . . . uur komen halen
What will it cost?	Hoeveel kost dat?
May I park here?	Mag ik hier parkeren?
Axle (back)	Achteras
Axle (front)	Vooras
Bearing	Lager
Body	Carrosserie
Bonnet (hood)	Kap
Brake	Rem
Carburetor	Carburator
Clutch	Koppeling
Crankshaft	Krukas

Cylinder	Cylinder
Dashboard	Instrumentenbord
Exhaust	Uitlaat
Bumper	Bumper
Gear box	Versnellingsbak
Headlights	Koplampen
Ignition	Ontsteking
Jet or carburetor	Sproeier
Number plate	Nummerplaat
Oil can	Oliekan
Petrol tin (gas can)	Benzineblik
Spark(ing) plug	Bougie
Speedometer	Snelheidsmeter
Steering wheel	Stuurwiel
Tyres (tires)	Banden
Tail light	Achterlicht
Valve	Klep (van de motor)
Wheel (spare)	Wiel (reserve)
Windscreen wiper	Ruitenwisser
The toolbox	Gereedschapskist
Bolt	Bout
File	Vijl
Hammer	Hamer
Jack	Crick
Nail	Spijker
Nut	Moer
Pliers	Buigtang
Screw	Schroef
Sound your horn	Klaxoneren, signaal geven
Slow	Langzaam
Proceed at walking pace	Stapvoets rijden
To the right	Naar rechts
To the left	Naar links
Crossroads	Kruispunt
No admission	Verboden toegang/inrit
Keep to your right	Rechts houden
Level crossing	Spoorwegkruising
Road up for repair	Opgebroken rijweg
Road blocked	Versperde weg
No traffic allowed	Verboden voor alle verkeer
One-way street	Eenrichtingverkeer
Traffic lights	Verkeerslichten
Turn	Keren
Straight ahead	Rechtuit of Rechtdoor
Maximum speed	Maximum snelheid

DAYS OF THE WEEK

Monday	maandag
Tuesday	dinsdag
Wednesday	woensdag
Thursday	donderdag
Friday	vrijdag

| Saturday | zaterdag |
| Sunday | zondag |

NUMERALS

one	een (ayn)
two	twee (tvay)
three	drie (dree)
four	vier (feer)
five	vijf (fife)
six	zes (sess)
seven	zeven (zayfern)
eight	acht (ahgt)
nine	negen (nayghen)
ten	tien (teen)
eleven	elf (elf)
twelve	twaalf (tvahlf)
thirteen	dertien (derrteen)
fourteen	veertien (fairteen)
fifteen	vijftien (fifeteen)
sixteen	zestien (zessteen)
seventeen	zeventien (zayfenteen)
eighteen	achttien (ahgteen)
nineteen	negentien (nayhgenteen)
twenty	twintig (tvintuhk)
twenty-one	een en twintig (ayn en tvintuhk)
twenty-two	twee en twintig (tvay en tvintuhk)
thirty	dertig (derrtuhk)
forty	veeertig (fairtuhk)
fifty	viftig (fifetuhk)
sixty	zestig (zesstuhk)
seventy	zeventig (zayfentuhk)
eighty	tachtig (tahktuhk)
ninety	negentig (naygentuhk)
one hundred	honderd (hondert)
one hundred and ten	honderd tien (hondert teen)
two hundred	tweehonderd (tvay hondert)
one thousand	duizend (doyzent)

MAP OF HOLLAND

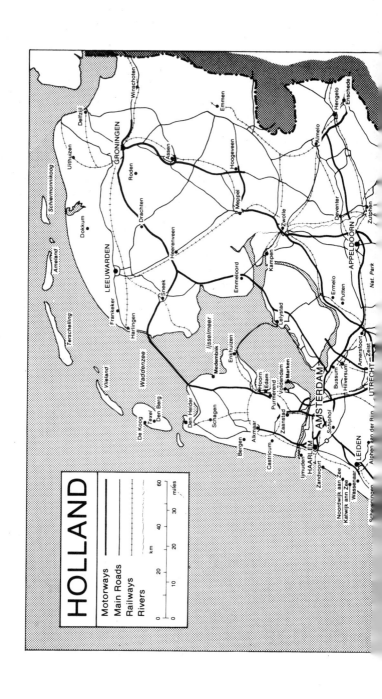

HOLLAND

Motorways
Main Roads
Railways
Rivers

km 0   10   20   30   40   60 miles
    0   20   40

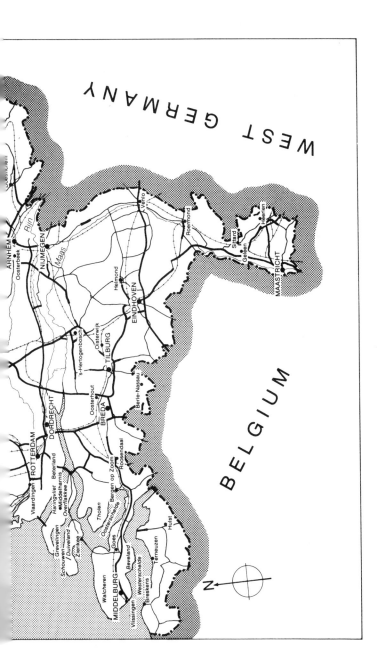

Index

Index

**The letter H indicates hotels and other accommodations.
The letter R indicates restaurants.**

General Information

See also Geographical Index which follows for specific details

Geographical Index

FODOR'S TRAVEL GUIDES

Here is a complete list of Fodor's Travel Guides, available in current editions; most also available in a British edition published by Hodder & Stoughton.

U.S. GUIDES

Alaska
American Cities (Great Travel Values)
Arizona including the Grand Canyon
Atlantic City & the New Jersey Shore
Boston
California
Cape Cod & the Islands of Martha's Vineyard & Nantucket
Carolinas & the Georgia Coast
Chesapeake
Chicago
Colorado
Dallas/Fort Worth
Disney World & the Orlando Area (Fun in)
Far West
Florida
Forth Worth (see Dallas)
Galveston (see Houston)
Georgia (see Carolinas)
Grand Canyon (see Arizona)
Greater Miami & the Gold Coast
Hawaii
Hawaii (Great Travel Values)
Houston & Galveston
I-10: California to Florida
I-55: Chicago to New Orleans
I-75: Michigan to Florida
I-80: San Francisco to New York
I-95: Maine to Miami
Jamestown (see Williamsburg)
Las Vegas including Reno & Lake Tahoe (Fun in)
Los Angeles & Nearby Attractions
Martha's Vineyard (see Cape Cod)
Maui (Fun in)
Nantucket (see Cape Cod)
New England
New Jersey (see Atlantic City)
New Mexico
New Orleans
New Orleans (Fun in)
New York City
New York City (Fun in)
New York State
Orlando (see Disney World)
Pacific North Coast
Philadelphia
Reno (see Las Vegas)
Rockies
San Diego & Nearby Attractions
San Francisco (Fun in)
San Francisco plus Marin County & the Wine Country
The South
Texas
U.S.A.
Virgin Islands (U.S. & British)
Virginia
Waikiki (Fun in)
Washington, D.C.
Williamsburg, Jamestown & Yorktown

FOREIGN GUIDES

Acapulco (see Mexico City)
Acapulco (Fun in)
Amsterdam
Australia, New Zealand & the South Pacific
Austria
The Bahamas
The Bahamas (Fun in)
Barbados (Fun in)
Beijing, Guangzhou & Shanghai
Belgium & Luxembourg
Bermuda
Brazil
Britain (Great Travel Values)
Canada
Canada (Great Travel Values)
Canada's Maritime Provinces plus Newfoundland & Labrador
Cancún, Cozumel, Mérida & the Yucatán
Caribbean
Caribbean (Great Travel Values)
Central America
Copenhagen (see Stockholm)
Cozumel (see Cancún)
Eastern Europe
Egypt
Europe
Europe (Budget)
France
France (Great Travel Values)
Germany: East & West
Germany (Great Travel Values)
Great Britain
Greece
Guangzhou (see Beijing)
Helsinki (see Stockholm)
Holland
Hong Kong & Macau
Hungary
India, Nepal & Sri Lanka
Ireland
Israel
Italy
Italy (Great Travel Values)
Jamaica (Fun in)
Japan
Japan (Great Travel Values)
Jordan & the Holy Land
Kenya
Korea
Labrador (see Canada's Maritime Provinces)
Lisbon
Loire Valley
London
London (Fun in)
London (Great Travel Values)
Luxembourg (see Belgium)
Macau (see Hong Kong)
Madrid
Mazatlan (see Mexico's Baja)
Mexico
Mexico (Great Travel Values)
Mexico City & Acapulco
Mexico's Baja & Puerto Vallarta, Mazatlan, Manzanillo, Copper Canyon
Montreal (Fun in)
Munich
Nepal (see India)
New Zealand
Newfoundland (see Canada's Maritime Provinces)
1936 . . . on the Continent
North Africa
Oslo (see Stockholm)
Paris
Paris (Fun in)
People's Republic of China
Portugal
Province of Quebec
Puerto Vallarta (see Mexico's Baja)
Reykjavik (see Stockholm)
Rio (Fun in)
The Riviera (Fun on)
Rome
St. Martin/St. Maarten (Fun in)
Scandinavia
Scotland
Shanghai (see Beijing)
Singapore
South America
South Pacific
Southeast Asia
Soviet Union
Spain
Spain (Great Travel Values)
Sri Lanka (see India)
Stockholm, Copenhagen, Oslo, Helsinki & Reykjavik
Sweden
Switzerland
Sydney
Tokyo
Toronto
Turkey
Vienna
Yucatán (see Cancún)
Yugoslavia

SPECIAL-INTEREST GUIDES

Bed & Breakfast Guide: North America
Royalty Watching
Selected Hotels of Europe
Selected Resorts and Hotels of the U.S.
Ski Resorts of North America
Views to Dine by around the World